FOOTBALL IN T

ABDULLAH AL-ARIAN

Football in the Middle East

State, Society, and the Beautiful Game

OXFORD
UNIVERSITY PRESS

Oxford University Press is a department of the
University of Oxford. It furthers the University's objective
of excellence in research, scholarship, and education
by publishing worldwide.

Oxford   New York

Auckland   Cape Town   Dar es Salaam   Hong Kong   Karachi
Kuala Lumpur   Madrid   Melbourne   Mexico City   Nairobi
New Delhi   Shanghai   Taipei   Toronto

With offices in

Argentina   Austria   Brazil   Chile   Czech Republic   France   Greece
Guatemala   Hungary   Italy   Japan   Poland   Portugal   Singapore
South Korea   Switzerland   Thailand   Turkey   Ukraine   Vietnam

Oxford is a registered trade mark of Oxford University Press
in the UK and certain other countries.

Published in the United States of America by
Oxford University Press
198 Madison Avenue, New York, NY 10016

Library of Congress Cataloging-in-Publication Data is available
Abdullah Al-Arian.
Football in the Middle East: State, Society, and the Beautiful Game.
ISBN: 9780197659670

Printed in the United Kingdom on acid-free paper
by Bell and Bain Ltd, Glasgow

CONTENTS

CONTENTS

ACKNOWLEDGEMENTS

This book is the result of a two-year research initiative undertaken by the Center for International and Regional Studies (CIRS), Georgetown University in Qatar. My thanks to Mehran Kamrava, former Director of CIRS, and Zahra Babar, Associate Director, for initiating this research and inviting me to serve as the project's faculty lead and volume editor. I am grateful to the staff at CIRS— Elizabeth Wanucha, Misba Bhatti, and Maram Al-Qershi—for their impeccable organization of the working group meetings, and to Suzi Mirgani for her editorial assistance. Finally, I extend my thanks to Ziad Abu-Rish, Yousuf Al-Bulushi, Sonia Alonso, Mariya Petkova, Murat Yildiz, William Youmans, Ali Al-Arian, Laila Al-Arian, Jonathan Brown, Muriam Haleh Davis, Thomas Serres, Shadia Mansour, the Real Football Group, and The Spanish Football Podcast (#TSFP).

ABOUT THE CONTRIBUTORS

Niki Akhavan is an Associate Professor and Chair of the Media and Communication Studies Department at the Catholic University of America. Her research areas include Iranian digital cultures, state-sponsored media, and cinema. She is the author of *Electronic Iran: The Cultural Politics of an Online Evolution* (Rutgers, 2013). She has also published on Iranian narrative and documentary cinema, the intersections of Iranian media and gender, and information warfare in the age of digital media.

Abdullah Al-Arian is Associate Professor of History at Georgetown University in Qatar where he specializes in the modern Middle East and the study of Islamic social movements. He is the author of *Answering the Call: Popular Islamic Activism in Sadat's Egypt* (Oxford University Press, 2014). Previously, he was the Carnegie Centennial Visiting Fellow at the Josef Korbel School of International Studies at the University of Denver. He is also editor of the Critical Currents in Islam page on the *Jadaliyya* e-zine.

Zahra Babar is Associate Director for Research at CIRS at Georgetown University in Qatar. Her current research interests include rural development, migration and labor policies, and citizenship in the Persian Gulf states. She has published several articles and chapters, most recently, "Im/mobile Highly Skilled Migrants in Qatar," with M. Ewers and N. Khattab, in *Journal of Ethnic and Migration Studies* (2019); "Enduring 'Contested' Citizenship in the Gulf Cooperation Council," in *The Middle East in Transition: The*

Centrality of Citizenship (2018); "The 'Enemy Within': Citizenship-Stripping in the Post-Arab Spring GCC," in *Middle East Journal* (2017); "The 'Humane Economy:' Migrant Labour and Islam in Qatar and the UAE," in *Sociology of Islam* (2017); and "Population, Power, and Distributional Politics in Qatar," in *Journal of Arabian Studies* (2015). She served as editor for *Arab Migrant Communities in the GCC* (Oxford University Press/Hurst 2017), and coedited, with M. Kamrava, *Migrant Labour in the Persian Gulf* (Columbia University Press/Hurst 2012).

Aubrey Bloomfield is an independent writer and researcher based in Aotearoa, New Zealand. His work focuses on international relations and the intersection of sport and politics, and his research interests include sport and human rights; the relationship between sport, identity, and nationalism; and sport as a site of both normalization and resistance in the Moroccan occupation of Western Sahara and the Israeli occupation of Palestine. In particular, he has previously written about the role of sport in the Palestinian-led Boycott, Divestment, Sanctions (BDS) movement. His writing has been published in *The Nation*, *Mondoweiss*, *Africa is a Country*, *Palestine Square*, *Jadaliyya*, *Al Jazeera*, *The Guardian*, the *Oxford Research Encyclopedia of African History*, and the *Journal of Palestine Studies*, among others. He has also been a freelance proofreader and copy editor for the *Journal of Palestine Studies* since 2016.

Simon Chadwick is Global Professor of Sport and Director of the Centre for the Eurasian Sport Industry, Emlyon, France. He also serves as Professor of Sports Enterprise at Salford University Manchester, where he is Co-director of the Centre for Sports Business. In addition, Chadwick is Senior Fellow of the University of Nottingham's China Policy Institute, where he is Founding Director of the China Soccer Observatory. His academic research has appeared in journals including *Sloan Management Review* and the *Journal of Advertising Research*. He has published numerous books on sports, including coediting the *Handbook of Football Business and Management* (Routledge, 2016). He authored "The Business of Sports in the Gulf Cooperation Council Member States" in *Sport, Politics, and Society in the Middle East* (Hurst/OUP 2019). He is a sports business columnist, and regularly appears on television, commenting on sports for broadcasters such as CNN, Al Jazeera, and the BBC. He previously worked as Director of Research for the Josoor Institute in Qatar, part of Supreme Committee for Delivery and Legacy, the ministry organizing the 2022 World Cup.

Ibrahim Elhoudaiby is a doctoral candidate in Columbia University's department of Middle Eastern, South Asian, and African Studies. A graduate of the American University in Cairo (2005), he holds a BA in political science and an MA in political science and development studies (2012). He also holds a diploma in Islamic studies from the High Institute of Islamic Studies. His research focuses on the encounter between the modern corporation and the premodern political and legal structures of the Middle East.

Thomas Ross Griffin is Assistant Professor of Postcolonial Literature in the Department of Literature and Linguistics at Qatar University. His research interests include the portrayal of the Arab world in Western media, the relationship between sport and postcolonial society, and national identity in the Gulf. He has published on a broad range of subjects ranging from Orientalism in the British press in the twenty-first century to the soft power implications of the Marvel Superhero Universe in peer-reviewed journals. He is author of "Football in the Hands of the Other: Qatar's World Cup in the British Broadsheet Press," in *The Arab World Geographer* (2017) and "National identity, Social Legacy, and Qatar 2022: the Cultural Ramifications of FIFA's first Arab World Cup" in *Soccer & Society* (2019). He has edited university press collections and for international news media, and has contributed articles to *Middle East Eye* and *Al Jazeera*.

Craig L LaMay is a journalist and Professor in Residence at Northwestern University in Qatar, and Faculty Fellow at the Northwestern Institute for Policy Research in Evanston, Illinois, where he is on the faculty of the Medill School of Journalism. Previously, he was Editorial Director of the Freedom Forum Media Studies Center at Columbia University, where he was editor of the *Media Studies Journal*. He teaches courses in comparative media law;

sports media and intellectual property; and sports diplomacy and sport and human rights. Research interests include media development in democratizing and post-conflict societies; broadcast regulation and televised leader debates; and sport as a social institution. He is on the board of the Center for International Media Assistance, a program of the National Endowment for Democracy. He is author of "The World Cup and its Challenge to Free Expression Norms in Qatar," in *Sport, Politics, and Society in the Middle East* (OUP/Hurst, 2019). He has contributed chapters to a number of edited volumes, and his articles have appeared in *The New York Times*, and *The Wall Street Journal*, among others. He is the former Middle East editor of the *International Journal of the History of Sport*.

Maher Mezahi is an independent football journalist based in Algiers. He examines the relationship between politics and sport, and his research interests include North African politics, history of colonial sport in Africa, and football. He covers North African football extensively, and his work has been published in the international media including the BBC, *The Guardian*, *The Telegraph*, ESPN Africa, Al Jazeera English, and *New Frame*. He covered the 2017 African Cup of Nations (AFCON) in Gabon and in Egypt in 2019. He has an active social media presence on Twitter and YouTube, where he presents on football, sports, and social issues. He produced the video "How Algerian Football Fans Helped Topple a Dictator" for COPA90 digital content company (May 14, 2019), and recent articles include "Football Fans, Algeria's Invisible Catalyst" for *New Frame* (March 20, 2019).

Yağmur Nuhrat is a cultural anthropologist and Assistant Professor at Istanbul Bilgi University, in the Department of Sociology. After completing her doctorate in anthropology at Brown University, she worked as a postdoctoral fellow in the Istanbul Studies Center at Kadir Has University. Her research interests include the anthropology of ethics and morality; sports and football anthropology; gender, language, and women's football; and urban anthropology. She has published on football in edited volumes and peer-reviewed journals including in *American Ethnologist* (2018), where she examined the concept of love vis-à-vis the commodification of football in Turkey. In *Fashion Theory* (2019), she wrote about how football jerseys contribute to the making of men through accentuating their bodies. In the *Journal of Middle East Women's Studies* (2017), she wrote about language and women football fans in Turkey; and in *Sport in Society* (2017), she focused on Ultras in Turkey. She has recently completed ethnographic research on a private women's football tournament and league in Istanbul.

Danyel Reiche is a Visiting Associate Professor at Georgetown University—Qatar, where he leads the Center for International and Regional Studies (CIRS) research initiative on the FIFA World Cup 2022. He published the books *Success and Failure of Countries at the Olympic Games* (Routledge, 2016) and, together with P. Brannagan, *Qatar and the 2022 FIFA World Cup: Politics, Controversy, Change* (Palgrave Macmillan, 2022); he co-edited the volumes Sport, *Politics and Society in the Middle East* with T. Sorek (Hurst/OUP, 2019) and *Routledge Handbook of Sport in the Middle East* with P. Brannagan (2022).

Ramón Spaaij is Professor in the Institute for Health and Sport at Victoria University in Melbourne, Australia, and Visiting Professor at the Utrecht University School of Governance, the Netherlands. His research focuses on questions of social cohesion, conflict, and social change. He has two established fields of research that address these questions: the sociology of sport and the sociology of terrorism. His work has contributed to contemporary academic and public debates on diversity, social inclusion, community development and violence by bringing sport into view as an analytical lens through which to study and better understand these complex social issues. He also conducts internationally recognized research on violent extremism and lone wolf terrorism. He coedited *The Palgrave International Handbook of Football and Politics* (2018), *Routledge Handbook of Football Studies* (2016); and coauthored *Sport and Social Exclusion in Global Society* (Routledge, 2014), among others. He has contributed to a wide range of media including *The New York Times, The Guardian*, and *The Australian*, among others.

INTRODUCTION

Abdullah Al-Arian

Far and away the most popular sport in the world, football has a special place in the states and societies of the Middle East. The beautiful game has a rich and vibrant history in the region and continues to be the single most unifying cultural force in the realm of sports. Football brings together families as they pass down their support for clubs from one generation to the next. The sport brings cities out in full force to celebrate their local team's most memorable victories. It mobilizes entire nations beneath the badge of their country on football's largest stage, the Fédération Internationale de Football Association (FIFA) World Cup. Football fandom has also been channeled in the course of popular revolutions, while authoritarian rulers have relied on it to bolster support for their regimes. It has been invoked in the relations between states, both in times of cooperation and in times of conflict. As the brief sketches below demonstrate, the story of football in the Middle East is inseparable from the broader experiences of the region and the destinies of its people.

Against all odds, the Iraqi national football team defeated the likes of Australia and South Korea to reach the 2007 final match of

1

the Asian Cup, where it would face perennial favorite and three-time winner of the tournament Saudi Arabia. Even under ideal conditions, reaching a first-ever final would be an impressive feat for Iraq, but in this moment, the cup final matchup represented what one writer observed as "the side without a country, against the most well-funded national side in the world."[1] Since the 2003 invasion of Iraq by the United States, which followed more than a decade of debilitating economic sanctions, the Iraqi national team had faced perilous conditions that tempered any footballing ambitions the country may have held. In the leadup to the tournament, the team was forced to train in neighboring Jordan to escape the ravages of military occupation and sectarian violence back home. Then, on the eve of the opening group stage match, the team's physiotherapist was killed by a car bomb in Baghdad while attempting to rejoin the squad.[2]

The Iraq team lifted the cup in Jakarta, following a narrow 1–0 win over Saudi Arabia in the final. The victory, however, had been overshadowed by the news from home, as a series of bombings killed fifty Iraqi fans while they celebrated their team's semi-final win over South Korea. Subsequent news reports juxtaposed the team's remarkable achievement with the adversity it faced. The blending of the two produced narratives about the unity displayed "across Iraq's sectarian divide" and "the healing power of sport."[3]

Three years later, in 2010, world football's governing body, FIFA, would declare that it had accepted Qatar's bid to host the 2022 FIFA World Cup. The announcement was at once met with jubilation and incredulity. Qatar would become the smallest country to ever host a World Cup and the first in the Middle East to do so. Buoyed by the country's natural gas wealth, Qatar's leaders positioned their nation as a technically advanced site to host a tournament that "created new concepts" and "pushed the boundaries," while also pledging to be more inclusive than conventional tournaments—"a World Cup for everyone," according to the chairman of the Qatar bid, Sheikh Mohammed bin Hamad Al-Thani.[4] Sheikha Moza bint Nasser, the wife of the country's ruling emir at the time, added, "this is an opportunity to eradicate misconceptions, not just about Qatar, but about the wider Islamic and Arab world."[5]

Elsewhere, FIFA's announcement elicited considerable outcry. Critics questioned every facet of the decision, from Qatar's lack of a strong footballing pedigree, to concerns over climate conditions during the desert country's intensely hot summer months (in which the games are traditionally played).[6] Others expressed skepticism toward Qatar's ability to pull off the logistical feat of constructing new stadiums, training facilities, hotels, and a public transit system, among other infrastructure requirements, even with the tournament being twelve years away.[7] Cultural arguments advanced the notion that a Muslim country that limited the sale of alcohol could not possibly host a global event in which alcohol consumption was a central feature of the fan experience.[8] Some even questioned the integrity of the process itself in which "an unlikely nation" was awarded the World Cup, amid allegations of vote-buying and corruption within FIFA.[9] Most of all, however, Qatar would face intense scrutiny over the conditions of its migrant labor force, which formed the backbone of the country's ability to build the infrastructure vital to the delivery of the games.[10] In light of persistent accusations that it was practicing "modern-day slavery," Qatar faced intense pressure to reform its labor system to bring it in line with international human rights standards.[11]

Only a few months after Qatar's successful World Cup bid made headlines, a wave of popular uprisings swept the Middle East and North Africa. As one authoritarian regime after another faced the prospect of being overthrown in favor of a more representative political order, observers shifted their focus to examining the various social movements that mobilized in opposition to deeply entrenched dictatorships. In Egypt, which saw the three-decade rule of Hosni Mubarak upended by an eighteen-day mass protest, the role of football Ultras was noted for defending protesters confronted by state violence. In their storied past, devoted fan groups such as the Al-Ahlawy Ultras (of Al-Ahly Sporting Club) were no strangers to repressive crackdowns. As one member of Al-Ahlawy recounted, "it wasn't just supporting a team; you were fighting a system and the country as a whole. We were fighting the police, fighting the government, fighting for our rights."[12] That experience proved valuable when Mubarak sent both police forces and plain-clothed gangs to disperse the protesters at Tahrir Square in Cairo and elsewhere across the country. The Ultras repelled attacks by government forces, protected civilian protesters, and maintained the pressure on the regime that ultimately led to Mubarak's removal.

During the transitional period that followed, the Ultras continued to be a fixture at the mass protests objecting to the military's domination of the political process. Then, following a match at Port Said Stadium in February 2012, seventy-four Al-Ahly supporters were killed in attacks by armed thugs as police stood by and did nothing. The assault was likely premediated—retribution for the Ultras' anti-regime activism. The massacre was by far the largest instance of violence in Egyptian football history. In the words of one observer, the Port Said tragedy "transformed a football fan club of revolutionaries into a political entity."[13] The Ultras' efforts to seek justice for the victims through Egyptian courts were denied. Instead, the government issued a ban on all fans in football stadiums that was only partially lifted in 2018.[14] As for the Ultras, the revived authoritarian regime led by President Abdel Fattah el-Sisi outlawed all organized fan groups as part of its broader efforts to suppress independent political currents within Egyptian society.

Football in the Middle East Through the Decades

In the shadow of these and other developments, it is no surprise that over the course of the past decade, football in the Middle East has emerged as the subject of both impassioned political and cultural expression as well as academic study. Historian Rashid Khalidi identified the problems in defining the "Middle East" as a self-contained unit of analysis, owing to the lack of precision in determining its physical boundaries, the colonial origins of the term, and its continued political uses in the service of neo-imperial interests.[15] He also noted the failure to account for economic, social, and political processes that transcend regional confines, and called upon scholars to seek the connective tissue between phenomena with roots in the region and their manifestations beyond narrowly defined geographies.[16] There are few developments in the modern era that rise to this call more than football, a sport that originated elsewhere, and has captured the imaginations of populations across all continents, but nevertheless developed deep political, cultural, and social roots in the Middle East. The studies presented here reflect an understanding of the region as a porous unit of analysis with processes that can be traced to regions beyond, observed in part through the universality and permeability that football offers.

This volume aims to build upon the recent surge in interest in football as the leading sport in the Middle East, while also high-lighting its longstanding presence as a political and cultural force for over a century. To be sure, the beautiful game has roots in the region that date back to the era of European colonial rule, state-building, and modernization. The introduction of football as a leisure activity and an organized sport was part and parcel of broader efforts by officials to transform colonized subjects into "properly obedient individuals" whose physical conditioning formed an integral part of colonial educational.[17] Local elites inter-nalized discourses on organized sports as a mark of cultural and civilizational advancement.

Egyptian nationalists believed their country's participation in the 1920 and 1924 Olympic Games represented Egypt's arrival as a full-fledged member of the global community of nations.[18] In mandate Palestine, organized football matches were alternately used by colonial officials "to pacify the anger of the Arab popula-tion who opposed the pro-Zionist British policy," as well as by Zionist settlers and indigenous Palestinians to assert competing nationalist claims.[19] The establishment of an annual football tour-nament in the mid-1940s aided the Hashemite monarchy in its consolidation of Jordanian national identity, while in Sudan, col-lege graduates' assumption of leadership in the national football association represented "an early exercise in mass politics and popular government."[20]

As scholars have noted, football's central place in public life across the Middle East and North Africa continued well into the era of anti-colonial revolution and radical politics. As part of its revolutionary struggle against France, the Front de Liberation

(FLN) assembled a football team to advocate on behalf of Algerian independence while competing internationally.[21] Upon leading the military's overthrow of the Egyptian monarchy, Gamal Abdel Nasser went to great lengths to enlist the Egyptian Football Association in mobilizing mass support for the newly established republic, using it to empower the armed forces and legitimize the dominant role it came to play in governance.[22] So too was football considered a liability to more pressing political demands. In the aftermath of Egypt's defeat in the June 1967 war with Israel, Nasser suspended the Egyptian league, labeling it a "distraction" from the goal of national liberation.[23] Similarly, in the lead-up to the 1979 Iranian Revolution, opponents of the ruling monarch argued that the national obsession with football represented a deliberate attempt by the Pahlavi regime to subdue the population into quiet obedience in the face of government corruption and repression.[24]

By the late 1990s, amid emerging discourses on the impact of globalization on local societies, football was frequently invoked as a device to understand international relations, neoliberal economics, and the homogenization of popular culture. "Football as peacemaking" became a frequent refrain, with the United Nations establishing a series of programs promoting football as a tool for conflict resolution and economic development.[25] More than just another game, the group stage match between the United States and Iran at the 1998 World Cup carried the weight of nearly twenty years of hostile relations between the two states. The drama surrounding the match, which Iran won 2–1, played out in the realm of global public opinion and in conciliatory statements by the heads of state of both nations.[26] Emboldened by the perceived political opening posed by the globalization of football, one prominent writer envisaged a "football revolution" in the Middle East that would displace the forces of political Islam and anti-Americanism.[27]

Furthermore, the acquisition of a number of high profile European clubs by multinational corporate conglomerates, coupled with the increased commodification of football on a global scale, saw the Middle East develop into one of the most promising consumer markets for the sport in the twenty-first century.[28] Some

INTRODUCTION

critics warned that the market-driven and individualistic nature of neoliberalism would pose a direct threat to the "collectivist values" historically embedded in football competition and fandom.[29] Alternatively, these scholars appealed to the notion of "glocalization" as an interpretive tool that would at once highlight:

> how globalization is marked by trends towards both commonality or uniformity *and* divergence and differentiation. These interdependencies are more fully captured by the broad opposition between "homogenization" and "heterogenization", which registers trends towards cultural convergence and divergence. To pick the most elementary illustration, while football's global diffusion points towards a worldwide convergence over the popularity of particular sports, many societies display divergence in how they organize, interpret, and play the game.[30]

In contrast to the more expectant voices that positioned the sport as a transformative force within society, this approach seeks to underscore football's centrality as part and parcel of broader social phenomena. Put another way, "in the realms of politics and economics, it is easier to see how [football] reflects political and economic globalizations more than it contributes to them."[31] This point rings true in the various developments that followed, particularly when charting the recent evolution of football in the Middle East.

Beginning with the 2008 purchase of Manchester City FC by an Emirati royal investment group, Gulf states would flex their economic muscle in the realm of world football, reviving the competitive fortunes of a number of European clubs in the process.[32] Heated rivalries between national football teams and their supporters represented broader political conflicts between states and the cynical attempts by authoritarian rulers to deflect attention from their own failures, as occurred in 2009 when Egypt and Algeria battled for one of the final spots in the following year's World Cup. The qualification matches sparked hypernationalistic rhetoric by media and state officials in both countries, and saw the outbreak of violence among fans.[33] Indeed, the experiences of football fans in the Middle East have frequently offered a reflection of political and socioeconomic realities of the states in the region, from their mobilization against authoritarian rule, to their efforts to challenge economic corruption and gender discrimination.[34] The above sentiment is equally apparent in the campaign to host the 2022 World Cup in Qatar, a $200 billion endeavor that reflects less upon the sporting ambitions of a country than its leveraging of unrivaled economic standing to advance critical national interests.[35]

Scholars Take the Field

All of these developments have ushered in a voluminous rise of scholarship around the subject of football in the Middle East. Books, blogs, special issues of academic journals, and international conferences have explored the topic, partly in an effort to enhance more generalized discussions surrounding world football by examining its development in an understudied region, and by finding within the sport a unique method of taking the pulse of the Middle East.[36]

It is in that spirit that this collection of chapters has come together. Each contribution to this volume has developed, in part, as an extensive conversation with the existing body of literature in the field, as well as by introducing original research questions that seek to push the study of football in the Middle East into new avenues. The question of the game's historical development in the region is crucial to the understanding of how football continues to manifest as a site of mass mobilization and political contention today. Using the formation of the Egyptian league as a case in point, Chapter 1 explores the linkages between the establishment of some of Egypt's most iconic clubs and the negotiation of national identity in the context of British colonialism. The chapter identifies the broad array of actors responsible for the development, dissemination, formalization, and organization of the game in Egypt. In describing the complex relationships between football players, club officials, fans, and nascent state institutions, Ibrahim Elhoudaiby makes the critical point that football is not merely a platform upon which external political interests compete, but rather, owing to its power within society, football exists as a site of political contestation in its own right.

INTRODUCTION

That historical analysis and contextualization offers significant grounding for the discussions that follow. In Chapter 2, I challenge recent analyses that position football in the Middle East as a site of soft power demonstration among the region's ruling elites. Instead, I propose that the politicization of football be examined through its perceived ability to legitimate regimes, particularly authoritarian systems of governance. Whether through their direct participation in regional and international tournaments, significant investments in European clubs, or serving as hosts for mega events, states have enlisted their footballing interests to acquire legitimacy in the face of internal and external threats. Using a variety of examples from recent history, the chapter showcases the ways in which state instrumentalization of football has attempted to legitimize neo-imperial control, facilitate transitions of power, insulate regimes against external attack, isolate and target opposition groups through securitization policies, and deflect criticism of unpopular practices through "sportswashing." As the chapter notes, that many of these attempts have ultimately fallen short in their political objectives is not due to the limits of the sport or its place in society. On the contrary, the failed co-optation of football by regimes that enjoy the full range of coercive instruments of power is a testament to football's transcendent quality as a sociocultural force that cannot be easily bent to the will of the state.

Further expanding upon this latter point in Chapter 3, Maher Mezahi offers a look at the mobilizing power of football in the face of longstanding political repression. The Hirak mass protest movement that launched in Algeria in 2019, and succeeded in terminating President Abdelaziz Bouteflika's plans to run for a fifth consecutive presidential term, featured chants, songs, and artwork popularized by supporters of football clubs. Mezahi's richly descriptive analysis underscores the significance of football fan culture as a rare site of collective political expression in an otherwise stifled and securitized climate. The interplay between fan behavior and broader cultural expression presents football as a permeable cultural force, as seen during the protests in the utilization of *Chaabi* folk music by football Ultras, and in turn, the unveiling of *tifo* visual displays normally reserved for stadiums on match day.

Upon further exploration of football's position as a site of contention, it becomes increasingly clear that in most cases, it is neither strictly the domain of state power nor purely a source of popular empowerment. In Chapter 4, Yağmur Nuhrat examines the power dynamics at play in Turkish football, through the lens of gender inequality. As both the research data and shared experiences demonstrate, women footballers experience massive wage disparities, inadequate medical care, and greater career insecurity compared to their male counterparts. Administrators often treat women's football as a "social project"—another avenue to enforce patriarchal gender norms—rather than a space for competition and collective achievement. Even the physical landscape of the game becomes a site of contestation, as women footballers confront a lack of access to football pitches and training facilities. By mapping the numerous ways in which women's football in Turkey is trivialized, Nuhrat also sheds light on the role that various actors play in that process. From corporate sponsors, male coaches, and league administrators, to media professionals and state officials, women's football reflects broader structural challenges in confronting gender inequality across the political, socioeconomic, and cultural spheres.

National football associations have long been studied as a conspicuous stage for the expression of national identity. In Chapter 5, Thomas Ross Griffin tests the limits of the existing scholarship by examining the complex case of the Qatar national football team. The squad is composed of players who embody three distinct categories of citizenship: full Qatari citizens, long-term residents who were born in the country, and naturalized citizens who hail from elsewhere. Individual players' performance of nationalism, as expressed in team celebrations, media appearances, academic interviews, and social media posts, challenges conventional wisdom regarding the exclusionary nature of national identity in Gulf states. Indeed, as Griffin argues, the differences in national identity performance across the "thick" to "thin" spectrum of citizenship types are far less apparent than prevailing analyses would suggest. Moreover, in light of the porous and overlapping nature of the identities in question, the research goes further in challenging rigid designations of citizenship.

In sharp contrast to the role of football as a path to national inclusivity, the next chapter presents an example of football as a force for national exclusion. Chapter 6 details the Lebanese state's restrictive policies and practices toward Palestinian football players. In what he refers to as the "triple periphery," Danyel Reiche explains that Palestinian residents of Lebanon face multiple obstacles in their pursuit of competitive football: as non-citizens, they face major legal restrictions that limit their ability to join domestic clubs; as stateless Palestinians, they are also denied the opportunity to represent their nation in international competitions; and as refugees, they face numerous hurdles in seeking footballing opportunities abroad. The chapter positions these restrictions partly as an extension of the broader discriminatory policies that Palestinians face in Lebanon. For instance, following a strange provision passed in the late 1990s, "goalkeeper" was added to the list of nearly forty professions from which Palestinians have been barred. At the same time, Reiche notes that the discrimination against Palestinians in the realm of football also exhibits unique features stemming from intricacies in the structure of the Lebanese Football Association and its attempts to grow the game nationally, even at the expense of promoting a higher level of competition, through quotas on the number of Palestinian players, higher registration fees, and other restrictions.

Zooming out from the case of Palestinians in Lebanon, Chapter 7 looks at the question of refugees and football more broadly. As a region with one of the highest concentrations of refugees in the world, the Middle East has been surprisingly understudied in explorations of football as a medium through which to navigate the obstacles brought on by forced displacement. Ramón Spaaij documents the array of programs utilizing football as a source of support for resettlement, particularly among children and youth. Often designed under the rubric of "football for development," these initiatives represent a range of institutional actors, from state-supported agencies and international bodies like the United Nations, to non-governmental organizations, multinational corporations, and major football clubs. Notwithstanding the stated goals of these programs, Spaaij amplifies the questions raised by scholars in the field of development studies concerning the neo-imperialist implications of initiatives designed in the Global North for application among the most vulnerable populations in the Global South. These critiques underscore the need for more empirical research on the impact of the instrumentalization of football on refugee communities throughout the region.

The next two chapters delve more deeply into the propensity for football to serve as a tool in global humanitarianism and campaigns for justice, liberation, and respect for human rights. In Chapter 8, Aubrey Bloomfield examines the role of football in the Palestinian-led Boycott, Divestment, Sanctions (BDS) movement targeting Israeli occupation and discriminatory practices. Modeled after the sports boycott of apartheid South Africa, the BDS movement has begun to utilize the ubiquity of football as the most popular sport in the world to mobilize global support in favor of a boycott. Campaigns targeting Israel's hosting rights of the 2013 UEFA European Under-21 Championship and a friendly match in Jerusalem between Argentina and Israel ahead of the 2018 World Cup served to raise awareness of Israeli human rights abuses. The latter also succeeded in canceling a high-profile match. As Bloomfield notes, placing football front and center in the boycott movement has raised the cost of Israel's policies toward Palestinians and offered an avenue to both educate fans and channel global solidarity.

In granting Qatar the right to stage football's centerpiece event, FIFA inadvertently presented labor rights activists an unprecedented opportunity to shine a light on the working conditions of migrant laborers in the Gulf. In Chapter 9, Zahra Babar dissects the global campaign to uphold the rights of migrant workers, tens of thousands of whom would be enlisted in the major construction projects necessary for Qatar to host the 2022 World Cup. The chapter presents Qatar's resulting labor reforms over the course of the past decade as the product of a multiplicity of factors, including domestic political considerations and international pressures stemming from Qatar's isolation during the blockade led by regional rivals Saudi Arabia and the United Arab Emirates. While playing a crucial role in highlighting the concerns surrounding migrant labor conditions and setting clear targets for reform, Babar argues that the global campaign fell short by limiting its focus to the role of the state in initiating reforms, bypassing domestic civil society, and failing to account for structural factors in the global economy that have given rise to mass inequality.

The chapter that follows shifts the focus to fans, whose active support of clubs and national teams often acts as a significant measure of their success. In Chapter 10, Simon Chadwick argues that scholars who study fan engagement should take local conditions into account rather than simply apply measures of consumer behavior designed primarily to gauge fan engagement in a North American or European setting. As one of the fastest-growing markets for football fandom by far, owing in large part to their economic prosperity, the six countries that form the Gulf Cooperation Council (GCC) present a unique case of fan engagement. Testing conventional approaches to the study of fan behavior, this chapter presents the multiplicity of unique factors in the case of the GCC that necessitate rethinking how fan engagement is assessed. Alternative modes of consumption, aside from match attendance (which tends to be quite low), the localization of global brands (including clubs whose ownership resides in the GCC), and the impact of cultural norms on collective expressions of fan support, present just some of the emerging challenges to the study of fan engagement.

The final two chapters examine the increasingly intertwined relationship between football and media. Chapter 11 looks at football in Iran as a site of contestation between fans aiming to challenge the state's practice of banning women from stadiums and the state's determination to impose its vision for Iranian society, particularly in the regulation of one of the country's most popular sports. As Niki Akhavan demonstrates, this tension played out in a series of confrontations over the admission of Iranian women into football matches. However, in the high-stakes competition for control over the ensuing narrative, the state's ability to leverage its control over sports television broadcasting granted it the ability to impose its values by incorporating them directly into the most popular medium for the consumption of football. As Akhavan also notes, however, attempts to consolidate the state's position through the media have only served to expose internal divisions within the ruling elite and continue to be undermined by popular challenges to authority.

Sports media networks have come to play a far greater role in the production, distribution, and consumption of football globally. As Craig LaMay explains in Chapter 12, Qatar expanded its influence in the realm of football through its purchase of BeIN Sports network and its acquisition of the rights to broadcast many of the leading European leagues and global competitions. With the launch of the blockade against Qatar by several of its GCC neighbors in 2017, BeIN was caught in the crosshairs of attempts to undercut Qatar's economic interests and tarnish its reputation. A Saudi-based network, BeoutQ, pirated BeIN's signal and offered it as a low-cost alternative to audiences throughout the Middle East. The resulting broadcast wars played out within international courts, in the court of global public opinion, and across the airwaves. While the battle of the broadcasters ended following the lifting of the blockade against Qatar and the restoration of diplomatic relations with its neighbors in 2021, the reverberations to this major challenge to BeIN's previously unmatched dominance are certain to be felt by football fans across the region. The race for the region's mammoth football viewing audience is likely to be decided by a combination of factors: access to new technological modes of delivery, the cutthroat competition for the acquisition of broadcast rights at increasingly exorbitant costs, and the overriding struggle for political control of the region's burgeoning media landscape.

As we hope the chapters enclosed in this collection demonstrate, football is not only an explanatory tool to assist in the understanding of broader political, cultural, and socioeconomic forces at work in the Middle East. Rather, it exists as a site of contestation in its own right. States view football as an avenue to accumulating power, whether in the face of popular resistance or at the expense of rival regimes. Corporate interests assess its seemingly limitless potential for commodification and profitability. Meanwhile, whether in the course of a revolutionary struggle, a momentary escape from their tribulations, or just another match day, people project onto football their hopes and fears, anxieties and aspirations. As the legendary manager of Liverpool FC Bill Shankly once said, "Some people believe that football is a matter of life and death...I can assure you, it is much, much more important than that."

1

THE POLITICAL GAME

A GENEALOGY OF THE EGYPTIAN LEAGUE

Ibrahim Elhoudaiby

Introduction

October 22, 1948. Egypt was going through an extended period
of crisis. Six different cabinets had been formed since 1940, and
the newly formed government, led by Nuqrāshī Pasha, was far
from stable. Beginning in the summer of 1948, a series of explo-
sions over several months terrorized Cairenes, leaving dozens dead
and hundreds injured. A column of the Egyptian military was con-
temporaneously besieged in al-Faluja, 30 kilometers northeast of
Gaza City in Palestine. It had been dispatched in May, after Zionists
began their ethnic cleansing of Palestinians. A truce had been in
process for some time, and, on that day, it finally went into effect.

October 22, 1948. Bani Suwayf, Upper Egypt; a sunny Friday
afternoon. Twenty-two players, hundreds of spectators, a handful
of club administrators, and a few journalists convened for a highly

17

anticipated sporting event. It was the inaugural game of the Egyptian football league: Fārūq (a club named after the king; now named Zamālek) vs. Dakhliyya ([Ministry of] Interior). The game ended with an astounding victory for Fārūq. Moḥammad Amīn, Fārūq's striker, scored the tournament's first goal, and his team scored three more times before the guests pulled off one face-saving goal. Final score: Fārūq 4, Dakhliyya 1, but neither team won the league. While Fārūq ended in fifth place, Ahly ended the season on top of the table and went on to win nine consecutive titles, before Fārūq won their first title in 1959/60.

On October 24, 1948, the events of Friday were reported in the newspapers. Because they belonged to the supposedly distinct realms of politics and sports, they were told separately. In Al-Ahrām, for example, news from the war in Palestine made the headlines, while the game result, alongside a photo of the governor of Bani Suwayf kicking off the football season, was covered in the sports section on page 8. The organization of academic disciplines reinforces this separation, and politicians and sports officials are keen on demarcating the fields within which they operate, insisting that sports are apolitical. For example, the Olympic Charter bars athletes from making political statements at the Olympic Games;[1] and the Fédération Internationale de Football Association (FIFA), the "United Nations of football," prohibits the display of "any political … statements or images" on players' equipment.[2] While admitting that sports and politics do sometimes overlap, these overlaps—such as the cancellation of a league, political chants at a stadium, or a war erupting in the aftermath of a football match— are dismissed as aberrations to be condemned and fixed.

But what if the interplay of sports and politics was not an aber-ration, but an essential feature of professional sports? George Orwell famously described sports as "war minus the shooting."[3] It is a domain in which friends and foes are demarcated, hence falling squarely within Carl Schmitt's definition of politics.[4] Critical schol-arship therefore regards organized football as a stage on which politics plays out. Take the Egyptian league's inaugural game. The competing teams were named after two powerful political symbols (the king and the ministry of interior), and the winners had to change their name a few years later, when a coup d'état abolished King Fārūq's monarchy and established a republic. Following the same logic, some scholars take the centennial rivalry between "Cairo's Giants" Ahly and Zamalek to be an extension of the Wafd Party's tensions with the palace, pointing to the heavy presence of Wafd Party leaders in the former's board, and the latter's name before the coup-cum-revolution.[5] Other scholars take these rival clubs to represent different social classes in colonial Egypt.[6]

While accepting the inseparability of professional football and politics, I contend that such a view falls short of capturing the politics of the game. It characterizes professional football as a platform on which national and international politics (the purview of formal political institutions) plays out, and not a political terrain in its own right. However, professional football is not just a sport played by athletes. More importantly, it is a game organized by clubs, associations, and other corporations that are invested in forming subjects, distributing power, and organizing the collective lives of teams and fans alike—all of which are political matters par excellence. Professional football does not therefore merely overlap with politics: it *is* politics.[7] The latter historical narrative is thus doubly political: the organization of a professional football league is ipso facto political, and both the truce in al-Faluja and the league's inaugural game are integral to the contestations of power that culminated in the birth of an independent, postcolonial state.

Rejecting the dualism of politics and professional football, this study explores the genealogy of Egypt's football league—the oldest league in Africa and the Middle East. National leagues are the most salient feature of professional football. While European leagues (notably the English Premier League, Bundesliga, Serie A, and La Liga) are the most successful in drawing talent, investors, and spectators from around the world, leagues exist in all 211 FIFA member nations. This universality offers ways to remain silent about the league's genealogy. With its existence deemed natural, the Egyptian league's history is only told teleologically. Instead, I take the league's inauguration to be an uncertain outcome of a complex historical process, at the heart of which was the emergence of clubs as sites for negotiating Egyptian nationalism and for organizing sports and youth under British colonial rule. While associated with the nationalist project, club directors were also invested in configuring power relations within their respective clubs, negotiating their position vis-à-vis other clubs and institutions, and establishing their collective hegemony over other forms of play. It is through these multiple negotiations that both the politics of the game and the specific form of the national league are best understood.

This chapter is divided into five sections. In the first section, I study the early days of football in Egypt. I explore the diverse forms of play expanding at the turn of the twentieth century, analyze their social and political significance, and identify the institutions supporting them. The second section focuses on the nationalization of football in the aftermath of the 1919 revolution, which gave rise to a nationalist, anti-colonial movement and, subsequently, a constitutional monarchy with compromised sovereignty and de facto British occupation. I scrutinize the attempts of middle-class Egyptians to expand the nation to include rural and working-class populations, the role of football and mass media in these endeavors, and their implications on the politics of the game. The third and fourth sections center on club politics. In the third section, I examine both the ascent of clubs to a hegemonic position in organizing the football game and the shifting distribution of power within these clubs. In the fourth section, I trace these clubs' role in organizing the nation, demarcating their members from others, negotiating hierarchies, and assigning roles to different social groups. In the final section, I outline the developments of the professional football landscape dominated by these clubs, and the interclub power contestations that culminated in the establishment of the national football league in 1948.

Genesis: From Play to Game

Football was introduced in Egypt by the British military. The occupation of 1882 brought to the country military officers who had previously participated in the British championships. The subsequent defeat of the Mahdist uprising of 1885 in Sudan gave the

occupying troops more time to spare. Football games and tournaments were routinely organized in camps, and some games were
played in public squares in major cities, where neighboring
Egyptian peasants, workers, urban poor, and passersby watched.[8]
It was not long before these spectators appropriated, creolized, and
played football.

The game played in military barracks was alien to Egypt's contemporaneous, physical culture. Scholarship on both Mamluk and
peasant/countryside leisure suggests that precolonial and subaltern
sport was less bureaucratized.[9] There were no strict rules, record
keeping was minimal at best, and games did not necessarily result
in winners and losers—at least not definitively. When *awlād al-
balad* (the poor urban masses, literally "the country's sons") played
football,[10] hitherto referred to as the "British game,"[11] they applied
their norms of play, significantly relaxing the rules of the game
played by soldiers. There were no strict rules other than kicking
the ball using feet and attempting to get it between the designated
goal posts; "all other rules, including offside, penalty kicks, the
number of players on each side [and whether it should be the same
for both sides], were relative, negotiable and changeable, and could
be agreed upon either before or during the game."[12] If one team
significantly outplayed the other, teams were reshuffled in the
middle of a match to balance it out. Players were not always dis-
tinguishable from spectators: games took place in alleyways where
play was interwoven—and had to negotiate space—with other
social activities. It was common for a passerby to stop to kick the
ball around, before walking away. Young boys played in their traditional garments (*jallābiyya*s), some "begging their mothers to
make them shorter" so that they could move and kick the ball
around with ease.[13] The creolized, *awlād al-balad* football, in other
words, was not primarily about winning—it was a means of social-
izing. Friend and foe, or teammate and rival, were not therefore
clearly demarcated, and competitiveness, while an essential part of
the sport, remained marginal.

This street football therefore stands in stark contrast with the
formal football game, largely confined to British and effendi circles.
For the British colonial officers, football served two purposes.

First, it was a means of inculcating discipline through the rules of the game.[14] Targeted colonial subjects were not peasants or urban poor playing on the streets, but effendis—the colonially educated middle-class men who were to be disciplined into civilized imperial citizens. Second, mixing with the colonial subjects on playing fields was a means of emphasizing colonial difference. It was an expression of British superiority manifest in their mastery of team tactics and individual self-discipline.[15] Colonial discourses had deemed the Egyptian body "weaker, less disciplined, and insufficiently masculine" and therefore unfit for national service,[16] and British superiority on the field validated these claims. By and large, however, and while the emphasis on physical culture was manifest in most media outlets of the era, this "disciplining through football" was initially confined to a small segment of the effendi class—those in direct contact with military camps. Beyond this domain, effendis were hardly interested in football.

But a football game that took place in 1895 turned the world upside down. Moḥammad Effendi Nāshid, an administrative employee at a British military workshop, assembled a team of Egyptian effendis to play against a British military team. The game took place at a square near the Citadel, and a few effendis watched. It was not intended to be a big night; a British victory was expected. Against all odds, however, the effendis' team scored twice, and the British failed to equalize. As soon as the (British) referee blew the final whistle, news of this unthinkable victory spread throughout neighboring coffeehouses where effendis spent their afternoons. Even if they knew next to nothing about the rules of the game, these effendis were proud. Having "suddenly discovered that defeating the English was possible," they took interest in football as a domain of rivalry in which they could assert themselves. The colonial strategy of using the game to demonstrate differentiation was turned on its head. Since that day, football for the effendis "was no longer just a game."[17] Or did it just *become* a game?

Notwithstanding its popularity, *awlād al-balad* football was not a game. As David Graeber notes, play and game are not the same. Games have certain common features: "they are clearly bounded in time and space, and thereby framed off from ordinary life ...

There are also rules ... And, critically: that's all there is. Any place, person, action, that falls outside that framework is extraneous; it doesn't matter; it's not part of the game."[18] Play, in its ultimate form, is the exact opposite of that; it is unrestricted improvisation in the complete absence of rules. The vernacularized street football was not ultimate play, for it did have some minimal rules that constituted a common language for the competing teams. It was not, however, a game.

As the football game became more popular among effendis, play and the game became demarcated both socially and geographically. Play, on the one hand, took place in streets and was associated with the ("uncivilized") masses. The game, on the other hand, became increasingly integral to the emergent effendi ideology that took corporal self-disciplining, or *riyāḍa*, to be a measure of civilization and the ability to self-govern.[19] Because playing on the streets and mixing with the masses was deemed too dangerous,[20] effendis established enclosed spaces for the game. Their youth practiced football at schools, where they also studied British curricula.[21] Newly formed school teams participated in games and tournaments against other school teams. With football being a measure of civilization, school officials took pride in their respective football teams' performance and were keen on attracting and retaining talent.[22] To be sure, effendi interest in football was not uniform; some segments of the elite were critical of this focus on physical culture. They saw it as a distraction and a deviation from the intellectual and spiritual pedagogy necessary for building (or reviving) a strong nation. "Prince of Poets" Aḥmad Shawqī, to take one example, composed a poem on the occasion of Lord Cromer's departure in 1907, criticizing his educational policy, which "turned schools from the pursuit of science to 'football.'"[23] This dissent notwithstanding, the football game was becoming increasingly central to the effendi world.

The year 1907 saw another development in the bureaucratization of football. On April 24, 'Umar Effendi Luṭfi called for a meeting to discuss his proposal for establishing a sports club. Luṭfi, one of nationalist leader Muṣṭafa Kāmil's closest associates, had previously founded the Higher Schools Students Club (HSSC) in

1905. Intended to "facilitate communication between Kāmil and the [effendi] students,"[24] the HSSC had a prestigious building surrounded by a spacious garden for social gatherings, but no sports facilities. Kāmil encouraged the progression from this HSSC to the (national) Ahly Sporting Club, which he saw as a "more mature form of organization,"[25] adding sport to the social gatherings. It was also more mature in its institutional form.[26] Building on the contemporaneous proliferation of corporations, and Luṭfi's earlier interest in associations, manifest in his writings and contributions to the establishment of several "cooperative companies" (*sharikāt taʿāwuniyya*),[27] Ahly was established as a joint-stock company.

Ahly was not the only club formed in this period. In the preceding decade, both British and Egyptian clubs were formed. But Ahly was unique in two ways. First, it was the first *sports* club to be formed primarily—even if not yet exclusively—for Egyptians.[28] It was therefore the first embodiment of the new effendi interest in *riyāḍa*. The club established facilities and hosted games for different sports, namely football, tennis, billiards, and gymnastics,[29] football being by far the most popular.[30] Its membership was restricted to effendis, constituting a small minority of natives,[31] and the intention was to drive them away from the "destructive habits" of smoking all afternoon and evening in coffeehouses, and to encourage them instead to engage in *riyāḍa*.[32] Second, and further illustrating the intertwining of sports and nationalism in effendi ideology, Ahly was founded and directed by leaders of the nascent nationalist movement. In addition to Luṭfi, the list of founders and directors includes Saʿd Zaghlūl, Amīn Sāmī, Moḥammad Maḥmūd, Abdel-Khāliq Tharwat, Ṭalʿat Ḥarb, and Aḥmad Ḥishmat, all key figures in the subsequent 1919 revolt.

Ahly's football team would be later recognized as the most successful African club in the twentieth century, but when the club opened its doors to members in 1909, it did not have a football team. It did have a football pitch, and eventually built a stand for 200 spectators in 1924.[33] This pitch was initially used for intra-club games in which teams representing students of different schools played against each other. These games became bureaucratized in 1913, when Board Member Aḥmad Ḥishmat donated a silver cup for an annual football competition between teams representing different high schools. The Mixed Football Association (MFA), which was founded in 1910 by representatives of seven European countries, organized its first tournament in the same year, but Ahly declined to participate. Football games took place primarily within the club, with directors mostly interested in promoting *riyāḍa* among Egyptians.[34] It was not until 1916 that Ahly formed a team to participate in the Sultanic Cup, organized by the English Egyptian Football Association (EEFA) that was created in the same year.[35] Even then, school and club teams overlapped: of the thirty-eight games Ahly's team played that year, only thirteen were against English sides. The remaining fifteen games were against high school teams comprised of the same body of players that formed the club's team, and competing for the Ḥishmat Cup.[36] Contrary to standard (and rather anachronistic) historiographical accounts, the club was not established primarily to compete against the British. It was a space for effendis to compete in physical games. Effendi interest in this physical culture remained limited, and club memberships are a case in point: Ahly, the club most interested in recruiting effendis, had 228 members in 1915 and 263 in 1919.

At the cusp of the 1919 revolt, *awlād al-balad*'s play remained the hegemonic form of football. Effendis interested in the game played in enclosed spaces, clubs, or schools, and were not interested in extending it to the masses. Their imagined community was limited to effendis, who took interest in *riyāḍa* (and consequently, football) as a measure of civilizational progress.

The Making of a National Sport

On March 8, 1919, British colonial authorities arrested and exiled nationalist leader Sa'd Zaghlūl, and two of his associates, who were demanding independence. The arrests sparked a wave of protests across the country, in which hundreds of protestors were killed within two weeks. Ahly, and probably other clubs, acted as launching pads for many effendi protests, but this was far from an effendi revolt. Not only did urban middle-class women participate in protests, but also workers and peasants in different provinces. The

25

masses, including effendis, were involved in the struggle against
the British colonizers, and increasingly they saw themselves, with
all their differences, as constituting a single body politic. The contemporaneous collapse of the Ottoman Empire contributed to the
naturalization of the nation-state as the ultimate political community. Anti-colonialism and nationalism therefore became syn-
onyms. The nation, defined in opposition to the colonizer,[37]
encompassed more than its effendi core, and was now struggling
to restore its sovereignty manifest in an independent state.

Redefining the nation to include the masses necessitated redefining the national sport. The effendi interest in *riyāḍa*, expanded
since the turn of the century, had become "a matter of common
sense to elite and middle-class Egyptians" by the 1920s.[38] This had
allowed the colonizers and effendis to share the love of the game,
and exhibit their sportsmanship on the field. However, the nation
now included other social groups that were united against the
British. The "primary contradiction" was no longer between game
and play, but between the nation and the colonizer. For football to
retain its position as a national sport, it needed to exclude the
British, and include non-effendis at least partially.

Excluding the British took place through the Egyptianization
(*tamṣīr*) of football. This process finds its roots in the 1907 establishment of Ahly, which institutionalized effendi participation in
the game. A handful of foreigners had initially joined the club; in
1920, however, the club revised its policy, restricting membership
to Egyptians.[39] Other Egyptian clubs were also established, notably
Ittiḥād (Union) in Alexandria, and Maṣrī (Egyptian) and Nahḍa
(Renaissance, later renamed Ismāʿīlī) in the Canal Zone. Yet perhaps the most consequential club nationalization is that of Zamālek,
initially known as Qaṣr Al-Nīl Club. Established in 1911 by George
Marzbach, a Belgian lawyer at the mixed courts, the club soon
changed its name to Mukhtalaṭ (Mixed). It is not clear whether the
club's membership was initially limited to foreigners,[40] or whether
it was an exception to that rule and became a place for "Western-
educated Egyptians" to interact with "colonial administrators and
European industrialists."[41] In any case, foreigners, especially those
associated with mixed courts, formed the majority (at least) of club

members, and Egyptians—who were allegedly denied member-ship—joined the club as football players.[42] This was part of a broader phenomenon of European clubs allowing "'servant teams' comprised of local Egyptians to play against other clubs," and tak-ing pride in organizing such events.[43]

Foreign control over the "mixed" club came under fire in the years leading up to the 1919 revolt.[44] As the club opened its membership to Egyptians, who gradually constituted a plurality of members, the foreign directors (especially the French) main-tained their autocratic control, until an Egyptian takeover in 1927.[45] Three years later, the club decided to restrict its mem-bership to only Egyptians,[46] and elected Minister of War Ḥaydar Pasha as president. The collapse of the Ottoman Empire and the reconfiguration of rulers—as patrons of the nation and members of the body politic—encouraged them to "provide patronage in an attempt to demonstrate their national character,"[47] and national clubs were key beneficiaries of this new interest. Even the club's name was Egyptianized. No longer "mixed," Mukhtalaṭ was renamed after King Fārūq, the "first Arabic-speaking" leader of the ruling dynasty in 1940, just one year after the king placed the club under his "royal guardianship," and four years after the ratification of the Montreux Convention, which provided for the abolition of mixed courts.

Egyptianizing football was not limited to clubs. The sport's governing bodies underwent the same process. Ahly and other Egyptian clubs were critical of the MFA's exclusion of Egyptians from its bodies from the start, and did not participate in organized games and tournaments. Ahly did participate, however, in the competitions organized by the EEFA, notably the Sultanic Cup, as did other "Egyptian" clubs. However, in the aftermath of the revolt, the Egyptian Football Association (EFA) was established in 1921. In a letter to *Al-Ahrām* newspaper on October 3rd that year, the association's assistant secretary wrote that the "sports com-munity in Egyptian clubs decided to establish for themselves a union ... Clubs have ... agreed that the *ittiḥād* will represent the Egyptian nation (*al-umma al-miṣriyya*) in the Olympics."[48] In 1923, the EFA finally secured its oversight over twenty-four clubs.

The EFA soon began creating a national football domain. Instead of competing against the British, Egyptian teams could now have their own, exclusively Egyptian, tournaments. The Prince Fārūq Cup was organized for the first time in 1922. Mukhtalaṭ won the first title after an astounding victory over the Alexandrian team Ittiḥād: 5–0 in the final game. Three other teams (Ahly, Ittiḥād, and Tirsāna [Arsenal]) won the title in the following four years. Several other competitions were organized in the 1920s, notably the different provincial leagues inaugurated between 1922 and 1924. The Sultanic Cup competitions continued until 1938, and available records suggest (albeit inconclusively) that it had been Egyptianized as well, with the Sherwood Foresters' 1920 title being the only title won by an English team post 1919.

In addition to Egyptianizing clubs and competitions, assembling a national team was another focal point of Egyptianization efforts. First constituted in 1920, the team competed in the Summer Olympics of 1920, 1924, and 1928. In 1934, it became the first African and Middle Eastern team to participate in the FIFA World Cup. Throughout the 1920s, the team was almost exclusively comprised of effendis, but the post-1919 nation was not limited to these effendis. For the team to become truly national, non-effendis had to take part. While they did not initially join effendis on the field, they were invited as spectators.[49]

Arabic newspapers, proliferating in the aftermath of 1919, began dedicating pages to the coverage of sports. While literacy levels were relatively low,[50] newspapers were "often read aloud in coffeehouses and other public spaces, making it available to a broad cross-section of Egyptian men."[51] Appearing in newspapers and being communicated orally on a large scale was the news of the football game, not the street sport. Shaun Lopez's study of *Al Ahrām*, the largest Arabic newspaper of the time, outlined some central themes of its coverage of sports in the 1920s. It "associated both itself and the national team with the Egyptian people as a whole," described matches "as if they were a military battle," and displayed "intense preoccupation with the European gaze."[52] Football, in other words, was the nationalists' battlefield in which they play-fought against their colonizers to assert themselves.

While "print capitalism" played a central role in ensuring the hegemony of the effendi game,[53] high levels of illiteracy meant that, for the effendi game to penetrate the non-effendi world, print had to be coupled with the more hegemonic oral transmission.

Delimiting Competition, Entrenching Clubs

Expanding the nation beyond its effendi core took place through an uneven negotiation, one in which clubs played a central role. Like other corporations, clubs were unique in their ability to link their members (and affiliates) into a unified body politic, hence providing a solution to the problem of liberal governmentality.[54] This is particularly true of the metropolis, where, as Michel Foucault reminds us, the state was bound by the imperative of not governing too much.[55] In this European context, as one 1933 article in a specialized Egyptian sports magazine put it, clubs are "supported by government power and the money of the rich, and therefore increase in power over time." They are "organized, luxurious, and equipped with all means of leisure and training," and have "all the technical coaches and trainers they need."[56] The situation in Egypt was different. Corporations did not rise as a response to the imperative of not ruling too much, but as a response to the problem of compromised state sovereignty. With the nation being defined primarily as against its British colonizers, and with these colonizers significantly controlling the state, anti-colonial (read: national) elites had to resort to corporations (including clubs) as a means of formulating and organizing a body politic. It is in this context that Luṭfi called for the establishment of Ahly. These native clubs did not have government support—at least not at the level they needed.[57] They had "little capital, and therefore appeared deficient."[58] Club directors had to at once expand their club's presence and role in organizing Egyptian youth and establish their own power within these clubs, all without the support provided to their European counterparts by their respective governments.

The power of club directors over members and teams was initially minimal. While these directors were authorized to approve new membership requests, hence delimiting the community, few rules organized the relationship between directors and members. This is especially true in the case of Egyptian/effendi clubs: as long as the members abided by the effendi ethics, it seems, from Ahly's archives, that they could do whatever they pleased. Clubs did not initially form football teams, and when they did, teams were loosely defined. Directors had little control over players who could (and did) play for more than one team at the same time.[59] It took over a decade for Ahly to begin regulating, but not entirely restricting, these "poly-clubic" affiliations, which are best understood in light of directors' efforts to consolidate power.

Ḥussein Ḥegāzī's journey offers insight into this consolidation. Born in 1889,[60] Ḥegāzī started playing football in the streets of Cairo, before joining a school team. After failing his high school exams in 1910—allegedly due to his obsession with football—his father sent him to study engineering in London, where he soon joined the football team. He also joined the English professional league, playing for Dulwich Hamlet and then Fulham. In 1912, Ḥegāzī was selected to join the Wanderers in their friendly games against different European sides.[61] His football career peaked, however, when he played and studied at Cambridge. In the 1913–14 season, his performance solicited countless compliments from *The Times*, which called him the "most conspicuous,"[62] and "most promising" player,[63] and the "mainstay" of the Cambridge side.[64] Ḥegāzī, already recognized as an effendi icon for the European compliments he received, returned to Egypt in the summer of 1914 and formed a team to play against different British regimental teams. His team, known as the Ḥegāzī Eleven, won several games, further boosting his popularity and that of the sport among the effendi class. Contemporaneous teams, including Team Nāshid, were also named after their captains.[65] Although Ḥegāzī was a club member since 1914,[66] it was after only a year later that he succumbed to pressures from Ahly and joined the club's team, along with several members of his team. The club helped him organize these games, which took place on its football field.[67] At Ahly, his team—as the club's archives make clear—was known as both Ahly, and Team Ḥegāzī.[68] In 1919, Ḥegāzī was ready for his next move. When Mukhtalaṭ offered him a better deal for the distribution of match revenues, he immediately accepted, and many fans followed him.[69] When the club later moved to its new premises, which did not have a billiards hall, Ḥegāzī, an avid billiard player, joined Sikka Ḥadīd (Railways), again followed by some fans. He rejoined Ahly in 1924, but when the directors suspended him for refusing to accept the second-place medal after losing to Tirsāna in the 1928 Sultanic Cup final,[70] he moved once again to Mukhtalaṭ, where he retired in 1931. Ḥegāzī also captained the national team at the Olympics in 1920 and 1924. Throughout most of his career, Ḥegāzī not only moved freely between clubs, but also assembled his own team that was independent of all clubs, organized games, and negotiated his team's share from match revenues.

None of the subsequent football stars enjoyed such power. By the late 1920s, football teams had club affiliations, and players, no matter how talented, were only members of these teams. Ḥegāzī's reportedly unmatched skill had little to do with that. Rather, it was the consolidation of club power that both restricted footballers' involvement in organizing the game and shifted fan loyalty from player to club. At least three factors contributed to this consolidation. First is the longevity of clubs' existence compared to individual players. Being established as corporations, clubs were legal persons, and therefore potentially immortal. This meant that they could outlive their players. Fans may have followed Ḥegāzī from club to club because of his wins against British teams, but unlike him, these clubs never retired. Team Ḥegāzī lasted for a decade, but the Ahly, Zamālek, and Sikka Ḥadīd teams he played for still exist. He may have won numerous titles and trophies, but even Sikka Ḥadīd, the least successful of these teams (now playing in the third division), won titles. Some, such as the Sultanic Cup and the Cairo League of 1924, were won early enough to establish a historical legacy, and others, such as the Sultanic Cup of 1936, were won late enough for subsequent generations to remember. Because fans favored the immortal—with which they could build memories, sometimes across generations—the fan versatility characteristic of Ḥegāzī's era was on the decline, even before he retired.

Traditions "invented" by these clubs contributed to the shift in fan loyalty from player to club. In 1917, and shortly after Ḥegāzī joined the club, Ahly's logo was designed.[71] In the aftermath of the 1919 revolt, the club's general assembly meetings were occasions for its board of directors to educate members (including players) about the club's patriotic origins and founding fathers.[72] Be it Ahly, Zamālek, Ittiḥād, or Maṣrī, different clubs developed their foundational myths, all (unsurprisingly) about the respective club and its founders' role in resisting colonialism. Clubs did not simply replace their retired players with younger ones—for example, in the case of Ahly, replacing Ḥegāzı with Mokhtār El-Tetsh—but they also amassed a set of symbols, rituals, and narratives that buttressed fan loyalty. Because clubs were not just premises for *riyāḍa*, but were now also political communities, loyalty was expected of players, too. Therefore, despite his outstanding skill, El-Tetsh is more often praised for his loyalty to Ahly.[73] In refusing to play for any other team throughout his career, he wrote his own name into Ahly's tradition.

The consolidation of club identity was coupled with bureaucratic measures that gradually buttressed directors' power over teams. In the case of Ahly, bureaucratization started with the club's decision to assemble a team in 1913. A football secretary was appointed the same year, and his office was soon formalized with the club directors decreeing the members of the football committee. The secretary's first task was to organize an election for the team captain, who would then join the football committee and report on its activity to the club's directors in bimonthly reports.[74] The team was also bureaucratized. In addition to selecting players to fill in different positions in the team (and reporting their names and positions to the board), the football secretary also assigned regular training hours for the club's team. The club's board decided to provide the team apparel, "except shoes," on the condition that it remain the club's property.[75] This bureaucratization demarcated the team players from other club members, and, as the club's board of directors provided more assistance for the former—also subsidizing the cost of their "trips" and matchday expenses—it had more power over the team.

In 1915, Ḥegāzī and other players were warned against violating the club's bylaws, which allegedly "do not permit a [club] player to play for any other team."[76] This rule almost amounted to each club having a monopoly over its players, except for two caveats. First, such restrictions only applied when these teams played against Ahly. When other players submitted a request to partake in a game at Sikka Ḥadīd a few months later, the directors approved, noting that as long as they did not "play against the club," nothing in the bylaws prohibited them from partaking in the game.[77] Second, and as Ḥegāzī's journey makes clear, directors had control over team players only insofar as they chose to be part of the team. But they could not restrict them from resigning from the club's team to join others.

The restrictions imposed by the club boards on the participation of their team members with other teams soon came under attack from all sides. The bureaucratization of competitions with the emergence of the MFA and EEFA led to a more expansive interpretation of these restrictions. Not playing against the club in this context meant not playing for any of the teams participating in these competitions. As the competitions proliferated, more games fell under this category, and the "friendly" (read: standalone) games in which a club player could participate became scarce. Each player was now associated with one team. For skilled players like Ḥegāzī, this was hardly a problem. Others, however, protested. In March 1918, Ahly team member Ibrāhīm Osmān submitted a formal complaint to the club's board. Throughout the season of 1917–18, Osmān claimed he only participated in a mere four games. He felt wronged because as a team member, he was barred from representing other clubs. After investigating and deliberating, directors issued their resolution, which was based on the club records. Osmān, the resolution read, had actually played ten (not four) of the twenty-five games that the team had played that season, a number determined to be "not too bad for a substitute." But the player's grievances were heard: the directors decided to form another team "to allow players who are not part of the first team" to participate in football games.[78] Since then, and for a few years, Ahly (and later, Zamālek) had two teams.

Two other sets of measures strengthened the grip of the club's directors over their football team members. First was the consolidation of EFA power. The teams participating in the MFA and

EEFA competitions represented either clubs or British regiments. When the EFA was established in 1921, it limited its membership to Egyptian clubs, hence provoking strong opposition from Ḥegāzī, who was still interested in participating in competitions with his clubless team.[79] With clubs not clearly defined, however, this was hardly considered a barrier to entry. It was only eight years later that these barriers to entry became significant,[80] when the EFA defined a club as, among other things, a "sports establishment, with bylaws enforced by a body of directors, and premises that include sports facilities, and a football pitch compliant with the EFA specifications." While some temporary exceptions were made to extend membership to establishments with non-compliant pitches, these exceptions were exactly that: temporary. The line separating clubs from (now informal) teams had been drawn, and, unsurprisingly, it mapped perfectly on to the line demarcating the football game from street football.

Second were the growing restrictions on the transfers of players. When Ahly suspended Ḥegāzī in 1928, he moved to Mukhtalaṭ, and there was nothing that Ahly could do to stop him. Player transfers remained unregulated for a few more years. In the 1930s, an entente between club directors emerged, leading to the involvement of the directors of the two clubs involved in the transfer. Already in 1925, the EFA started issuing player identification cards, with each player affiliated with one club at a time.[81] By the early 1930s, these IDs were made valid for one year, restricting transfer during football season. The grip clubs had over their players was further strengthened when, in January 1935, the EFA extended the validity of players' IDs, making them good for two years.[82] Even in the 1930s, Egyptian clubs compared poorly to their European counterparts, but the power they consolidated over both semi-professional footballers and the football scene in Egypt was significant. It is from this position of strength that clubs negotiated the expansion of the nation.

Negotiating the Nation

The 1919 revolt transformed the meaning of nationalism. The earlier "moment of departure," nationalism was an elitist project in which national identity was confined to effendis. The nation now broadly included other participants in the revolt. Effendis needed to maintain their hegemony while mobilizing and organizing the masses for the nationalist project. In the maneuver that followed, they needed to integrate the masses while keeping them at arm's length from the nation's core. The negotiation therefore entailed both "the development of the thesis [effendi football in this case] by incorporating a part of the antithesis [or street football],"[83] and developing a set of pedagogical practices that aimed at civilizing the non-effendis. This negotiation took place, in part, through football. Substantively, and thanks to print capitalism, the effendi game emerged as the proper *fuṣḥā* (standard/classical Arabic)—like football to be used in official occasions, even if the vernacularized, colloquial street football was more popular. It was therefore the game, now confined to clubs, that defined the nation. The negotiation was largely confined to questions of access to this football nation, and clubs played a central role in it. Two questions defined this negotiation: extending the national game to non-effendis, and consolidating and expanding the national football space. The inauguration of the national league and the specific form it took emerged as the unintended outcome of this negotiation.

Non-effendis were initially invited to football clubs not as players, but rather as spectators supporting both national and club teams competing against foreign sides. Football stadiums therefore emerged as sites of national unity. This unity, however, did not entail equality. In fact, the setting of stadiums provided a model for the ordering of the nation, reflecting the hierarchies therein. Not only were tickets divided into three price categories, but the expected fan attitude and attire in each category was different. First-class seats were first-row hardwood chairs with armrests and backrests, and were reserved for pashas (elites) and well-established effendis, who attended games in their suits. Second-class seats had only backrests and were reserved for effendis who were seated, in their suits, behind those in first class. Pashas and effendis had been attending football matches for over a decade, but in the aftermath of the 1919 revolt the masses also attended. Standing behind the pashas and effendis in the seatless third-class zones in their *jallābiyya*s, these fans were constantly condemned for their uncivilized conduct.[84] Therefore, while gathering to support the national team, the nation—in terms of appearance and conduct— was far from homogenous, and was clearly segregated. In fact, police forces were mobilized to separate peasants from the pashas and effendis attending the games.[85]

The masses were not only integrated as fans. Confining non-effendis to spectatorship risked both alienating them and wasting a valuable disciplining opportunity. It also deprived clubs of talent and fans. Several effendi clubs, including Ahly and Mukhtalaṭ, gradually opened their doors to street talent, extending their membership to non-effendis who proved their competence on the field. Ahly also hired a coach to discipline the talented street players into professional footballers, and Mukhtalaṭ soon followed suit. This disciplining was not limited to the football field. As non-effendis joined club teams, they were introduced to the effendi social world. In addition to sportsmanship, disciplining the body, and respecting hierarchies and order, these players also learned effendi etiquette, and acquired effendi sensibilities. Upon retiring, many of them secured effendi governmental jobs through their club connections. Football remained an effendi game, but it was also a civilizing apparatus that now produced effendis in the same way that schools did, as the growing discourse on sportsmanship indicates. And just like schools, calls were made for opening clubs for all: "the youth, the weak, and those with special needs. For the entire population; old and young, women and children." If *riyāḍa* was the accepted measure of civilization, it was argued, the nation did not need a handful of champions to progress, but an entire population engaged in physical activity.[86] However, these calls came to no avail. The non-effendi inclusion was a means of social mobility in a hierarchal system that maintained the supremacy of effendi culture and guarded against elevating the vernacular culture to a normative position. It is this keenness to preserve the game/effendi-play/ masses hierarchy that explains the decision made by some clubs, notably Gezira, to not hire non-effendi talents, or not join football tournaments altogether.

Also partially integrated into the national football milieu in the aftermath of the 1919 revolt was the Coptic Christian minority.

Coptic clubs were established alongside Jewish, Greek, Italian, Levantine, British, and other local and foreign community clubs at the turn of the twentieth century.[87] In the following years, tensions between Muslim and Coptic elites were building, and eventually climaxed with the 1910 assassination of Christian Prime Minister Butrus Ghali.[88] The assassination proved to be a turning point in two ways. First, it led the state to adopt a zero tolerance policy towards the National Party with which the assassin, as well as Kāmil and Luṭfī, were affiliated. This gave rise to a new national leadership that was keen on integrating Copts into the national movement.[89] Second, and consequently, the assassination contributed to the watering down of the religious content of nationalist discourse, allowing for the emergence of a "religiously neutral" nationalist space.

Physical culture was already a central theme in contemporaneous religious discourses, both Muslim and Christian. Effendi clubs provided a venue for members of these communities to participate in *riyāḍa* outside their narrow configurations. Islamic and Coptic clubs and associations persisted (and, in the case of Islam, proliferated after the Ottoman Empire collapsed), but were marginalized from the football domain. Many Copts simultaneously migrated to the effendi clubs; Ahly archives, for example, show a significant growth in Coptic membership after 1919.[90] However, Copts, while becoming club members, seldom made it onto teams. They occupied their diverse class positions in the stands, they were members of effendi clubs, and they faced no legal obstacles in attempts to join teams, but these teams were de facto confined to Muslim effendis or those who had become so.

Another form of marginalization took place with respect to women. If non-effendi men could join the team through discipline, women, despite their strong appearance on the national stage in 1919, could not. Since the turn of the century, strands of the emergent effendi ideology insisted that "a successful civilization must have physically fit women as well."[91] Young women therefore formed sports teams in primary and high schools.[92] Among the leading advocates of this idea was Luṭfī, a close associate of Qāsim Amīn, who, like his friend, published a treatise on women's rights. As early as December 1907, Luṭfī advocated for women's *riyāḍa*.

Maintaining effendi-cum-Victorian morals, he proposed to Ahly's executive committee "choosing two days a week in which only women would be allowed entry" to the club's premises.[93] The committee postponed discussing his proposal, and the available records make no mention of women's participation in any club activities until after the 1919 revolt, in which women's participation yielded a handful of iconic national martyrs. In 1922, eleven years after Luṭfi's death, his proposal resurfaced, and foreign relatives of club members were allowed to use the club's tennis courts. A year later, the club finally designated two days a week (Mondays and Wednesdays) for women's riyāḍa. On these days, no men were allowed to enter the club until noon.[94] The following year, Saturdays were also designated for women's riyāḍa. Very little is known about the kind of sports women played during those days, but records show that Ahly had only eleven women members, made up of six foreigners and five Egyptians,[95] hence ruling out football (at least in its bureaucratized form). While riyāḍa was therefore not the purview of men, professional football was.

The football nation was thus a nation of men. The game, as depicted by popular media, was a form of war in which the national team (not unlike the military) thrived to maintain national pride. But women were now part of the nation represented by this national football team. While excluded from the field, they were still encouraged to attend games and support the team. When a Yugoslavian team was invited to play some friendly games against a team assembled of players from different Cairene clubs in 1926, women were among the crowd. It was not, of course, the first time that women attended football games, but this time they came in large numbers, and a pavilion (surādiq) was installed for them.[96] While keeping them at arm's length, effendis negotiated a formula whereby women (albeit not on the field) were members of this nation represented by the muntakhab, i.e., the national football team.

Peripheralized for the Nation

The Egyptianization of football clubs and competitions did not entail the consolidation of a nationwide football domain. The "foot-

ball nation" was, in fact, disconnected: every urban center constituted a stand-alone football zone with its own nationalist politics
and interclub rivalries. Friendly games were mostly intra-zonal,
and while nationalist club directors were invested in the geographical connectedness and expansion of their football nation, the financial and administrative costs of travelling meant that, before 1919,
such efforts remained scarce. Take the case of Ahly: the Port Said
and Asyut clubs invited the Ahly team for friendly games in 1917.
In both cases, the team's trip became a major social event. Officials
of the host clubs received their guests at the railway station and
organized banquets, and the club's delegation, including players
and officials, stayed for a few days before and after the games.[97]
The cost of these games was so burdensome that club directors had
to negotiate their respective shares in covering them.[98] Internally,
directors negotiated the division of costs between the club and its
players. Most friendly games therefore took place between clubs
of the same urban center, while inter-province games were largely
limited to the Sultanic Cup. Being a knockout tournament, the
number of games a team played was contingent on its success, and
even the winner played only four to six games annually. Sultanic
patronage for the tournament, as well as the limited revenues from
match tickets, helped subsidize these games.

The post-1919 Egyptianization efforts were thus primarily
focused on consolidated provincial football zones. The nationwide
Prince Fārūq Cup was inaugurated in 1922, but its significance
remained secondary to provincial leagues that were organized by
the EFA that were inaugurated starting in 1922. The EFA designated Cairo, Alexandria, and the Canal Zones as the nation's football zones, and the different clubs within each of these zones competed for a provincial league title. Each zone therefore emerged as
a football center in its own right, its "Egyptianness" consisting
primarily of the exclusion of British clubs. Because playing within
these football centers entailed no significant travel and transportation costs, different clubs, irrespective of the scale of their membership or the abundance of financial resources, were on equal
footing. Records on the Alexandria and Canal Zone tournaments
are scarce, but the Cairo records indicate that no single club domi-

nated the competition. In its first eleven years, Ahly and Mukhtalaṭ won four titles each, Sikka Ḥadīd won two, and Tirsāna one. Of the six teams competing, four won titles—an indicator of the competitive balance of these provincial leagues.

These football zones delimited the nation. Because competitions took place on a provincial level, so clubs located outside these urban centers were at least partially excluded from the football nation. The status of these clubs, especially clubs from Upper Egypt, such as the Asyut Club, remained ambiguous. While excluded from the provincial leagues, they still participated in the Prince Fārūq Cup. These peripheral clubs lobbied to participate in provincial leagues. The Zagazig club, located midway between Cairo and Ismailia, requested to join the Cairo League. Its request was denied, and, consequently, it joined the Canal Zone league. Because these peripheral clubs had to travel to play their games, they were at a significant disadvantage. This, in turn, had significant impacts on their results. As a result, it should come as no surprise that when the EFA clustered its member clubs into three tiers in 1929, only three of the fifteen Tier A clubs were from outside the EFA-designated football zones.[99]

Clubs were not only integrated into the national football space through non-provincial competitions. In 1922, and alongside the provincial competitions, the Prince Fārūq Cup was inaugurated, setting the stage for a national game. The cup is significant in that it was the first nationwide competition that was exclusively Egyptian. It was not, however, the most important tournament in the season. Due to the high cost of travelling, only a few clubs participated. As a knockout competition, participating in the cup entailed playing a limited number of games. The 1923 finalists, to take one example, played only six games. A knockout tournament was apt for the national level because playing more games—and therefore incurring more travel costs and logistical hardships—was contingent on success. While contributing to the connectedness of the nation of football, the Cup tilted the playing field. Because more clubs were located in Cairo than in other provinces, the probability of Cairene teams playing locally in this national competition was significantly higher. Of the six games Ahly played on its way to winning the 1923 title, five took place in Cairo.[100] Of the cup's first twenty titles, Cairene teams won fifteen of the first twenty titles, with Ahly winning eight titles, Mukhtalaṭ five, and Tirsāna two. The other five titles were won by Alexandrian teams (Ittiḥād and Olympic Club winning two titles each, and Terām one). The nationalization of the sport, in other words, was an uneven process in which Cairo emerged as the center, and other cities, hitherto urban centers in their own right, were rendered peripheries.

A club and city hierarchy therefore emerged. The 1929 clustering of clubs is a case in point. With seven Tier A teams and another three in Tier B, Cairo emerged as the unchallenged football capital. Alexandria and the Canal Zone competed for second place: the former with seven Tier B clubs and two Tier A clubs, and the latter with three clubs apiece. All other clubs belonged to Tier C. The club hierarchy was therefore a city hierarchy. While keen on competing nationally to improve their national standing, clubs emphasized the primacy of the provincial competition in which they were not peripheralized. Throughout the 1920s and early 1930s, provincial and national competitions overlapped; the national cup only complemented the more important provincial leagues. Clubs were deeply immersed in their respective communities, for whom they sometimes opened their pitches, and from whom they recruited players and developed a fan base. While winning more titles than any other club, Ahly and Mukhtalaṭ maintained a predominantly Cairene fan base, comparable to that of provincial icons such as Ittiḥād, Ismāʿīlī, and Maṣrī in their respective cities.

May 31, 1934. *Hunā al-Qāhira* (This is Cairo). These were reportedly the first words uttered in a studio somewhere in Cairo, to be broadcast across Egyptian Radio. Throughout the preceding and following years, colonial infrastructure, notably roads and railways, facilitated the project of connecting the football nation by bringing down the cost of travel and reducing its duration for club teams. Similarly, the national radio, run by a British company, popularized national sports. Just as the transportation infrastructure needed mobile customers and goods to profit, the radio needed popular content for people to tune in to,[101] and football, the national game, was the content of choice. Egyptian cup matches were broadcast as early as 1934. Live coverage meant that fans no longer had to wait for the newspaper to be read aloud to know about the results. The former effendi game was popularized through "media capitalism,"[102] and was now followed even beyond the urban centers. With the nation broadened, new football zones were added in Upper Egypt and the predominantly rural Delta. Radio broadcasting reinforced the existing hierarchies. Based in Cairo, radio primarily broadcasted Ahly and Mukhtalaṭ games. Clubs were paid for the coverage,[103] so they increased their revenues and, in having their games broadcast beyond Cairo, expanded their fan base. Ittiḥād, Ismāʿīlī, and Maṣrī and other provincial leaders were peripheralized. Denying them the status of top tier clubs, and, through Cairo-centric narratives, marginalizing their role in the making of a nation best explains their hostility towards Cairo-based clubs, notably Ahly. The reinforcement of this hierarchy was reflected by the number of titles won by different clubs. Whereas six different teams won the Prince Fārūq Cup prior to 1939, the title became the purview of Ahly and Mukhtalaṭ (now Fārūq) in the following decade.

Radio contributed to the connectedness of the football nation. Fans could easily follow their teams to stadiums, follow their games from afar via radio broadcasting, and follow their news in widely circulated newspapers. If the bureaucratized competition was, in part, about comparison and measurement, widely circulated newspapers and radio broadcasting and the resulting emergence of the national economy meant that the nation was now the appropriate unit for this measurement. Subsequently, the Prince Fārūq Cup gained currency, and as any quick survey of contemporaneous newspapers suggests, it established itself as the most important competition.

But the provincial leaders in Alexandria and the Canal Zone (the only football zones invited to the national league) were not willing to accept their peripheralization, or give up their provincial leagues without a fight. When the EFA approved plans for organizing the national league in January 1935, the announced plans reflected the tensions between Cairene clubs and other clubs. The national league was not a stand-alone tournament, nor did it replace provincial leagues. The first leg of these provincial leagues (which were being played as the plans for a national league were being discussed) defined league contenders, with the top four teams from Cairo, and the three top teams from both Alexandria and Canal qualifying for the competition. According to the announced plans, the five games each team played in the second leg of its provincial league would also count towards the national league.[104] The number of additional games each team would play was still limited (six for Cairene teams, and seven for others). This plan never materialized. It is not clear whether it was the heavy costs of playing more national games, club directors resisting peripheralization, or the EFA director (also Mukhtalaṭ's director) not following through because Mukhtalaṭ, ranking fifth in the Cairo League, that led to the postponement.

October 22, 1948. The inaugural game of the league finally kicks off. The expansion of railway networks and the reduced cost of transportation, the securing of revenues through advertisements and radio broadcasting returns which increased club revenues, the popularization of national competitions, and the consolidation of a set of criteria to determine the participants (the EFA club's hierarchy), all contributed to making this day possible. Importantly, however, this new national league did not replace provincial leagues. Of the twenty games Fārūq (formerly Al Mukhtalaṭ) played in the inaugural season, the six that were played against Cairo also counted towards the provincial league. While ending the season in fifth place, the team also won the Cairo League, having outperformed all Cairene teams in their head-to-head games. The overlap of provincial and national competitions allowed provincial leaders to deliver some titles to their fans while being nationally peripheralized. The national league did not map onto the emergent political nation. The eleven clubs competing for the first title were all located in the three football zones initially established by the EFA. The national game was only played in urban centers.

Conclusion: Politics of the Postcolonial Game

When Fārūq hosted Dakhliyya for the league's inaugural game in 1948, Colonel Gamal Abdel Nasser was besieged in al-Faluja. Soon after his return, he joined a small group of dissenting officers in forming an underground organization to topple the regime. Less than four years later, the Free Officers staged a coup d'état that ousted the king, abolished the monarchy, and drove out the British troops, concluding the 70-year occupation. Within two years, the new republic dissolved all political parties, passed land reforms, and revoked civil ranks. In June 1956, Nasser, the de facto ruler since the revolution, finally assumed the presidency. Nationalist discourse in the "moment of arrival" is conducted in a "single, consistent, unambiguous voice ... [successfully] glossing over all earlier contradictions, divergences and differences and incorporating within the body of a unified discourse every aspect and stage in the history of its formation."[105] Official national history celebrating national heroic figures therefore celebrated footballers, whose accomplishments and talent were among the ideological components of this nationalist discourse.[106] Streets were named after sport icons, including Luṭfī, Ḥegāzī, and Tetsh, and the performance of the national team became a matter of national pride.

It was not long before the postcolonial regime took an interest in football. Having controlled the state apparatus, the junta strengthened its grip over professional football institutions, hence changing the politics of the game. In 1958, and shortly after Egyptian, Sudanese, Ethiopian, and South African delegates to FIFA agreed to establish the Confederation of African Football (CAF), Minister of War Abdel-Ḥakīm 'Āmer was appointed EFA director. The regime's policy and interest in football also manifested in the composition of clubs and leagues. The postcolonial state's interest in education gave rise to an unprecedented urban middle class, and heavy state regulations kept the cost of joining clubs reasonable. These clubs had been hitherto directed to effendis and pashas, but the revocation of civil ranks allowed different social groups to assume leadership. In Ahly, despite the absence of legal restrictions to the election of others, all club presidents between 1909 and 1952 were pashas. In the immediate aftermath of the coup-cum-revolution, however, a police officer and then a military official assumed the presidency. Four of the last five club presidents, including the incumbent Maḥmūd al-Khaṭīb, are football legends who initially joined the club as players. Professional football as a vehicle for social mobility was therefore expanded. Clubs also proliferated in the Delta and Upper Egypt, and it was not long before some of these clubs—notably, those representing the state's interests in heavy industry, such as Ghazl al-Maḥalla—had made their way to the league's first division.

This is not to suggest that football was simply controlled by the state, however, or that the politics of the game mirrored that of the state. In fact, professional football remained a terrain of political contestation throughout Nasser's reign, with different actors striving to assert their power and defend their interests. These contestations took place on several fronts; the first being interclub rivalry. Within the context of the emergent clientelist regime, club directors saw in the political leadership a resource to be exploited. Ahly thus named Nasser honorary president, and Fārūq changed its name to dissociate itself from the ancien régime. With strong fan bases, both clubs had enough leverage to negotiate their interests with the regime. As a result, they emerged as the uncontested leaders of Egyptian football. They also developed strong lobbies, significantly shaping the laws that came to regulate their activities. In 1957, for example, new regulations were passed giving clubs even more power over player transfers.[107]

Another area of contention and contestation was the conceptualization of professional football. As mentioned above, one strand of anti-colonial thought was critical of the exaggerated focus on football. Their vocal (albeit marginal) critique kept the question of whether football was "just a game" or rather a civilizational apparatus open for debate. In the aftermath of the 1967 military defeat, Nasser banned the football league, deeming the game "a distraction" from the real, military struggle.[108] This ban created an existential threat to clubs, whose directors pursued different strategies to highlight their importance for the nation. In October 1967, only four months after the military defeat, Ahly's board mandated that all club youth join military training camps, and encouraged them to volunteer in the army.[109] Football may have been "just a game," but its infrastructure proved its usefulness on other fronts. Clubs and their leaderships thus maintained their relevance in a moment of crisis.

In this chapter, I have argued that professional football is, by definition, political, and that its politics are best explored through centering on the institutions that govern it—most importantly clubs. The relationship between politics and sports is the subject of a growing body of scholarship. The operative question in this literature, as Victor Cha suggests, is "How does sport 'fit' into our understanding" of politics?[110] The answer is straightforward: there is hardly any meaningful space for football in an understanding of politics that confines it to formal political institutions, the political actors operating within them, and the processes leading to formal political outcomes. Notwithstanding the importance of formal politics in shaping the football terrain, football players, directors, clubs, and federations are not proxies for state power. They are involved in political contestations that revolve, for the most part, around clubs and associations. These corporations should be moved back to the center of their own political and intellectual histories; they should not be treated as imitations, extensions, or reflections of state power, but as political communities in their own right.[111] Their relationship with the state is one site for exploring their politics—a significant one in postcolonial settings in which power is largely concentrated, as in the case of post-1952 Egypt—but the politics of the game cannot be reduced to this aspect.

Nor is it possible to understand the politics of football without interrogating the relationship between play and game. It is precisely the conditions under which the former is transformed into the latter that define the politics of the game. Questions of access, rules, institutions invested in football, the balance of power within these institutions, the regulations governing them, and competing projects for subject formation and identity-making—all integral to transforming play to game—are all political matters par excellence. They demarcate the professional football domain, define its place in society, and determine the distribution of power within the sport's domain. James Dorsey's claim that politics is "written into the DNA of soccer" therefore ought to be qualified:[112] it is written into the DNA of professional football. In settings in which power is largely concentrated, the role of formal political institutions in determining the politics of the game is less subtle. Yet a full appreciation of these politics necessitates interrogating both the boundaries of professional football and the relationship between game and play. This interrogation should neither take the game to be orthodox football and play to be a residual category, nor assume that play is game in the waiting room.

2

BEYOND SOFT POWER

FOOTBALL AS A FORM OF REGIME LEGITIMATION

Abdullah Al-Arian

On February 8, 1957, Egypt was one of four countries to spearhead the establishment of the Confederation of African Football (CAF), the latest continental confederation recognized by the Fédération Internationale de Football Association (FIFA), the global football governing body. Two days later, the first African Cup of Nations kicked off in Sudan with just three teams participating: Egypt, Sudan, and Ethiopia, after South Africa was disqualified when it stipulated that it would be fielding an all-white team.[1] Egypt defeated Sudan 2–1 in the semifinal before going on to beat Ethiopia 4–0 in the final and lift the inaugural cup in front of 20,000 fans in Khartoum. Egyptian President Gamal Abdel Nasser was particularly enthused about the rise of African football as an act of decolonization. He had called for the meeting of the various national federations and insisted that the first continental tournament be held as soon as CAF's membership in FIFA had been approved.[2] As a country that had only recently forced the withdrawal of British forces, Egypt, like many other postcolonial states, sought to affirm its place in the world not only by joining international bodies such as the United Nations—which it did in 1945—but also through membership in sporting organizations such as FIFA, becoming the first African nation to do so.[3]

Domestically, Nasser understood the power of football to mobilize Egyptians. Al-Ahly Sporting Club had deep anti-colonial roots, and, in 1956, Nasser was chosen to become its honorary president.[4] Field Marshal Abdelhakim Amer, who commanded Egypt's armed forces, was also entrusted to take over the Egyptian Football Association (EFA) and oversee its growth as a predominant force in popular culture.[5] The integration of football with the aims of the state was virtually seamless, as Amer granted military honors to some of the domestic league's star players.[6] On the eighth anniversary of the July 1952 coup that brought the military regime to power, Egypt's president inaugurated Nasser Stadium (later renamed Cairo International Stadium), an impressive feat of state modernization that would boast a 120,000 spectator standing-room capacity. Nasser proclaimed that the stadium's construction was a symbol that Egyptians had become free "to develop our country as we see fit."[7]

On the international stage, Nasser maintained that football had the power to withstand efforts to marginalize and isolate states. The establishment of CAF occurred just months after the tripartite attack on Egypt by British, French, and Israeli forces following Nasser's nationalization of the Suez Canal. Establishing strong links of solidarity across the African continent was a central tenet of Egypt's post-revolutionary foreign policy. Africa comprised the "second circle" of Nasser's outlook on international solidarities as laid out in *The Philosophy of the Revolution*.[8] Through CAF, football provided a platform from which to establish stronger relations with states such as Sudan and Ethiopia, with whom cooperation over access to Nile waters was a critical component of Egypt's regional security. Football also established a mechanism to form a united stand in opposition to the racist practices of apartheid South Africa, which was expelled from CAF and only readmitted following the fall of apartheid more than three decades later. Along with the pursuit of strategic political goals, venues such as CAF also aided in the quest for regime legitimation. In 1959, Egypt hosted the second African Cup of Nations and competed under the flag of the United Arab Republic—the newly formed union between Egypt and Syria. The cup holders defeated Sudan 2–1 in the final match to retain the trophy on home soil and offer a major boost to Nasser's ambitions as a regional leader in the face of rising Cold War tensions.

Developments in recent years have seen a growing interest in exploring the connections between international politics and football, particularly in the Middle East and North Africa (MENA) region.[9] As the above examples from Nasser's Egypt demonstrate, states have historically explored the variety of ways that football, as a powerful cultural form, can be utilized "to advance particular policies, gain legitimacy, increase public support, or pacify the restless masses."[10] When examining this notion over the course of the past decade, there has been a considerable shift in attention toward the role that state appropriation of elite sports plays in the promotion of soft power politics. This has occurred as a result of several considerations. The concept of soft power, as put forward by international relations theorist Joseph Nye Jr., gained considerable traction as an explanatory tool of US power projection in the post-Cold War global order. Contrasting it with hard power, Nye defined soft power as "the ability to get what you want through attraction rather than coercion or payments. It arises from the attractiveness of a country's culture, political ideals, and policies."[11] By subsuming the notion of "culture" writ large beneath the category of soft power, many analyses of state utilization of cultural institutions, such as sports, have tended to view them purely through the lens of "attracting" other states and populations. Taking it a step further, another scholar and former diplomat suggested that sports as a form of soft power can bring together political adversaries, raise the national profile, sell the national brand, and possibly even bring world peace.[12]

The Limits of Soft Power

Nevertheless, consigning all instances of cultural exchange between states, including in the realm of elite sports, to this framework can become problematic, in that it overlooks other possible political ends served by such institutions. In observing the MENA region in particular, the soft power explanation has become increasingly fashionable considering the role that wealthy Gulf states have played in the world of football. Headlining the list of recent achievements was FIFA's decision in 2010 to award its landmark event to Qatar. Along with the 2022 World Cup, Gulf states including Qatar, the United Arab Emirates (UAE), and Saudi Arabia have hosted several major regional and international football tournaments, such as the Asian Football Confederation's Asian Cup and the FIFA Club World Cup. In 2019, Saudi Arabia even hosted the Spanish Super Cup and the Italian Super Cup, domestic tournaments organized by football federations in Spain and Italy respectively. Transforming the Gulf region into a global football hub has been coupled with efforts by Gulf states to expand their reach into Europe's elite leagues. Ranging from highly lucrative kit sponsorship deals to outright ownership of some of the world's most high-profile clubs, Gulf states have emerged as game-changing players in European football.

When examining the causes and consequences of these and other similar developments, most analyses have focused almost exclusively on the question of soft power. The aggressive transfer policy of Qatari-owned French club Paris Saint-Germain (PSG) was described as a "high-profile soft power play."[13] Emirates Airlines' kit sponsorship deals with several elite European clubs reflected a soft power strategy to market the UAE as "a global example of prestige and excellence."[14] Abu Dhabi's ownership of Manchester City FC has served as "an incredibly powerful tool to mold an image on an international stage."[15] Even Qatar's $200 billion investment to host the 2022 FIFA World Cup has been explained as an effort to raise "brand awareness" of the country.[16]

While not dismissing the significance of deploying football in the service of national branding, regional and global integration, and positive image cultivation, this chapter proposes to go beyond soft power explanations to explore other ways in which football serves the political interests of states. Specifically, it argues that states have found uses for football as a tool for acquiring legitimacy in the face of internal and external threats. If legitimacy in nondemocratic contexts is understood as "something that autocracies attempt to acquire or cultivate through legitimation claims, symbols, narratives, and/or procedures," it is clear that various forms of cultural expression—particularly those around which populations have demonstrated an ability to rally, unite, and mobilize—can serve as powerful tools to regimes.[17] Dukalskis and Gerschewski have proposed four mechanisms for autocratic legitimation, of which two are most relevant here. The "passivity mechanism" aims to demobilize potential opposition through cultivating "a sense of resignation to the regime's rule by conveying its power, cohesion, and unassailability."[18] As the authors demonstrate (in part) through the work of Lisa Wedeen on Syria under the rule of Hafez al-Assad, passivity can operate through "displays of regime power, but can also take the form of distraction, discrediting political alternatives as unrealistic or, in Wedeen's words, disseminating government ideology that 'clutters public space with monotonous slogans and empty gestures, which tire the minds and bodies of producers and consumers alike.'"[19] By contrast, deriving from rentier state theory, performance legitimation relies on a regime's ability to deliver "order, stability, and growth."[20] As we shall soon see, depending on a regime's needs, co-optation of elite sports by states can alternately serve as a pacifying measure or a confidence-boosting measure to both domestic and international audiences.

Forms of Football as Legitimation

The following sections explore the variety of forms that the legitimation process can take. In the same way that Nasser deployed Egyptian football as a form of resistance against colonial domination, states can also employ football as a mode of legitimizing neoimperial control, such as in the aftermath of the 2003 US-led invasion and occupation of Iraq. Unlike the other case studies discussed here, this case ostensibly featured an occupying power utilizing the success of Iraq's national football team to legitimize a nascent democracy rather than an authoritarian system of rule. Nevertheless, as numerous scholars have shown, US policy in the aftermath of the Iraq invasion was far more concerned with justifying an illegal occupation than with propping up Iraqi democracy. One scholar noted of the US mission that "the basic problem lies in the contradictions of a democratizing project militarily imposed by an outside power, which Iraq has had the misfortune to demonstrate in an archetypical fashion."[21] In this regard, attempts to legitimize neo-imperial control through sports have far more in common with legitimation efforts of authoritarian regimes than it may seem at first glance.

States can also channel popular sentiments toward the national football team as an extension of authoritarian control during periods of political transition, as in Egypt during both the latter years of Hosni Mubarak's rule as well as the early years following the military coup that brought Abdel Fattah el-Sisi to power. States can turn to their investments in football to ward off specific threats during times of crisis—as Qatar did in the summer of 2017, following the launch of a blockade against it by a quartet of states led by Saudi Arabia and the UAE. As the UAE demonstrated during the same period, states can leverage their economic power in the high-stakes world of European club football to extract political concessions in pursuit of their securitization goals.[22] Finally, states can also use their promotion of football to counteract international isolation and negative publicity resulting from damaging policies in other arenas, a practice known as "sportswashing."[23] In recent years, Saudi Arabia has actively stepped up its investments in football, for instance by hosting both the Italian and Spanish domestic cup final matches and the purchase of English club Newcastle United by the state-owned Public Investment Fund. Concurrently, the Saudi regime has waged a destructive war in Yemen and carried out a violent campaign to repress dissent at home and abroad.

It should be noted that these categories are not mutually exclusive, and states can employ more than one at any given time. Saudi Arabia's active sportswashing of its unpopular policies, for example, is also a feature of states pursuing legitimacy by other means. Even analyses that invoke the soft power framework have acknowledged that, in some cases, it is worth looking beyond that theory's central tenets at other strategic motivations. One study of Qatar's investment in sports suggests that it is insufficient to examine it solely through the lens of "improving relations between nations," the stated goal of Qatar's Olympic Committee.[24] Rather than simply framing such policies from the perspective of "gaining international prestige," it is worth considering how they contribute to Qatar's geostrategic and security priorities, especially in relation to its neighbors in the Gulf Cooperation Council (GCC).[25] Others have argued that Nye's notion of "smart power," which combines elements of soft and hard power, offers a more accurate description of state investment in mega sports events, particularly because of the immense financial assets required—a feature of hard power politics.[26]

Another caveat worth mentioning concerns the degree of agency that organized sports institutions maintain within an otherwise state-centered lens of analysis. To echo the argument put forward by Ibrahim Elhoudaiby in this volume, club teams and national federations are not simply apolitical entities upon which states play out their competing political interests. Rather, they too are political actors with interests that either align with or diverge from those of state power, depending on the objective. The political outcomes discussed here are often the product of processes of negotiation between state actors and the sporting institutions in question. As Elhoudaiby demonstrates, Nasser-era Egypt featured political contestations at the levels of interclub rivalry, club membership and directorship, and even in the very conceptualization of organized football.

As the cases presented here illustrate, regimes may employ football as a form of legitimation irrespective of the degree of authoritarian behavior that they exhibit. In contrast to Natalie Koch's assertion that "soft" authoritarian regimes are more likely to utilize elite sports as "a tool to elicit respect and legitimacy on the global stage" than "hard" authoritarian regimes that rely more heavily on "naked coercion," this chapter contends that repressive authoritarian regimes can be just as likely to deploy the use of sports in concert with their hard authoritarian toolkit.[27] Indeed, the el-Sisi regime in Egypt, as well as Saudi Arabia under the rule of Crown Prince Mohammed bin Salman, have exhibited some of the most repressive behavior in the modern history of their respective countries, and yet they have also leaned more heavily on their national footballing interests as a means to acquire legitimacy on the domestic and international stages. Eva Bellin has laid out a series of factors that have facilitated what she refers to as the "robustness" of authoritarianism in the Middle East. Among others, these include the ability of rent-seeking states to support coercive apparatuses through state revenues, as well as their ability to maintain international support from powerful states with aligned interests.[28] Whether materially or in terms of forging relations globally, state investment in football has been employed for precisely the same purpose: the maintenance of power.

Football as a Form of Neo-Imperial Control

At the 2004 Summer Olympic Games in Athens, the Iraqi national football team took the competition by storm, defeating Portugal 4–2 in its opening match, before beating Costa Rica 2–0 to go into the quarterfinal stage after winning the group. The Iraqis continued their unexpected run, eking out a narrow 1–0 victory over Australia to set up a semifinal matchup against Paraguay, and a chance to compete for Olympic gold. The Iraqi team's impressive run was all the more compelling due to the country's recent history of repression and violence at the hands of local rulers and foreign powers. The players, nearly all of whom were under twenty-three years of age, had grown up in a state ruled by the authoritarian dictator Saddam Hussein. The nation was wracked by a destructive war against Iran in the 1980s and a military confrontation with a US-led coalition in 1991, followed by over a decade of devastating UN sanctions that cost the lives of over half a million Iraqi children. Then, in the spring of 2003, George W. Bush launched a military invasion and occupation of Iraq under the guise of combatting global terrorism and promoting democracy in the

Middle East. Barely a year since the US occupation of their country, Iraqis struggled with the absence of basic government services, the exploitation of their natural resources, and the exacerbation of political divisions that had spilled over into militant violence, often due to a process of "sectarianization" enflamed by local elites and the occupying power.[29]

Against this backdrop, the performance of the Iraqi team offered a narrative of perseverance in the face of adversity and national unity at a time of deep social and political division. It was a narrative that would be eagerly exploited by the Bush administration at a crucial moment, when the Iraq War was proving to be deeply unpopular among Americans and threatening Bush's prospects for reelection. For over a year after the invasion, Iraq was still governed by the US-led Coalition Provisional Authority. Elections had proven impossible to hold under the cloud of violence and instability, making a mockery of Bush's infamous "Mission Accomplished" speech in May 2003.[30] And so, for those two weeks in the summer of 2004, the Iraqi national team captured the American imagination. On the eve of the Iraqis' semifinal match, the *Los Angeles Times* called them "the darlings of the Summer Games."[31] News reports drew sharp contrasts between the brutal conditions athletes had to endure while competing when Saddam Hussein's son Uday oversaw national sports and the optimism offered by their recent liberation.[32] Another piece showcased the "new Iraq" represented by a team that drew on athletes of different ethnic backgrounds: "they were just a bunch of kids from war-torn stadiums with guts and heart. They were Arab and Kurd, from Fallujah and Najaf and Sadr City, carrying all the anxiety over events back home, the burning refuse and shot-up things that those city names conjure."[33] Later, one book romanticized the experience as follows: "Iraqi sports. It once meant death and destruction under Uday Hussein. Now it means life and a new found freedom. . . . It provides a link that helps bring down terrorism and helps in uniting a country in the name of democracy."[34]

The Bush administration sought to apply the success of the Iraqi team toward its own political goals. As the players were racking up victories, Bush began to cite them in his reelection campaign stump speeches. In a national radio address following the team's opening match win over Portugal, he declared, "for the first time in decades, the world will see Iraqi Olympians free from the brutal punishment of the dictator's son .... Twenty-nine athletes from Iraq are competing in Athens, including the Iraqi soccer team, which thrilled the world by winning its first game."[35] When the team neared the semifinal, Bush's reelection campaign released a television advertisement that used the Iraqi team's success to justify the US invasions of Iraq and Afghanistan in dramatic fashion. Over images of Olympic athletes competing with the flags of Iraq and Afghanistan in the foreground, a voiceover narration declared: "Freedom is spreading throughout the world like a sunrise. And this Olympics, there will be two more free nations—and two fewer terrorist regimes. With strength, resolve and courage, democracy will triumph over terror—and hope will defeat hatred."[36]

The Iraqi team lost its final two matches and settled for a fourth-place finish, causing the Bush campaign to veer away from its appropriation of the team's successful run. Nevertheless, some reports suggested that in the event that Iraq reached the gold medal match, Bush intended to fly to Athens to be in attendance, an honor usually reserved for the heads of state of the competing countries.[37] According to an official with the Iraqi Olympic Committee, the team was even asked by US officials to display the flag of Afghanistan alongside its own at the final match.[38]

It is difficult to ascertain what impact the Bush campaign's instrumentalization of the Iraqi football team had on Bush's 2004 reelection victory. However, happening as it did less than three months before the US presidential election, the public relations campaign certainly offered a rare glimmer of optimism to an otherwise precarious situation. Having failed to stabilize conditions in Iraq following a war of choice that was deeply divisive both at home and among US allies in Europe, the Middle East, and elsewhere, the US believed it needed to justify the initial intervention as well as its continued military presence at a moment when the legitimacy of its mission was highly in question. For the Bush administration, the success of Iraqi athletes was held up as validation of its decision to go to war. The war's defenders pointed to both symbolic and material benefits represented in the Iraqi team's footballing success. The same president who four years earlier ran on a platform of opposition to the concept of nation-building was now claiming victory in rebuilding the Iraqi nation.[39] Whereas leading Middle East scholars were cautioning that Iraq was far more on its way to becoming a failed state than a functional democracy following the overthrow of the Ba'athist regime, Bush's supporters advanced a narrative that a positive sporting display on a global stage served as proof that democracy was taking root.[40] They claimed credit in no uncertain terms, stating that "the Iraqis could not have accomplished what they did without other countries' assistance. The Coalition altogether spent $10 million rebuilding the sports program in Iraq from the ground up."[41]

Within Iraqi society, the US narrative and its associated policies did not appear to have the desired effects. Coalition officials had taken great care to showcase the occupation's support for the revival of football in Iraq. They distributed footballs to children on religious holidays, established 5,000 local amateur teams, and lobbied the International Olympic Committee to readmit a post-Saddam Iraq following a lengthy suspension of Iraq's membership.[42] However, such goodwill gestures paled in comparison with the daily miseries endured by most Iraqis under military occupation. To top it off, the Olympic team's time in Athens was closely stage-managed by officials expecting the athletes to act as ambassadors for a vision of their country produced by the Bush administration. As one sports columnist noted, "No doubt the coalition government back home would like them to represent the 'new' Iraq, one that's free of torture and corruption, an Iraq that's not particularly ethnic or too radically religious, a national icon and rallying point that's not a mosque."[43] Despite that, and much to the chagrin of those officials, several members of the football team spoke out in opposition to the Bush campaign's tactics. Speaking to an American sports journalist, midfielder Salih Sadir said: "Iraq as a team does not want Mr. Bush to use us for the presidential campaign. He can find another way to advertise himself." He added, "We don't wish for the presence of Americans in our country. We want them to go away."[44] Another player, Ahmad Manajid, went further, declaring that if he were not playing for the national team, he would have joined the resistance as a fighter to defend his homeland.[45] Even the team's coach, Adnan Hamad, condemned the US occupation for having "destroy[ed] everything" in the country.[46] Naturally, Iraqi Olympic Committee officials protested the publication of those comments and attempted to limit media access to the team thereafter. But the anger and frustration expressed in their words offered a stark contrast to concerted efforts by US officials to seize upon the Iraqi team's moment in the sun to legitimize an ongoing military occupation.

Legitimizing Hereditary Rule

In late 2009, Egypt and Algeria competed for one of the final spots at the 2010 FIFA World Cup in South Africa. It had been nearly two decades since the Pharaohs had last qualified for the competition, and a victory by more than two goals in Cairo would have seen them win their group outright and punch their ticket to South Africa. But the Egyptians only managed a 2–0 victory in the November 14 match, meaning that Egypt and Algeria had tied at the top of their group, necessitating a one-match playoff to be held at a neutral site four days later. In the decisive match in Sudan, Algeria advanced with a 1–0 result, shattering Egyptian hopes of ending their World Cup drought. Overshadowing the football, however, was the alarming rise in tensions between the two sides. Disruptive behavior by some unruly fans, including an attack on the Algerian team bus in Cairo that caused injuries to several players and team personnel, threatened to suspend the first match before it was played. Then, after the replay in Sudan, riots broke out in Cairo as over one thousand fans gathered in front of the Algerian embassy to burn Algerian flags in protest over reports that Egyptian fans were assaulted in the stadium.[47] Egyptian officials deployed security personnel after the Algerian embassy was firebombed and the subsequent clashes led to dozens of injuries.[48] The conflict eventually died down, but only after a very public war of words between officials from both states, the withdrawal of the Egyptian ambassador to Algeria, and mutual economic reprisals.[49]

Although fan violence has long been an unfortunate side effect of the sport, particularly in historic football rivalries the world over, what stood out in this instance of violent mobilization of supporters was the clear role that the regime of Hosni Mubarak played in stoking the flames of jingoistic nationalism to serve its own ends. A deeply unpopular authoritarian ruler for nearly three decades, Mubarak seized upon a moment of national unity by mobilizing Egyptians in opposition to a constructed enemy. More significantly, the Algeria matches served as an opportune moment to advance the regime's plans for Gamal Mubarak to succeed his aging father as president.

The elder Mubarak tapped into a longstanding rivalry between the two nations that dates back to the 1950s, when Nasser refused to allow the Egyptian national team to play Algeria's revolutionary football team at a time when Algeria was fighting for independence from French colonial rule. Later, the two countries had locked horns in a bid to qualify for the 1990 World Cup, which the Egyptians did at the expense of Algeria.[50] In the lead-up to the 2009 matches, Egyptian fans were ramping up the rhetoric through online taunting of Algerian fans and cyberattacks on their websites.[51] But the heated exchange of words soon left the realm of online fan behavior to the far more visible state media apparatus. Following the first match in Cairo, reports emerged that Algerian fans were rioting and attacking Egyptian businesses in Algiers. TV presenter Amr Adib expressed outrage, asking "why do the Algerians hate us?" while airing videos of Algerian hooligan behavior.[52] Other TV programs claimed Algerians were "terrorizing" Egyptians and subjecting them to a "bloodbath."[53] State newspapers published unsubstantiated accusations that the Algerian government was emptying its prisons and sending thousands of criminals to wreak havoc on Egyptian fans in Sudan, attacking them with "knives, nails, daggers, switchblades, scalpels and heavy wooden sticks."[54] As one observer noted at the time, "elsewhere in the Egyptian media, Algerians have been described, en masse, as 'uncivilized,' 'violent,' and 'sick.'"[55] Prominent celebrities and retired football stars also contributed to the mass hysteria, using their platforms to enflame passions and rally around the Egyptian national team.[56]

Attempting to seize upon the rising tide of nationalist sentiment, the Mubarak family positioned itself at the head of the charge. Gamal Mubarak possessed no military background, but nonetheless aspired to inherit a police state ruled exclusively by former military officials. Sure enough, the footballing clash with Algeria was characterized in the language and imagery of war. Photographs of Gamal from the matches made the rounds in the Egyptian media. Dressed in a suit and draped in an Egypt football scarf, the younger Mubarak cheered on his team from the stands like a general leading his army into battle. He struck an ominous tone in his TV interviews, declaring that "Egypt is a major power that should not be taken lightly."[57] Gamal's older brother Alaa was even more brazen in his words, leading a *New York Times* report to remark that he "sounded as if he were calling his nation to war."[58] Calling into a popular program, Alaa justified the emotional reactions to the events in Sudan: "We have to take a stand. This is enough. That's it, this is enough. Egypt should be respected. We are Egyptian and we hold our head high, and whoever insults us should be smacked on his head."[59] Elsewhere, he continued to escalate the verbal attacks on Egypt's football nemesis, proclaiming that, "there is nothing called Arab nationalism or brotherhood.... When Algerians learn how to speak Arabic they can then come and say that they are Arabs."[60] Not to be outdone, shortly after Egypt's exit from World Cup qualification, Hosni Mubarak delivered a speech to a joint session of parliament in which he declared that "Egypt does not tolerate those who hurt the dignity of its sons."[61] Egypt withdrew its ambassador from Algeria and threatened to boycott international football for the next two years if FIFA did not take action against Algeria's fans.

In the short term, the Mubarak regime's ability to rally support for itself clearly proved effective. Its allies within the media, popular culture, and broader society mobilized heavily in support of the national team and offered little opposition to the emergence of Gamal Mubarak as the face of Egypt's short-lived "war" with Algeria. As one Egyptian fan was quoted as saying, "I didn't fight in 1973, but I will be there in 2009."[62] Efforts to legitimize the regime's hereditary project proved far more difficult. Enflaming passions around football offered little more than a brief distraction from the climate of repression, lack of political freedoms, and dire economic situation that characterized the late Mubarak era. In fact, the mission likely backfired, as Egypt's failures on the pitch and the upheaval that followed paved the way for broader discussions regarding the government's failure to provide adequate education, employment, and housing.[63] Meanwhile, the crackdown on rioting fans by security forces served as a reminder of the regime's willingness to resort to violent repression as a means of maintaining order. The theory around legitimation processes suggests that, as military regimes contend with growing demands among segments of the population most disaffected by prior regime legitimation efforts, they face a challenge "to adapt the regime's legitimacy claims and public policies in order to incorporate new elements of political freedom or public welfare."[64] In this instance, the Mubarak regime's legitimation efforts fell flat, as they offered nothing that fundamentally differed from a status quo whose conditions had only worsened over time. One commentator observed that: "The government's lack of legitimacy was highlighted by the chaos in Khartoum; aiding and abetting the crudest nationalism, while blocking all forms of real political participation, is a shortsighted tactic that doesn't address the population's underlying discontent."[65] Western media outlets covering these developments identified deep-seated frustrations among the Egyptians they interviewed. In a sign of things to come, one Egyptian quoted in the *New York Times* was far more critical, reflecting, "If we are infuriated, it is not over soccer, to hell with the game, we are infuriated over our dignity."[66]

Legitimizing A Post-Coup Order

In October 2017, Egypt finally realized its dream of returning to the World Cup. At a qualification match versus Congo, star forward Mohamed Salah converted a dramatic stoppage-time penalty to give Egypt a 2–1 victory and secure its place in Russia the following summer. Egyptians were particularly elated at this achievement given the turmoil that they had endured over the previous five years. Following a popular uprising that overthrew the Mubarak regime in 2011, a short-lived democratic transition was upended by a military coup. The July 2013 intervention that brought Field Marshal Abdel Fattah el-Sisi to power was accompanied by a wave of violent repression that aimed to throttle the revolutionary hopes of millions of Egyptians. Security forces killed over a thousand protesters at an anti-coup sit-in.[67] Tens of thousands more Egyptians were imprisoned on politicized charges, with hundreds of them sentenced to death in mass trials that abandoned all pretense of judicial procedure.[68] Under the guise of fighting terrorism, a series of hastily approved laws governing public gatherings, political organizing, humanitarian advocacy, and media reporting effectively destroyed all prospects for civil society to participate in political life. Even the nation's vibrant football culture was not spared. Club Ultras, many of which had been politically mobilized during the revolution, were outlawed and declared to be terrorists.[69] The ban on match attendance by fans, following the violent clashes with state security forces at Port Said stadium in 2012 that left seventy-four fans dead, remained in effect, and was not lifted until late 2018. The regime also targeted one of the most storied players in Egyptian football history: Mohamed Aboutrika, who led his nation to two African Cup titles, was added to a terror list for having expressed support for the democratically elected government led by the Muslim Brotherhood's Mohamad Morsi.[70] His assets were frozen by the courts and the state media led a barrage of attacks against his character.

It was against this backdrop that el-Sisi attempted to co-opt the Egyptian national team's appearance on the world's biggest stage in a bid to legitimize his precarious rule. In the months before the World Cup kicked off in Russia in 2018, Egyptian Football Association (EFA) President Hany Abo Rida held a press conference offering his endorsement of el-Sisi's reelection. Though the election results were a foregone conclusion (the regime had arrested, intimidated, or otherwise disqualified all possible challengers), el-Sisi happily accepted the fawning praise and pledges of fealty expressed by Abo Rida and the presidents of some of the country's most prominent football clubs. The speakers took turns professing their support for the regime as they stood before a banner that read: "Egyptian Football Association backs and supports president Abdel Fattah el-Sisi to lead the country through continuous achievements."[71] State media commended the sports figures for taking a "historic stand," although FIFA announced that it was considering possible sanctions against the EFA for the blatant violation of its policy against football associations taking explicitly partisan political stances.[72] However, FIFA took no action, and the EFA's website and promotional materials continued to place el-Sisi at the center of its celebration of the Egyptian national team's success story.

Led primarily by the EFA, the regime also attempted to exploit Salah's status as global superstar. Having won the 2017–18 English Premier League Player of the Year award after a record-breaking first season with Liverpool FC, Salah was poised to lead the national team to success in Russia, for which the regime expected to claim full credit. However, the EFA's overtly exploitative behavior toward its star player became its own undoing. Salah's face adorned the side of an EgyptAir aircraft, for which the player's agent filed a complaint before FIFA's disciplinary committee over the violation of his client's image rights. In a letter detailing the allegations against the EFA, Salah's agent claimed that Abo Rida had previously requested that Salah allow his image to be used by the national team's corporate sponsors. Despite Salah's flat refusal, the EFA proceeded anyway, sanctioning the use of his image by Telecom Egypt and EgyptAir.[73] In a rare public criticism of officials, Salah himself issued a statement calling his treatment at the hands of the EFA "extremely insulting."[74]

Reports later emerged that Salah was also frustrated with the poor management of the Egyptian national team in the lead-up to its group stage matches in Russia.[75] In a concern that later proved warranted based on the team's performance on the pitch, the EFA had seemingly placed far greater emphasis on staged publicity events than on proper training and match preparation. The team's hotel was overrun by celebrities and Egyptian business and political elites seeking to mingle with the players. The EFA also appeared to be using Salah as a political pawn in its attempts to forge ties with Ramzan Kadyrov, the warlord ruler of Chechnya, where the Egyptian team was based during the tournament. Images of Salah being paraded by Kadyrov went viral on social media, and Salah was even granted honorary Chechen citizenship.[76] Ultimately, the team lost all three of its group stage matches, including a humiliating final match defeat at the hands of Saudi Arabia, finishing bottom of the group. In the aftermath of the team's poor showing, Salah reportedly considered retiring from national team duties.[77] He later publicly expressed his dismay at the EFA's lack of protection of its players from the "many disturbances" to which they were subjected, and their exploitation through excessive public appearances.[78]

In the end, the Egyptian regime's overzealous attempts to exploit the national team's footballing success to legitimize itself proved to be a spectacular failure. Its desperation stemmed from el-Sisi's inability to pursue other means of stabilizing a new authoritarian system of rule following the country's brief revolutionary moment. Fearful of creating new avenues for mass mobilization, el-Sisi neglected to pursue the traditional modes of regime legitimation, such as constructing a mass political party apparatus or co-opting business elites. Instead, along with the robust security apparatus that maintained a climate of fear, he oversaw the aggressive reentry of Egyptian military interests into the public sphere. This included the takeover of Egyptian Media Group, the company that managed sole sponsorship rights for the EFA, by Eagle Capital, a front organization owned by Egypt's General Intelligence.[79] This gave the regime direct access to key decisions governing the EFA's World Cup preparations, including where the team would be stationed during its time in Russia and players' media availability and obligations to corporate sponsors. In typical fashion, the el-Sisi regime attempted to deflect all criticisms of its role in the Egyptian national team's failures and to lay the blame squarely on its political foes. In comments made to state media, Abo Rida inexplicably held the Muslim Brotherhood responsible for the World Cup debacle.[80] How the outlawed Islamist movement determined the course of Egypt's World Cup was not explained. However, the regime had long struggled in its efforts to utilize the lure of football for its own ends. Earlier that spring, during el-Sisi's sham reelection, over one million Egyptians reportedly cast their ballots for Mohamed Salah.[81]

Warding Off Threats

In the summer of 2017, PSG made headlines by shelling out €222 million to FC Barcelona to add Brazilian star Neymar to the team's forward line. The exorbitantly high transfer fee shattered the previous world record of €105 million that Manchester United paid Italian club Juventus for midfielder Paul Pogba one year earlier. Not content with its historic signing, by late August, PSG fought off interest from the likes of Real Madrid and acquired electrifying French striker Kylian Mbappe from Monaco on a loan deal that became a €180 million permanent transfer one year later. Although the football arms race among Europe's elite clubs was nothing new, the massive surge in transfer fees in this instance was largely due to recent geopolitical developments in the Middle East. In early June, the governments of Saudi Arabia, the UAE, Bahrain, and Egypt cut off all relations with Qatar amid accusations that it was supporting terrorism and interfering in their internal affairs. As the weeks dragged on, the ensuing blockade represented the deepest crisis in the history of the GCC. In response, Qatar strengthened its relations with regional powers Turkey and Iran, and appealed to the Trump administration to bring its influence to bear over the blockading states to ease tensions.

Historically, Qatar had long maintained existential concerns regarding Saudi hegemony, and went to great lengths to neutralize those threats—in part by emerging as a major global actor in its own right. Beginning in the late 1990s, Qatar played a critical role in resolving regional conflicts, established a global media network in Al Jazeera, allowed the United States to maintain a military base on its soil, and became a hub of culture and education. Nonetheless, no achievement put Qatar on the global map quite like winning the right to host the 2022 World Cup. Soon after Qatar won the bid in 2010, it embarked on major sports investment projects, including the 2011 purchase of PSG by Qatar Sports Investments (QSI).[82]

Two years later, Qatar Airways reached an agreement with Barcelona to become the first corporate sponsor to appear on the club's iconic blue and red striped shirt.[83]

While all these developments point to the typical soft power tactics in which all states engage, the events of summer 2017 belong in a category of their own. For one, the considerations that went into the Neymar transfer exceeded those of typical footballing priorities. To be sure, PSG chairman Nasser al-Khelaifi had long expressed an interest in the player, believing him to be the clear successor to Cristiano Ronaldo and Leo Messi, the two best players in the world for most of this century. However, the mechanics of launching a successful bid were highly complex. Neymar had recently signed a five-year contract extension and Barcelona was not in the business of selling its best players in the prime of their careers. In fact, the €222 million buyout clause included in his contract was intended to be a prohibitive warning to would-be suitors.

For Qatar, the blockade upended the prior calculus. The blockading states had not only mobilized all of their diplomatic and economic might, but had also waged an aggressive media campaign to isolate Qatar and diminish its reputation globally. Accusations that it supported terrorism—unsubstantiated as they were—went hand in hand with questions surrounding Qatar's ability to host a successful World Cup.[84] Adding to the rising tensions, US President Donald Trump appeared to lend his initial endorsement to the blockade, accusing Qatar of funding "radical ideology" following a high-profile visit to Saudi Arabia.[85] The Qatari response ran a wide spectrum, from concluding an agreement to station Turkish troops in Qatar as a deterrent to possible military action by Saudi Arabia to tapping into its deep currency reserves in order to stabilize its economy. Qatar also pursued alternative trade routes and developed domestic industries seemingly overnight.[86] Additionally, it tackled the blockade on a public relations front, attempting to shift the narrative toward its many achievements.[87]

The Neymar deal should be viewed in the same light. The exorbitant cost defied the fiscal conservatism prior to the blockade that had led to budget cuts across all sectors, including those involved in World Cup preparations.[88] The structure of the deal ensured Neymar's commitment to Qatar's overarching goals. QSI paid the player a total of €300 million, an excess of €78 million over the buyout clause. In turn, Neymar signed a five-year deal with PSG (through 2022) and agreed to act as a spokesman for the World Cup taking place that same year. In making the statement signing, not only did PSG secure the services of one of the brightest stars in world football, but Qatar also acquired a symbol of its defiance against its attempted isolation.

The effectiveness of the strategy remains an open question. A French government official acknowledged that the Neymar deal had clear diplomatic aims for Qatar, but asserted that it was unlikely to change the outcome of the GCC crisis.[89] Elsewhere, regional analysts appeared in agreement that the deal at least had the effect of shifting the narrative away from Qatar's alleged misdeeds to its latest high-profile achievement.[90] As one football writer noted, despite the exorbitant expense, the move was intended "to prove to its neighbors that whatever blockade they put up, they can still operate as before, if not stronger…. In those terms, half a billion dollars is peanuts."[91] In that respect, PSG's improbable acquisition of two of football's biggest stars in Neymar and Mbappe clearly demonstrated that Qatar had no intentions of retreating from its ambitious goals. This acted as a vocal response to doubts raised about Qatar's ability to proceed with its World Cup preparations while under blockade. Nevertheless, among some critics, those transfers, along with PSG's signing of Leo Messi in 2021, continued to highlight persistent questions about the role of cash-rich states in world football amid financial fair play regulations and recurring critiques surrounding the political, economic, and social welfare conditions under which the 2022 World Cup has been organized.[92]

Securitization Strategies

On the other side of the GCC crisis, the UAE also employed its footballing interests in pursuit of concrete political objectives. Rather than warding off the threat of external intervention, however, the Emirati government attempted to leverage its stake in what became one of the most powerful football clubs in Europe to support its regional securitization policies. In the wake of the Arab uprisings that aimed to dismantle the ruling order in much of the region, the UAE positioned itself at the head of the counterrevolutionary forces committed to maintaining the authoritarian character that defined most states in the region.[93] Led by Crown Prince Mohammed bin Zayed, the UAE played a critical role in the coup that upended Egypt's democratic transition and brought the el-Sisi regime to power.[94] The UAE served as the leading backer of the military warlord Khalifa Haftar in Libya and a key player in the destructive civil war in Yemen.[95] The UAE has also been accused of attempting to derail Tunisia's nascent transition to democratic rule.[96] Indeed, one would be hard-pressed to find any corner of the Arab region that has not been impacted by aggressive Emirati diplomatic, economic, or military intervention over the past decade. As the *New York Times* wrote of Mohammed bin Zayed, "he seems to believe that the Middle East's only choices are a more repressive order or a total catastrophe."[97]

In late 2015, *The Guardian* reported that the Emirati government had threatened to block arms purchases and energy deals worth billions of pounds if the UK government did not take decisive action against the Muslim Brotherhood.[98] As one of the more organized political actors in post-authoritarian transitions in Tunisia and Egypt, and a prominent actor within civil society throughout the Arab region, the Islamist movement was identified by the counterrevolutionary forces as the actor best positioned to bring about substantive changes to the ruling order in a number of states. As such, the UAE led an aggressive crackdown against the Muslim Brotherhood at home, banning the organization, imprisoning accused sympathizers, and constructing "a hypermodern surveillance state where everyone is monitored for the slightest whiff of Islamist leanings."[99] Around the region, the UAE led a campaign to see the movement and its various offshoots excluded from political life and banished from society, through force if necessary. Mohammed bin Zayed also strongly believed that the cooperation of Western governments was critical in his broader war against civil society forces in the Arab region. Government documents obtained by *The Guardian* showcased several instances of Emirati officials communicating to their British counterparts their demands that Britain take concrete measures to crack down on the movement, by supporting the repressive policies of Arab states and denying the Muslim Brotherhood safe haven in the UK.

The UAE relayed its demands, in part, through Abu Dhabi's ownership of Manchester City FC. In 2012, Simon Pearce, a member of the Manchester City board of directors, put forward a series of economic incentives for British companies and the military in exchange for taking decisive measures against the Muslim Brotherhood. The desired measures included purging the BBC of Islamist infiltration and a crackdown against prominent figures and organizations in the British Muslim community. In exchange, the government of David Cameron was promised energy contracts for BP, an order of military hardware worth £6 billion, and an enhancement of the two nations' military and intelligence cooperation.[100] Two years later, when no decisive action was taken, Khaldoon al-Mubarak, Manchester City's chairman and close confidant of Mohammed bin Zayed, delivered a message to Britain's ambassador to the UAE, warning that British inaction against the Muslim Brotherhood had raised a "red flag" due to the fact that "our ally is not seeing it as we do: an existential threat not just to the UAE but to the region."[101] The British government responded in part by conducting a lengthy inquiry into the activities of the Muslim Brotherhood in Britain. Its final report offered some critiques of the movement, but was ultimately inconclusive, and apparently not to the liking of Emirati officials, who continued to withhold the government's financial incentives.[102]

Abu Dhabi's 2008 takeover of Manchester City was initially viewed as a project in Emirati "state-branding" that featured "both a sporting and an urban transformation" for the city of Manchester.[103] The club's stadium was renamed for Abu Dhabi's flagship airline, Etihad, and Emirati officials later pledged to invest £1 billion to redevelop the city's infrastructure and construct thousands of new homes.[104] In 2013, Human Rights Watch issued a report revealing Emirati human rights abuses and condemned efforts to use Manchester City to "construct a public relations image of a progressive, dynamic Gulf state, which deflects attention from what is really going on in the country."[105] As can be seen from the campaign to shift British security policy, however, Emirati investment in Manchester City extends far beyond enhancing the UAE's reputation. The club's personnel were similarly enlisted in UAE attacks on Qatar that predated the start of the GCC crisis. A 2016 report revealed that Pearce helped facilitate the UAE's hiring of Quiller Consultants, a UK public relations firm that worked to plant negative stories against Qatar in the British press. One newspaper subject to the secret lobbying published thirty-four articles over a two-month period accusing Qatar of supporting terrorism.[106] Similarly, in Fall 2017, a little-known British consulting firm named Cornerstone Global Associates issued a widely publicized report calling into question Qatar's ability to host the 2022 World Cup, concluding that it should either be stripped of the tournament or forced to share it with its neighbors. Extensive investigations and media leaks later revealed that Cornerstone was likely acting at the behest of the UAE.[107] The World Cup served as an underlying factor in the GCC crisis, with the Emirati foreign minister at one point suggesting that Qatar's right to host the tournament should be directly linked to its meeting the demands of the blockading states.[108] Dubai's security chief put it more bluntly, writing, "If the World Cup goes out of Qatar … the crisis in Qatar will end because the crisis was made to break it."[109]

Sportswashing

State footballing interests have historically played a critical role in masking destructive or unpopular government practices. Infamously, the 1978 World Cup was played in Argentina at a time when the ruling military junta was disappearing thousands of Argentine citizens in concentration camps and summary executions.[110] As a country with far less investment in football than its Gulf neighbors, Saudi Arabia in recent years has scrambled to grow its domestic league and establish links with major leagues and clubs the world over. During the 2017–18 La Liga season, nine Saudi players were sent to join a number of Spanish clubs on loan as part of a "multiyear marketing and licensing arrangement."[111] While the move was ostensibly to give the players valuable experience in one of the world's top leagues, only one Saudi player ever featured in a match. Spanish league officials hoped their addition would expand the appeal of Spanish football in the Middle East, and clubs benefited from the fact that the Saudi federation was paying the players' salaries. The following year, after having recently hosted the Italian Super Cup, Saudi officials reached a three-year €40 million deal to host the Spanish Super Cup. Real Madrid lifted the trophy in Jeddah following its victory in an expanded tournament that featured the Spanish league's top four teams. In early 2020, Saudi Arabia launched a domestic league for women's football as part of a broader effort to relax rules that uphold gender discrimination across Saudi society.[112] That same year, the English Premier League received a £300 million takeover bid of Newcastle United by Saudi Arabia's Public Investment Fund (PIF).[113] Following some backlash and significant pressure on the Premier League to block the deal, the sale of an eighty percent stake to PIF was finalized in late 2021.[114]

This bold shift in Saudi posture stemmed from the broader developments underway in the country since the rise of Crown Prince Mohammed bin Salman. Hailed in Western capitals as an aggressive modernizer who sought to liberalize Saudi society and reclaim its place in the region, particularly in the face of Iranian hegemony, Mohammed bin Salman undertook several aggressive policies, with cataclysmic consequences that reverberated throughout the region. These included crucial Saudi support for the military coup in Egypt, the humiliating detention and forced resignation of Lebanon's prime minister, and the waging of a devastating war in Yemen that has cost thousands of lives, unleashed a cholera epidemic, and put twelve million people at risk of starvation.[115] Internally, Mohammed bin Salman reordered the structure of the Saudi state to concentrate power more in his own hands, and unleashed a violent purge of opposition forces, including within the royal family. Powerful princes and business elites were detained and interrogated, many of them only freed upon handing over billions of dollars in cash and assets.[116] Following a wave of violent repression at home, Saudi security forces pursued dissidents abroad, most prominently in the killing of journalist Jamal Khashoggi in the Saudi consulate in Istanbul in October 2018. As grotesque details of the murder became publicized, Mohammed bin Salman was roundly condemned, in some cases by American politicians, business elites, celebrities, and journalists who had only recently feted him during a high-profile visit to the United States. In April 2019, the US Congress passed a resolution to end the US role in the Yemen war, a development that was unthinkable only a year earlier.

Saudi Arabia's sudden investment in football cannot be considered separately from these broader developments. Having spent millions in public relations and marketing ahead of his US tour, Mohammed bin Salman had clearly demonstrated a strong interest in maintaining a positive image in the face of reports surrounding his suspect policy choices.[117] One of his crowning achievements, the annual investment conference dubbed "Davos in the Desert," was largely abandoned by companies and prominent investors following the Khashoggi killing.[118] While consistently a feature of Saudi diplomatic and economic policy priorities, leveraging Saudi Arabia's financial clout in the realm of cultural exchange became an even more pronounced feature of the kingdom's outreach efforts following its growing isolation. Along with a number of concert performances, professional wrestling exhibitions, and tennis matches, hosting the likes of Leo Messi and Cristiano Ronaldo as they competed for real silverware offered a major boost to the country's image problems. When the deal was finalized to make Newcastle "the richest club in soccer," fans were instantly enlisted in showcasing their support for the new ownership, donning *thobes* and waving Saudi flags on matchdays, while echoing regime talking points online.[119]

These initiatives may have yielded tangible results in the form of global partnerships and marquee events that defied efforts to isolate Saudi Arabia. However, they also came with their share of critiques and condemnations. Ahead of the Spanish Super Cup's opening matches, Amnesty International's Spain director used the occasion to question the Spanish Football Federation's decision to partner with Saudi Arabia, writing, "Before deciding the venue, the federation should know the details and history of human rights violations in Saudi Arabia, including discrimination against women, freedom of speech restrictions, participation in the war in Yemen, extensive use of the death penalty and torture of prisoners."[120] The Spanish league's chief executive, who has often been at odds with the federation president, also voiced his displeasure with the Super Cup plans, telling journalists, "The Saudi Arabian government has a policy whereby they improve the image of the government through sport, whitewashing their image, and we all have a responsibility there."[121] Other critics pointed to widespread reports that Saudi officials had sanctioned the piracy of Qatari network BeIN Sports' broadcasts through a channel called BeoutQ based in the kingdom, arguing that Saudi Arabia should not be rewarded with hosting duties as a result of such blatant disregard for another rights holder.[122] In fact, a ruling by the World Trade Organization holding Saudi Arabia responsible for the piracy threatened to undo the Saudi government's Newcastle bid.[123] As many observers have noted, efforts to legitimize the Saudi regime fell flat when confronted by the reality of the state's continued human rights abuses. At the same time that Mohammed bin Salman sought acknowledgment for his decision to grant Saudi women the right to drive, he oversaw the imprisonment and torture of women's rights activists. In the same vein, launching Saudi Arabia's first women's football league could do little to mask the reality of the state's treatment of women and its broader disregard for human rights.

Conclusion: The Limits of Football Legitimacy

The widespread appeal of football as a cultural touchstone across the MENA region has shaped a contentious dynamic described as "a battleground for control between rulers looking to enforce order and fans who want to bring about change."[124] From the perspective of the state, football has more often than not represented an avenue by which to pursue strategic goals. It has been employed in the quest to justify an imperial intervention and stabilize an ongoing foreign occupation in Iraq. Authoritarian rulers, including Egypt's past and present dictators, have leveraged mass support for the sport into legitimizing their own rule as the regulators and purveyors of the game. They have claimed their nation's footballing successes as their own, while attempting to diminish the impact of failures on the pitch on their claims to authority. As Qatar and the UAE have alternately shown, states have similarly utilized their footballing interests to maximize their positions vis-à-vis rival states, either to neutralize threats emanating from hostile regimes or elicit specific policy changes in their attempts reshape regional security in their image. Additionally, states such as Saudi Arabia have engaged in sportswashing in an attempt to turn popular love for football into an armor to shield themselves from criticism for violations of human rights and other transgressions.

Though they have occurred under different circumstances and have taken on a variety of forms, all these state uses of football share the desire for legitimacy. Owing to their shortcomings in other, crucial areas, from providing for the welfare of citizens to observing the norms of international behavior, states in the MENA region have clearly viewed the sport as a convenient vehicle to make legitimation claims on the domestic and international fronts. While the examples in the categories above have noted a degree of success in the achievement of specific aims related to these legitimation claims, they have also demonstrated, without exception, the limited utility in exploiting football to make those claims. As powerful an appeal as the sport can have for audiences the world over, it has proven no match for the persistence of the underlying issues that raise questions of state legitimacy in the first place.

3

A STUDY OF FOOTBALL CHANTS AS POLITICAL EXPRESSION IN THE ALGERIAN HIRAK

Maher Mezahi

Introduction

This study examines football-related chants used as political expression in the 2019 Hirak demonstrations in Algeria. When mass protests spilled out onto the streets of Algiers on Friday, February 22, 2019, the air was palpably tense with nervous anticipation. Social media was rife with rumors of anti-government demonstrations, and there were very real fears that the protests would be violently repressed. Public gatherings had been de facto prohibited in Algiers since 2001, when tens of thousands marched on Algiers to protest the killing of unarmed, eighteen-year-old Massinissa Guermah in a gendarmerie base.[1]

Independent journalist Nabia Lahchi recalled an eerie silence ahead of the Friday prayers on that day, after which a group of young men marched from the working-class neighborhoods of the Casbah and Bab El Oued, chanting: "There is no president, there is only a photo" and "there will not be a fifth term, oh Bouteflika."[2] The chant embodies football-related art as political expression in the 2019 demonstrations. It refers to a song titled "Y'en a marre" ("Fed Up") by Mouh Milano, a musician and supporter of Union Sportive de Medina d'Alger (USMA), which quickly became a hit on YouTube and in the terraces of Stade Omar Hamadi, USMA's home stadium.[3] The line "There is no president, there is only a photo," was Milano's answer to an unpopular practice propagated by a group of Algerian politicians in the lead-up to the 2019 Algerian presidential elections. Several members of the political establishment had the habit of honoring an absent President Abdelaziz Bouteflika by presenting gifts to a portrait of him after he suffered a debilitating stroke in 2013, severely limiting his motor functions and slurring his speech.[4]

The most salient example occurred at an event in the La Couple Arena in the heights of Algiers on February 10, 2019, when Bouteflika's presidential campaign honored a framed portrait of him in his absence while announcing his intention to run for reelection. General Secretary Moad Bouchareb, of the incumbent ruling party, Front de Liberation (FLN), announced on stage: "I am honored to announce that the FLN presents the revolutionary, Abdelaziz Bouteflika, as a candidate for the next presidential election, as a sign of recognition for his good governance, his wise choices and the achievements reaped by Algeria under his presidency."[5] Following the ceremony, photographs emerged of Bouchareb saluting members of the FLN party with one hand and hugging a portrait of Bouteflika in the other. What transpired at La Coupole would spark spontaneous weekly protests across the country, giving birth to a movement that would eventually be dubbed the "Hirak" movement (literally "movement" in Arabic). The movement emerged organically and never appointed a leader. Throughout 2019 and the early part of 2020, Algerians of all walks of life marched through city centers on Friday afternoons chanting slogans and displaying signs and flags. The cessation of weekly protests only came into effect when the danger of public assembly became clear with the advent of the COVID-19 pandemic in March 2020. From February 2019 to March 2020, the Hirak leveraged enough pressure to force Bouteflika's resignation, and to spur a crackdown on corruption and a revision of the constitution. The objective of this chapter is to examine the historical roots of the creation of football-related political art in Algeria and then illustrate how it was adopted by the Hirak movement of 2019–20. For the purposes of this chapter, football-related art is defined as music, large choreographic displays (or *tifos*), and graffiti—all of which were used to organize and galvanize protestors as well as make public statements. Ultimately, the findings of this chapter reveal that football fans in Algeria were not only actively protesting within the Hirak, but that their songs and displays were adopted by the general public on a massive scale.

Due to how recently the Hirak movement manifested, it has yet to yield significant scholarly analyses of the ties between football and the movement. As a result, this work rests on a considerable amount of primary material relevant to the Hirak movement, such as newspaper articles, songs by football supporters, and my experience covering football matches and Hirak protests as a journalist. In addition to covering more than thirty anti-regime protests across Algeria, I attended more than a dozen local football matches throughout 2019. These trips helped provide a clear context of what the protestors' concerns were, and how they were using football-related art to express them. In addition to speaking to several members of Ultra groups about the Hirak movement, I also visited Casa Verde, the locale for Mouloudia Club d'Alger (MCA) Ultras, to do the same. The photos included in this chapter were taken by me while covering the protests. All translations of lyrics of supporter chants and Ultra group chants related to the Hirak movement are my own. Secondary material related to the broader political history of Algerian football was easier to obtain, and the work of Mahfoud Amara was particularly useful.[6]

A Brief History of Algeria's Politicized Football Stadiums

In Algeria, football supporters have a history of expressing themselves through football-related art, including *tifos*, or choreographed fan displays in stadiums that are unveiled before and during football matches. These displays are often used to spread a message on television and social media. Just as graffiti in working-class neighborhoods has long been a credible indicator of working-class political perspectives, artistic displays and stadium songs remain the oldest and most authentic method of disseminating a public's point of view. Football stadiums have, therefore, always been places of resistance, identity affirmation, and truth-telling in Algeria.

During the colonial period, from the end of the nineteenth century until independence in 1962, Muslim-Arab football fanatics sang *anasheed*, or traditional Islamic songs, in the stadium as a way of supporting indigenous Muslim-Algerian clubs against colonial "European" clubs, which for long periods of time abided by quotas, capping the number of indigenous Algerian players on a single team.[7]

The first Muslim-Algerian sporting association, Mouloudia Club d'Alger (MCA), was created in August 1921 in the Lower Casbah of Algiers. Its name, "Mouloudia," comes from the Muslim holiday "Al Mawlid An-Nabawy," which marks the birthday of the Prophet Muhammad.[8] Mouloudia's color profile of green and red also reflects indigenous culture and religion; according to one of the founders, Abderrahmane Aouf, "Green represents paradise, and red is for generous blood."[9] Other club founders confirm that green was also chosen as the color of Islam, and red because it was Prophet Muhammad's favorite color.[10] The crescent moon and star, symbols of Islam, are also included in the logo. To this day, more than forty sporting associations around the Maghreb have proudly adopted the "Mouloudia" name, tying clubs to local identity.

In 1956, two years after the start of the Algerian war of independence, the FLN ordered all indigenous clubs to pull out of leagues operated by the French Football Federation, a decree that was eventually observed by clubs in all divisions in Algeria.[11] Two years later, the first Algerian national team was created when thirteen professional Algerian footballers decided to leave their clubs in France to form the FLN team, which was based in neighboring Tunisia. Some players, such as Rachid Mekhloufi of A.S. Saint-Etienne and Mustapha Zitouni of A.S. Monaco, were expected to feature during France's 1958 World Cup campaign, but turned down that opportunity to constitute the FLN team instead. The

Fédération Internationale de Football Association (FIFA) threatened member associations with sanctions were they to partake in
matches against the FLN team, yet the team still managed to play
more than ninety matches against national teams, club teams, and
labor union teams across a four-year timespan.[12] The campaign was
extremely successful in raising awareness for the Algerian struggle
to the extent that Algerian revolutionary Ferhat Abbes went so far
as to say that the FLN team advanced the cause of Algerian independence an entire decade.[13]

After independence, politically contentious stadium chants
began to permeate the public sphere in the 1970s when JS Kabylie
(JSK) supporters affirmed their cultural identity in front of
President Houari Boumediene during the 1977 Algerian Cup
final, pitting their side against N.A. Hussein Dey. Boumediene
was not popular amongst large parts of the Kabyle population in
Algeria due to his strict 'Arabization' policy,[14] which made the
Arabic language Algeria's sole official language, repressing
Amazigh language partisans.[15]

On the day, JSK supporters saw their opportunity to express
their sentiments to Boumediene by singing "Anwa wigui? Imazighen"
("Who are we? Amazigh people") and booing the national anthem.
Mouloud Iboud, JSK's captain on the day, narrated the scenes of
that ground-breaking final in a 2014 interview with *LeButeur*:

> I think everyone remembers the wave of people that had reached
> the capital (Algiers) on the day of the final. In addition to the
> purely sporting challenge, that is to say: we had to offer the JSK
> and all of the Kabylie its first cup in history; the final of '77 was an
> occasion for reclaiming the Amazigh cause. The thousands of sup-
> porters who invaded July 5th Stadium did not stop asking
> Boumediene for recognition of the Berber cause, with the famous
> slogan "Anwa Wigui D Imazighen" which gave goosebumps to all
> players on the pitch. Throughout the match, supporters kept talk-
> ing to the president, who was in the VIP stand.[16]

Mahfoud Amara notes that JSK supporters continued to demand
language rights in football stadiums during the Berber Spring of
1980.[17] "Banners were deployed during football matches with slogans in favor of Tamazight (Berber language): 'Nous ne sommes

pas des Arabes, Tamazight dil likoul' ('We are not Arabs, Berber language in schools')."[18]

In the late 1980s, Algerian youth became deeply frustrated with the single-party rule of the FLN, and thousands rioted on the streets in October 1988.[19] The Algerian government's heavy-handed response killed hundreds. The aftermath effectively ushered in a new era of politics, ending one-party rule in Algeria. Soon thereafter, stadiums around the capital sang: "Bab El Oued chouhada" ("[those in] Bab El Oued are martyrs"), a chant that can still be heard in stadiums today.[20] At the final sitting of the FLN Central Committee under single-party rule in Algeria, Bendjedid spoke of the "violence in our stadiums," validating the popular sentiment that the stadium spoke for the majority of Algerians.[21]

In Algeria's first set of transparent elections in the early 1990s, the newly formed Islamic Salvation Front (FIS) handily won municipal elections and the first round of legislative elections. Acting swiftly before the second round, the Algerian military interrupted the democratic process and dissolved parliament, plunging the country into civil war.[22] Nevertheless, football leagues operated consistently, and during the 1990s sympathizers of the FIS sang their displeasure at the army's assault on democracy. As if addressing the party's imprisoned leadership, some fans sang: "Oh Ali [Belhadj], oh Abbass [Abassi Madani]; The [Islamic Salvation] Front is doing well."[23]

Music groups proliferated across the country in the 2000s and, with the advent of the internet, they began to recount the highs and lows of their daily lives. For example, in 2014 the "Torino," "Palermo," and "Catania" musical groups produced a song entitled "Babour Casanova" ("Casanova Boat"), which brings up themes of emigration and disgust at the political elite. As a result, criticism of socioeconomic policies and the realities of young people in Algeria became more pronounced, coming to a crescendo during the Hirak movement in 2019.

Chaabi Music: Football's Working-Class Soundtrack

The earliest original musical expressions in Algerian football came in the form of *Chaabi*—a unique genre of working-class music that

emerged from the Casbah of Algiers at the beginning of the twentieth century. The term *Chaabi* comes from the Arabic word for
"people" (*sha'b*), indicating that the genre was open and accessible
to anyone. Algerian *Chaabi* traces its roots back to classic Berber
and Arab-Andalusian melodies, yet it provides room for improvisation and interpretation by coupling melodies with classical and
urban poetry. The music is usually composed by a group headed
by a "master" who interprets social issues and imparts wisdom
upon those present. *Chaabi* groups also use local instruments such
as violins, Spanish guitars, North African lutes known as "oud," and
goblet drums called "darbuka."[24]

The grand master and inventor of *Chaabi* music is El Hadj
M'hamed El Anka, a native of the Casbah.[25] El Anka managed to
vulgarize prestigious Andalusian music by introducing fewer
instruments, by using local vernacular in lyrics, and by framing his
interpretations of classical Arabic poetry (*Qaṣīda*) in accessible contexts.[26] Though initially rejected by upper-class society as controversial, El Anka and his acolytes were immediately popular
amongst the working classes that loved football. In addition to
sharing the same demographic, football and *Chaabi* also shared the
same space: cafés.

In his essay "From the Moorish Café to the Sports Café," Youcef
Fates illustrates how the Moorish café, an import from the
Ottoman Empire, and a place that was most frequented by the
indigenous working-class population, became a place where politicians, artists, athletes, and passionate supporters would congregate.[27] It was in these cafés that a strong link between working-
class men and football was developed. Besides being a place to
socialize, cafes also rented out their address for the registration of
sporting associations, and posted updates and scores of domestic
and international football results when recounted by radio.

> In Jijel, it is a kiosk operated by a former sportsman, a footballer
> of the first football team of the Jeunesse Sportive Djidjellienne,
> Mr Moussaoui Messaoud, which crystallizes the male sociability of
> Jijel, thanks to a carefully updated table of all the information on
> football in Algeria and abroad. Jijel's youth gathered there to com-
> ment on these events. In Oran, another kiosk (cafe) brings together

MCO (M.C. Oran) members and supporters. Friendly gatherings are held around the leaders, the oldest of whom are seated on carpets in the traditional way and the young ones on chairs... This is the case, for example, of the Cafe des sports in Mostaganem.[28]

In the Casbah of Algiers, Café Malakoff (which El Anka owned), Café des Sports, and Café Tlemcani, were all spaces where the world of *Chaabi* music and football collided. El Anka is on record giving private shows at these cafes, the proceeds from which were directly transferred to Muslim-Algerian clubs in Algiers.[29]

It would only be a matter of time before *Chaabi* artists began singing about football. The earliest track can be traced to as far back as the 1930s, when Saoud L'Oranais, an Algerian-Jewish composer, published songs such as "Gheniet U.S.M.O" ("The songs of U.S.M. Oran"). The track is likely the first ever football vinyl record captured on 78 RPM in North Africa. The lyrics call on the listeners to celebrate USMO's 1933 victory in the regional Oran Cup. As Chris Silver notes:

> On Gheniet U.S.M.O (the Song of Union Sportive Musulmane d'Oran), Saoud l'Oranais invites the listener to celebrate the soccer club's triumph in the Oran Cup of 1933. As the "Champion d'Oranie"—the phrase l'Oranais invokes again and again on the 1934 recording—the U.S.M.O was catapulted into the North African championship, where it would face and ultimately lose to the rather fierce *l'Union Sportive Marocaine de Casablanca*. Nonetheless, traces in the archives and in popular memory make clear that Saoud l'Oranais Arabic-language panegyric to U.S.M.O hardly disappeared—being sung or hummed for years to come.[30]

It is noteworthy that Saoud chose to sing about USMO, a Muslim club that would soon after recruit an influx of Jewish players, and not a "European" club created by and for the settler population.

In 1951, *Chaabi* master Hadj Mrizek, who later purchased Café Malakoff from El Anka, published a short song entitled "Mouloudia." Throughout the recording, Hadj Mrizek repeats: "Oh you who love sport, sign up with Mouloudia, the most famous club in North Africa." Expressing support for MCA, the doyen of all Muslim-Algerian sporting associations at the time, was an explicitly political act. Dahmane El Harrachi, Mahieddine Hadj

Mahfoud, Ammar Ezzahi, El Hachemi Guerouabi, and other masters of the craft also performed songs of support for their favorite football clubs. As *Chaabi* grew into an accepted discipline in the 1950s, it became, like football, a revolutionary activity. Private *Chaabi* concerts provided cover for revolutionaries who needed to meet in the Casbah, and coded messages were disseminated through the lyrics of *Chaabi* songs.[31]

Nowadays, the *Chaabi* genre is sometimes perceived to be less popular amongst young Algerians vis-à-vis newer local genres, such as Rai music or Gnawa music. However, football supporters continue to have strong ties to *Chaabi* figures and their compositions. When Ammar Ezzahi passed away in 2016, USMA supporters organized a *tifo*, which spelled out "Adieu l'artiste" ("so long, our artist"), along with a portrait of the *Chaabi* master.[32] In any Algerian stadium in any given week, it is common to see supporters playing *Chaabi* instruments, drumming up a rhythm, and improvising slogans during the match. The historic relationship between *Chaabi* music and football in Algeria largely explains the musical tradition of football supporters in the North African country.

Structuring Football Support in North African Stadiums

After *Chaabi* masters released the first football tracks during the colonial period, a culture of informal musical groups came to the fore in the 1980s with the Virage Electric Orchestra of USMA.[33] The "Virage" is analogous to the Italian football concept of the "Curva," i.e., a curved section of the stadium that passionate supporters claim as their own. The Virage Electric Orchestra was a loose, informal group of USMA supporters at Stade Omar Hamadi in Bologhine, Algiers. It is from that rich musical tradition that the USMA group, "Ouled El Bahdja" ("Sons of Algiers") emerged. They are widely considered to be the most creative and politically active musical group in Algeria, and one of the most in North Africa.[34]

In an interview with national newspaper *El Watan*, Oussama, one of the founding members of Ouled El Bahdja, noted that his group actively strives to preserve the musical tradition of past supporters: "Our slogan is 'USMA fans are conservative.' One of our main objectives is to preserve the musical heritage of the supporters before us."[35] Pointing to their cultural heritage, Ouled El Bahdja refuse the "Ultra" tag that is sometimes placed on them, claiming that they are not emulating an Italian trend, but, rather, reviving an Algerian tradition. However, there can be no denying that the Italian Ultra movement did indeed influence Algerian football supporters in the way they organized and created their art. Mark Doidge presents a thorough definition of Italian Ultra groups, noting that "the term has been adapted to refer to all hard-core football fans that demonstrate an unwavering support of their team.... This support is highly ritualistic and is characterized by the extensive displays of flags and banners, igniting of flares, and chanting of songs."[36] With the advent of the internet, the Ultra movement spread across the Maghreb in the early 2000s, effectively structuring passionate North African supporters. Supporter groups formed leadership committees, designated specific places to sit in the stadium, established well-defined codes to abide by, and synchronized clothing apparel. The first Ultra group to appear was in Tunisia with the Esperance de Tunis group: L'Emkachkhines. Morocco's first Ultra group, Green Boys, formed in 2005, before the movement spread to Algeria and Egypt in 2007 with Ultras Verde Leone (MCA) and the Al-Ahlawy Ultras.[37]

European Ultra influence is reflected in the names and conduct of new North African groups. Italian or English is often used in Ultra group names, such as Verde Leone (MCA), Loca Ragazzi (CS Constantine), Fanatic Reds (CR Belouizdad), Winners (Club Africain and Wydad Casablanca), and Eagles (Raja Casablanca). Some Algerian clubs will often unofficially pair their club with that of a European club with the same colors. USMA supporters often refer to their own club as "Milano" because of the red and black color profile. It is common to see the Turkish league's Galatasaray kits during an NA Hussein Dey match, a team that also dons yellow and red.

Yet, what makes North African Ultras unique is that each has its own accompanying musical group which composes and records songs for the team. These songs are then published on social media, where supporters can listen and memorize lyrics ahead of singing them in the stadium.[38] One well-known USMA musical group with connections to Ouled El Bahdja is Groupe Milano. MCA's musical groups include Groupe Torino, Groupe Catania, and Groupe Palermo that were affiliated with Ultras Verde Leone. Other groups are direct subsidiaries of Ultra groups, such as Dey Boys of NAHD and Fanatic Reds of CR Belouizdad (CRB).

Politicization of Ultra Groups in North Africa

A notable trend over the past decade is that football songs composed by supporter groups have taken on regional popularity across North Africa. This was first properly observed when Raja Casablanca's Ultra group, the Ultras Eagles, and the musical group affiliated with them, Gruppo Aquile, released "Fi Bladi Dalmouni" ("In My Country They Have Oppressed Me"). The song evokes a lack of opportunity and economic mobility in Morocco, government corruption, and the proliferation of drugs.[39] The general themes of the track so resonated with audiences across the Maghreb that it was eventually covered by an Algerian Rai singer Mohamed Benchenet and became very popular in Algeria in the months leading up to the Hirak movement. Some of the lyrics state:

> Oh, in my country they have oppressed me; Oh, who can I complain to?
> To the lord the Most High; Only he knows (my situation).

> They've spent on Hachich; And abandoned us like orphans; We'll get our due in the afterlife; You've wasted talents; With drugs, you've crushed them; Is that not the truth?

> You've eaten the state's money; Given it to foreigners; An entire generation's been suppressed.[40]

In Tunisia, Club Africain's Ultra group, African Winners, released a song called "Ya Hyetna" ("Our Life"), which also touches on a similar host of socioeconomic problems:

> You brought drugs into the country and you have ruined it!
> You pushed people to immigrate, you forced them!
> You smothered them! In a wooden raft, you threw them![41]

Common themes of a lack of opportunity, drug scandals, and prioritizing foreigners over local populations seem to resonate the loudest. "Ya Hyetna" and "Fi Bladi Dalmouni" are two examples of how musical groups attached to Ultras can touch on political issues not only in one country, but across a region.

As large crowds of people from all walks of life gathered to demand freedom, dignity, and democracy during the Arab uprisings that began in late 2010, football stadiums across North Africa transformed into sites of violent clashes with security forces, enhancing the politicized nature of Ultras and their music. In Egypt, the Ultras were more explicitly involved in the protests against the regime of Hosni Mubarak. Witnesses describe the Al-Ahlawy Ultras as creating a frontline between protestors and security forces, bringing their knowledge of dealing with the police to Tahrir Square. Dag Tuastad documented the role of the Al-Ahlawy Ultras in Tahrir Square:

> They knew how to act collectively, to hit and run, to survive and escape prolonged exposure to tear gas, to change their front fighters so as to rest them periodically, to bang the drums to warn of police attacks, to identify provocateurs, to cheer and whistle when in need of tactical withdraws, to avoid collective running knowing the danger of stampings and panics, to regroup, and return fireworks, to suffer and endure pain as many having been subject to mistreatments and even torture at the police stations.[42]

It is widely believed that the Port Said Stadium massacre of 2012, in which seventy-two Al Ahly supporters were killed (two more would later succumb to injuries) occurred as an act of deliberate retribution by the regime. Reports point to the fact that supporters were barely searched upon entering the stadium, and that police stood idly by as Al Masry fans attacked Al Ahly fans with machetes and knives. James Dorsey writes of that tragedy:

> The brawl was widely seen as an attempt by the military and the security forces that got out of hand to cut down to size a force that played a key role to the toppling in 2011 of President Hosni Mubarak and subsequent opposition to military rule... Fiercely independent, passionately loyal to their club, and aggressive in support for their team, the ultras constituted the one force that

refused to shy away from sustained confrontation with security forces whose strategy was limited to intimidation and brute force.[43]

Later, President Abdel Fattah el-Sisi, who claimed power following a 2013 military coup that upended the post-Mubarak transition, went so far as to ban Ultra groups altogether, seeing them as a threat to stability. "In banning the ultras—groups of fervent, well-organized, street battle-hardened soccer fans—authorities would outlaw a social force that rivaled in appeal the Muslim Brotherhood that was criminalized last year as a terrorist organization with the military coup that toppled Mohamad Morsi, the country's only democratically elected president."[44]

In Morocco, Ultras in Tangier, Casablanca, and Rabat have drawn the fascination of international media in recent years, especially with regards to the political critiques present in their songs. For instance, Ultras Los Matadores of M.O. Tetouan protested the death of Hayet Belkacem, a young migrant from Tetouan who wanted to cross into Spain illegally and was killed by Moroccan Royal Marine forces a few days before the start of the 2018–19 football season. Ahead of their first home fixture of the season against Kawkab Marrakech, Los Matadores published a Facebook post calling for adherents to assemble on a main boulevard, dressed in dark colors of mourning.[45] Police quickly dispersed the gathering, but not before the Ultras chanted: "With our souls, with our blood, we will avenge you Hayet… The people want the person who killed Hayet." The Ultras in Tetouan, which sits a few miles from the Strait of Gibraltar, also chanted of their desire to emigrate by singing "Viva Espana." Before the match, the Moroccan national anthem was booed.[46]

As a result of political contestation across the region, several governments responded by setting attendance caps or by outright banning Ultra groups. In Tunisia and Egypt, attendance caps remain strictly enforced with few exceptions. In Casablanca, Ultra groups were banned in 2016 following violent events between two groups of Raja Casablanca supporters. A minister delegate, Najib Boulif, went so far as to call Raja Ultras "terrorists."[47]

Football-Related Art as Political Expression in the Hirak Movement

As the political discourse surrounding football supporters in Morocco, Tunisia, and Egypt continued to grow, Algerian Ultras became more politicized after the retreat of the Arab uprisings elsewhere, responding to domestic political events by releasing music that addressed these issues in explicit terms. For example, after Bouteflika suffered a stroke that consigned him to a wheelchair and limited his public appearances,[48] the Dey Boys released a song before the 2016 Algerian Cup final with a punchline stating: "The president in a wheelchair; a puppet holding on to power."[49] The following year, Ouled El Bahdja, Algeria's most infamous football musical group, released a song titled "Qilouna" ("Leave Us Alone") in the midst of reports that the Algerian government was exploring the possibility of fracking for shale gas reserves in the Sahara. In a piece dedicated to attacking government corruption, they sang: "The people don't hear what's happening in the Sahara."[50] Further, in 2018, when 701 kilograms of cocaine were seized at the port of Oran, which was eventually linked to entourages of ministers, mayors, governors, and even the head of the national police,[51] Mouh Milano's song "Y'en a marre" expressed its alarm, stating: "the state is wild, [importing] hash and cocaine."[52]

Although Algerian Ultra groups did not overtly oppose Abdelaziz Bouteflika's decision to run for a fourth term in 2014, it seemed only a matter of time before they would respond to his eventual plans to run for a fifth term. The incumbent president had ruled Algeria since 1999, when he was elected in controversial elections, and despite a two-term presidential limit, Bouteflika led efforts for a constitutional amendment that would allow him to run for additional presidential terms. The amendment was ratified by the two houses of parliament in 2008.[53] The decision to run a severely ill president—Bouteflika had not addressed the nation directly since 2012 and had not made a public appearance since 2017—for an unprecedented fifth term at La Coupole was not well-received by many Algerians,[54] triggering protests in different regions of the country in the lead-up to February 22, 2019.[55] Hundreds of protestors voiced their discontent in Bordj Bou Arreridj, Kherrata, Algiers, and Khenchela.

As Algerians around the country mobilized to oppose Bouteflika's reelection, the defining characteristic of the Hirak movement was its nonviolent nature, which some pundits attributed to the memory of the bloody 1988 riots and subsequent Black Decade, fearing that the same scenario would be repeated with clashes between protestors and security forces. Instead, the demonstrations would become weekly occurrences characterized by peaceful protest, chanting, and collaborative discussion. Some protestors even dubbed it the "revolution of smiles."[56]

No Ultra group made an appearance at any Hirak protest in a formal capacity. However, football fans did find ways to come together organically and sing their songs in public spaces. As football supporters sit in certain areas within the stadium, they also occupied certain spaces during the Hirak movement. The stairs adjacent to the Barberousse high school on the main avenue of Didouche Mourad and the stairs of the Grande Poste were temporarily transformed into locations supporters could congregate

Figure 3.1: A Friday Hirak protest in the Algerian province of Bordj Bou Arreridj, 200 kilometers from Algiers in April, 2019. Photo by Maher Mezahi.

within, akin to the stadium.[57] As the Hirak movement gained momentum during the month of March, "La Casa Del Mouradia" ("The Mouradia House") emerged as an anthem for the protestors.[58] The song, created by Ouled El Bahdja, was named after the popular Netflix series "Money Heist" that depicts a hold-up at the Royal Mint of Spain. The chorus dissects Bouteflika's four terms in office from the point of view of a football supporter.

> It is dawn and I cannot sleep
> I am slowly getting high
> Who are the causes, who can I blame [for my problems]
> We are sick of this life we are living
>
> In the first [term] we can say they tricked us with "reconciliation"
> In the second [term] it became clear that this was La Casa Del Mouradia
> In the third [term] the country suffered because of personal interests
> In the fourth [term] the puppet died and our issue persists.[59]

In these lyrics, Ouled El Bahdja displays a keen understanding of political history and current affairs. "Reconciliation" refers to Bouteflika's policy of presidential amnesty during the Algerian civil war;[60] the atmosphere of reconciliation meant that for many Algerians it was not the right time to contest policy in the political arena. The song also touches on the numerous corruption scandals that rocked the Bouteflika regime, and calls the president a "puppet" because his ill health did not permit him to run the country, instead conferring power on his brother, a group of shadowy military officials, and various oligarchs.

Protestors of all ages and social classes learned the lyrics of "La Casa Del Mouradia" and sang it in large numbers. However, other stadium songs were also adopted by the Hirak movement on a smaller scale. USM El Harrach's "Chkoun Sbabna" ("Who is the Cause of our Problems) was also widely memorized and sung during Hirak protests.[61]

> And if they say, "You want to wreak havoc"
> It has been a long time since havoc has been unleashed
> You have sold Algiers and split it up

You have bought all the villas in Paris
These are the sons of Harkis ("traitors") who sold it (Algiers)
The poor man in his country is renting

Who is the cause [of our problems]
The government, they are the cause
The cause of our misery
Algeria has worn us down.[62]

Another song, "Ultima Verba" ("Last Words"), by Ouled El Bahdja, became so popular that Algerian hip-hop sensation Soolking adapted it and achieved major commercial success.[63] The song's title is derived from a poem by Victor Hugo, dispelling the myth that because most football supporters come from the working classes, they must be uneducated and uncultured. Soolking's version, "Liberté" ("Freedom"), has amassed hundreds of millions of views on YouTube, and has had success with protests around the world.

The government will fall
And so will the one who built the highway
Freedom, Freedom, Freedom
The "virage" is singing

And we are the obstacle to you, Oh government
And our fire will not be extinguished.[64]

The first line cited is particularly significant because it targets Ali Haddad, a Bouteflika oligarch and owner of Ouled El Bahdja's own club. Besides owning USMA, Haddad was the president of the Forum de Chefs d'Enterprise (FCE), an Algerian business forum and a symbolic ally of the Bouteflika regime.[65] Haddad's flagship company, Entreprise des Travaux Routiers, Hydrauliques et Bâtiment—known colloquially as ETRHB—was awarded large contracts in the construction of the national East-West highway in Algeria, which was riddled with scandals.[66] As the protests continued to grow, Haddad was intercepted attempting to flee to the Tunisian border. He was charged with illegally possessing two valid Algerian passports simultaneously and placed in provisional detention.[67]

In addition to songs, football supporters also choreographed stadium behavior by unveiling *tifos* during demonstrations. This phenomenon started in the city of Bordj Bou Arreridj, where a group of young volunteers named "Ouled El Djebasse ("Children of Djebess"—a neighborhood in Bordj Bou Arreridj) created their own *tifos* and unfurled them from an unfinished construction site near the old marketplace. Besides hanging the 15 by 13 meter tarp, the volunteers also lit flares and fireworks, and sang football songs.[68] Most *tifos* made reference to some type of confrontation between Algeria and a detested opposing force that sometimes took the form of the Algerian government, the French government, or—simply—"the gang," referring to Bouteflika and the oligarchs that backed him.[69] Some of the designs staked specific political positions, like at the end of March, when the *tifos* read: "Justice is the base of governance." Others depicted a card game and a football match, where the protagonists represent the people, and the opponent represents the government.[70]

Over one month, in April 2019, *tifos* were displayed in seven different provinces: Touggourt, Relizane, Algiers, Chlef, M'sila, Djelfa, and Bordj Bou Arreridj. For Doidge, these displays directly correlate with the behavior of Ultras:

> Banners or striscione are unfurled across the curve. These depict membership of the group, political messages or taunts to rivals. In

Figure 3.2: A group of young volunteers named "Ouled El Djebasse" unfurl a *tifo* near the city's old marketplace in late April, 2019. Photo by Maher Mezahi.

addition to the visual display, the fans produce an aural performance through orchestrated choruses and combined with drums and trumpets, in some cases. Many of the songs reinforce the aesthetics through expressing support of the team, city or political views. The choreography is often supplemented with flares and smoke bombs that add to the aural and visual spectacle.[71]

Giant flags also made appearances during the Hirak movement, which did not necessarily reveal a slogan, but rather illustrations of symbolic figures in Algerian history. Over the previous decades, reclaiming symbols of Algeria's past became a popular practice among football supporters. Some Ultra groups are even named after popular figures. For example, MO Constantine's sole Ultra group is Ultras Ouled Ben Badis, after reformist Muslim scholar Abdelhamid Ben Badis—a figurehead of Algerian cultural nationalism in the 1930s. Stadiums in Algeria are almost all named after a revolutionary figure or significant date. Banners of Ali La Pointe, a protagonist of the Battle of Algiers, hang in front of Mouloudia supporters at every match. CR Belouizdad, a club named after Mohamed Belouizdad, a forefather of organizations that led to the FLN, has supporters that tag graffiti of his silhouette across the neighborhood. Yacef Saadi and Zoubir Bouadjadj, two leaders of the Autonomous Zone of Algiers (ZAA), an armed subdivision of the FLN, played for USMA before the Algerian war of independence broke out. Supporters continue to hang ZAA banners wherever they play in homage to their revolutionary past.

Just as football supporters began to reclaim national, historic, and revolutionary personalities, this was also one major characteristic of the Hirak movement. Protestors seemed galvanized when former revolutionaries of the Algerian War of Independence, such as Djamila Bouhird, Lakhdar Bouregaa, and Louisette Ighilahriz participated in Hirak protests.[72] When Friday protests coincided with the birthdays or death anniversaries of democratic revolutionary figures, such as Abane Ramdane or Hocine Ait Ahmed, protestors would create signs, flags, and banners celebrating their legacies.[73] The reclaiming of national symbols is another characteristic the Hirak shares with local football supporters.

95

Conclusion

This chapter has illustrated the various forms by which Algerian football supporters have historically expressed their political views. From the middle of the twentieth century, working-class football supporters, including grand masters of *Chaabi* music such as Hadj Mrizek, began using music to support their team. With the advent of recording equipment, television, and, eventually, social media, football supporters gained the ability of transmitting messages— during and beyond the matches themselves. Heavily influenced by other North African Ultra groups and the political transformations they experienced during the Arab Spring, Algerian football fans also began relaying political messages in their art. Whether they voice their opinion through music, *tifos*, or other methods, there can be no denying that football-related art has transcended the game and has taken on explicitly political dimensions. Due to the political and popular nature of football-related music, some Hirak protestors, who may not have shared a passion for football, learned the lyrics of football songs and began to identify with them. Songs such as "La Casa Del Mouradia" or "Pouvoir Assassin" ("Regime of Assassinations") became anthems during the Hirak movement, attributing power and status to otherwise disenfranchised working-class supporters in Algeria. In addition to songs, *tifos* were used to send messages to a disconnected ruling elite and to the wider world via public media outlets and social media. For a period of several weeks during the months of April and May, massive *tifos* were unfurled in several cities across the country. Within working-class neighborhoods, graffiti was also utilized to anonymously and pub-licly express dissenting opinions. From February 2019 to March 2020, anti-regime protests have radically changed the political landscape in Algeria. Former president Abdelaziz Bouteflika was forced to abandon his plans to run for a fifth presidential term and to approve ostensibly democratic reforms such as the constitutional referendum and legislative elections in 2020. There can be no denying that, in employing the use of football-related art, football supporters played a key role in the Hirak movement of 2019–20.

4

THE TRIVIALIZATION OF WOMEN'S FOOTBALL IN TURKEY

Yağmur Nuhrat

Introduction

Typically associated with boys, men, and hegemonic masculinity, football presents numerous challenges for women participants.[1] Even in the United States, where women's football is more developed and successful than in many other contexts, there is still palpable wage disparity between male and female practitioners.[2] Social scientific literature on football offers several accounts that demonstrate how women are "othered" in football,[3] wherein the sport supposedly contradicts feminine nature or aesthetics,[4] by way of trivialization, devaluation, and eroticization,[5] as well as downright underestimation of rigor and competence.[6] This chapter conceptualizes inequality and othering through trivialization. I describe the context and dynamics of how women's football is trivialized in Turkey on varying scales, from mundane match day procedures to larger-scale labor exploitation. I demonstrate how these dynamics produce women's football as a space of insecurity and precarity for footballers and deprive them of the means necessary for oppositional mobilization.

The chapter is based on four months of qualitative research between November 2019 and February 2020.[7] During this time, I interviewed active and former women footballers, coaches, federation and club administrators, media representatives, and what was the only major sponsor associated with a team during the time of my fieldwork. This chapter also benefits from my observations at five football matches in Istanbul and a training session in Izmir. As part of this project, I also spoke to five women academics who work on sports and gender and I benefit from their insights.[8] Overall, thirty-eight people participated in this research, thirty-one of whom were women.[9]

For this project, I took extensive notes during the interviews but did not record them—precisely because of the deep sense of insecurity and anxiety I discerned and elaborate upon in this chapter. I realized that any attempt to record the sessions would silence the interlocutors about issues they were already reluctant to discuss—issues like labor exploitation, mistreatment by superiors, enduring homophobia, etc. As such, the quotations here are not verbatim, but I did work diligently to reproduce them as I heard them based on my notes, which I redrafted immediately after any given interview.

There are multiple ways in which gender inequality may be conceptualized in this context: by comparing football to other sports; by comparing the situation in Turkey to other places; and finally by comparing men's and women's football in Turkey. As my interlocutors described unequal conditions, they predominantly spoke in (covert or overt) relation to men's football in the country and pointed to moments of trivialization, which deemed the women's sport unequal. As such, this is the lens through which this chapter engages the subject. I start by providing a brief history of women's football in Turkey and club dynamics to contextualize trivialization, before I move on to discuss trivialization on various scales.

TRIVIALIZATION OF WOMEN'S FOOTBALL IN TURKEY

A Brief History of Women's Football in Turkey

The first recorded instance of a public conversation about women playing football in Turkey was in 1929, when there was some speculation in a newspaper as to whether or not women could play.[10] The first women's game on record took place in 1954 in Istanbul, between an Izmir team and an Istanbul team—although, according to Murat Toklucu, the Izmir team never appeared, and the Istanbul team had to divide into two teams of eight to carry on. When the first application was submitted to form a women's team in March 1968, potential club members or players were required to bring written consent from their husbands or—if single—from their fathers.[11] This team never actually formed.[12]

It was at the beginning of the 1970s when the first women's team was established within the auspices of the Kınalıada Sports Club as a football team "for girls." The team, whose name was later changed to Dostlukspor, is on record for complaining about not finding any other women with whom to compete.[13] In the 1980s, the number of women's teams proliferated due mainly to a rise in the number of Astroturf fields in major cities.[14] The players began to voice their desire to form a league. The Turkish Football Federation (TFF) did try to initiate one in 1985, but the quality of football was found insufficient and the project was thereby postponed.[15] The women's league was founded almost a decade after that first attempt, in March 1994, with sixteen teams organizing under the name Bayanlar Futbol Ligi ("Ladies' Football League").[16] The games would last for eighty minutes with two forty-minute halves.[17] The most prominent team during that era was Dinarsu, a team founded by a major carpeting firm. Dinarsu claimed the title for four consecutive years and competed in various tournaments in Europe but had to pull out in 1997 due to lack of support and funding—a familiar pattern in women's football.[18]

The women's national team was founded in 1995 and the league continued steadily until 2003, when it was suspended.[19] The league was reinitiated in 2006 and carries on today with three divisions. The first division is composed of two groups of twelve teams each; the second division, thirteen teams; and the third

99

division includes nine groups, each with between six and eleven teams. Including the younger women and leagues, the number of athletes recorded by TFF was over 3,500 at the end of 2019.[20] There is still not a separate women's football division or department at TFF, although I have been told that this is under way. Currently, the Football Development Directorate and the managing unit of the national team are in charge of administering or guiding women's football.

Football in Turkey falls beneath the purview of the Union of European Football Associations (UEFA) and has been oriented towards Europe since its inauguration. The title winners compete in European championships, and TFF considers UEFA to be a source of guidance and inspiration. Given the popularity and success of European teams, many footballers dream of playing in Europe and consider it a significant milestone of having "made it." As such, even though this chapter does include references to women's football in the Middle East, much of the academic framing is informed by literature on women's football from Europe.

Club Dynamics and Contextualizing Trivialization

Although I have gathered some insights into the second and third divisions, my research has been based predominantly on first division women's football, which at the time of my research included a single group of 12 teams. During my fieldwork, four of the twelve teams in the first division were Istanbul-based and a fifth was based in Kocaeli, in a province just outside of Istanbul. Turkey's second, third, and fifth major cities, Ankara, Izmir, and Adana respectively, each had a team. There was a team from Zonguldak in northwestern Turkey and there were three teams in the southeastern region, from Diyarbakır, Hakkari, and Gaziantep.[21] As of June 2022, all these teams still compete in the first division.

Three of Istanbul's four teams (Kireçburnu, Fatih Vatan, and Ataşehir), and the teams from Ankara (FOMGET), Izmir (Konak), Zonguldak (Karadeniz Ereğli), and Hakkari (Hakkarigücü) are all municipality based. During my fieldwork, Istanbul's Beşiktaş was the only one among the more prominent sports clubs in Turkey to have a women's football branch. Turkey's other leading clubs—Fenerbahçe (FB), Galatasaray (GS), and Trabzonspor (TS)—each founded (FB) or re-inaugurated (GS and TS) their women's football division in 2021. Gaziantep's ALG Spor is an initiative of the ALG textile business. Amed Sportif Faaliyetler was founded in the 1990s as Diyarbakır's municipal team. They changed their name to Amed in 2014 and lost municipal support in 2017 when the government-appointed mayor insisted on reversing the name change to no avail.[22] The clubs based in Adana (İdman yurdu) and Kocaeli (Bayan) were both founded through personal initiatives. Historically, since the re-inauguration in 2006, it has been Ataşehir (three titles) and Konak (five successive titles between 2012 and 2017) that have been most successful. Beşiktaş claimed the title in 2019 in the third season of their ascendance to the first division; they were ousted by ALG, their fiercest competition, in 2020, and regained the title in 2021.

Beşiktaş, decidedly the most prominent of women's teams during my research, with a professional men's team that has traditionally ranked among the first three in Turkey's top division, offered pronouncedly better conditions for their players (in terms of training, facilities, or public visibility) as compared to many of the rest. In 2019, it was the only team with a major sponsor, the team with the most recruits on the national team, and the team whose captain (Didem Karagenç—also the captain of the national team) had a sponsorship deal with Visa and had been profiled by the *The Guardian*. The club has an official agreement with a major hospital chain in Turkey, which allows for rigorous healthcare for its athletes. Finally, Beşiktaş's larger prominence in Turkey's football scene has allowed them to build relations with TFF that, according to some of my interlocutors (from rival teams), helps Beşiktaş move more swiftly in women's football. Still, women's football ranks quite low within the club hierarchy, especially when compared to men's football.

The other major team that was reported to enjoy high standards in terms of physical infrastructure and facilities, players' financial situations, and moral support, was ALG Spor from Gaziantep. Here, the provisions were less corporate and more based on the individual prosperity of the president—a well-to-do textile merchant. ALG also stands out because its staff are in close communication with a women-oriented sports nongovernmental organization (KASFAD—Sports and Physical Activity Association for Women, based out of Ankara's Hacettepe University), and its academic cadres.

As such, Beşiktaş and ALG Spor clearly stood out in my interlocutors' descriptions. Nergis was a 26-year-old player who played for an Istanbul club when we met in 2019.[23] She started football at around age fifteen or sixteen, which I found to be typical for her generation. She has played for multiple clubs in Istanbul and has international experience. I asked her to compare clubs in terms of the resources or the opportunities they provided. She explained the following:

> There is Beşiktaş, but that is a wholly separate category. They have all kinds of resources there; they are a brand in and of themselves. It is a different situation there… Having a stadium, regular and rigorous training sessions, food delivered to your facilities, a massage therapist, a physiotherapist, doctors, etc. It is only Beşiktaş which provides all of this consistently. Then you have ALG, things are good there too. They pay you well, you do not have to spend anything. They give you accommodation. They pay you on time.[24]

Her teammate Seda's descriptions corroborated hers:

> There is incredible investment on the part of ALG. They provide all sorts of resources. They have a gym, a pool even. They are paid on time. The club president attends the games. They provide accommodation for the players. They have healthcare professionals onboard.[25]

These accounts show that players on other teams most often cannot take for granted basic provisions such as having a gym in which to exercise or healthcare professionals to attend to them when necessary. Indeed, compared to these two teams, many others provided far less for their players and did so far less consistently. This included everything from the availability of training grounds or camps, the cleanliness of changing rooms, paying wages on time, regular physiotherapy, or immediate healthcare in the case of an injury.

Women received such meager wages—roughly between 2,500–5,000 TL per month (around $400–800 USD) if they were Turkish nationals, and up to 7,000 TL (around $1,120 USD) if they were foreigners—that almost all of them were required to work second jobs as physical education teachers or fitness instructors. Very few of them envisioned a career in football, simply because it was not realistic for a woman to plan her livelihood around football—a comparable (but not identical) dynamic with women footballers' career visions in European contexts.[26] Note that in contrast, male footballers in the first division have salaries in the hundreds of thousands to millions of Euros; they certainly do not need second jobs, because football is their career.

Male domination in sports governance in general and especially football extends into women's football.[27] Of the twelve first-division teams, only two (ALG and Hakkarigücü) had women as their head coach during my research. The clubs were predominantly run by male administrators; TFF cadres in charge of organization were also composed largely of men. Moreover, although stadiums in general appear to be more diverse compared to men's football, many fans of women's football were men.

This dominating male gaze can translate to seeing women's football as a device for women's empowerment, a discourse I encountered at three separate clubs. At one of them, I was told specifically that the women's team was part of the "social-minded municipality" approach where the municipality carried out social projects for the betterment of specific communities. The team itself was founded from within disadvantaged girls' dorms to "save" them from potential crime or other deviance. At TFF, I was also told explicitly that sporting success ranked second in women's football, where it was more about the "social side" of the issue—equipping women with certain skills and abilities.

This approach extends from how women's sports in general has been treated as a "symbol of modernity," development, and progress in Turkey.[28] With regard to football in particular, this outlook has been critiqued because of its insistence on instrumentalizing football at the expense of foregrounding women's sporting careers or abilities. Treating women's football as a social project also results in narrowly defining the parameters of success—producing future mothers (an ongoing designation for a final destination for women) who have received some sort of formal education so they can integrate into the existing capitalist system.[29] I found that when individual men personally take on this mission, they also begin to see themselves as protective father figures in charge of guarding "vulnerable girls." As such, the hierarchical relation between men and women in football manifested in the social project formulation is simulated on the everyday through men whose authority derives not from sporting command but from some sort of fatherly bene-factor relationship.

Trivialization Unpacked

Sexism, including normative assumptions regarding ideal male and female activities, has largely impacted women's experiences play-ing football around the world and, as such, a considerable part of scholarly literature discussing this phenomenon. Women's football is documented as devalued and trivialized in the everyday and in media discourse,[30] including in contexts where football is consid-ered more a woman's game like the US.[31] Women footballers confront "othering" most often because playing football contradicts normative femininity and amounts to "unsafe femininity."[32] As such, playing football has led to multifarious moments of negotia-tion for women in regard to gender roles.[33] Particularly in the Middle East, this process has also manifested as one, which tackles religious and political norms.[34] Here, I dwell on the notion of inequality—as stemming from sexism—based on a specific cate-gory: deeming women's football as trivial.

I use the concept of trivialization to mean women's football is largely neglected, forgotten, ignored, or considered unimport-ant.[35] I was able to gather several everyday and relatively small-scale reminders of this from my observations during fieldwork. For example, even though the match fixture was announced three weeks prior to the season, the specific times were only finalized a couple of days in advance of any given game. In addition, games hardly ever started on time, because they mostly took place on municipal pitches that were booked throughout the day with no gaps. When a single game ran over time, it affected every successive match. Many pitches lacked scoreboards. Sometimes there were extra goalposts lying arbitrarily and confusingly on the sidelines. The sidelines also regularly witnessed the following games' athletes' warm-up, which I was told can include men verbally harassing the women players on the pitch. The games were free to attend, and security was minimal. My interlocutor, who has played in both the first and third divisions, told me that in the third division, it was almost as if a group of friends had gathered to kick the ball around—there would be no signals at all that a match was happening within a structured or organized league.

My interlocutors have described larger obstacles in the face of equality that also stem from trivialization. The players of even the more successful teams complained about not being able to book training camps. Many of the goalkeepers told me that their team did not staff a goalkeeping coach, meaning they had to train by themselves or personally hire a trainer. During the four months that I conducted research, more than one team's players had not been paid in over two months. Some players told me that they spent years playing without receiving any wages at all because they were younger or less successful. Finally, women's football received virtually no media coverage; there were sporadic and unreliable sponsorships, with the exception of Beşiktaş's deal, and the league was not included in official betting programs. Indeed, for many of my interlocutors, exclusion from the interlinked media/sponsorship/betting triangle was foremost proof that women's football was trivialized.[36]

Men's first-division football, in contrast, can easily be distinguished in all these parameters. The league, the teams, and individual players have numerous sponsorship agreements between them. Broadcast rights, purchased for around $500 million, belong to BeIN Sports.[37] The league and the teams have the basic organizational components and amenities lacking for women, as discussed above. In addition, men's football arguably constitutes the most popular pastime in Turkey. Teams and footballers have an immense following, celebrity status, and fandom attached to them. As such, much of the above conditions are remarkably different for men. However, what lies at the basis of the trivialization of women's football—and the most prominent difference to the men's sport— is the absence of professional contracts for women footballers. Women's football is considered an amateur sports branch and even though the footballers are technically "professionals," they do not sign binding contracts. The few players who actually did have contracts explained that they were rather meaningless. This affects, among other things, their health. Nergis told me:

> We are at the mercy of individuals' own conscience. We are not considered professionals. It is an amateur branch. So, for example, the club does not provide us with insurance. Only if something happens during a game that necessitates a surgery ... but even then, they would not pay for it. We have insurance from our other jobs.[38]

Elif, who plays for a team outside of Istanbul, told me that while it was a requirement for their club to provide insurance for the men's teams, the same did not apply to women. Selin, a goalie based in Istanbul, told me:

> We do not have a doctor. We do not have a physiotherapist. We have to take care of each other. It has to be something really serious for them to take us to the hospital, like a broken bone or ruptured tendons or torn muscles. I think we had a hospital sponsor once, but nothing really happened, they just took the money. We all have sports degrees so we take care of each other, in terms of massage or physiotherapy. Our outfitter sometimes serves as the health staff.[39]

Selin's teammate Nil told me that clubs especially hesitate before paying for the surgery of a player who is approaching age thirty, because her bodily capital is no longer as prized as a younger player's. Indeed, I have heard a coach brag about how his club paid for an older player's knee surgery instead of firing her—almost as a favor rather than as complying with her rights.

Selin described their contracts as "verbal agreements, which are supposed to be a little bit more reliable than the spoken word." Nil stressed that this supposedly reliable contract did not give them any power to mount challenges to their working conditions—not about missing wages, nor being fired, nor lack of healthcare. She said:

> Even if there is a contract, it's just like a meaningless piece of paper. It's not approved by a notary or anything. It's not official. It's like a verbal agreement between two people. You can't use it to object to anything. There is no basis for any objections. It's not official.[40]

I was told that players could be fired and rehired quite frequently and rather arbitrarily. Nil told me that she has been fired "many times" for tardiness or absence: "They would say, 'OK you are fired. Do not come again.' And then they'd call me back."

The absence of professionalization goes hand in hand with and reinforces the conception that for women, football is not and cannot be work. My interlocutors told me repeatedly that their families generally view their footballing as a derailment of their career, and they themselves do not consider football to be a career path, because they are unable to make a living with their earnings from football. Nil said she only finished university because she knows that pursuing a career in football in Turkey is not realistic. Selin explained that she was waiting for her appointment as a physical education teacher so that she could settle somewhere and start her career. The sexist perception in relation to who can claim football professionally has made it so that women, including those who play professionally in the first division, see it, at best, as a hobby. Writing about Palestinian women's football, Kenda Stewart has argued that it is precisely this designation as "hobby" that can, to some extent, create a space for women to claim football and thereby contravene normative ideals.[41] What I found, in contrast, was that the "work vs. hobby" dichotomy worked to further legitimize the exploitation of women footballers. This is because it contributed to not taking their work seriously or even valuing it as work.

I also observed that in the absence of professional contracts, the above-mentioned authority relations between male coaches or administrators and female players could serve to mask labor exploitation through kinship terminology. This is especially the case given how women's football is not considered legitimate work. Jessaca Leinaweaver demonstrated, through the case of child circulation in

Peru, that a child's status in a home, whether or not they are considered to "accompany" an elder, a server, or a helper, is tenuous, given the blurriness of boundaries regarding what constitutes work and non-work in domestic life.[42] I found that as male superiors in women's football formed these "fatherly" relations with their "girls," it became easier to take arbitrary decisions and reinforce the precarity of the players' general situations. Seda told me that she was sick of everyone "pretending to be family ... your father or big brother."[43] She did not want another father; she wanted a coach she could count on. She said that these kinds of pseudo-intimate relations paved the way for exploitation, including unwanted sexual advances (perhaps counter-intuitively) based on a level of trust and rapport established through a sense of intimacy.

Literature on women's football from around the world suggests that issues related to professionalization are shared across multiple contexts—but that it, in and of itself, cannot automatically bring equality. The latter is obvious, especially considering the regulatory impacts of "professionalization from above" in Denmark and Sweden and the struggle to achieve equal pay in various parts of northern Europe and the US.[44] As such, rather than idealizing professionalization as the key to equalization, I propose it be situated as a node that must be disentangled in its complexity.

To some extent, male youth squads suffer from similar conditions where they are not allocated as extensive resources or support as the men's first team. However, young male footballers are not trivialized—at least not in the same way as the women athletes. They may be considered less important or less worthy than the men's first team, but as Nil told me, with men the objective is to train footballers. In general, boys are being invested in as future footballers and many imagine themselves (and their whole families) thriving on footballer salaries in the future. In contrast to the TFF official's description of women's football mentioned above, with men, it is sporting success that matters and not some "social aspect." Therefore, while some features of women's football and boys' academies might resemble each other at face value, my findings show that trivialization, as I describe it, pertains only to women.

It is a common manifestation of sexism against women to create an atmosphere where women must continually prove their credentials in order to sustain themselves or move forward in professional environments. I have heard countless stories of women in playing and non-playing roles recount relevant experiences—having to prove they know the rules of the game, how to play it, talk about it, etc. Having to prove oneself has also been emphasized as a condition to overcome trivialization. A woman coach told me:

> Support only comes if you succeed. There will be no support unless we prove ourselves. Women have always had to prove themselves to get anything done. It is the same here. Look, I asked for an additional camp. I did not get it. I am not going to sit around and cry about it. When we prove ourselves, it will come.[45]

Of course, according to some, it is impossible to succeed without that initial support—"you need such a big push to get such little done," as one player told me. The coach quoted above seemed to have internalized this dynamic of which she was acutely aware, attempting to work through it to counter dynamics of trivialization.

Overall, the lack of professional contracts marks women's football in Turkey as a site of inconsistency, unreliability, and utter precarity and insecurity. This reflects on how hesitant and at times timid some of my footballer interlocutors were. Some had to keep our interviews a secret from their coaches; others refused to give me contacts of potential participants when I requested to reach more interviewees. Yet others had to convince their mates that they really did not need their coaches' permission to speak to me, that I was not recording interviews, and that their names would not appear in anything I wrote. They kept glancing at my notes to check what I was writing.[46] They hesitated even as they described quite basic dynamics like not being offered substantial support or funding by governing organizations. As such, I found the general sense of insecurity, anxiety, and mistrust to be pervasive among the players.

Potential for Change

Maud, who played in Turkey in the 1990s, said that during her time, coaches and clubs used to "toy" with players, that "no one was sure of a position or its continuation. They paid very little money, withheld payments arbitrarily, and all the governors were older men."[47] On the one hand, women's football in Turkey continues to present a bleak portrait, as described in the preceding section where a sense of insecurity and precarity remains.

On the other hand, this bleak vision appeared to be more pronounced in the words of my older interlocutors—those above the age of twenty-five. The younger generation—footballers around eighteen to twenty-two—had a relatively more positive outlook, and I did not sense that this related to youth or lack of experience. I believe that some concrete developments in the past couple of years in Turkey and abroad may have contributed to shaping their trajectories differently, including the heightened visibility of the Fédération Internationale de Football Association (FIFA) Women's World Cup, agents coming in to watch games, players from Turkey being recruited to play in the USA or in Spain in the last couple of years and Karagenç's sponsorship deal with Visa mentioned above.

Still, even the younger players were not under the illusion that it would be possible for women to pursue football as their only career in Turkey any time soon. However, they were better able to situate themselves in the burgeoning field of global women's football and thereby maintain a somewhat more secure sense of their footballing endeavors and practices. As such, while the portrait during my research was bleak, the new generation did appear to have points of reference that could allow them to conjure alternative trajectories. As I have indicated above, two years after my research, certain steps were taken to encourage and increase the visibility and popularity of women's football, mainly with the foundation of new teams and new sponsorship deals. At face value, it appears that various agents, including the federation, clubs, and sponsors, have begun to attach more importance and value to women's football, perhaps convinced by its rising popularity around the world. However, it is too soon to conclude that these very recent changes will effectively combat trivialization. We have yet to see what these developments will mean in terms of the fair inclusion of women in football. Support in the form of popular clubs and money being invested in the sport may counter trivialization trends on some level, but this may also reinforce already existing inequalities between some of the more prominent clubs and actors and the less visible or resourceful.

In 2019, my non-footballer interlocutors referred to two potential initiatives, one foreign and one local, which might help improve the situation. I was told that UEFA was in the process of imposing certain standards regarding women's football, although rather inconsistently, including the criterion of professional contracts for teams to be able to qualify for European tournaments. Some administrators were hopeful that such an imposition could profoundly reform the women's game. Others were more cynical, because they did not believe that clubs were financially strong enough to implement many of the changes (some of which pertain to costly infrastructure) and believed that the TFF would be unwilling to offer support. Some were entirely unaware of developments, even though TFF representatives were said to hold meetings with each club to communicate these ideals. As of June 2021, professional contracts were still lacking. I was also told of the potential foundation of an independent association to advocate for the rights of women athletes, especially in recognition of labor exploitation (as described here). Given the athletes' lack of means to organize, to be discussed in the conclusion, this might prove to be an effective channel, but once again such an association is yet to be formed as of 2021.

Conclusion

Global football's gradual evolution into a lucrative enterprise with numerous shareholders and stakeholders results in its actors of varying resources and affiliations having diverse priorities and experiences concerning the game. FIFA administrators in Switzerland have a vastly different experience of football than Bangladeshi workers building stadiums; fan rights organizations combating commercialization have entirely different appreciations of football than major corporate sponsors, media networks, or betting agencies; countries from South America to the Middle East bank on football financially and socially, continuing to develop the game as a business and impacting the lives that center on it.

Gender inequality is part and parcel of this large picture whereby women's football is at once working to accommodate global football's commercial thrust and tackling age-old stereotypes around normative gendering and sexualities. In Turkey, on the one hand, there is the federation, which is bound by European regulations and influenced by the market within which football is situated. On the other hand, there are prominent clubs with their administrations, sponsors, staff, and players that feel more implicated in this global conversation. Then, there are smaller localities and their clubs and players, to whom much of this corporate glitter is distant and removed. All these actors are situated differently vis-à-vis the media, civil society organizations, and supporters or "consumers."

The women I talked to, although officially part of the larger corporate enterprise, dealt mainly with their club administrators and coaches, and had day-to-day issues and priorities that were marked by the nature of those immediate relations. This became clear to me when I incessantly inquired into whether they had been involved in any mobilization efforts to address some of the inequalities described here. They had not. They felt too disposable to constitute any kind of real risk for their superiors. They thought they, unlike their male counterparts, would immediately be fired and replaced. This, to some readers, might be negligible, since the potential gains for the women (economic, social, or psychological) appear to be so meager when they do play, but neither my interlocutors nor their peers were willing to take this risk. KASFAD has been engaged in organizing events to bring together academics, women's football actors, and civil society actors to resolve some of the issues discussed here.[48] However, even though as I described above, some of the younger players did have an easier time thinking past the immediate and situating themselves in the blossoming field of global women's football, I did not find any of them referencing these civil society mobilizations towards effective change.[49]

Nil's account as to the lack of mobilization revealed the hierarchy within which the players were situated and its implications. She explained that many of these women began to play as teenagers in their respective middle schools or high schools where their male coach would simultaneously be their physical education teacher—sometimes even their headmaster. As such, the coach would have double or triple coats of authority over the young girl player where she could even risk being expelled from school if she raised her voice. She said:

> I had an injury once. He [the coach] scolded me for not giving it my all. I said I was injured. So then, the national team, the U17, had a camp. They called me, and I had recovered by then. But he forbade me from going, and of course you can't say anything. He does not allow you the right of speech. If he was not connected to the school, maybe you could. But then if you did, you would be at risk at school too, because he was also the headmaster you see.[50]

This narrative shows that the existing hierarchies between younger women players and older male coaches points to historically damaging and unfair relations within which women have acquired their footballing practices and been molded as footballers. It is such learnedness, such historical carving, that limits them today, as much as (and I believe more than) any manifest obstacle. Therefore, multiple layers beneath global corporate football, the local everyday of gender inequality continues to mark women's footballing presence and experience. Women's football is a rather claustrophobic space with everyone "inside each other's business" as one of my interlocutors put it, with many footballers residing together in clubhouses, and with kinship metaphors liberally employed to supposedly encourage warmth and closeness. This only contributes to maintaining the status quo with its existing power dynamics and to reinforce the players' sense of insecurity and precarity, making it all the more difficult to envision change.

The last half of the 2010s saw recurring discussions around how equality pertains to gender relations in Turkey—in various domains of public space, including academia, women's organizations with different political agendas, and politics itself. Briefly, a more creationist stance has put forth that the concept of "justice" is more applicable to thinking about gender since gender "inequality" is supposedly natural and therefore irrelevant to thinking about justice. This point of view, incurring a divorce between equality and justice, has been widely contested by feminists, who have made it a point to stress the notion of "equality" as a precursor for any kind of justice. As such, the public debate around what constitutes the just treatment of men and women extends to fields beyond football.[51] Football is definitely the most popular sport in Turkey which, I believe, means that disentangling the nodes and manifestations of inequality here can shed light on how we might conjure, conceptualize, and discuss gender inequality in other social spheres.

5

HOMELAND

NATIONAL IDENTITY PERFORMANCE
IN THE QATAR NATIONAL TEAM

Thomas Ross Griffin

Introduction: Identity as Survival

Given Qatar's shared cultural heritage with the other nations of the
Gulf, its rulers, upon announcing its independence in 1971, quickly
realized that a distinct national identity would be essential if the
country was to successfully establish itself as a sovereign state. This
desired identity would describe a modern, open society keenly
aware of its Islamic values and cultural traditions, but also one that
"was somehow 'different' from other states in the Middle East and
North Africa."[1] Seldom has this difference been more apparent than
on June 5, 2017, when Saudi Arabia, Bahrain, and the United Arab
Emirates (UAE) launched an unprecedented land, sea, and air
blockade of Qatar.[2] The aftermath of this event saw the re-emer-
gence of a historical rivalry between the blockading nations and

Qatar, one that had become increasingly bitter since Hamad bin Khalifa Al-Thani assumed control of the country from his father in 1995 and set it on a course that would move Qatar further away from Saudi hegemony. As Qatar resisted growing pressure to return to the fold, the following years saw the simmering hostilities between Qatar and its neighbors fully exposed during the 2017 blockade. When the Qatar national football team travelled to the UAE to participate in the 2019 Asian Cup, they often did so in front of extremely hostile crowds, as all Qataris had been denied entry to the UAE since the blockade began. It quickly became clear that many of those historical animosities remained, and that there was more than just sporting pride and a trophy at stake for Qatar.

Rank outsiders before a ball was even kicked, Qatar upset blockade rivals Saudi Arabia and the UAE, as well as Asian football heavyweights South Korea and Iraq, to reach the final against tournament favorites Japan. For many, however, Qatar's unexpected 3–1 victory in the final would become just another footnote in the overall narrative of the blockade. As both citizens and residents took part in unprecedented celebrations on the streets of Doha, in keeping with what had become the tit-for-tat nature of blockade politics, Qatar's beaten semi-final opponents, the UAE, lodged an official complaint with the Asian Football Confederation (AFC) that Qatar had fielded two ineligible players in that match. The UAE claimed that neither Almoez Ali, born in Sudan, nor Bassam Al-Rawi, born in Iraq, had been Qatari residents long enough to play for their adopted nation. As is ever the case in the increasingly globalized world of twenty-first century sports, what had long been considered rigid markers of identity were once again called into question. Although the AFC dismissed their complaint, the Emirati objections shone an uncomfortable light on the presence of other non-Qatari players in the team, such as Portuguese defender Pedro, and the Algerian duo of Karim Boudiaf and Boualem Khoukhi. But how do these players, drawn from a diverse array of countries and cultures, properly represent or "perform" the identity of Qatar, both on and off the pitch? To answer this question, this chapter examines the performances of nationalism by several of the Qatar national team players to suggest that each performative iteration forms a praxis that contributes to the construction of what Norbert Elias calls "the national habitus," or national character of the nation.

Sports as a Mirror

While competitive sports are viewed by many critics as providing the spectator with a physical manifestation of the nation, as Alan Bairner notes, "it also forces us at times to consider the precise nature of our own national identity."[3] The media attention that the marketization of sporting citizenship by Gulf nations has received in recruiting African long-distance runners to compete at various Olympiads has increased significantly in recent years.[4] Such an examination has the potential to be an uncomfortable one, particularly for Qatar, whose 2019 Asian Cup squad contained fifteen players eligible to play for another country.[5] Yet Qatar's preponderance of "outsiders" is often overstated and oversimplified, and is by no means the first time such practices have occurred in world football.[6] Of the twenty-two players the Republic of Ireland brought to Italia 90, sixteen were born in the United Kingdom. Similarly, nine of France's World Cup-winning squad in 1998 were either immigrants or the children of immigrants. This number would rise to seventeen when France won the tournament for a second time in 2018.[7] The explanation offered by the football associations of both the Republic of Ireland and France reflected the internal dynamics of each society at the time. Forced to emigrate in search of employment for generations, the Football Association of Ireland (FAI) contended that there existed an enormous diaspora of Irish people overseas, primarily in the UK, who were eligible to represent Ireland. When challenged about the lack of native French players in light of their victories in 1998 and 2018, French administrators, commentators, and players alike argued that the ethnic diversity of the "Rainbow Team" of 1998, and their successors in 2018, was the reality of modern French society.[8]

The Qatar 2019 Asian Cup squad is similar in how it reflects the social dynamics of the Gulf state. Qatar is a country of approximately 3 million people, and studies have reported that only

approximately 10 percent of the population is Qatari.[9] Such a figure is massively overshadowed by the Gulf state's migrant labor
force.[10] Blue-collar workers from India, Nepal, Bangladesh, and Sri
Lanka comprise over 50 percent of the country's population. The
other dominant social groups in Qatar are citizens from other Arab
states (approximately 16 percent) and the Philippines (approximately 7 percent). The remainder of the population is a mixture
of expats drawn from all over the globe. Qataris are very much a
minority in their own country, an issue exacerbated by the country's strict citizenship laws which insist on parental birth right as a
pathway to citizenship, thus excluding the swathes of children born
in Qatar to these economic migrants who would be considered
Qatari citizens if geographical birth right was considered.[11] Given
the relatively high percentage of economic migrants in Qatar
drawn from other Arab states, it is understandable that they are
similarly represented in the national football team.

The obvious discrepancy is the complete absence of players of
South Asian descent in the team, an anomaly that challenges the
argument that Qatar's Asian Cup squad reflects the social dynamics of the Gulf state. The vast majority of these residents occupy
a liminal space in Qatari society. While they reside in the country,
for the most part confined to their compounds beyond working
hours, this portion of the population exists outside many of
Qatar's social structures.[12] Sport is one such structure. The result
is that despite there being approximately 3 million people at any
one time in Qatar, over 50 percent of those people are overlooked
when a national team is selected. The largest social groups beyond
the South Asian population are long-term Arab residents, Qataris,
and short-term white-collar (and predominantly Western) expats,
and it is players from these three social groups that comprise the
national team.

This research focuses on these three "kinds" of player who represented Qatar in the 2019 Asian Cup; full Qatari citizens (*jus
sanguinis*), long-term residents born in Qatar (*jus soli*), and players
naturalized to represent Qatar (*jus talenti*). The criteria differentiat-
ing these three categories of player is derived from Gijsbert Oonk's
"thick and thin citizenship" which, as can be seen in the model, uses

Figure 5.1: Gijsbert Oonk's Model of "Thick and Thin Citizenship."

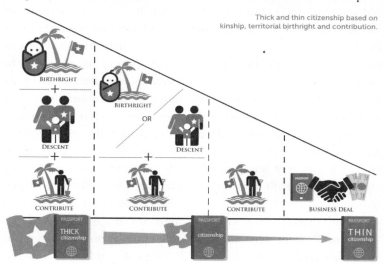

Source: Gijsbert Oonk, "Who Are We Actually Cheering On? Sport, Migration, and National Identity in a World-Historical Perspective," 2019, https://repub.eur.nl/pub/123010.

kinship, territorial birth right, and what he describes as "contribution" to create a sliding scale of citizenship.[13]

The *jus sanguinis* group are those with the thickest citizenship. The *jus soli* group, born in Qatar to non-citizens, has a thinner claim to citizenship than the *jus sanguinis* group, despite having spent most or all of their lives in Qatar. With no prior links to Qatar, the *jus talenti* group are those considered to have the thinnest claim to citizenship. Table 5.1 shows a clearer breakdown of the 2019 Asian Cup squad into these three categories. The table also reflects the stratified nature of Qatar's citizenship laws. This chapter is not suggesting that any of the players discussed are not eligible to represent Qatar, or that some players are more eligible than others. Each player adheres to guidelines regarding eligibility as stated by the Fédération Internationale de Football Association (FIFA). However, according to Law 38 on the acquisition of Qatari nationality (passed in 2005), the majority of the players selected for the Asian Cup squad would not be considered full citizens of

Qatar.[14] How does this impact their performance of nationalist fervor? Does their citizenship status influence their performance? Does the performance differ between those who are full Qatari citizens and those who are Qatari residents? How do the origins of those naturalized to play for Qatar impinge on how they perform their adopted identity? How do these players generate what Elias describes as the "I-we identity" essential to the formation of national habitus, that allows us to identify and co-exist with those like us and differentiate ourselves from those who are not, when such disparity exists amongst the players themselves?[15] As all identity performances are a dialectical process, what is the public's perception of these performances?

Table 5.1: Citizenship Breakdown of the Qatar Asian Cup Winning Team, January 2017

Player	Position	Citizenship		
		Jus Sanguinis	Jus Soli	Jus Talenti
Saad Al Sheeb	GK	▓		
Yousef Hassan	GK		▓	
Mohammed Al Bakri	GK	▓		
Abdelkarim Hassan	Def		▓	
Boualem Khoukhi	Def			▓
Pedro	Def			
Tameem Al-Muhaza	Def	▓		
Tarek Salman	Def		▓	
Bassam Al-Rawi	Def			▓
Hamid Ismaeil	Def			
Abdelrahman Moustafa	MF		▓	
Abdulkarim Al-Ali	MF	▓		

Name	Position			
Khaled Mohammed Saleh	MF		■	
Karim Boudiaf	MF			■
Abdulaziz Hatem	MF		■	
Assim Madibo	MF			
Salem Al-Hajri	MF	■		
Ahmed Fathi	MF		■	
Ahmed Alaaeldin	FW			■
Hassan Al-Haydos	FW	■		
Akram Afif	FW		■	
Almoez Ali	FW			■
Ali Hassan Afif	FW		■	

Source: Data collected by author from various sources.

Qatar's 2019 Asian Cup Squad

This chapter builds upon the work of theorists of sports and nationalism, such as Alan Bairner, who argued that national football teams and their athletes represent a physical embodiment of what Benedict Anderson termed the "imagined community."[16] This chapter examines the methods used by Qatar national team members to express this national identity. It argues that how the players perform Qatari identity, in their social media and their actions (both on and off the pitch), are contributions that integrate them further into Qatari society, and can be seen as truly representative of Qatar as a nation.

Methodology

One-to-one interviews with members of the Qatar national men's team, verified social media (Twitter) accounts, and player interviews given to television, newspaper, and online media provide the material upon which this research is based. The focus is solely on the men's national team, as Qatar does not have an active women's national team at present.[17] Player interviews were conducted in English and took place in Qatar. To protect the identity of participants, pseudonyms are used, and all player interviews were conducted individually. During the interviews, the broad topics discussed included:

- The players' motivations for representing the State of Qatar.
- The means players use to express nationalism.
- How players see themselves representing Qatar.

As highlighted by Nida Ahmad in her work on the use of social media by amateur sportswomen in the MENA region, a project such as this gives rise to ethical concerns related to digital lurking—the practice of joining in social media forums to observe but not participate.[18] As the online material used here is from the verified accounts of professional athletes that are in the public domain, ethical problems of this nature are redundant. Yet there are other concerns. When social media was in its infancy at the end of the 2000s, theorists such as Brett Hutchins noted that the opinions expressed on platforms such as Twitter presented an accurate and authentic appraisal of the athlete's true feelings on a subject. For Hutchins, it was a means of genuine "self-representation and personal expression," and this is frequently how such posts continue to be read.[19]

Banal and Social Nationalism

But given the commercialization of social media in recent years, whether such statements accurately reflect a player's true feelings towards a given subject is now up for debate, as third parties such as public relations representatives and business managers often function as caretakers and filters of an athlete's social media profile. Valid questions may also be asked about the efficacy of such performances, isolated as they are to social media platforms, and whether material published on the profiles is influenced in some fashion by state or federation officials in order to portray a specific image of Qatar's national football team as a social construct that is identifiably Qatari in every sense. However, the intent of this chapter is to examine the performance of identity rather than appraising the authenticity of such a performance. To do so, two differing forms of nationalism—banal nationalism and social nationalism—are used as theoretical frameworks. Michael Billig explains banal nationalism as the methods and means whereby "daily, the nation is indicated, or 'flagged,' in the lives of its citizenry" rather than something that only emerges in times of crisis.[20] Billig emphasizes that this form of nationalism is by no means neutral. Even the most mundane actions can often be understood as "a continual 'flagging,' or reminding, of nationhood."[21] Billig argues that practitioners are still "participating within ... nationalism's tradition of argumentation."[22] By way of their actions, they "advocate a particular vision of who 'we' are, and what 'we' should be like."[23] Banal nationalism is at the opposite end of the spectrum to what Billig describes as the "violent passions" of hot nationalism.[24] The latter predominantly occurs "in times of social disruption" and is much more likely to be a communal effort caused by a specific catalyst rather than a multitude of isolated actions.[25] Such group performances of nationalist zeal, provoked by specific and extraordinary circumstances, can be read as social nationalism. This is a form of nationalism "which defines itself by social ties and culture rather than by common descent," permitting outsiders to join the nation if they identify with and adopt the social behaviors of the dominant in-group.[26]

Digital Identities / Banal Identities

While sports are still predominantly produced for and consumed by a traditional television audience, social media platforms such as Twitter and Instagram now frequently act as secondary sources of supplementary information to the spectacle shown on screen. This section builds on Nida Ahmad's work on the everyday use of social media by female athletes in the Middle East and North Africa to self-brand in a manner that reflects the region's predominant cultural values. But here, the argument is that the digital identities performed by the Qatar players are an example of what Elias described as the "process of national habitus/character formation," one that "is framed, constructed, and represented by and through discursive practices."[27] Specifically, the argument here suggests that the identities performed on social media by the Qatar players are not done so primarily with commercial gain in mind, but rather more as a means of presenting a Qatari identity in keeping with the predominant post-blockade discourse.

Jus Sanguinis

Born in Doha to Qatari parents, and thus occupying the thickest end of Oonk's scale of citizenship, national team captain Hassan Al-Haydos is an example of a *jus sanguinis* footballer currently representing the Gulf state. When examining Al-Haydos's digital identity, the most striking aspect of his profile is the image shown in Figure 5.2—one that has become synonymous with Qatar since the start of the blockade in June 2017.

Known as تميم المجد, (Tamim Al-Majd, or "Tamim the Glorious"), this portrait of the Emir became the face of Qatar as a modern, open, Arab, and Muslim nation in the aftermath of the blockade, that could not only survive, but thrive on its own.[28] It is not surprising that this image was used by a player at the thickest end of Oonk's scale. Equally unsurprising are more verbal performances of patriotism, as shown by the example in Figure 5.3.

The post is captioned by a hashtag that translates as #TamimAlMajd and a single word in Arabic: فداءً. Transliterated as "fidaa," this old, romantic Arabic term often conveys feelings of undying love and a willingness to sacrifice oneself for another. However, buttressed as it is by two Qatari flags, and placed above a photo of Al-Haydos waving aloft a t-shirt with the Tamim Al-Majd image emblazoned across it, the context is clearly patriotic. Threaded throughout his profile is a series of similar posts that reflect an obvious sense of pride and loyalty to ruler and state. These sentiments are mentioned once more in a 2019 interview, when Al-Haydos spoke of how he was both "honored and proud of

Figure 5.2: Hassan Al-Haydos Twitter Profile Image

Alsadd club and Qatar national team player

Source: Hassan Al-Haydos, Twitter post, October 1, 2019, https://
twitter.com/hassanalhaydos/photo.

Figure 5.3: "I will sacrifice myself for you #TamimtheGlorious"

Source: Hassan Al-Haydos, Twitter post, July 28, 2017, https://twitter.
com/hassanalhaydos/status/890695998628147200.

being Qatari," and of the importance of serving his country and raising its status through sporting success.[29] As a *jus sanguinis* player, there is little surprise that the profile of Al-Haydos reflects prominent markers of Qatar's national habitus; a sense of national pride combined with a declared fealty towards ruler, country, and religious faith. However, Figure 5.4 shows also a concern for a sense of Khaleeji identity.

What is important to note is the date of this post, June 7, 2017. Here, accompanied by flag emojis representing each of the Gulf states, Al-Haydos modifies a prayer two days after the Saudi-led blockade began, saying: "O Allah we entrusted you the Gulf countries, its leaders, and its people. O the one with whom all the trusts are safe, protect and safeguard them with your eyes that know no sleep." As such, Al-Haydos's profile presents to the viewer an image of Qatar as a sovereign state, defiant in the face of the ongoing embargo by its neighbors, but still intertwined with a sense of

Figure 5.4: Al-Haydos's Response to the 2017 Blockade—"O Allah we entrusted you with the Gulf countries, its leaders, and its people. O the one with whom all the trusts are safe, protect and safeguard them with your eyes that know no sleep."

حسن الهيدوس
@hassanalhaydos

اللهم إنا استودعناك دول الخليج وقادتها
وأهلها فاحفظهم بحفظك يا من لا تضيع
ودائعه ، وأحرسهم بعينك التي لا تنام 🖤

Translate Tweet

16:09 · 07 Jun 17 · Twitter for iPhone

belonging to a greater Khaleeji and Arab community. In many ways, it mirrors Matthew Gray's assessment of Qatar as "a country with a specific national identity but that nonetheless forms part of a wider Arab and Muslim identity."[30] Such sentiments are not confined to the captain of the national team, however. The profiles of other *jus sanguinis* players from the 2019 Asian Cup team, such as Tameem Al-Muhaza (Instagram) and Salem Al-Hajri (Instagram), show much of the same.

Figure 5.5: Hassan's Response to the 2017 Blockade—"O Allah make this land safe and secure."

Source: Abdulkarim Hassan, Twitter post, June 13, 2017, https://twitter.com/ABDULKARIM_QAT/status/874674830087524353.

Jus Soli

Having won Asian Footballer of the Year awards in 2018 and 2019, respectively, two of the most celebrated players of the *jus soli* group are Al-Sadd duo Abdulkarim Hassan and Akram Afif. Born to non-Qatari expatriates resident in Qatar, both Hassan and Afif would be placed somewhere to the center of Oonk's model of "thick and thin citizenship," further to the right of the scale than players such as Hassan Al-Haydos. What is interesting to note is that being a member of the *jus soli* group seems to have little impact on the national identity that either Hassan or Afif perform on social media. As can be seen from the example given in Figure 5.5, Abdulkarim Hassan's performance of Qatari identity demonstrates many of the same tropes and motifs as that of his *jus sanguinis* captain.

It becomes immediately apparent when viewing Hassan's profile that his identity as an Arab and a Muslim are key components of his digital identity. Yet what is interesting to note is how these transnational identities are presented in parallel with a clear affirmation of Hassan's identity as a citizen of Qatar, something that becomes particularly more evident in the weeks and months after June 2017 and the beginning of the Saudi-led blockade. This sense of pronounced patria is highlighted by a series of religious calls to protect Qatar and repeated postings of the Tamim Al-Majd image scattered throughout his profile. An example of such is shown in Figure 5.5, as Hassan prays to keep Qatar safe while the viewer's attention once more centers on Tamim Al-Majd.

However, unlike the much more neutral بلد (*balad*, "land" or "country") used in Figure 5.5, after defeating the UAE 4–0 in the Asian Cup semi-final, references to Qatar are made using the much more forceful phrase وطن (*watan*, or "homeland"), as can be seen in Figures 5.6 and 5.7.

The combination of picture and text in each post is equally significant. Figure 5.6 shows Hassan posing in military salute alongside *jus sanguinis* player Hassan Al-Haydos under the caption "God, the homeland, the Emir," while Figure 5.7 proclaims fealty to the Emir, saying "we are your supporters Tamim. We're always there

Figure 5.6: "God, the homeland, the Emir"

Source: Abdulkarim Hassan, Twitter post, January 30, 2019, https://twitter.com/ABDULKARIM_QAT/status/1090501591663284226.

Figure 5.7: "We are your supporters #TamimtheGlorious. Although our flag is not with us, although we are not in our land, you can still count on us"

Source: Abdulkarim Hassan, Twitter post, January 29, 2019, https://twitter.com/ABDULKARIM_QAT/status/1090314109105639425.

for you and the country" above a picture of Hassan celebrating with several of his teammates. Quoting from a well-known poem, Henna Ahl Al-Samla ("We are the People Who Stand Their Ground"), there is clear inference that Hassan and his fellow players are willing to assume the role of proxy soldiers of Qatar in hostile territory during the Asian Cup.

It is evident that Hassan's association with Qatar goes much deeper than the idea of "sporting citizenship" discussed by David Storey in relation to the national allegiances and identity choices of African footballers.[31] Fawaz is one example of a *jus soli* player. Although born in Qatar, he is of Sudanese parentage. When asked about this in an interview, *jus soli* player Fawaz emphasized his commitment to Qatar, the nation of his birth.[32] Regardless of citizenship status, he insisted that it was "an honor and a pleasure to represent your country," and being selected to play for Qatar was essentially an act of duty, stating that "you fight ... to give all your best for this country because this country gives us a lot." Speaking in an interview, fellow *jus soli* player Ahmed also verbalized this digital performance of patriotism. Another player of non-Qatari parentage born in Qatar, he stated that "it's an honor and a pleasure to play for your country ... for a player to fight for his country and to make his country proud of him."[33] Much like the sense of Qatari identity exhibited by the *jus sanguinis* players, there is a clear and explicit sense of belonging evident in both the words of the *jus soli* players and the Twitter profile presented by Abdulkarim Hassan.

Born in Doha in 1996, Akram Afif is the son of a Yemeni mother and a Tanzanian footballer father who migrated to Qatar in the 1970s. Although Afif grew up in the emirate and spent the lion's share of his career playing there, as is the case with Abdulkarim Hassan, Afif's citizenship status is thinner than that of his *jus sanguinis* teammates. But as Figures 5.8 and 5.9 show, much like Hassan's profile, Afif's profile reflects similar expressions of loyalty to religion, nation, and ruler, with the latter two again becoming much more frequent in the months after the blockade. Figure 5.8 echoes Hassan's prayers to keep Qatar safe, while Figure 5.9 is an example of one of several posts containing the Tamim Al-Majd portrait as a

Figure 5.8: Afif's Response to the 2017 Blockade—"O Allah make this land safe and secure, Amen."

Source: Akram Afif, Twitter post, June 11, 2017, https://twitter.com/akramafif_/status/873860923504689152.

Figure 5.9: Akram Afif's T-shirt Protest versus South Korea, June 2017

Source: Akram Afif, Twitter post, June 20, 2017, https://twitter.com/akramafif_/status/877220565450342400.

131

show of support for the emirate during the tense first few days of the blockade.

However, Afif's profile also includes a much more subtle performance of Qatari identity worth discussing, one demonstrated by his longstanding use of a profile picture, shown in Figure 5.10, that shows him dressed in the traditional *thobe* and *gutra* (robe and headdress) of the Khaleeji Arab. As noted by Miriam Cooke, the *thobe* and *gutra* are more than everyday clothing. She states that they have become "the *sine qua non* of national performances," and argues that, particularly in the Gulf, clothing has become an essential part of marking out national identity in public spaces.[34] Afif's profile image in Figure 5.10 shows evidence of this practice. Adopting a plain white "*gutra egal*" and a white *thobe* with buttoned

Figure 5.10: Akram Afif in Formal Qatari Attire

Source: Akram Afif, Twitter post, December 10, 2019, https://twitter.com/akramafif_/status/1204443310212993024.

collar and cuffs, his appearance in this image is immediately identifiable as Qatari to Khaleeji Arab society. This is a powerful and deliberate act in the context of the Gulf. To refer to Cooke once more, "this national uniform is out of bounds for foreigners" and "replacing the tie and suit in the twenty-first century, 'tribal' dress is modern, national but, above all, it is also patriotic."[35] Despite his citizenship status being thinner than the accepted archetype of an idealized Qatari citizen, Afif still presents an image of this archetype in social media posts.

This practice is not limited to Akram Afif. Others, including fellow *jus soli* player Abdulkarim Hassan and *jus talenti* players Basam Al-Rawi and Almoez Ali, post similar images of themselves wearing national dress on their social media profiles. In doing so, each football player is participating in the politics of exclusion that allows them to identify as part of the in-group of Qatari society. The idea of a society being divided into in-groups and out-groups is an integral part of Anh Nga Longva's analysis of Kuwaiti society, a study that, if used as a synecdoche for the wider Gulf, can also be applied to Qatar. The premise of Longva's argument is that Kuwaiti society is built upon "a politics of exclusion" that categorizes the population of the country into an "in-group" and an "outgroup."[36] Visualizing Kuwaiti society as a series of concentric circles, Longva argues that the greater a person's compatibility to the accepted archetype of an idealized citizen—an Arab Muslim living in Kuwait and born to Kuwaiti parents—the closer to the centermost circle, or in-group, that person becomes. However, Longva acknowledges that identity is a dialectical process. She notes that it "cannot be conceptualized only in terms of the actor's consciousness of self, but also in terms of perceptions of the actor's self by others in relation to whom he or she holds these roles and statuses."[37] Understanding this dialectic is crucial to understanding the significance of clothing in Qatar. It essentially becomes the costume used to convince those watching this identity performance of the wearer's belonging to the in-group. That these players dress in this fashion demonstrates that there is a deliberate decision made to reflect a specific Qatari identity. As a performance of national identity occurring in such an ordinary circumstance, this small act, represented on the everyday mundanity of social media, is in its essence a form of banal nationalism.

Jus Talenti

Occupying the thinnest end of Oonk's model are the *jus talenti* group. These are players naturalized because of their talent. This group, containing some of Qatar's most high-profile players, including Almoez Ali, Pedro, and Basam Al-Rawi, has frequently drawn the most controversy. Some athletes cite close cultural ties and economic factors as motivation. Others, as Danyel Reiche discusses in his chapter in this volume, cite the desire to escape discrimination in their own countries. Yet, despite their diversity, the examples shown below relating to the digital identity performances of the Sudanese-born Almoez Ali and the Baghdad-born Basam Al-Rawi demonstrate a keen similarity to the *jus sanguinis* and *jus soli* groups in how they perform Qatari identity.

The examples shown in both Figures 5.11 and 5.12 demonstrate many of the previously discussed tropes performed by *jus sanguinis* and *jus soli* players and are also replete throughout Ali and Al-Rawi's profiles.

Almoez Ali's affection for Qatar is clear in Figure 5.11, declaring that "I congratulate his highness the Emir, and the people of Qatar, both citizens and residents, on this achievement, and with God's will, what's coming is going to be better!" Figure 5.12 shows how both Ali and Al-Rawi adopt the Qatari style of national dress to perform the exclusionary politics that identify them as part of the "in-group" of Qatari society. Posts requesting God's blessing and reflecting admiration for and loyalty to the Emir, akin to the example provided in Figure 5.13 below, also pervade both player's feeds, in a similar fashion to their *jus sanguinis* and *jus soli* teammates. Here, Al-Rawi is offering birthday wishes to the Emir, wishing him a long and healthy life for the sake of the people of Qatar. These profiles highlight an overriding attachment or commitment to Qatar.

However, it is equally interesting to note the minute identity disturbances that emerge in the *jus talenti* performances of national-

Figure 5.11: Ali's Affection for Qatar—"I congratulate his highness the Emir and the people of Qatar, both citizens and residents, on this achievement, and with Allah's will, what's coming is going to be better."

Source: Almoez Ali, Twitter post, January 25, 2019, https://twitter.com/Moezali_/status/1088833251639214080.

ism that are not so apparent in the other groupings. What becomes visible, as shown in Figures 5.14 and 5.15, is a much more tangible sense of these disturbances as each player balances his relationship with Qatar against his country of origin. Figure 5.11 provides an example of such a disturbance, as Ali makes a distinction between the citizens and residents of Qatar when he specifically mentions مواطنين (muwatinin, or "citizens") and مقيمين (muqimin, or "residents") in his post. While Ali is demonstrating an awareness of the makeup of Qatari society, his post also speaks to the legislative construction relating to full Qatari citizenship.

Citizenship by birth, or *jus soli*, is not recognized. It is only possible through the *jus sanguinis* principle of being born to a Qatari father, or, in very rare circumstances, by Emiri decree, one can be granted Qatari citizenship for having "rendered great service to the

Figure 5.12: Al-Rawi and Ali as Part of Qatar's "In-Group"—"With my brother Moez and the dear Adel."

Source: Basam Al-Rawi, Twitter post, February 19, 2019, https://twitter.com/basam_97/status/1097774332917567489.

Figure 5.13: Al-Rawi's Birthday Wishes to HH Shaikh Tamim bin Hamad Al-Thani—"May you stay well, healthy, and safe in all your years. May Allah give you a long life for our sake."

Source: Basam Al-Rawi, Twitter post, June 3, 2019, https://twitter.com/basam_97/status/870989617771753472.

Figure 5.14: Ali's Prayers for Sudan—"O God, in these blessed days, protect Sudan from those who plot against it, and from those who are envious of it, and grace them with security and peace. #Sudan."

AlMOI'ZZ ✓
@Moezali_

اللهم في هذه الأيام المباركة احفظ
السودان وشعب السودان من كيد الحاقدين
والحاسدين وانعم عليهم بنعمة الأمن
والسلام #السودان

Translate Tweet

18:35 · 03 Jun 19 · Twitter for iPhone

Source: Almoez Ali, Twitter post, June 3, 2019, https://twitter.com/
Moezali_/status/1135570641577566210.

Figure 5.15: Al-Rawi's Prayers for Iraq—"I ask Allah the greatest to protect beloved Iraq."

Basam Al-rawi ✓
@basam_97

أسأل الله العظيم ان يحفظ العراق الحبيب

Translate Tweet

22:27 · 07 Oct 19 · Twitter for iPhone

Source: Basam Al-Rawi, Twitter post, October 7, 2019, https://twitter.com/basam_97/status/1181290049855467521.

country."[38] Even then, it is all but impossible for a resident to be awarded the full citizenship rights that an indigenous citizen would have. Requiring twenty-five years of continuous residency, and other factors relating to income, criminal history, reputation, and knowledge of Arabic, short of doing the state an outstanding service, naturalization is beyond the means of most long-term residents, forever placing them in the out-group of Qatari society.[39] By acknowledging the distinction between the two, Ali subtly acknowledges the disturbed identity that is evident in the identity performances of both the *jus talenti*, and in some cases, the *jus soli* players. Both groups contain players who have lived either all or nearly all their lives in Qatar. Yet due to the nature of Qatar's nationality laws, as noted by Castles and Davidson, their status as "quasi-citizens," created by the distinction made between citizen and resident, essentially alienates them from the dominant in-group of that society.[40]

Figure 5.14 provides a second and more explicit illustration of such disturbance. Here, during the unrest that occurred in the East African nation in June 2019, Ali writes "Please God, in these holy days, protect Sudan and the Sudanese from the plotting of the malicious, and give them the blessing of safety and peace." Similar sentiments, albeit in relation to his home country of Iraq, were echoed by Al-Rawi some months later, as shown in Figure 5.15 when he states, "I ask God to protect beloved Iraq." While other players, notably Akram Afif and Assim Madibo from the *jus soli* group, make similar posts professing support for Sudan, neither do so to the degree of Almoez Ali or Basam Al-Rawi. Given that both players lived in their respective home nations for a number of years before coming to Qatar, this noticeable disturbance of their performance of Qatari national identity is understandable. As is widely acknowledged, identity is not a binary. Rather, it is something that can manifest itself on a multitude of levels simultaneously. However, what many theorists also note is that when several identities emerge into the same social space, one always tends to become salient over others. Despite the controversy surrounding the origins of *jus talenti* players such as Al-Rawi and Almoez Ali as to whether they had been resident long enough to be considered

Figure 5.16: "Congratulations and Rejoice Qatar"

Source: Basam Al-Rawi, Twitter post, January 22, 2019, https://twitter.com/basam_97/status/1087779302576410624.

eligible to represent Qatar, it is clear that the salient identity emerging from their performances of nationalism on social media is a Qatari identity.

Perhaps the most indicative example of this salience is the tweet shown in Figure 5.16 that was pinned to the top of Al-Rawi's profile for over a year in the wake of the Asian Cup. The first post the viewer saw when examining his digital identity, it contains a short video clip of Al-Rawi's winning free kick in the closing minutes of Qatar's last-sixteen match in the 2019 Asian Cup.[41]

What is crucial to note here, however, is that this goal was scored against Al-Rawi's birth nation Iraq, eliminating Iraq from the competition and sending his adopted nation Qatar into the quarterfinals.

139

Figure 5.17: Al-Rawi's Defence [Tweet translated in below paragraph].

بسم الله الرحمن الرحيم
مبروك لمنتخب #قطر والشعب القطري الغالي
الفوز و التأهل لربع النهائي و هاردلك لمنتخب
العراق و الشعب العراقي الغالي

بالأمس لعبت أهم مباراة في مشواري الكروي
وسجلت الهدف الأكثر قيمة منذ أن بدأت ممارسة
كرة القدم ، أريد هنا أن أوضح بعض الأمور ، أنا من
مواليد #العراق و من أسرة عراقية أعتز و أفتخر
بجذوري و أصولي ، لكنني بدأت ممارسة كرة القدم
في دولة قطر و أكملت دراستي في مدارس قطر ثم
في أكاديمية أسباير و ساهم نادي الريان ثم احترافي
في سلتا فيغو الإسباني عبر أسباير في تطوير
موهبتي الكروية و انتهى بي المطاف في نادي
الدحيل ، لقطر فضل كبير علي لن أنساه أبداً ، أما
بما يخص احتفالي فبعد تسجيل أهم أهداف
مشواري فمن حقي أن أفرح و أحتفل و من حق
زملائي في المنتخب و شعب قطر علي أن أقدم كل
ما أستطيع لإسعادهم مع كل المحبة و التقدير
للجمهور العراقي ، فقبل أن أكون لاعباً محترفاً أنا
إنسان لدي مشاعر و أحاسيس تجاه من عملت
معهم و ساعدوني في كل لحظة تعثر في مشواري

Source: Basam Al-Rawi, Twitter post, January 23 2019, https://twitter.
com/basam_97/status/1088013477883596801.

Al-Rawi's obvious delight, one underscored by the caption of
the post, "congratulations and rejoice Qatar," is manifestly clear.
What is of even greater interest is the defense of this goal and
subsequent celebration that Al-Rawi posted the day after the victory over Iraq, which is shown in Figure 5.17.

Here, Al-Rawi begins by congratulating the people of Qatar for
their victory while also consoling the Iraqi players for their loss.
The disturbances in Al-Rawi's identity are made manifestly clear
by the player himself as he declares pride in his Iraqi origins.

However, he also goes to great lengths to explain how Qatar has played a critical role in allowing him to succeed as a footballer. He specifies the education, coaching, and support he received at the Aspire Academy that enabled him to achieve his sporting ambitions in Qatar and overseas. What is significant to note here is how Al-Rawi states that he "cannot forget Qatar's favors" and as such he feels compelled "to offer [the people of Qatar] what I can to make them happy." In essence, he is saying that while Iraq created him, Qatar made him who he is. Qatar provided him with the opportunity to become a professional footballer.

Both online and in person, Al-Rawi acknowledges his Iraqi heritage, and professes both an identity with and concern for the Iraqi people. In each of these instances, the importance of these players' citizenship towards their home countries of Sudan and Iraq becomes increasingly clear. Citizenship, at its most basic psychological level, is a sense of belonging to a particular social group that provides the fundamental aspects of a greater identity. While traditional ideas of citizenship once linked the concept to a singular national identity, in an increasingly globalized world, it is clear from the identity performances contained in the profiles of Almoez Ali and Basam Al-Rawi that differing interpretations of citizenship are prevalent in the sporting world. Yet while each player has maintained a bond to some degree with his respective home country, even after Qatari naturalization, it is clear that his performed identity demonstrates an obvious fealty towards Qatar.

Such disturbances were revealed in an interview with two other *jus talenti* players, Khaled and Abdullah. Although neither use the Twitter platform, both players stress the importance of their native identity, but see it as one that exists in parallel with, and not in place of, others. When asked in January 2020 to describe what playing for Qatar meant to him, the response given by *jus talenti* player Khaled mirrored that given by one of his *jus sanguinis* and *jus soli* teammates when he declared: "It is an honor to represent this country ... It's very good. It is a pleasure ... there are no words to explain. It's so good to represent the Qatar national team."[42] If a situation arose in which he would have to play against his native country, Khaled commented that while "it would be amazing," his efforts would be directed towards helping Qatar win.[43] Abdullah, who was placed in the unusual position of actually playing for Qatar against his country of origin, also reiterated these sentiments in an interview. He acknowledged that while it was strange to hear his own national anthem being played while wearing the jersey of another country, he was completely happy with the decision he made to represent Qatar.[44]

This is the salience of a Qatari identity coming to the fore that was often expressed in interviews. While playing for Cultural y Deportiva Leonesa in 2016, Ali spoke of his pride at being the first Qatari to score in Spain's La Liga, despite his Sudanese roots.[45] Similarly, when questioned about his background by Al Jazeera during the 2019 Asian Cup, while acknowledging Iraq as the country of his birth, Al-Rawi stated unequivocally that "I play for the Qatar national team and I am proud to be a part of this country. I am happy to live in Qatar and play for the team … I don't care what people say about where I come from."[46] Regardless of what group they belong to, what becomes increasingly clear is that the players use social media to perform their Qatari identity in similar ways. Regardless of origin or citizenship status, this cross-section of players reflects a similar affection for state, "performing" a relatively homogenous identity to each other. This performance has the potential to do one significant thing. In reflecting their multitudinous sub-identities as citizens, residents, Arabs, or expats, the umbrella under which all these myriad identities gather is that of a Qatari footballer.

These conclusions mirror those suggested by Irene Bloemraad in her study of dual nationality. Here, Bloemraad notes that even if immigrants initially see themselves as dual nationals, over time "most people will recognize the need to adopt one primary identity and political loyalty and they will transfer their subjective and objective attachments to their new home."[47] This is exactly what is occurring amongst the *jus soli* and *jus talenti* players of the Qatar national team. Although they may have originally belonged to a social out-group within Qatari society, their performances on social media are allowing them to move steadily inwards towards the social in-group. The performances of *jus sanguinis*, *jus soli*, and *jus talenti* players show little or no discernible difference. Although there are brief disturbances in the performance of identity of *jus soli* and *jus talenti* players, these are quickly overshadowed by their deliberate and repeated performances of a Qatari identity. The politics of exclusion that Longva and Cooke identify as segregating the respective societies of the Gulf are thus being challenged by these performances of banal nationalism as players from these two groups begin to be viewed in the same light as the *jus sanguinis* group—those with the thickest ties to Qatari society.

More than Just Footballers

The performance of identity, as previously stated, is an immensely dialectical process. To be successful, these identities must be appraised and deemed worthy or convincing enough to allow the actor to become a part of the in-group. While this is difficult to determine without the use of extensive survey data, it is possible to garner a general idea of the initial sentiment by examining the responses to some of the selected performances posted on Twitter. In doing so, it becomes clear that many people see the national team players from non-Qatari backgrounds as more than just sporting citizens. Some players, including *jus sanguinis* Hassan Al-Haydos and Saad Al Sheeb, *jus soli* Assim Madibo and Hamid Ismail, and *jus talenti* Boualem Khoukhi, Pedro, and Basam Al-Rawi, announced on social media that they were waiving part of their salaries to contribute to the fight against COVID-19, describing it as an undertaking for الوطن (*alwatan*, or "the homeland"). The public response to this action, as shown in the replies to Hassan's post, was overwhelmingly positive.[48] In addition to this pay cut, other players used social media to promote safety messages and were lauded publicly in response. Abdulkarim Hassan, for instance, tweeted his registration for a national volunteering campaign aimed at combatting COVID-19 and requested that many of his followers do the same.[49]

Given that these efforts directly benefit Qatari society, positive public sentiment is expected. However, what is also important to note is that this positive reaction is a general constant.

When Almoez Ali posted support for Sudan in Figure 5.14, the feedback received from users who state their location to be in Qatar was also predominantly favorable. Al-Rawi's explanation of his reasons for representing Qatar also garners a similar response. While many Iraqi fans express disappointment and anger at what they see as Al-Rawi's betrayal of his home nation, responses from Qatar fans are almost entirely positive, congratulating Al-Rawi for his achievements and describing him as a hero and the future of Qatari football.[50]

Social Nationalism and the Blockade

As argued by Billig, the potency of banal nationalism lies in how it conveys a sense of patria in the mundanity of normal life. However, on occasion, extraordinary circumstances encourage or enable citizens to project a very explicit kind of "hot" social nationalism that is the opposite of banal nationalism's deceptive ordinariness. One such moment was the 2017–2021 blockade of Qatar. Feelings of confusion, distress, and ultimately anger erupted in Doha as it became apparent that Saudi Arabia, the UAE, Bahrain, and several other nations had severed all ties with Qatar, and the only route to repair them was surrendering the state to Saudi hegemony. Suddenly, the 2018 World Cup qualifier between Qatar and South Korea due to be held a little over a week after the start of the blockade took on much greater significance than just another football match. It became an opportunity for a very public demonstration of support for Qatar and its emir, and an open show of defiance in the face of regional pressures to recommit to Saudi hegemony. The face of this protest was the portrait of Tamim Al-Majd, the image that had become a synecdoche of the nation itself.

Throughout the warmup, the Qatar players wore t-shirts with the Tamim Al-Majd image emblazoned across the front, a garment Hassan Al-Haydos was quick to grab when celebrating what was to be the winning goal in the 75th minute as Qatar won 3–2. What is crucial to note in this performance of social nationalism during such an extraordinary moment in Qatar's history is that every player participated in this very public performance of Qatari identity. It was not just those in the *jus sanguinis* group, occupying the thickest end of Oonk's scale of citizenship. The players involved became a physical embodiment of a society that was not afraid to choose its own path. This shared sentiment of support for Sheikh Tamim and the small state of Qatar from such a diverse groups of players, before and during this game, was a very visible expression of social nationalism that helped to reframe the narrative of the blockade for those who lived in Qatar.

Shoomilah Shoomilah

Given its occurrence before and during a World Cup qualifier, Qatar's t-shirt protest quickly drew the ire of FIFA, whose insistence that there be a separation between football and politics prevented the repeat of such explicit demonstrations of nationalism. The Qatar players were not easily deterred, however, and consequently, what were deemed as acceptable displays, such as the singing of anthems, were suddenly instilled with increased importance. In their study of national identity performance in international rugby, Jason Tuck and Joseph Maguire cite player responses that identify feelings of positivity and pride associated with singing the anthem. When discussing "Flower of Scotland," several Scottish players stated that they recognized key tropes that allowed them to conceive of a specific identity for their nation that they would seek to imitate upon the pitch.[51] Qatar's anthem, "As-Salam al-Amiri" ("Peace to the Emir"), allows a similar calculus to be performed.[52]

> Swearing by God who raised the sky,
> Swearing by God who spread the light,
> Qatar will always be free.
> Elevated by the souls of the loyal,
> Follow the path of the ancestors,
> And the prophets' guidance.
> In my heart,
> Qatar is an epic of dignity and glory.
> Qatar is the land of the forefathers,
> Who protect us on call-up to sacrifice.

Dovish at times of peace.
Hawkish at times of sacrifice.

Much of Qatar's desired identity can quickly be detected here. Those who sing the anthem pronounce a dedicated Muslim state that is also aware and proud of its Arab past. What is also important to note are the tropes that underscore Qatar's modern vision of itself since its independence in 1971, and that these tropes became ever more crucial to the identity of the state throughout the blockade. It describes a nation that is dignified and free, and one whose people are committed to ensuring its survival by fair means or otherwise if the situation demands.

While the anthem is an important part of Qatari identity performance, unifying each of the players under one lyrical banner, its expected and routine occurrence before every international football match challenges its effectiveness as an extraordinary display of social nationalism. The same, however, cannot be said for "Shoomilah Shoomilah," a song that has emerged as an alternative anthem amongst the Qatar players in recent years. As explained by the lyricist, Ayed bin Ghayda, when translated into English, the song tells the story of a beautiful woman looking to attract the attentions of a worthy partner by promising to commit her life to him.[53]

> Rise up to him, O girl with beautiful eyelashes, rise up to the level of the swordsman.
>
> Rise up to him.
>
> The Shaikh whose stands pleases the people around him. Rise up to him.
>
> Different from his generation, even in his young age.
>
> The one who stands by his words, and whose stands were evident among his generation.
>
> We are going to show those who showed greed towards our homeland. We will.
>
> His (the enemy's) strength and tricks are not going to benefit him (the enemy).
>
> O the breeze after the rain, take ...

… to him the salute of people whose intentions are sincere.

We bend for him with our souls and spears. We bend for him.

We are the supporters of his rule and we are his army. We bend for him.

Tell him that your people pledged loyalty to you. Tell him

Tell him that we are the protectors of "The Glory." Tell him.

Usually played at weddings to celebrate the bride's wisdom in choosing a suitable husband, its meaning quickly changed when a video went viral depicting the Qatar players singing the song in the changing room after their semi-final victory over the UAE.[54] The wedding metaphor remained, but now the marriage described became one between Qatar and the current emir, Sheikh Tamim, her worthy and noble partner. What is notable here is the explicit statement of support for the emir by all of the players. Just as the woman swore to sacrifice her life to protect her sheikh in the original version, in performing "Shoomilah Shoomilah," the players demonstrate their willingness to defend the emir and their homeland in the closing quatrain. Describing Sheikh Tamim as the "the breeze after the rain," the players to a man are "the supporters of his rule and … his army." Regardless of their status as *jus sanguinis*, *jus soli*, or *jus talenti* players, by participating in the singing of "Shoomilah Shoomilah," they perform this role which tells the listener that "they will bend for him" in order to protect the homeland.

As was seen after the decisive group game against the UAE in the Gulf Cup held in Qatar in December 2019, the players sang the song directly to the emir from the pitch in a performance led by *jus soli* player Abdulkarim Hassan. It is interesting to note how the song became a feature of the national team. Speaking to *jus soli* player Fawaz, he revealed that he introduced the song to the changing room and insisted that it become a part of who they were as a representation of Qatar. He stated that

it started from me, because I did the words and I organized it. The words take the heart of the player and everyone liked it [sic]. So I made a deal with my teammates that we have to sing this one. Even

147

before the game, before we start the game, we put Shoomilah on to give us motivation and also after the game to celebrate.[55]

Jus soli player Fawaz describes the song as something even more inspiring than "As-Salam al-Amiri," saying that it "touches you, your heart about Sheikh Tamim, about the country, so for me it gives me motivation, even for me, more than the national anthem."[56] *Jus sanguinis* player Ahmed reiterates these views, stating that "Shoomilah Shoomilah" "makes you want to go deep for the country and you go deep." Ahmed goes on to say that once he hears "Shoomilah Shoomilah," "it makes me go deep and go happy. I know success is coming and I'm doing something positive."[57] These views are understandable given that all players in the *jus sanguinis* and *jus soli* groups would have grown up and been educated in Qatar, and thus were exposed to these facets of Qatari culture organically from an early age. While this is not the case for the *jus talenti* group, Khaled states that when he hears the song, "it gives us more and more power to represent the country and to represent Qatar and the country."[58] What is significant about Khaled's statement is that he is one of the few players in the team unable to speak Arabic fluently. When asked about whether he understood the lyrics of the song, he replied "I don't understand anything, but when I listen to this music before the game with the lyrics, I become more powerful, more motivated to play the game."[59] For Khaled, "Shoomilah Shoomilah" acts as a unifier that transcends potential cultural barriers that naturalization could bring and instils within him a sense of *patria* towards Qatar akin to that of his *jus sanguinis* and *jus soli* teammates.

It is clear that for each of the players above, "Shoomilah Shoomilah" is every bit the source of motivation and pride that Tuck and Maguire discovered when examining the responses of international rugby players to the singing of their anthems. While "As-Salam al-Amiri" is a song for the people of Qatar, "Shoomilah Shoomilah" is a song for the team of the people of Qatar. Entwined with the events of the blockade and the patriotic zeal they inspired, the song's public demonstration of many of the key tropes of Qatar's post-blockade identity is a pressing example of social nationalism. Representing an open, independent, modern, Arab society to the world, those who sing it are very visibly not just the *jus sanguinis* players within the team. "Shoomilah Shoomilah" has become an anthem of its own, representing all the people of Qatar.

Conclusion

Whether banal or social, it is clear that the nationalist performances by each of these Qatar national team players demonstrates both a homogeneity and salience that challenges the gradient of the sliding scale of Gijsbert Oonk's model of thick and thin citizenship. This chapter argues that the differences between the thickest and thinnest forms of citizenship are less than expected. A suggested reason for this is the contribution element of Oonk's model. Contribution is a common factor across all three categories of player (*jus sanguinis*, *jus soli*, and *jus talenti*), and plays a significant role in shaping the perception of an athlete in the community. Contribution describes how players integrate into the society in which they are living, and how they actively seek to increase the wellness of that society. Very public shows of support for the emir and Qatar on social media and during international football matches, as well as other contributions, such as Abdulkarim Hassan's active participation in national volunteering campaigns, are examples of the myriad contributions made by the footballers of Qatar. In allowing some players an opportunity to demonstrate a loyalty that may not have been as "thick" as previously realized, these performances continue to flatten the gradient of Oonk's model even further.

It is my hope that this chapter is read as a preliminary study into the issue of sport and identity in the Gulf. It became clear throughout the project that there is little difference in the performance of national identity amongst the different categories of players in the Qatar national team. However, what also became increasingly apparent is that the boundaries identified here—between *jus sanguinis*, *jus soli*, and *jus talenti* players—are incredibly porous, often overlapping, and reflecting the myriad complexities that arise when attempting to determine nationality, particularly in Qatar and the Gulf. Transnational tribal links, Qatar's complex, innately stratified laws of citizenship, and forced economic migration both to and from the Gulf state are just some of the reasons why it could be argued that several of those who identify as *jus sanguinis* in this study could also occupy the *jus soli* category. Likewise, there is also a convincing argument to place several of the *jus talenti* players in the *jus soli* category. Some players came to Qatar with their families as young children, and it would be inaccurate to suggest that anything other than a desire to represent their adopted country is their motivation to play for Qatar. The common denominator between nearly all these players, it seems, is a lifetime spent as an integrated part of Qatari society. If some of these athletes are not citizens in the fullest legislative sense, it is not because they do not "feel" Qatari.[60] It is not because they do not contribute to the society that has shaped them, supported them, and celebrated them. It is because the laws relating to Qatari citizenship promote those with the deepest ties to the state. It is within these knowledge gaps that possibilities for further research lies.

Once the headlines denouncing Qatar's national team selection policy as a mixed bag of mercenaries and domestic talent are stripped away, what is left is a group of players who represent the diversity of Qatari society today in the very same manner that Paul Pogba, Kylian Mbappe, and Antoine Griezmann represented the ethnic diversity of French society during the 2018 World Cup in Russia. What this is doing in and of itself is pushing back against the exclusionary nature of Qatar's citizenship laws that attempt to recreate the "imagined community" of the state, to present a social construct in keeping with the realities of Qatari society. Whether performing national identity on social media, or in front of thousands of spectators, by reflecting the state's values, ideas, and its vision of itself, these players move from "thinner" to "thicker" forms of citizenship and contribute very publicly to the identity of a contemporary Qatar. Publicly acclaimed for the efforts and the sacrifices they make, the commitment these players show to Qatar elides any concerns about the distinction between *jus sanguinis*, *jus soli*, and *jus talenti* players. Their nationalism constitutes a performance that acts as a panacea towards those who doubt the integrity of their motivation on the pitch. When such actions are viewed in tandem with the contributions that many of these players make to enhance the wellness of their society, it is clear that the phrase "homeland," though used often, is not used lightly.

6

PLAYING IN THE TRIPLE PERIPHERY

EXCLUSIONARY POLICIES TOWARDS PALESTINIAN FOOTBALL IN LEBANON

Danyel Reiche

Introduction

This chapter explores Palestinian football by focusing on the case of Lebanon, one of the largest host communities for Palestinian refugees. In comparison to other Palestinian diaspora communities, Palestinians in Lebanon have a limited presence in football. While in countries such as Chile and Jordan football has served as a tool for integration, Lebanese football has reflected the exclusion of Palestinians in society. This study argues that Palestinian footballers' lack of access to Lebanese citizenship—which is different from the experience of Palestinian immigrants and refugees in Chile and Jordan—is the main reason for the absence of Palestinian football success stories in Lebanon.

This chapter examines how Palestinian football players in Lebanon are operating in a triple periphery. First, they are excluded from Lebanese football through lack of access to Lebanese nationality, which creates football-specific obstacles, such as a cap for Palestinian players in Lebanese leagues. Second, their status as stateless persons prevents Palestinians in Lebanon from representing their country of descent in international competitions. Finally, being stateless refugees restricts their potential movement to other football leagues abroad.

Before examining the case of Palestinian football in Lebanon in particular, the chapter begins by comparatively reviewing the academic literature on the recognition of the Palestinian Football Association (PFA) at the international level, the accomplishments of the Palestinian national men's football team, and the experiences of Palestinian football players in other diaspora communities. According to Almond et al.:

> Comparing our experience with that of other countries deepens our understanding of our institutions. Examining politics in other societies permits us to see a wider range of political alternatives. It illuminates the virtues and shortcomings of our own political life. By taking us beyond our familiar arrangement and assumptions, comparative analysis helps expand our awareness of the possibilities of politics.[1]

This chapter thus contributes to our understanding of the Palestinian diaspora experience through the lens of football. Before delving into a more in-depth discussion of Palestinian football in Lebanon, the following is an overview of Palestinian football in other parts of the world.

Palestinian Football in Israel

There are 1.42 million Palestinians inside Israel and 281,000 in East Jerusalem (which was annexed by Israel), making up around twenty percent of Israel's population.[2] For Sorek, Arab football in Israel represents an "integrative enclave" and "a sphere which permits a limited and well-bounded inclusion in Israeli citizenship." There is, according to Sorek, an increasing visibility of Arab soccer players in the Israeli public: the number of Arab teams is "more than double the relative share of the Arab population in Israel."[3] In the 1996–97 season, the first Arab team, ha-Po'el Taibeh, started playing in Israel's top football league. In 2004, Sakhnin was the first team from an Arab city to win the Israeli Cup, and was eligible to represent Israel, making it the first Arab club in the UEFA Cup European club competition.[4] Given the presence of Arab soccer players in Israeli teams, these attract a significant number of Arab fans.[5] Starting with the participation of the Israeli national men's football team in the 1976 Montreal Olympics, "the most symbolically significant phenomena was the prominent presence of Arab players in the Israeli national team."[6] For Sorek, "the Israeli national soccer team played an inclusive role with regard to the state's Arab citizens."[7] However, Shor and Yonay take a more critical stand in their article "'Play and Shut Up': The Silencing of Palestinian Athletes in Israeli Media," arguing that there is a "no-politics rule" for Palestinian football players in Israel. They note that "while the Palestinians are not allowed to mix sport and politics and complain about discrimination, Jewish speakers do mix the two spheres in order to 'prove' that discrimination does not exist."[8] The work by Shor and Yonay, which is based on an analysis of articles in the Israeli media over a period of five years, concludes that Palestinian football players in Israel "are expected by the journalists to draw a strict line between themselves, 'the Israeli Arabs', and the Palestinians in the occupied territories, but also between them and Palestinian identity, which is associated only with violence and terror attacks."[9]

The experience of football players who are residents of the occupied territories deviates considerably from that of Palestinian football players who are citizens of Israel. The PFA has repeatedly protested Israel's efforts to hinder football development in the occupied territories and the inclusion of six teams from settlements into Israeli football leagues. While the Fédération Internationale de Football Association (FIFA) refused to rule on the settlement teams, arguing it would be beyond its ability to resolve the matter,[10] the world governing body of football established the FIFA Monitoring Committee Israel-Palestine in 2015 "to monitor Israeli commitments to ease athletes' travel through checkpoints and border crossings, remove tariffs on the import of sports equipment, and help build fields and facilities in the West Bank and Gaza Strip."[11] However, the case of the Palestine Cup Final in 2019 shows that not much progress has been made. There are two separate Palestinian football leagues, one in Gaza and one in the West Bank. The champions of both leagues planned to play a two-leg final against each other to determine the Palestinian champion and representative for the Asian Champions League. After the first match took place in 2019 in Gaza between Khadamat Rafah and West Bank champion Balata FC, ending in a draw, Israel denied travel visas to most players from Khadamat Rafah. The final had to be postponed several times and was finally cancelled. No Palestinian champion could be determined in the year 2019.[12]

Palestinian Football in Jordan and Chile

The Palestinian diaspora is larger than the population at home. According to the Palestinian Central Bureau of Statistics, there were 12.5 million Palestinians in the world in 2017.[13] Some football club teams associated with the largest Palestinian diaspora communities have gained notable achievements. What they have in common is a display of Palestinian nationalism, ethnic affiliation, and historical heritage, but also resistance to Israel's colonization of their homeland: "This kind of nationalism is crystallized mainly as a reflection of the meeting or clash with the 'other.'"[14]

Palestinian football has made positive headlines in recent years: The men's national team qualified for both the 2015 and 2019 editions of the continental football championship Asian Football Confederation (AFC) Asian Cup, as well as the FIFA Arab Cup in 2021. This was a remarkable success for Palestine, a country of only 5 million people that FIFA (Fédération Internationale de Football Association) only recognized in 1998.[15] The PFA is one of forty-six member associations of the AFC.[16] The fact that in 2015 only sixteen AFC member associations could participate in the Asian Cup—and in 2019, only twenty-four—shows how remarkable it is that Palestine qualified for the event. "Although their on-field success has been limited, the presence of a Palestinian national team allows to compete [*sic*] and participate like any other country and this has helped retain a sense of national identity," concludes Duerr.[17] Dart notes that "football represents a promising opportunity to promote Palestine on an international stage" and "is being used to draw attention to the Palestinian struggle for a homeland."[18]

Jordan is home to the largest Palestinian diaspora community, with approximately 2.29 million people.[19] The football club al-Wehdat SC, founded in 1956, represents Palestinian Jordanians. After the 1970 civil war between the Jordanian Armed Forces (JAF) and the Palestinian Liberation Organization (PLO) in which the PLO lost its main base and had to reorganize in Lebanon, an "East Bank first policy" was employed in Jordan. According to Tuastad, "the only arena where Palestinian national identity could be openly expressed became, from then on, the football arena."[20] By January 2020, the club had won sixteen national championships and contributed to "forming Palestinian identity in Jordan."[21]

The largest population of Palestinians outside of the Middle East, made up of around 500,000 people of Palestinian descent, live in Chile. In football, they are represented by Club Deportivo Palestino, which was founded in 1916 by Palestinian immigrants. According to an article in *Haaretz*, about 95 percent of the "Chilestinians" are Christians whose origins lie in the Jerusalem-area triangle of Bethlehem, Beit Jalla, and Beir Sahour, with most families having emigrated before the 1930s. "The main impulse for those early waves of emigration was the Ottoman conscription law. Christians were drafted at an early age and sent to the front, sometimes unarmed, to serve as cannon fodder in battles against other Christians, in the Balkan wars and in World War I."[22] The article concludes that Palestinians have integrated into Chile more easily given that most of these Palestinians are Christians, like most Chileans.

Club Deportivo Palestino is one of the top teams in Chile and has even won the national championship twice. In international football, players from Club Deportivo Palestino can choose to represent either Chile, as their country of birth, or Palestine, as their country of descent.[23] The President of the Palestinian Authority (PA), Mahmoud Abbas, has even called Club Deportivo Palestino a "second national team,"[24] and Schwabe similarly notes that Club Deportivo Palestino has assumed the "position of ambassador for Palestine."[25] Schwabe goes on to argue that "for Santiago's Palestinian-Chileans, soccer has become a means of expressing cultural pride" and "solidarity with the people of Palestine."[26] For instance, in 2014, international media reported that the club "has been fined by the country's soccer league for wearing game jerseys in which the No. 1 was depicted by a 1947 map of Palestine before the creation of Israel."[27]

The Case of Lebanon

Lebanon is a major host community for Palestinians, although the precise number of Palestinians in Lebanon is disputed. According to the Palestinian Central Bureau of Statistics, there were 514,000 Palestinians in Lebanon in 2017. By January 2019, there were 470,000 refugees registered with the United Nations Relief and Works Agency for Palestine Refugees (UNRWA) in Lebanon, with about 45 percent of them living in the country's twelve refugee camps.[28] According to the Lebanese government's first-ever census of Palestinian refugees in Lebanon, they numbered 174,422 in 2017, with an additional 18,601 Palestinians living in camps in Lebanon after fleeing the conflict in neighboring Syria.[29]

When it comes to football, Lebanon deviates from Israel, Jordan, and Chile. While Palestinians face discrimination in those countries—particularly in Israel, as an ethnic democracy with legislation that discriminates against the native Palestinian population—football is a sphere in which Palestinians can attempt to feel equal. Sport provides opportunities as an arena of meritocracy.[30] However, there are no success stories about Palestinian football in Lebanon as there are in Israel, Jordan, and Chile. There are exclusionary policies towards Palestinians in Lebanese society, but especially in the football sector. Hence, the presence of Palestinians in Lebanese football is limited. There is no Palestinian flagship team in Lebanese football leagues, and Palestinians from Lebanon represent neither Lebanon nor Palestine in international football competitions. In comparison, there were four Israeli-born Arab players in the Palestinian squad for the 2015 AFC Asian Cup.[31] However,

Arab Israelis transferring to Israeli teams are no longer nominated for the Palestinian national team. For example, Abdallah Jabar, a player who represented Palestine in several international games, was kicked out of the squad after joining the Israeli team Hapoel Hadera in May 2020.[32]

Palestinian football players in Lebanon are marginalized both at the domestic level and the international level, given the absence of successful Palestinian clubs in Lebanese competitions and the lack of representation of Palestinian football players from Lebanon in the national teams of both Palestine and Lebanon. Consequently, this section is structured in two parts, taking both those levels—national and external policy processes—into consideration. The first part looks at the domestic level; it shows how access to local competitions is limited for Palestinian football players and analyzes the reasons for this discriminatory policy. The second part looks at external discriminations by analyzing why Palestinians from Lebanon are widely excluded from Palestinian and Lebanese participation in international football competitions. Both sections follow the approach of Houlihan, who differentiates between "politics and sport" and "politics in sport." "Politics in sport" looks at the role of national and international sports governing bodies, while "politics and sport" analyzes interventions by the government and supranational political bodies.[33]

This research is based on a review of two bodies of academic literature: first, studies on Palestinian football in diaspora communities and the process of international recognition for the Palestinian football federation.[34] This body of literature mainly deals with men's football, reflecting the fact that Palestinian football is predominantly a male sphere. An exception is an article by Stewart on the Banat Sakhnin team, the only Palestinian Arab team in the Israeli women's soccer league, which was established in 1998 to comply with FIFA and Union of European Football Associations (UEFA) regulations.[35] The second body of research relates to the living conditions of Palestinians in Lebanon, and mainly focuses on the various forms of discrimination they face in Lebanese society.[36] While the general literature on Palestinians in Lebanon focuses on the harsh conditions in refugee camps and discriminatory policies, such as the prohibition on acquiring property and on working in a wide range of professions, research specific to Palestinian football has focused on major diaspora clubs in Chile, Israel, and Jordan, as well as the struggle for international recognition of the PFA by the world governing body of football, FIFA.

Palestinian football in Lebanon is an underresearched aspect of the academic literature on both Palestinian football and the living conditions of Palestinians in Lebanon. A notable exception is Fogliata's ethnographic work on Al-Aqsa, a football team from the Palestinian camp Bourj el-Barajneh. The camp was established in 1949 and is located in a southern suburb of Beirut, four kilometers from the capital's downtown. Its population increased from 3,500 people in 1949 to 18,351 in 2020.[37] Fogliata's main research interest was Palestinians from Syria living in that camp and playing in the Al-Aqsa team.[38] Fogliata's work shows how "Palestinian clubs turn into an alternative space where Syria's refugees can find an alternative chance to show their talent" and serve as an "entry-point" to be recruited by Lebanese teams."[39]

The new dimensions of the current study are to link literature on the discrimination against Palestinians in Lebanon with research on the sports sector; to identify general political as well as sport-specific reasons for exclusionary policies in football; and to analyze and explain the different experiences of Palestinian football in Lebanon compared with other Palestinian diaspora communities.

Research Methodology

While the discussion of Palestinian football in general (and of discriminatory policies towards Palestinians in Lebanon in particular) is based on a review of the academic literature, there are hardly any secondary sources for the current case study: Palestinian football in Lebanon. Therefore, the main body of this work relied on the collection of primary data by conducting nine in-depth, semi-structured interviews between July 2019 and July 2020. Apart from one researcher, who specialized in Palestinian affairs and football in Jordan and other Middle Eastern countries, all interviewees are key stakeholders in Palestinian football or Palestinian affairs in Lebanon, with long-term experience and first-hand knowledge of the game. Five interviews were held in person and four interviews were held via telephone, Skype, or WhatsApp, and some sources were interviewed on more than one occasion. The chosen format of asking a series of open-ended questions allowed for more fluid interactions between the researcher and respondents and provided a multi-perspective understanding of the topic by not limiting respondents to a fixed set of questions.[40]

The main purpose of most interviews was to acquire the respondents' knowledge, views, and personal experiences regarding the historical development of Palestinian sport, with a particular emphasis on football in Lebanon. Two interviews conducted with researchers who specialized on Lebanese politics and Palestinian affairs in Lebanon went beyond football and sought to better understand the discrimination of Palestinian football players in the general context of exclusionary policies towards Palestinians in the country.

The interviewees are as follows: 1) an American University of Beirut (AUB) sociology professor, who has widely published on the living conditions of Palestinian refugee camps in Lebanon and on the various discriminations Palestinians face in Lebanese society; 2) an AUB political science professor, who has published on Palestinian issues in Lebanon and the region; 3) a social anthropologist from Norway, who has widely published about Palestinian issues, including the al-Wehdat football club representing the Palestinian community in Jordan; 4) a Palestinian from Lebanon who has played for various Lebanese football clubs—at the time of the interview, for a second league team—and was the most recent Palestinian from Lebanon to be nominated for the Palestinian national team; 5) a Palestinian from Lebanon who switched to another sport—rugby—after encountering frustrating experiences when playing football in the third Lebanese league; 6) the coach of the Palestinian national team in Lebanon and a formerly successful player, who was naturalized by Qatar to play in the Qatari national football team; 7) the chair of the Palestinian rugby league federation in Lebanon, who provided information about the different legal frameworks for Palestinian athletes across major sports in Lebanon; 8) a PhD student, who manages a social media account on Lebanese football and was able to provide detailed information on specific Palestinian players; and 9) the press officer of the Lebanese Football Association (LFA), who explained the historical development of the rules for Palestinian players in Lebanese football.

Domestic Discrimination in Lebanese Society

Palestinians in Lebanon face many forms of discrimination as a result of the Lebanese state's exclusionary policies. Palestinian refugees in Lebanon "enjoy neither the civil rights of Lebanese, upon whose territory they reside, nor those of foreigners living in Lebanon."[41] According to UNRWA, Palestinian refugees in Lebanon are prevented by Lebanese law from employment "in at least 39 professions (such as medicine, law, engineering, etc.)," and cannot join labor unions and syndicates.[42]

As a result of Israel's refusal to allow Palestinian refugees to return to their homeland, these Palestinians have lived in Lebanon for more than seventy years. Most of them still live in poverty, as "much of the employment available to Palestinians is of low status, precarious, and insufficient to lift them out of poverty."[43] Palestinians in Lebanon "earn lower wages than the Lebanese for the same level of education and occupation" and are not enrolled in the country's social security system.[44]

There was a period when Palestinian refugees were entitled to property ownership in Lebanon. However, following a change of law in 2001, Palestinians in Lebanon have been unable to acquire property ownership rights.[45] They have no access to public services in the country and are dependent on humanitarian assistance for education and healthcare, which is mostly provided by UNRWA and nongovernmental organizations. UNRWA schools are over-crowded, which also impacts sports. According to a study on school dropouts in Palestinian refugee camps,[46] some of the reasons why many students do not consider UNRWA schools attractive and drop out—at far above the average rate of other schools in Lebanon—

160

include: a lack of extra-curricular activities during school hours; an absence of proper physical education classes, if they exist at all; limited space for sporting competitions; and an insufficient number of qualified instructors. In their work on Palestinian refugee camps in Lebanon, Hanafi et al. note: "accounts from Palestinian camp dwellers in Lebanon show that they refer to themselves as the 'forgotten people,' feeling that they live in a hostile environment where basic human rights, including the right to work, have no effective means of representation or protection."[47]

Domestic Discrimination in Lebanese Football

In the 1970s, not only did many Palestinians play for Lebanese clubs—which had no restrictions against Palestinian players at that time—but Lebanese players were also eager to play for Palestinian clubs, which were well funded at that time. The Lebanese and the Palestinian leagues coordinated their schedules, and some players would play for both Palestinian and Lebanese clubs.[48] Support from the Palestinian Liberation Organization (PLO) was a key reason for the temporary success of Palestinian football clubs in Lebanon, which attracted the best Lebanese and Palestinian players. Their matches were hosted in Lebanon's major stadiums in front of large audiences. The PLO was primarily based in Lebanon for twelve years after being expelled from Jordan in 1970 and before Israeli troops invaded Southern Lebanon in 1982, which forced the organization to leave Lebanon and to move to Tunisia.

> The expulsion of the Palestinian leadership, and militants in general, from Lebanon, and the removal of the Supreme Council and sport associations to Tunis in particular, stumbled the progress of the sport movement, and had its impact on club teams and activities. What was built through a period of fourteen years was destroyed in a few days. The invasion was a blow for every sphere of life of the Lebanese and Palestinian people, including the athletic movement.[49]

Starting in 1985, the Lebanese Football Association introduced a cap of three foreigners for match day squads. Up until then, there had been no restrictions on the number of foreign players—including Palestinian refugees, who were regarded as foreign. In the 1970s, when football was not as televised and globalized as it is today, many Lebanese clubs, including major ones like Nejmeh, recruited a significant number of locally based Palestinians. Even after the introduction of the cap in 1985, many of the spots reserved for foreign players were filled by Palestinians. However, after the Lebanese civil war ended in 1990, the country's economy recovered, and clubs received more support from sponsors who were able to attract international players now willing to come to a pacified Lebanon. Gradually, Palestinian players were replaced by other foreigners, particularly from North Africa and other Middle Eastern countries, as well as from Armenia and Brazil.

Starting from the 1998–99 season, a small improvement compared with the post-1985 situation was introduced. "Since then, one Palestinian is counted as Lebanese, and only additional Palestinian players are counted as foreigners. This rule applies to all divisions. The first league allows three foreigners. The second, lower leagues permit two foreigners," explained the press officer of the LFA, when interviewed for this research. He elaborated further details of the rule: the one permitted Palestinian player must have been born in Lebanon, otherwise he is counted as foreign. Hence, a Palestinian from abroad would be considered a foreigner. Lebanese clubs can sign as many Palestinian players as they want, but only up to four can be included in the eighteen-man match day squad: one as a local player and three as foreigners. However, it is no longer common to recruit Palestinians in the three spots allocated for foreign players.[50] One of the major pre-match responsibilities of referees in Lebanese football is to ensure that the number of Palestinian and foreign players does not exceed the cap.

The cap on Palestinian football players in Lebanese football is also called the "Kippa law," as the LFA press officer explained to the researcher:

> Mr Rahif Alameh, the former LFA general secretary, took this decision. There was at that time a famous Palestinian player with the club Ansar, Hussein Kippa. Some of Alameh's critics charged that the LFA took this decision to strengthen the Ansar Club.

However, it was a sport decision in general and all clubs subsequently benefited from it. For example, Tadamon Sour Sporting Club had the Palestinian player Ibrahim Manasri.

In the 2019–20 season in Lebanon,[51] there were, according to the LFA press officer, 157 football clubs playing in four divisions, with twelve clubs in the first and second divisions respectively. The twenty-four clubs in the third division and the 109 clubs in the fourth division are divided into groups.[52] This means that on each match day only 157 of the 2,826 spots are available for Palestinians. The limitation to 157 spots for Palestinians—twenty-four of them in the first and second leagues, where appropriate payments are more common than in the third and fourth leagues, which comprise the vast majority of football clubs in Lebanon—has intensified intra-Palestinian competition. One of my interviewees was a Palestinian footballer who played for the Armenian club Homenmen in the third Lebanese league. Armenians account for around four percent of the Lebanese population, and there are three major Armenian sports clubs: Homenetmen, Antranik, and Homenmen, which operate at different locations in Lebanon.

Homenmen had signed my interviewee and another Palestinian player for the 2018–19 season, despite the fact that Lebanese clubs pay the federation a higher registration fee for Palestinians than for Lebanese—50,000 Lebanese pounds (LBP) compared with 20,000 LBP.[53] The player noted that "there was a lot of competition between me and the other Palestinian player since only one of us could make it into the eighteen-men match-day squad. We liked each other but of course I was always disappointed when I was not nominated."[54] After the season, he stopped playing football and started a career as a rugby union player in Lebanon. He was even selected for the Palestinian squad at the Arab Rugby Sevens in Amman, Jordan, in November 2019.

Starting from the 1998–99 season, another major shift occurred in Lebanese football with a rule that goalkeepers had to be Lebanese citizens. The reason for this rule was perhaps more practical than xenophobic: in the 1990s, most Lebanese clubs had Palestinian or foreign goalkeepers, resulting in a shortage of competitive goalkeepers for the Lebanese national football team. The LFA press officer confirmed that "today, all goalkeepers in Lebanese clubs are Lebanese."[55] Some might argue that this is a reason why the Lebanese national team has improved over time, reaching eighty-ninth in the FIFA World ranking of December 2019.[56] For comparison, twenty years earlier, the country was ranked twenty positions lower, at 109.[57] However, the fact that many of the Lebanese national team goalkeepers grew up abroad provides a counterargument: the "Lebanese-only goalkeeper" rule is an unnecessary discrimination against Palestinians. For instance, the two most capped goalkeepers for Lebanon in the last decade were Mehdi Khalil and Abbas Hassan. Mehdi Khalil, who played in all matches for Lebanon at the 2019 AFC Asian Cup, was born in Sierra Leone, while Abbas Hassan was born in Lebanon but grew up in Sweden and even represented the Swedish national youth team before switching allegiance to Lebanon.[58]

Palestinian Football in Lebanon

The discrimination against Palestinian football players in Lebanon has led to the emergence of an independent Palestinian football system separate from the Lebanese leagues. This became the main arena in which Palestinians could play football in Lebanon. There are thirty Palestinian football clubs divided between four geographical divisions: Beirut, Sidon, Tripoli, and Tyre. Additionally, in 2016, a Palestinian national team in Lebanon was formed, occasionally playing friendly matches against Lebanese clubs and Lebanese national teams such as the national military team or national youth squads.[59] Some of the Palestinian players who make it into major Lebanese football teams continue playing for their camp teams if there is no conflict in fixtures. Some of the clubs are affiliated with the Palestinian political parties Hamas and Fatah, showcasing the conflict over power and control in the camps. For example, Al-Aqsa, a football team from the Palestinian camp Bourj el-Barajneh, is associated with Hamas.[60]

There is a Palestinian championship—determined in matches between the champions of the four Lebanese regions—as well as a cup competition. However, because Palestinian football players in

Lebanon do not receive any support from the PFA or the LFA, both competitions were suspended at the time of this research. The last national championship took place in 2017–18 and was won by the Ahel team from the Ain al-Hilweh camp in Sidon. The last cup competition took place in 2016–17 and was won by the Burj Shemali camp from Tyre.[61] Consequently, competitions mostly occur at the local level.

The league of camps for male football players in Beirut commenced in 2004 with six teams from different camps in the Lebanese capital, rising to fourteen teams in 2017.[62] I accompanied the coach of the Palestinian national team in Lebanon to attend a match between two Palestinian camp teams in November 2019. The match took place on a municipal football field in Beirut in front of a majority male audience of approximately 100 people, with some young girls as the only exception. The absence of female spectators is a social norm and not a league rule. Interestingly, the teams were not named after their camps in Lebanon but contained references to Palestine: The Martyrs of Jerusalem were playing against Jericho, the latter referring to a Palestinian city in the West Bank. Although, according to UNRWA, more than half of all Palestinians in Lebanon—fifty-five percent—do not live in camps,[63] a vast majority of Palestinian football teams in Lebanon are based in camps where a football pitch is usually available. Not all of them are of original football field size: some are mini-fields, while others just have sand as a surface. However, non-camp residents are also eligible to play in camp teams—as long as they are Palestinian and are not simultaneously playing for another camp team. The eligibility also applies to Palestinians who escaped the civil war in Syria.[64]

Writing on Palestinian football in Jordan, Tuastad states that, "initially, the various refugee camps organized their own separate league system... From 1975, however, teams from the Palestinian refugee camps were admitted into the Jordanian league."[65] Lebanon deviates from the inclusive Jordanian example: there is no Palestinian team in any of Lebanon's four leagues, even though other communities have their own football clubs that are integrated into the national football system. For example, Safa Sporting Club represents the Druze community, Racing Beirut represents Orthodox Christians, and Homenmen is an Armenian football club.[66] The major difference between the Palestinians and other minorities in Lebanon, such as the Druze, Orthodox, and Armenians, is that the former are not permitted to obtain Lebanese citizenship, although some have been living in the country for four generations. If they had access to citizenship, Palestinians could form their own teams for Lebanese competitions, just as the Druze, Orthodox, and Armenians have done.

No Path to Lebanese Citizenship

Access to Israeli citizenship explains the success of Palestinian football in Israel; access to Jordanian citizenship explains the success of Palestinian football in Jordan; and access to Chilean citizenship explains the success of Palestinian football in Chile. The lack of access to Lebanese citizenship, combined with legal restrictions for Palestinians in Lebanese society, explain the absence of success stories regarding Palestinian football in Lebanon. There is no path to Lebanese citizenship for Palestinians, and "procedures to allow non-residents to apply for naturalization in Lebanon, Egypt and Saudi Arabia do not apply to stateless Palestinians."[67] An article in *The Arab Weekly* titled "In Lebanon, Rage for Jerusalem but not for Palestinians at Home" states: "Lebanon's politicians claim that giving Palestinians full citizenship within the country would undermine their right of return to land in the present-day state of Israel."[68]

According to Ghandour, there were only two instances of Palestinian naturalizations in Lebanon: a first wave began in 1948 and ended in 1958, marked by the end of the Camil Chamoun government, in which approximately 50,000 Palestinians were granted Lebanese citizenship. A second wave occurred through a naturalization decree in 1994 when late Prime Minister Rafik Hariri was in office. This allowed the naturalization of 154,931 foreigners, 32,504 of whom were Palestinian refugees.[69] While the majority of Palestinians in Lebanon are Sunni Muslims, it was mainly Palestinian Christians who were naturalized, arguably to increase the country's Christian demographic and to counter the mass Christian migration to Europe and the Americas.[70] "Some wealthy and urban Muslim Palestinian families were also naturalized, though their numbers were significantly less compared to their Christian compatriots."[71] In an op-ed in *The Daily Star*, Hanafi, a professor in sociology at the American University of Beirut, writes: "It is as if they were telling us that the liberation of Palestine were possible only through the further debilitation and humiliation of the Palestinian refugees."[72] Similarly, an article in *The Guardian* concludes: "Today, Lebanon is the most hostile country to Palestinian refugees after Israel."[73]

One of the interviewees for this research is the chair of the Palestinian rugby league federation, who grew up in Lebanon before studying in France. He had a successful period of playing basketball with Lebanon's leading club Al Riyadi. However, he stopped playing at the age of fifteen because of his limited career opportunities in the sport. In Lebanese basketball, Palestinians are considered to be foreigners. As opposed to football, basketball in Lebanon does not even allow one Palestinian player to be counted as a local player: "They would rather naturalize Americans than Palestinians," he said during our interview.[74] The coach of the national Palestinian football team in Lebanon played for the Qatari national football team in the mid-1970s. When interviewed for this research, he said: "I was born in Lebanon and was the best player in Lebanon but never got the nationality. I cannot even buy property. When I went to Qatar, I received after six hours the nationality. It even stated, 'born in Qatar.'"[75] Qatari nationality law allows the naturalization of foreign athletes, and the country makes ample use of this opportunity.[76]

There are different interpretations regarding discrimination against Palestinians in Lebanon. One is that the Lebanese society, across all political parties, punishes Palestinians for having participated in the Lebanese civil war.[77] Another interpretation is related to the fact that most Palestinians in Lebanon are Sunni Muslims: "There is a fear that if Palestinians are integrated, they will upset the delicate confessional balance that prevails here."[78] Lebanon has a unique political accommodationist system that is described in the academic literature as confessionalism, "a system of government that proportionally allocates political power among a country's communities—whether religious or ethnic—according to their percentage of the population."[79] By naturalizing Palestinians in Lebanon, Sunni Muslims would become the largest religious group in the country.

The discrimination against Palestinians in Lebanese football also affects which spectators are admitted to matches. In May 2019, *Middle East Eye* reported that Palestinians in Lebanon were denied entrance to the stadium in Beirut at an AFC Cup match between a Jordanian team and a Lebanese team. While "Jordanian Palestinians were allowed to watch the game between Jordan's al-Wihdat and the Lebanese club Nejmeh, Palestinians that lived in Lebanon were stopped at the entrance of the Camille Chamoun Sports City Stadium."[80] The online news outlet quoted a fan saying, "What kind of heights of racism is this when we are prevented from entering a football pitch to watch a game? None of us knows the reason behind this, except that we are Palestinian refugees in Lebanon."[81]

Palestinian Women's Football

Women and girls are widely marginalized within the Palestinian football system in Lebanon. Stewart notes that Banat Sakhnin, the only Palestinian Arab team in the Israeli women's soccer league, "struggles at organizational levels to establish itself as a team to be taken seriously."[82] She quotes a female player stating, "The majority doesn't accept a girl playing soccer. They refer to it as a masculine game."[83] Stewart goes on to argue that "soccer practices and games offer a liminal social arena for female players to contest the cultural and familial expectations placed upon them by their community, religion, friends or family."[84] If and when families accept that their daughters play football, it is considered "a hobby to keep them busy until they marry."[85]

Some nongovernmental organizations focus on promoting football activities for Palestinian women and girls in Lebanon. An example of a group working on women's football projects in Lebanon is the Canadian non-profit organization Right To Play, which organizes football for girls in Nahr al-Bared, a Palestinian refugee camp in the north of the country (near to Tripoli). According to an article in *The Guardian*, religious leaders in the community were opposed to girls playing football, and so Right To Play built a football pitch for the female players to be able to play without being seen by the community. The article concludes that "the battle is far from won. Girls may now be able to play football in one sequestered corner of Nahr el-Bared, but women remain prohibited, their participation limited to occasional tournaments staged outside the camp by Right To Play."[86]

In addition, other donors focus on women and girls in Palestinian camps by promoting sports other than football, such as a cricket project in Beirut's Shatila refugee camp.[87] Furthermore, UNRWA, with the support of the European Union, has launched the Palestiniadi (Palestinian Olympics) for Palestinians in Lebanon. The eleventh edition took place in July 2019 in Siblin Training Centre; across a three-day event, it featured competitions for boys and girls in various sports, including football, volleyball, basketball, running, table tennis, and chess.[88]

Statelessness and the Palestinian National Team

Based on the 1993 Oslo Accords between the Israeli government and the PLO, the Palestinian Authority (PA) started issuing passports to its residents in 1995.[89] However, Palestinians from Lebanon are not eligible for this passport. The PA passport requires presentation of a birth certificate that states "born in Palestine" and proof of residence in the areas under PA rule.[90] The PA passport was, by December 2019, accepted by forty-eight countries for visa-free travel, visa on arrival, or Electronic Travel Authorization.[91]

For Palestinians in Lebanon, and some other Arab countries, a Refugee Travel Document (RTD) is issued. According to Shiblak, Palestinians are the largest stateless community in the world, and "today more than half of the eight million or so Palestinians are considered to be de jure stateless persons."[92] Azzam even estimates the number of stateless Palestinians in the world at 6.3 million.[93] According to the United Nations Refugee Agency (UNHCR), there is in total an "estimated 10 million stateless people around the world… Stateless people are not considered as nationals by any state."[94] However, without citizenship, an athlete cannot represent a country in international sport; there are only a very few exceptions, such as rugby where proof of residence is, apart from citizenship and evidence of ancestry, a legitimate eligibility criteria according to the rules of the global governing bodies in rugby union and rugby league, World Rugby and Rugby League International Federation.[95] According to FIFA, "any person holding a permanent nationality that is not dependent on residence in a certain country is eligible to play for the representative teams of the association of that country."[96] The same applies for the Olympic Games. The Olympic Charter states that "any competitor in the Olympic Games must be a national of the country of the NOC which is entering such competitor."[97] Hence, Palestinians from Lebanon are legally not permitted to represent the Palestinian national football team for any FIFA-sanctioned competition or qualification for the Olympic football tournament.

Although some Palestinians are born and raised in Lebanon, and some even represent the fourth generation in the country, their status as non-citizens prevents them from representing Lebanon in international football. However, it is even more difficult for Palestinians from Lebanon to access their supposed home country Palestine and to represent it in international football competitions. Palestinians from Lebanon greatly identify with the Palestinian national team. For example, when a friendly match between Lebanon and Palestine was played in Beirut in November 2016, the website *Football Palestine* reported, "fantastic support from the refugee community in Lebanon meant this often felt like a home game in terms of support. The fans deserved the draw."[98] However, while Palestinians from Lebanon can cheer for the Palestinian team, belonging to the Palestinian team has become, for Palestinian football players from Lebanon (unlike for players from other diaspora communities), a distant dream.

Palestine is not a member of the United Nations, but it was granted the status of UN non-member observer state in 2012. Duerr notes that, "the rise of the Palestinian national team corresponds to a political campaign of increasing international recognition."[99] By December 2019, 138 of the 193 UN member states had recognized Palestine.[100] "The role of the national football team should be seen as a contributing factor to this effort."[101] The PFA was recognized by FIFA in 1998. According to FIFA, "Their national team played their first friendly matches against Lebanon, Jordan and Syria in July 1998 and first qualified for the AFC Asian Cup in May 2014" (the tournament itself took place in 2015). The FIFA website also highlights the fact that "the national team went on to reach an all-time high position of 73rd in the FIFA/Coca-Cola World Ranking in February 2018."[102] Dart notes that "for the Palestinians, the success of the men's national football team has contributed to the embodiment and promotion of a national consciousness and is used to generate greater international support for their human rights."[103] According to Duerr,

> Appearing on the world stage promotes an image of being as equal and legitimate as any other state. It also provides Palestinians with a sense of national pride as they play against other national teams. When the Palestinian team members wear their green or white jerseys (depending on the fixture), the team reinforces a sense of national identity. The flag is raised, the name "Palestine" is used, and the team competes against de jure states.[104]

Palestine's most remarkable successes were participating in both the 2015 and 2019 editions of the continental football championship, the AFC Asian Cup, and the FIFA Arab Cup 2021. Although the team did not make it to the second round in either instance, their performance improved in 2019 compared to 2015, when the team lost all three matches. In 2019, the team achieved two draws against Syria and Jordan, while losing to Australia.[105] At the FIFA Arab Cup 2021, the team lost against Morocco and Jordan but achieved a draw against one of the best Asian national teams, Saudi Arabia. Some players from the Palestinian diaspora—for example, those residing in Chile and the United States—belonged to the squads.[106] Duerr notes that "the mere existence of a separate team that plays international matches against foreign opposition provides a level of national consciousness, both inside the Palestinian territories and amongst neighboring states."[107]

Before the PFA was officially recognized by FIFA, it was common for Palestinians from Lebanon to represent the Palestine national team in friendly matches, which were often played in Jordan. Even after the FIFA recognition, there were a few cases of Palestinians from Lebanon representing the Palestinian national team, although this was legally problematic. I interviewed a player from a second league club in Lebanon who, earlier in his career, played for different first league teams in Lebanon. He said he was the last Palestinian from Lebanon to play in the national Palestinian team.[108] The Palestinian authorities had issued him a temporary Palestinian passport, which had expired at the time of the interview in November 2019. Officially, a Palestinian passport requires one to be born in Palestine and possess resident status in the areas under PA rule. However, naturalizations of elite athletes are common around the world, and a couple of exceptions have been also made in the past for Palestinian football, as in the case of the interviewed player, who played in the Palestinian national team from 2004–09. At that time, Palestinian home matches took place in either Qatar or Jordan. Financially supported by FIFA, a national PFA stadium in Al-Ram near Ramallah was officially inaugurated on October 26, 2008.[109] Tragically, what was considered a milestone for Palestinian football also marked the end of the meager representation of Palestinians from Lebanon in the Palestinian national team. To enter the West Bank from Lebanon, one has to travel through Israel and go through Israeli checkpoints. However, Palestinians in Lebanon are affected by the Lebanese boycott law that does not permit entering Israel.[110] The interviewed player commented that "the new home stadium in Palestine marked the end of my career in the national team."[111]

Overall, stateless Palestinian football players from Lebanon witness a triple periphery. First, they have limited access to domestic competitions in both Palestine and Lebanon, which introduced the cap on Palestinian players. Clubs in the West Bank, which pay decent salaries, have become popular destinations for players of Palestinian origin from all over the world.[112] However, Palestinians from Lebanon cannot even play for those Palestinian clubs, since their host country, Lebanon, does not permit entering Israel, and Palestine cannot be reached without passing through Israeli checkpoints. Second, there is no opportunity to represent either Lebanon or Palestine in international matches. And third, due to the limited mobility of their Refugee Travel Document, there is hardly any opportunity for Palestinians to play for professional football clubs abroad.

Conclusion

This chapter has shown that Lebanese football reflects the many discriminations Palestinians face in Lebanese society—particularly because there is no path towards Lebanese citizenship for Palestinians. At the same time, the significant Lebanese diaspora benefits abroad—in countries such as Australia, Brazil, and the United States—from liberal citizenship laws by obtaining a domestic passport. This marks a stark difference to the experiences of Palestinians in Lebanon.

Lebanon has not fared well in the international sporting arena. Other countries with smaller populations and lower Gross Domestic Product (GDP)—for example, Estonia, Georgia, and Jamaica—have won far more medals at the Olympic Games than Lebanon.[113] The exclusion of Palestinians from the Lebanese sport sector means there are few of the refugee success stories that occur in many other countries—achievements that would help Lebanon improve in international sports. Rather, in international sport, Lebanon relies on diaspora athletes who have never lived in Lebanon—as opposed to Palestinians who were born in Lebanon and grew up in the country—and who sometimes represent Lebanon only because they did not make it into the national team of their adopted country.[114]

This case study sheds light on the precarious situation of stateless athletes in international sport, which is characterized by its nationalistic architecture. Without belonging to a country, or a territory that is recognized by international sport federations, athletes cannot participate in international events, which are competitions between nation states. The number of stateless people in the world, around 10 million, is larger than the entire population size of more than 100 countries.[115] However, it is a small percentage in relation to the total global population of around 7.8 billion, which might explain the lack of interest in the topic in academia and global media as well as in international sport governing bodies.[116]

While this chapter has compared Palestinian football in Lebanon with other Palestinian diaspora communities, future research could look into the experiences of football players from other stateless communities and compare them with the circumstances of Palestinian athletes in Lebanon. An interesting comparative case would be the Rohingya people, a mostly Muslim ethnic minority group in Myanmar that represents about one million people out of the country's total population of 52 million, and that is not eligible for citizenship. The circumstances in which they live in Myanmar has caused most to flee to Bangladesh, where they are denied recognized refugee status.[117]

Another interesting topic for future research would be to analyze policies that have tried to integrate non-nationals and refugees into international sport: one is the residence rule in select sports, such as cricket, netball, rugby league, rugby union, and squash, where proof of residence, regardless of citizenship, qualifies a player to represent a country in international sport. Although stateless people might not have been a main motivation for introducing this rule, they can benefit from it. For example, there were some cases of Palestinian players in the Lebanese national rugby union team who benefited from the residence rule.[118]

A further topic to examine is the creation of the first refugee teams by the International Olympic Committee (IOC) at the 2016 and 2020 Summer Olympics. However, the weakness of the current concept of a "refugee team" is that it is limited to individual sports.[119] Adopting the residence rule into the IOC Charter would make the Olympic Games more inclusive, by also allowing refugees and other immigrants to play in team sports such as football.

Given the current rules in Lebanese football, lack of support from the PFA, and limited access to international sporting competitions, stateless athletes such as the Palestinians in Lebanon are forgotten people in international sports. This is a violation of one of the five fundamental principles of Olympism which are stated in the Olympic Charter: "The practice of sport is a human right. Every individual must have the possibility of practicing sport, without discrimination of any kind."[120]

7

REFUGEES AND FOOTBALL IN THE GLOBAL AND MIDDLE EAST CONTEXTS

Ramón Spaaij

Introduction

This chapter aims to explore the role of football in navigating the challenges associated with forced displacement and resettlement, both globally and within the Middle East context. This attention to the Middle East will help to fill a major gap in the contemporary academic literature: the discrepancy between the research sites of published studies and the locations where the majority of the world's displaced people actually reside, which include parts of the Middle East,[1] most notably Lebanon, Jordan, and Turkey.[2]

Forced displacement is a persistent global challenge. Currently at a record high, 70.8 million children, women, and men were forcibly displaced by early 2019.[3] The causes, drivers, and consequences of forced migration are complex and multidimensional.[4] Displacement experiences and settlement needs for refugees are equally complex and diverse. Amid political and social tensions, new arrivals continually seek new strategies to pursue viable futures.[5]

There are significant interrelationships between forced displacement and the world of sports. In different parts of the world, government and civil society have embraced sports as a space where the wellbeing and settlement of refugees may be supported. Settlement services have long recognized the value of sports in helping people navigate life in a new country. The current Western-centric refugee "crisis," which reflects the predominant context of the "Global North,"[6] has drawn increased attention to the potential contributions of sports and physical education in this regard, including at the supranational level. The year 2018 saw the launch of the "Sport for Protection Toolkit: Programming with Young People in Forced Displacement Settings," a collaboration between the United Nations High Commissioner for Refugees (UNHCR), the International Olympic Committee (IOC), and Terre des hommes.[7] This toolkit guides the work of the Olympic Refuge Foundation, and is used by a range of organizations and stakeholders to better understand and implement effective programming.

In December 2019, the UNHCR and the IOC led a pledge by more than eighty entities to provide access to sporting opportunities to young refugees.[8] The declaration acknowledged that:

> For children and youth uprooted by war or persecution, sport is much more than a leisure activity. It's an opportunity to be included and protected—a chance to heal, develop and grow. Sport can also be a positive catalyst for empowering refugee communities, helping to strengthen social cohesion and forge closer ties with host communities.[9]

Those making the pledge included governing bodies such as the football associations of Bangladesh, England, and the Republic of Ireland, the Council of Southern Africa Football Associations, and the AC Milan Foundation.

Another significant initiative occurred three years earlier when, for the first time in modern Olympic history, a Refugee Olympic Team comprising ten athletes competed in the 2016 Rio Olympic Games. IOC president Thomas Bach described the symbolic value of this initiative as follows:

This will be a symbol of hope for all the refugees in our world, and will make the world better aware of the magnitude of this crisis. It is also a signal to the international community that refugees are our fellow human beings and are an enrichment to society. These refugee athletes will show the world that, despite the unimaginable tragedies they have faced, anyone can contribute to society through their talent, skills and strength of the human spirit.[10]

The contrast between world leaders' enthusiasm for the Refugee Olympic Team and their apathy towards or even vilification of refugees more generally was not lost on some commentators. "The world loves refugees, when they're Olympians," wrote Roger Cohen in the *New York Times*.[11] Uri Friedman observed, "Affirming that 10 athletes are not officially dead to the world of Olympic competition just because they've been separated from their country is, without question, a very small step in addressing the refugee crisis. But it's a small step occurring on a big stage."[12]

Two Refugee Olympic Team members, both swimmers, originated from Syria. Rami Anis, who was born in 1991, fled from Aleppo to Turkey. He subsequently made his way to Greece in a dinghy and eventually reached Belgium, where he was granted asylum in late 2015. Anis trains at the Royal Ghent Swimming Club. The second young Syrian on the 2016 Refugee Olympic Team, Yusra Mardini, has since become a well-known refugee advocate. She and her elder sister fled the Syrian war in 2015, travelling through Lebanon to Turkey before departing for Greece by sea and eventually reaching Germany, where she now lives and trains. Mardini was appointed a UNHCR Goodwill Ambassador in 2017 and has addressed world leaders at various occasions. She was named one of *People*'s 25 Women Changing the World and one of *Time* magazine's 30 Most Influential Teens of 2016. Her book *Butterfly: From Refugee to Olympian, My Story of Rescue, Hope and Triumph* has been published in English and German, and her life story is currently being made into a film.[13] Mardini first and foremost identifies as a competitive athlete: "All of us in the water, you will forget who you are, what you did in your life, and which country you are from… You are a swimmer, and whoever is next to you is a swimmer, too, even if it is a world champion."[14]

She is also on a mission to alter global perceptions of refugees.[15] In her words,

> I want everyone to think refugees are normal people who had their homelands and lost them not because they wanted to run away and be refugees... But because they have dreams in their lives and they had to go. A lot of people in Syria forgot their dreams and I hope everyone will follow their dreams to achieve something good in the future.[16]

Mardini's remarks reflect the hope that drives refugees to seek a better future, which is what sport programs promote. Yet exceptional success stories in media, popular culture, and policy discourse regarding the power of sports to empower refugees may not reflect wider realities. Stone argues that the "role of community sport is in balancing the utopian compensatory desire for a different life with the possibility of shaping the realities of everyday lives to be closer to that which is hoped for."[17] From a critical perspective, the opportunities afforded to refugees in sports may in most cases constitute little more than moments of inclusion and belonging. They may enable refugees to survive as individuals within existing economic and cultural conditions, and to fit into a system that may have the effect of condemning them to a future of precarity.[18] A Somali community activist interviewed by the author expressed this conundrum as follows:

> If we talk about young Somali [refugees], I believe that there are also some negative aspects of sport. The way they think is that it's good to have fun, but many of them also think that it will help them to become millionaires. They look up to those who have built a better life through sport and say, "I want to become a millionaire like them." But very few of them can make it. They are not in a proper situation to live that position. They don't have good services and facilities and education for that. It's a lie. It's a false expression. ... It's good to have ambition but for that whole generation to have that same ambition is not good because they focus less on other ambitions and opportunities. For some young men, it's a way of justifying their failure in education.[19]

Notwithstanding the global attention for the power of sports as a stage or vehicle for hope, belonging, and social inclusion of refugees and asylum seekers, research and scientific knowledge on the topic is still limited. Indeed, there is neither robust evidence of outcomes nor systematic understanding of opportunities, challenges, and lived experiences associated with the role of sports in forced displacement and settlement journeys. Applied research is required to produce a much-needed evidence base to enhance programs, knowledge-sharing, and community capacity-building. Only in the last few years has scientific research on the topic evolved in earnest.[20]

This chapter is structured as follows. First, I will draw on the findings of a systematic literature review to explore the nexus between sports and refugees, with a particular emphasis on football, in the global context. Following this, I will position forced displacement and refugee settlement within the global "sport for development" movement, focusing on "football for development." This will include a critical discussion of the instrumentalization of sports for development purposes. The remainder of the chapter will specifically address refugees and football in the Middle East, by discussing past and present initiatives undertaken in the region. This chapter will provide examples of football-based programs that work with refugee youth in countries such as Jordan, Lebanon, and Turkey. These countries have featured among the main countries of asylum for refugees for some time.[21] This will provide an important corrective to the existing published research on refugees and sports, which is located almost exclusively outside the Middle East (with the exception of Turkey).

In this chapter, I define "refugee" as a person who is unable or unwilling to return to their country of nationality owing to a well-founded fear of being persecuted for reasons of race, religion, nationality, membership of a particular social group, or political opinion.[22] However, I acknowledge the problems with this definition, especially with regard to the risks of essentialization and generalization,[23] the potential failure to see the "normality" and agency of refugees, and the limits of policy categories.[24] For example, it is noteworthy that much scientific research in refugee and forced migration studies "has been conducted in more or less formal connection with (and often funded by)" governmental and nongovernmental organizations (NGOs) that are designed to manage refugee problems.[25] These institutional settings "have had subtle (and sometimes not-so-subtle) effects in shaping the questions that scholars have formulated about displacement and refugee settlement."[26] Bakewell makes the important point that if research uncritically accepts the boundaries of the field imposed by policy categories and priorities, it will tend to confirm and legitimize the assumptions made by powerful actors in the international refugee regime and ensure that these assumptions remain taken for granted.[27]

Forced Displacement, Refugees, and Football: The Global Context

The first comprehensive literature review on the topic, published in 2019, surveyed the state of play in this field of research. In this section, I will summarize the identified themes and research gaps in the global context, drawing on the literature. This will provide a backdrop and reference point for the discussion of refugees and sport/football in the Middle East. The review of contemporary academic literature, which I led with a team of staff and PhD students at Victoria University, comprised eighty-three publications published between 1996 and 2019, spanning fourteen languages.[28] The review included studies of any design that investigated the engagement of refugees and forced migrants in sport and physical activity, as either participants, volunteers, or fans.[29] Publications were identified using electronic databases.[30] The keywords "sport," "physical activity," "exercise," "movement therapy," and "leisure" were combined with refugee descriptor keywords "refugee," "asylum seeker," "forced migrant," and "forced migration" to gain a comprehensive coverage of the scholarly literature. Linguistically and culturally appropriate translations of these search terms were used for foreign-language publication searches. In addition, we searched the reference lists and bibliographies of publications for further relevant references that we followed up.[31] Existing bibliographies were also scrutinized for relevant references. Finally, we contacted researchers in other countries for advice on any additional publications in their native languages that they deemed relevant to the purpose of the review.

The current literature centers around three main themes: health promotion, integration and social inclusion, and barriers and facilitators to participation. There is considerable overlap between these themes in the literature, especially in studies that examine both barriers to participation and the outcomes and benefits of programs. Three main findings of the review are directly relevant for the purpose of this chapter. Firstly, as noted earlier, we found a stark gap between the research sites of the published research and the locations where the majority of the world's displaced people actually reside. The geographical distribution of the academic literature "appears to reflect the Eurocentric bias of global knowledge production in the social and health sciences ... and in sports studies."[32] The highest number of all refugees worldwide during 2018 came from Syria (6.7 million). The main countries of asylum for refugees in 2018 were Turkey, Pakistan, Uganda, Sudan, Germany, Iran, and Lebanon.[33] Lebanon continued to host the largest number of refugees relative to its national population, where one in six people was a refugee. Jordan ranked second (one in fourteen) and Turkey ranked third (one in twenty-two).[34] Yet Turkey and Germany are the only two countries on this list that were represented as research sites in the literature included in this review. None of the published, peer-reviewed literature in the fourteen languages examined had its empirical research located in the Middle East.

Secondly, we found that much of the literature was grounded (unintentionally or subconsciously) in a deficit model that associates refugee status with depressing circumstances, such as trauma, poor health, socioeconomic deprivation, and social isolation. The challenges that refugees face are clearly real and meaningful. However, there is a risk that by framing their experiences solely in those terms, we underestimate the agency of forced migrants.[35] This risk has been documented in refugee and forced migration studies—for example, by Liisa Malkki, who has critiqued the discourse that frames refugees as a "problem for development." In one of the few football studies to explicitly address this issue, Darko Dukic et al. note that "by foregrounding the barriers refugees and asylum seekers experience in sport and in other spheres of life, we, as researchers, tend to overlook and underplay their resilience and ability to overcome such barriers as they navigate life in a new country."[36] The authors sought to shift the lens from a deficit model to a strengths-based approach in order to hold space for what "we can learn from the stories and lived experiences of refugees and asylum seekers who *do* participate in [football]."[37]

In a similar vein, Clifton Evers argues that "sport-based intervention programs being mobilized to 'fix' young people [refugees] is a misplaced agenda."[38] He sensitizes us to our:

> obligation to become intimate with the young people's perspectives to the point of finding out not what the young people 'need' to know but what these young people's skills at life, settlement and well-being may teach us as researchers, as sports facilitators, as youth workers, as community development officers, volunteers, and the like.[39]

Evers' analysis draws attention to a third major finding of the literature review: the instrumentalist tendency in research on refugees and sports. Programs that involve refugees in football are often instrumental in nature and tend to align with contemporary policy priorities. Both policy and research frame football as a means for promoting the wellbeing and integration of refugees in conflict zones, refugee camps, or destination countries. From this perspective, football is essentially a means to an end, that is, "football as medicine" and "football for inclusion and peaceful coexistence." Some studies approach these goals inductively, by focusing on how refugees themselves feel about participating in football programs or how it benefits them. However, with few exceptions,[40] they tend to privilege cognitive perceptions over refugees' emotional and bodily experiences of football.[41] These sensory experiences are critical if we are to truly understand the meaning and impact of football in the everyday lives of refugees.[42]

I would add that these experiences are also key to understanding how football in the context of displacement may serve as a medium for belonging and identity, and a means by which refugees connect to their sense of selves before they became refugees, during their period of displacement, and afterwards during their time of resettlement. For example, Dukic et al. found that for those who grew up playing and watching the game pre-migration, "kicking the ball provided a space of familiarity, confidence and even freedom in the sense of movement and flow," within the context of everyday life in a new country that was "often fraught with uncertainty and full of misunderstanding."[43] They argue that football "acts as a form of expression, almost in the sense of a form of language. This is not, however, clumsy and uncertain attempts to use English, rather it is more akin to speaking one's mother tongue. Hence, even asylum seekers from different linguistic backgrounds can communicate with and through the ball." In doing so, playing football can strengthen elements of one's identity and contribute to "the resilience and confidence required to engage with the uncertainty presented by the host country."[44]

These findings are consistent with recent advances in the literature on "sport for development and peace" and "football for development." Notably, Spaaij and Schaillée, and Scott, have called for more research into participants' affective and bodily experiences in order to understand better the impact of programs in their everyday lives.[45] In the next section, I aim to position refugees within the "football for development" movement.

The Place of Refugees in "Football for Development"

Refugee youth participate in all levels of sports. Their experiences and achievements at the elite level have attracted considerable media attention, as in the aforementioned examples of Yusra Mardini and Rami Anis. At the other end of the spectrum, football and other sports have been shown to appeal to refugees and asylum seekers, especially young males, as a form of grassroots recreation, and as a setting where they can potentially experience a temporary escape from the strains of life,[46] experience moments of social inclusion,[47] and experience a sense of hope and belonging,[48] both in countries of resettlement and in refugee camps.[49] In all of these contexts, there is not a single, unitary "refugee experience."[50]

The gendered nature of sports programming is of particular importance in this regard. Historically, there have been fewer opportunities for girls and women to participate in sports. Refugee girls and women often face amplified barriers to participation—for example, a lack of culturally appropriate facilities, safety concerns, cost, and family and caring responsibilities. A prominent barrier tends to be the perception that may exist within their family or community that sports are not an appropriate activity for women. Research suggests that often it is not these women themselves who see sports participation as inappropriate, but rather others in their family or social environments.[51] Indeed, several young women indicated that they would like the opportunity to take part in sports just like their brothers, cousins, and other male relatives. As I will discuss in more detail below, in response to this demand there is now an increased sports provision for refugee girls and women. For example, PeacePlayers International has developed strategies to increase girls' enrollment among communities where female participation in sports is less common, such as providing sports equipment and culturally appropriate apparel, ensuring private playing space (out of view of men and boys), and increasing family buy-in by engaging them in the process (e.g., home visits).[52]

Prominent among the various manifestations of refugees' engagement in sports are community-based interventions or programs that offer sports (and primarily football) activities. This type of engagement has been the primary subject of scientific research on the topic, with nearly half of the published studies in this field being conducted in such interventions or programs.[53] Interventions or programs that work with refugees and sports are located in a range of settings, such as community health facilities, aid programs, settlement services, participatory action projects, refugee camps, and immigration detention centers. As discussed below, the objectives of these initiatives typically go beyond access to and participation in sports to address wider social, health, and educational goals. As such, they can be situated within the global "sports for development and peace" (SDP) movement.[54] Key development areas addressed in SDP include health, education, employability and entrepreneurship, women's rights, conflict resolution, and peaceful coexistence.

Despite their sometimes lofty ambitions, SDP programs have been criticized for often being little more than band-aid solutions to structural problems. Guest has articulated the critique that "simply distracting people provides only a temporary band-aid—it doesn't really lead to development at all."[55] In a similar vein, Spaaij and Jeanes have argued that SDP programs

> run the risk of being a "bandaid solution," leaving unchanged the root causes of deprivation and marginalization…. [They] may amount to little more than a political instrument for regulating the poor, with the purpose of moving workless young people into the dominant capitalist order, rather than contesting this order and opening up alternative realities.[56]

This critique echoes the broader developmentalist critique of humanitarianism that relief does not address the root causes of conflict and indeed may exacerbate the underlying inequalities that are generated through international economic and political dynamics.[57] I will return to this issue later in the discussion of current SDP programs in the Middle East.

SDP and Forced Displacement

SDP programs have been active in the Middle East for quite some time. One of the most publicized projects in the region is Football for Peace (F4P), a sports-based coexistence project that works with Israeli and Palestinian youth. This project is organized by the University of Brighton in partnership with the British Council. It has been running in towns and villages of the Galilee region of northern Israel since 2001. Coexistence projects of this nature fall under the category of the "normalization" of Israeli-Palestinian relations. As such, they can be critiqued from the standpoint that they work within, and hence reproduce, an oppressive system that, in this particular case, involves major human rights abuses toward Palestinians. F4P has attracted considerable research attention for more than a decade. This body of research has contributed significant insight into the benefits, opportunities, challenges, and limitations of projects of this nature that operate in complex and divided societies.[58]

Another high-profile example of SDP in the Middle East is the Qatari Supreme Committee for Delivery and Legacy's "Generation

Amazing" program, which delivers football facilities and training to vulnerable young people and promotes "sustainable behaviors among young people in Qatar and across the region."[59] A third example of an SDP project in the region is Sport and Play for Traumatized Children and Youth, implemented by the Swiss Academy for Development after the earthquake in Bam, Iran, in December 2003. The project sought to use sports as part of post-disaster psychosocial rehabilitation. Sport and play activities were considered to "fit well into the psychosocial approach because of their potential to build social cohesion, and to encourage community members to interact and communicate with each other."[60] Kunz found:

> The sport and play activities became an important part of the children's lives, bringing some stability into their shattered lives. Friendships emerged that spread into daily life. The activities were not only very much appreciated by the children themselves, but also by their parents, who were relieved to have educational and mental support for their children, thereby further stabilizing family relationships.[61]

Only a small proportion of SDP organizations and programs worldwide work specifically with refugees and internally displaced persons (IDPs). In a previous study, Spaaij and Oxford analyzed two websites to map and take stock of SDP initiatives that explicitly aimed to engage this target group: the International Platform for Sport and Development, and Beyond Sport.[62] Both online platforms provide a virtual space for the SDP community to network and share resources; the first had 532 registered organizations and the latter 2,158 registered projects at the time of the study. From this sample of SDP organizations and projects, we identified twenty-nine organizations and projects that explicitly focused on refugees and IDPs. The websites of these SDP initiatives were analyzed thematically for variables including geographic location, donor location, target population, objective, sports offered, and educational focus.

The SDP programs that work with refugees are diverse in size, structure, and application. Fourteen organizations work in multiple locations. For example, Capoeira4Refugees operates across

200 refugee camps and communities in twenty-one countries, while Right to Play works with more than one million children in twenty countries; both organizations operate in the Middle East. The locations of the SDP initiatives largely reflect where major humanitarian crises have occurred or are ongoing. For example, SDP programs are active in multiple locations in Jordan, Lebanon, Israel, the West Bank, and the Gaza Strip, reflecting the large numbers of people fleeing Syria, but also the long-term refugee status of many Palestinians.[63] The primary stated objectives of the initiatives in this region include providing fun activities to foster a sense of normalcy and distraction from the strains of life, life skills development, teaching resilience, empowerment, and promoting peaceful coexistence. In addition, there are various SDP initiatives in Central and Eastern Africa, which seek to promote peace/healing, social integration, teamwork, leadership, and overcoming boredom. Sports-based initiatives in Europe and North America created in response to the arrival of refugees, who have predominantly fled Syria, Iraq, and Afghanistan, tend to promote anti-racism, community integration, social inclusion, and educational support.

While SDP programs that work with refugees and IDPs utilize a variety of sports and games, football is the most popular sport in SDP programming.[64] Generation Amazing and F4P are cases in point. As O'Gorman and Rookwood posit, the "perceived simplicity, adaptability and global appeal and exposure of football have arguably positioned football as the most exploited sporting tool for development purposes."[65] They coin the term "football for development" to reflect this sentiment. Their work shows that the use of football in development work and corporate social responsibility (CSR) initiatives spans a myriad of organizations across the public and private sectors. This includes, most prominently, football federations and clubs (e.g., the Fédération Internationale de Football Association (FIFA), Asian Football Confederation, FC Barcelona), non-governmental organizations (e.g., Right to Play), international governing bodies (e.g., UNHCR, UNICEF), and multinational corporations (e.g., Adidas, Nike, BP). It also involves current and former star players whose philanthropic organizations support such projects, such as the Leo Messi Foundation and the Didier Drogba

Table 7.1: SDP projects that work with refugees in the Middle East

Organization	Project	Objective	Location	Sport
Right to Play, in partnership with, e.g., the Olympic Refuge Foundation	Multiple, e.g., Creating a Safe Play Space for Children	Education, peaceful coexistence, gender equality	Lebanon, Jordan	Multi-sports and games
Barça Foundation, Cross Cultures Project Association, Ministry of Education of Lebanon	FutbolNet	Peaceful coexistence, gender equality	Lebanon	Football
Spirit of Soccer, in collaboration with the Asian Football Development Project (AFDP)	Spirit of Soccer	Mine risk education	Multiple locations in northern Jordan, Iraq, Lebanon	Football
Capoeira4Refugees	Capoeira4Refugees	Psychosocial development and support	Syria, Palestinian territories, Lebanon, Jordan	Capoeira
Reclaim Childhood	After-school sports programming, summer camp, and coaching clinics	Peaceful co-existence, gender equality	Jordan	Football, athletics, basketball

Generations For Peace	Sport For Peace	Peaceful coexistence	Jordan, Iraq, Lebanon, Yemen	Multi-sports and games
Coaches Across Continents	Life Skills and Employment: Refugees Living in Lebanon	Education, social inclusion	Lebanon	Football, basketball, adapted sports
Taekwondo Humanitarian Foundation	Multiple projects	Education, health	Turkey, Jordan	Taekwondo
World Vision	Football program	Physical and mental health	Jordan	Football
World at Play	World at Play	Social inclusion	Turkey	Multi-sports and games
UEFA Foundation for Children and the Turkish Football Federation	Live Together	Peaceful coexistence, social cohesion	Turkey	Football

Source: International Platform for Sport and Development at www.sportanddev.org; and Beyond Sport at www.beyondsport.org.

Foundation. O'Gorman and Rookwood remind us that football federations have long been involved in activities attaching football with social development. At a club level, FC Barcelona is among the most active of any sports organization in this regard,[66] especially through the Barça Foundation. In the next section, I explore how these features of "football for development" play out in the Middle East. I will focus on the extent and nature of SDP programs that operate at the nexus of football and refugee youth.

Forced Displacement, Refugees, and Football in the Middle East

My starting point for the empirical discussion of refugees and football in the Middle East is a synthesis of the International Platform for Sport and Development website and the Beyond Sport website.[67] Both include comprehensive lists of SDP organizations and programs around the world. These websites enabled me to extract information on sport and football initiatives in the Middle East that work with refugees. The overview in Table 7.1 is not exhaustive and focuses primarily on formal activities; i.e., organized programs and interventions offered by a range of public and private actors. It does not include the full array of informal and semi-organized sports activities that refugees participate in across the region, such as informal play in refugee camps or after-school sports activities. The initiatives listed in Table 7.1 include some ongoing and sustainable projects as well as shorter-term projects. The SDP landscape is dynamic. Programs wax and wane due to short-term funding cycles and the challenging political and economic environment in which some programs operate.

Program Objectives and Approaches

Table 7.1 summarizes eleven SDP programs derived from the International Platform for Sport and Development website and the Beyond Sport website. Nine programs utilize football as part of the sports activities they offer refugee participants, and hence are situated within the "football for development" movement. Four programs are reported to exclusively use football: FutbolNet, Spirit of Soccer, World Vision, and Live Together. Another four programs offer football as part of a more holistic multi-sports and multi-game approach. The latter programs tend to use adapted games and modified rules that align with the program objectives and resonate with the target group. One of these programs, Generations For Peace (GFP), describes its approach as follows:

> Rather than pure sport activities following an official sport code, we use specifically-designed sport-based activities, games and drills which integrate peer-group peace-building education, because our objectives are peace-building outcomes rather than development of sporting skills or competitions. GFP Sport For Peace activities therefore harness the same energy of sport play, and the power of team dynamics and joint effort towards achieving a goal, but with the aim of changing attitudes, behaviour and relationships of the participants.[68]

This philosophy is consistent with what is often referred to in the SDP movement as "plus sport." This refers to projects that give primacy to social, educational, or health objectives, in which sports are used as an entry point or "hook" for development objectives.[69] Spirit of Soccer is another example of a "plus sport" program in the Middle East. The program offers clinics in schools, communities, and refugee camps to educate people about the dangers of landmines and Explosive Remnants of War (ERW). It also delivers safety messages using football games and drills. The football projects in the Za'atari refugee camp in Jordan also embody a "plus sport" philosophy, as the words of Bassam, a Syrian refugee living in Za'atari, illustrate:

> I'm learning how to transform the situation for Syrian children from the trauma they've experienced, creating fun activities for them through football… So we have rehabilitation for the Syrian refugees through sport and particularly football. The children arrive completely devastated. Many of them have seen family members killed before their eyes. The journey to Jordan is a difficult one. So what we're trying to do is through football to remove the sense of fear and give them some sense of normalcy. Football is the most popular sport; it plays the role of the mother. It's the only outlet that children have. It's a very difficult life here in the refugee camp and football alleviates their suffering.[70]

Akin to Bassam's comments, the objectives outlined in Table 7.1 highlight that sports, and football in particular, are considered a means or vehicle for development and change, not an end in themselves. The main stated objectives across the programs are peaceful coexistence (five), education (four), gender equality (three), health (two), social inclusion (two), and psychosocial support (one). These objectives are broadly consistent with the SDP goals discussed earlier, but peaceful coexistence appears to be a comparatively dominant theme in sports-based programs working with refugees and IDPs in the Middle East, relative to SDP programs worldwide. For example, the Union of European Football Associations (UEFA) Foundation and the Turkish Football Federation's Live Together project aims to stimulate peaceful coexistence and social cohesion by encouraging Turkish children and Syrian child refugees to interact while playing football together.[71]

"Plus sport" appears to be the dominant model for sports-based programs that work with refugees in the Middle East. However, some programs, such as Capoeira4Refugees and FutbolNet, also contain elements of "sport plus" in that they also emphasize the traditional sports-development objectives of increased participation and skill development. Capoeira4Refugees, which was founded in Syria in 2007, aims to improve the psychosocial wellbeing of young people impacted by conflict.[72] As part of this mission, the program works to strengthen the sustainability of the local and global capoeira community by supporting talented youth to become "Capoeira Community Changemakers." These objectives can be interpreted as a mix of "plus sport" (psychosocial support) and "sport plus" (capoeira community development). The attention to skill development in this program resonates with the emerging field of "physical literacy," which refers to "the motivation, confidence, physical competence, knowledge and understanding to value and take responsibility for maintaining purposeful physical pursuits/activities throughout the lifecourse."[73] The discourse of physical literacy is emerging in global policy and practice as a rationale for engaging migrants and refugees in sports and physical activity, but it is not (yet) explicitly used in the identified programs in the Middle East.

Gender

Football has traditionally been, and continues to be, a male-dominated industry, and SDP is arguably no different. A noteworthy feature of SDP programs working with refugees in the Middle East is their attention to gender. Three programs explicitly state as an objective the promotion of gender equality. For FutbolNet, this has specifically involved increasing football participation opportunities for girls and training female coaches in the Bekaa Valley in Lebanon.[74] Reclaim Childhood aims to empower refugee and at-risk women and girls in the Jordanian cities of Amman and Zarqa, and in the town of Madaba, through sports and play. It operates after-school sports programming and summer camps for girls and coaching clinics for local women. Even though gender equality is not a stated objective, World Vision's football program in the Azraq refugee camp in Jordan also pays close attention to providing participation opportunities for girls and young women. Its public documentation indicates deliberate efforts to train female coaches to make parents feel more comfortable about letting their daughters join the project and to create "role models" for the participating girls. The project also seeks to enable a "female friendly" environment by "adding plastic sheeting to the fences surrounding the pitches."[75]

These examples illustrate Saavedra's argument that female participation in gender-sensitive SDP programs "has the power to upend what is seen/presented as 'normal' and [has] become a major force for social change beyond sport by challenging gender norms."[76] Globally, there appears to be an increased presence of female participants within programs, either by including girls and women in a co-ed environment, or "empowering" them in a single-sex program.[77] Donors and SDP organizations have been quick to note, or assume, progressive gender-related outcomes. There are clear benefits pertaining to the improved health and education of girls and women by participating in SDP programs. However, critical research has pointed to the complexities of gender relations within football and SDP as a global industry.[78] Research has found that while girls and women can experience empowerment within sport programs, traditional social structures continue to maintain the gender status quo outside of the program.[79] As Hayhurst puts it, the women "must actively work within the constraints of neo-liberal development systems and alter such systems for their own benefit in order to gain increased autonomy: *the onus is on them to resist.*"[80]

Program Geographies

The geographical locations of the eleven programs listed in Table 7.1 broadly reflect the UNHCR statistics regarding which countries host the largest number of refugees relative to their national population, in which Lebanon and Jordan rank first and second, respectively. It also reflects Turkey's status as one of the main countries of asylum for refugees, especially refugees from Syria. Most of the programs operate in multiple locations and countries in the Middle East. Seven of the identified programs operate in Jordan, most notably in the Za'atari refugee camp. Six programs have a presence in Lebanon, especially in refugee camps (e.g., Nahr el-Bared) and in villages in northern and eastern Lebanon. Three of the listed programs are implemented in Turkey. Two programs deliver football and other sports in Iraq, while Syria, Yemen, and the Palestinian territories are each being serviced by one program in Table 7.1.

A contentious feature of "football for development" is that initiatives in the "Global South" are often led by agencies from the "Global North." These agencies include football federations and clubs, NGOs, foreign aid agencies, and educational institutions.[81] In fact, football for development originated as a Global North invention, and is typically justified on the basis of Global North rhetoric and research—though some exceptions exist.[82] Moreover, programs are "arguably delivered primarily for donors who hold unquestioned beliefs in the power of sport to 'do good' in Global South contexts."[83] This had led to considerable critique from scholars that football for development programs contain elements of neocolonialism.[84] On a broad level, many programs appear to perpetuate the neocolonial assumption that all young people from the Global South require saving or fixing,[85] and to undervalue local knowledge and the lived experience of recipients.[86] Moreover, several programs, especially those designed and run by Global North agencies, draw on professionals and volunteers from the Global North to facilitate social change in local communities. As Giulianotti et al. point out, "this approach can be in tension with the need to actively involve intended recipients and local communities in program design and implementation. Shared ownership and locally led and developed SDP projects are considered essential."[87]

Some of these features and tensions are reflected in programs that work with refugees in the Middle East. The types of public and private actors involved in the programs are diverse: international and local NGOs, football federations and clubs, government agencies, and multinational corporations. The two programs that have been designed by Global North actors, Right to Play and the Barça Foundation, operate in local communities and refugee camps in Lebanon and Jordan. FC Barcelona's CSR program is among the most extensive of any sporting organization,[88] whereas Right to Play is a global leader in SDP. The Barça Foundation's FutbolNet project has sought to "support the capacity of the Lebanese public school system to provide assistance to Lebanese host communities and to help refugees cope with the effects of displacement in the fields of education, trauma mitigation and social cohesion."[89] A difference with the heavily critiqued neocolonial approach, however, is that FutbolNet is run as a partnership model in which the Barça Foundation collaborates with an NGO, the Cross Cultures Project Association, and with the Ministry of Education of Lebanon. Similar forms of public-private and private-private partnership can be found in the Spirit of Soccer and Right to Play programs, and in the UEFA Foundation for Children's project in Za'atari refugee camp. The latter has provided football pitches for Syrian refugees in Jordan, followed by a joint effort by KIA Motors and the UEFA Foundation for Children touring around European cities to collect unwanted football boots to donate to Za'atari. Senior Vice President and Chief Marketing Officer Kong-Won Cho of Kia Motors referred to this campaign as "an illustration of the power that football holds."[90]

It is noteworthy that two programs were born in the Middle East: Generations for Peace is Jordanian, while the global Capoeira4Refugees (C4R) was founded in Syria. C4R is of particular interest in this regard because it deploys a martial art that originated elsewhere. Cofounder Ummul Choudhury describes this approach as follows:

> C4R Programmes have been designed for the particular contexts of conflict, war, and the cultural parameters within which we work. But we cannot take the credit for the unique artform that is Capoeira. Brazilian slaves developed Capoeira in the 16th century as a powerful response to their physical oppression: in mind and spirit they could still fight. Recognised by UNESCO for its unique cultural heritage, Capoeira is a living documentation of a people's struggle for freedom, and that specific heritage resonates with the students, those survivors of conflict, that C4R works with today.[91]

Programs like C4R and Generations for Peace are important because they can access and use local wisdom and contextual knowledge to ensure that they meet local needs and reflect local realities.

Conclusion

This study has sought to make a contribution to the knowledge base regarding the nexus between football and refugees, with particular attention being paid to how this plays out in sport/football for development in the Middle East. The empirical data on SDP and football-based programs in countries such as Jordan, Lebanon, and Turkey, coupled with critical examination of development, provides several insights that inform current scholarship on sports/football and forced migration. To date, very little scientific research has been undertaken on the topic in this region, and hence the assumptions and stated objectives articulated by relevant actors are still largely anecdotal and untested. Reflecting global trends, the findings suggest the diversity of development objectives for which football is used as an entry point or "hook," as well as the range of public and private actors that are engaged in this work. Based on the available data, it appears that SDP activity in the

Middle East increasingly engages refugee girls and young women, reflecting a global trend in SDP toward a focus on including girls and women in sport programs.

The limited empirical data suggest that a number of key questions and challenges surrounding the role of sports in empowering refugees and other marginalized population groups hold similar relevance in the Middle East context. The influence of Global North and non-local actors as program organizers, providers, and donors, for example, raises questions about their ability to decenter sport programs to address complex and locally identified problems. Their approach can be in tension with the need to actively involve intended recipients and local communities in programming, and may (inadvertently) further neo-liberal policies that have contributed to the weakening of community capacity. The scope that local stakeholders in affected communities must exert their own agency is a question that warrants further research.

A related feature of SDP programs targeting refugees in the Middle East is that they tend to operate within a discourse of individual empowerment. This reflects a broader concern that such programs place the onus on their targets to be the agents of social change by building their self-efficacy and self-responsibility, but without addressing the structural inequalities that continue to situate refugees in positions of marginalization.[92] Participation in sport can yield significant health, social, and—occasionally—economic benefits, as documented, for example, in the Sport for Protection Toolkit.[93] However, the opportunities afforded to refugees in sports may in most cases constitute moments of inclusion and belonging, or a temporary safe space. They may enable refugees to survive as individuals within, and adapt to, existing economic and cultural conditions, rather than work to challenge and alter those conditions. We thus need to be mindful not to engage in de-contextualized, romanticized generalizations about the "power of sports" for refugees.

Finally, this chapter has warned against framing refugees as a "problem for development," which we typically see reflected in a deficit model that associates refugee status with trauma, poor health, socioeconomic deprivation, and social isolation. The challenges that refugees face are both real and urgent. However, when we frame their experiences solely in those terms, we dismiss the agency of forced migrants. In giving voice to some of the stories and lived experiences of refugees in sports, this chapter has sought to advocate a more strengths-based perspective. At the same time, we need to be mindful that exceptional success stories in media, popular culture, and policy discourse regarding the power of sport to empower refugees may not reflect wider realities. There is, of course, no single, unitary "refugee experience." The different experiences of girls and women, who have only more recently gained access to sport programs, are a case in point.

Further empirical research is required to start addressing the identified research gaps in earnest. In the Middle East context, there is an opportunity to focus future research around two particular limitations of the international literature: firstly, to frame the relationship between refugees and football from a strengths-based perspective; and secondly, to move beyond the instrumentalist tendency in research and policy by prioritizing the lived experiences of participants, with a focus on the affective and embodied dimensions of their experience and the benefits they gain from playing football. Herein may lay some of the significant and original future contributions that research based in the Middle East can make to the study of forced displacement, refugees, and football. I would also encourage future research to engage with critique of the instrumentalization of football and of development and humanitarianism more broadly, in order to advance a more thorough understanding of the complexities of football and forced displacement.

8

MORE THAN JUST A GAME

FOOTBALL IN THE PALESTINIAN BOYCOTT, DIVESTMENT, SANCTIONS MOVEMENT

Aubrey Bloomfield

Introduction

There is an enduring misperception that sports and politics do not, or should not, mix. Despite this, there is a long history of sports being used by repressive regimes as a vehicle for normalization, and also by their challengers as a venue for political protest and activism, perhaps most notably in the international campaign against apartheid South Africa. The launch of the Boycott, Divestment, Sanctions (BDS) movement in 2005 by a coalition of over 170 Palestinian civil society organizations called for a global campaign of boycotts, divestment, and sanctions "against Israel similar to those applied to South Africa in the apartheid era," explicitly noting that it was "inspired by the struggle of South Africans against apartheid."[1] The sports boycott of South Africa is considered to have been one of the most significant aspects of the international anti-apartheid movement,[2] having a powerful psychological and reputational impact on the ruling regime.[3]

The BDS movement targets Israel for its ongoing violations of international law and Palestinian human rights. In particular, it calls for an end to the occupation and colonization of all Arab lands, full equality for Palestinian citizens of Israel, and the right of return for Palestinian refugees. It was born out of frustration with the continued failure on the part of the international community, as well as the Palestinian establishment, to hold Israel to account for its actions. It also represents a challenge to the ongoing evasion of responsibility by international parties to act against the occupation on the grounds that this would interfere with a "peace process" that would ostensibly produce a two-state solution—despite decades of negotiations yielding only an entrenchment of the occupation through expanded settlements. BDS seeks to raise the costs of the status quo for Israel in the same way that the anti-apartheid movement did for the South African regime. This is not to say that BDS is the same as the movement that targeted South Africa, or that South African and Israeli policies and practices are the same.[4] Instead, the South African example acts as both a source of inspiration to the BDS movement and a useful historical precedent for considering BDS strategies. While attributing the success of particular BDS actions directly to activist pressure is not always possible, a glance at even an incomplete BDS timeline reveals the breadth of its activities worldwide.[5] All these activities have led to growing negative publicity and pressure for Israel and those who are complicit in helping maintain or normalize its occupation.

This chapter examines the relationship between the BDS movement and the use of football, the world's most popular sport (and the most popular sport in both Palestine and Israel), as a site for activism against the Israeli occupation. As a New Zealander deeply cognizant of the importance of sport in the anti-apartheid movement given the history of sporting contact between New Zealand and South Africa, I aim to offer a global, outsider perspective on the role of football in BDS as an international solidarity movement.

In doing so, I will argue that the conditions exist to make a sports boycott of Israel a viable and effective part of the BDS movement, as it was in the campaign against apartheid South Africa.

The Palestinian BDS National Committee is the coalition of civil society organizations that acts as the focal point and coordination body for the global BDS movement, providing support to the various BDS campaigns around the world. Activists and groups within the movement can decide how best to apply BDS in their particular contexts, so long as they carry out their activities in keeping with the movement's principles and objectives. To date, BDS efforts have largely focused on divestment and consumer, academic, and (non-sports-related) cultural boycotts. Football, and sports more generally, have been underutilized and understudied aspects of the movement. However, in both areas, this has started to change, albeit to differing extents. Given the important psychological impact sporting boycotts and sanctions had on the identity of the ruling white regime in apartheid South Africa, they have the potential to significantly raise the cost of the status quo for Israel. Israel's political identity has always been grounded in deep identification with the West, and any challenge to Israel's place among or access to Western nation states prompts deep anxiety in the Israeli body politic. Israelis are thus particularly sensitive to anything that might jeopardize this connection, as would be the case if its sports teams were prevented from competing in Europe. They are also sensitive to anything that might disrupt Israel's connection to international sports more broadly and the impact this would have on the country's global image.

The BDS Sports Boycott

While not featuring as prominently as in the international campaign against apartheid South Africa, sports have not been entirely absent from the BDS movement. At least as far back as 2002, prior to the BDS launch, groups such as the Palestine Solidarity Campaign in the United Kingdom and the Muslim Association of Britain were calling for a sports boycott of Israel until it complied with international law and organized demonstrations when the

Israeli national football team and club teams played in Europe.[6] In 2010, a post on the website of the Palestinian Campaign for the Academic and Cultural Boycott of Israel, a key part of the BDS movement, speculated that a sports boycott "could exercise the same leverage on Israel that it did for nearly 30 years with South Africa" and would "intensify the world's spotlight" on Israel.[7] Despite this, prior to the campaign that began in 2011 against Israel hosting the men's 2013 UEFA European Under-21 Championship football tournament, the role of sports in Palestinian solidarity efforts was largely limited to isolated and infrequent calls for boycotts and sanctions, and protests at sports events. There was no concerted attempt by the BDS movement to capitalize on the potential of sports as a site for protest and resistance. But although the UEFA campaign did not succeed in having the tournament moved or boycotted, it did succeed in highlighting the potential for sports to increase pressure on Israel and drawing attention to Israel's treatment of the Palestinians.

Since then, sports have formed an increasingly significant part of the BDS movement. As I will discuss in more detail later, football has been at the heart of this. This has included a successful campaign against Israel hosting part of the men's UEFA 2020 European Football Championship, ongoing calls for Israel to be suspended from the Fédération Internationale de Football Association (FIFA), campaigns calling on other countries' national teams not to play football in Israel, campaigns against companies sponsoring the Israel Football Association (IFA), as well as regular pro-Palestinian demonstrations by football fans during games against Israeli teams. While sports boycott efforts have largely centered on football to date, other sports have also been important sites for activism and resistance. These include the decision in 2017 by six National Football League (NFL) players to boycott an Israeli government-sponsored public relations trip to Israel,[8] the campaign against Israel hosting the start of the 2018 Giro d'Italia cycling race,[9] and, in 2019, following activist pressure, the Portland Trail Blazers basketball team ending its partnership with a military contractor that supplied rifle scopes to the Israel Defense Forces.[10]

Although it is becoming a growing part of the BDS movement, the impact of the sports boycott, both real and potential, has received relatively little attention from scholars. Notable exceptions to this include Malcolm MacLean's discussion of sports boycotts targeting South Africa and their potential use against Israel; Jon Dart's work on whether a sports boycott of Israel would be anti-Semitic or anti-Zionist, the role of sport in Israeli soft power, and the motivations of activists involved in the BDS sports boycott; and Francesco Belcastro's examination of how sports are becoming an increasingly contested sphere in the Palestine-Israel conflict.[11] A number of journalists have also drawn comparisons between South Africa and Israel in highlighting Israel's possible vulnerability to a sports boycott.[12] Other studies have covered the place of sports in the Palestine-Israel conflict but have either not explicitly considered the role of the BDS movement or have not addressed it in detail.[13] MacLean's analysis is particularly instructive, highlighting important differences between the South African and BDS sports boycotts: that the groups calling for BDS are civil society organizations, not national liberation organizations as was the case in South Africa; that sports in Israel are less overtly discriminatory than they were in South Africa; and that because Israel and Palestine exist as separate political entities, the BDS movement is not able to point to alternative sporting bodies to replace Israeli ones in international institutions, as was the case with non-racial sporting bodies in South Africa. In addition, MacLean also points out that the geopolitical context was significantly different at the time of the anti-apartheid movement, when decolonization resulted in newly independent states often sympathetic to the cause, and the sporting world was less shaped by corporate and market interests. Nowadays, the waning significance of postcolonial solidarity and the greater corporate and market influence in sports mean that individual states are less likely to take direct action in support of a sports boycott of Israel. However, despite these differences constituting potential limitations for the BDS movement, MacLean did note in 2014 that given "the combination of football's cultural significance in Israel combined with Israel's powerful desire to normalise its global position and role," a sports boycott could potentially have a significant psychological effect on Israel.[14] Indeed, there is now a growing sports boycott, centered on football, that is increasingly challenging Israel's ability to successfully access the normalizing power of international sporting competition.

With the international community remaining largely indifferent or unwilling to act, Israel faces few real consequences for its occupation. As a mass spectacle and arguably the closest thing there is to a universal language, sports present a prime site for activism. As the US Campaign for Palestinian Rights argued after the NFL players boycotted the trip to Israel:

> the sporting boycott of South Africa played a critical role in de-normalizing apartheid by impacting the country where it would be felt most—teams and athletes refused to compete with the apartheid state in cricket, rugby, [football], many other sports, and the Olympics. The Palestinian call for the cultural and academic boycott of Israel includes the sports boycott as an extremely effective instrument of change.[15]

The BDS movement provides an outlet through which people around the world can engage in tangible actions designed to increase pressure on Israel.

The South African Sports Boycott

The international anti-apartheid movement began in the late 1950s as the repression of internal opposition to apartheid in South Africa continued to intensify. In 1958, African National Congress leader Albert Luthuli called for a global boycott of apartheid South Africa, and the anti-apartheid movement launched the following year. Although led by civil society, as the international movement grew it received support from countries around the world, including many newly independent nations. Sports were a feature in the anti-apartheid movement from the beginning, with efforts predating Luthuli's call. A 1956 announcement by the South African government that sporting activities should adhere to the policy of separate development helped to spur the growth of the sports boycott campaign.[16] This meant there was to be no interracial competitions, races were to organize their sporting activities separately, teams should not be racially mixed, and visiting athletes and teams should also respect these practices. The sports boycott campaign called for teams not to play in South Africa, to bar South African teams from playing in other countries, for South Africa to be expelled from international sporting organizations, and to cut off sporting ties with countries that continued to play against South Africa.

It achieved its first victory in 1956 when the International Table Tennis Federation expelled the white South African Table Tennis Union after black spectators were banned from a venue during an international tour and recognized the non-racial South African Table Tennis Board as the sole controlling body of the sport in South Africa.[17] Having been expelled earlier from the Confederation of African Football (CAF), the white Football Association of South Africa was then suspended from FIFA in 1961. Although it received a temporary reprieve in 1963 due to the support of the predominantly Western nations that held the power in the international organization, its suspension was reinstated in 1964. After previous failed efforts, South Africa was also excluded from the Olympic Games in Tokyo the same year, with the government refusing to abide by the International Olympic Committee's 1963 demand that it respect the policy of non-discrimination in the committee's charter.[18] The large number of former colonies, particularly in Africa, that achieved independence during the 1950s and 1960s aided these efforts. Many of these newly independent nations supported the anti-apartheid movement and as they joined international sporting institutions, they helped to shift voting power away from the white majority nations that tended to support the apartheid regime. Their presence was crucial to the reinstatement of South Africa's suspension from FIFA.

In addition to geopolitical changes, the sports boycott movement was also aided by organizational developments and political incidents. In 1959, Dennis Brutus and others established the South African Sports Association (SASA), which sought the proper recognition of black athletes by international sporting bodies and white sporting bodies in South Africa. Yet the lack of success with this approach, along with the Sharpeville massacre in 1960 and the arrest of several key leaders of the African National Congress (including Nelson Mandela in 1963), helped lead to the sports boycott movement adopting a more broadly political stance.[19] This was encapsulated under the rubric, "no normal sport in an abnormal society." In 1963, the leadership of SASA, including Brutus, formed the South African Non-Racial Olympic Committee (SAN-ROC), which sought the complete sporting isolation of South Africa.[20] Growing repression in South Africa, including the shooting and imprisonment of Brutus, led to SAN-ROC being forced into exile in England.[21] From there it linked up with other organizations in the United Kingdom and around the world and helped the sports boycott campaign grow in strength throughout the 1970s and 1980s. Importantly, the focus of the sports boycott campaign had now shifted from simply seeking the deracialization of South African sports to becoming one of a range of strategies in the broader effort to pressure the South African regime into abandoning the entire apartheid system.[22] South Africa was formally expelled from the Olympic movement in 1970, from FIFA in 1976, and from other international sporting bodies including boxing, basketball, swimming, track and field, weightlifting, and wrestling between the late 1960s and late 1970s.[23] The growing profile of the sports boycott was aided by the support it received from a number of international bodies and organizations, including the Organisation of African Unity (the precursor to the African Union) and the Supreme Council for Sport in Africa (formed by sports ministers across Africa), as well as agreements adopted by the United Nations and the Commonwealth Heads of Government intended to discourage sporting contact with South Africa. By the 1980s, South Africa's participation in international sporting competitions was increasingly difficult "and virtually the only teams entering South Africa were the rebel sides who received exorbitant sums to compete in pseudointernationals."[24]

Arguably the most significant aspect of the sports boycott campaign was the efforts to curtail bilateral sporting engagement with South Africa's traditional rivals Australia, New Zealand, and England. Controversies such as the Basil D'Oliveira affair in

England, and the South African requirement that no Māori players be selected for touring New Zealand rugby teams, significantly elevated the profile of the sports boycott and brought South Africa's apartheid policies into the general public's consciousness. D'Oliveira was a "colored" South African-born cricketer who had moved to England to play.[25] His non-selection for England's tour of South Africa in 1968–9 caused massive protests, and his eventual selection in place of an injured player led to the collapse of the tour following the South African government's opposition to his inclusion.[26] In New Zealand, opposition to the exclusion of Māori from touring teams was centered "on the claim that the South Africans were exporting apartheid with the result that New Zealand's allegedly exemplary race relations were being undermined."[27] The mass demonstrations in the United Kingdom against rugby and cricket tours in 1969–70 (with the latter being successfully stopped) and expulsion from the International Olympic Committee in 1970 were significant blows against apartheid sport. As international opposition to contact with South Africa hardened, anti-tour protests became less about selection policies (which South Africa relaxed to a limited extent) and more about apartheid as a whole. South African rugby tours of Australia in 1971 and New Zealand in 1981 were also greeted by massive protests involving tens of thousands of demonstrators, with MacLean arguing that "the 1981 anti-tour campaign in some ways represents the global apex of anti-apartheid solidarity protests around the cultural boycott."[28] It effectively forced the whole country to confront the apartheid issue and take a stance.

South Africa's international sporting isolation was never total, and it was an ongoing struggle to protect the gains that had been made and to advance the movement further. Yet, as noted earlier, sports are considered one of the most significant factors in generating attention and pressure regarding racial discrimination in South African sports and the system of apartheid more broadly. As John Nauright writes, "a measurable impact of sports sanctions is hard to determine as it is not possible to quantify an exact effect. It is possible to suggest, however, that the psychological impact of sporting sanctions had perhaps the most potent role in undermining white South African confidence and complacency."[29] Indeed, a survey of white South Africans in 1977 ranked the lack of international sports due to the boycott campaign as one of the top three most damaging consequences of apartheid.[30] MacLean argues that the "sports boycott was one of the major successes of the international anti-apartheid campaign."[31] Nixon notes that its power came from its ability "to grip the media by generating spectacle" and involve a "vast swath of society largely indifferent to international politics or ignorant of the issues at stake."[32] South Africa's sporting isolation helped to energize the wider struggle against apartheid and was arguably as powerful as the economic boycott because it disrupted South Africa's ability to take part in prestigious international sporting competitions.[33] This participation, and South Africa's membership in international sporting bodies as equals in the world of sports, had served to bestow a measure of respectability on the South African regime and its policy of apartheid.[34] The sports boycott alone did not bring about the end of apartheid but rather formed a highly effective part of the broader movement of boycotts, divestment, and sanctions targeting South Africa that went on for over three decades. In 1988, Sam Ramsamy, the executive chair of SAN-ROC, commented that while opponents of apartheid were under:

> no illusions that the sports boycott by itself can end apartheid ... the knowledge that the vast majority of sportspersons around the world would refuse to "play with apartheid" has greatly undermined the legitimacy of the government, boosted the morale of South African blacks, and encouraged the resistance at all levels.[35]

Football in Palestine and Israel

Despite their geographic proximity, Israeli football teams compete as part of the European football confederation, the Union of European Football Associations (UEFA), while Palestinian football teams compete as part of the Asian Football Confederation (AFC). Domestically, Israel and Palestine have separate football competitions, although Palestinian citizens of Israel (both players and coaches) have moved to Palestinian football leagues and Palestinian football players have also gone to play in Israeli leagues. In addition, Palestinian citizens of Israel play for teams in Israeli football competitions and even for the Israeli national team.

Football is the most popular sport in Israel and domestic competitions in particular have "become an integral part of the cultural life of many Israelis."[36] Israel has not enjoyed much high-profile success in international football—certainly not to the same extent as South African rugby and cricket teams. But there have been some limited successes with the men's national football team qualifying for the FIFA World Cup in 1970 and the Olympic Games in 1976. Israeli club teams also compete in European competitions after having been admitted to UEFA in 1994. While Yair Galily and Amir Ben-Porat argue that sports are not a primary concern in contemporary Israel, they go on to say that "sport in Israel is related to the national morale: the participation of the soccer selection in international games, the Maccabi Tel-Aviv basketball club in Europe, and athletes' achievements in the Olympic Games, were hailed as national successes. When an Israeli team is playing, the entire nation holds its breath."[37]

The prospect of a sports boycott is not new for Israel. Prior to the early 1970s, Israel was a member of Asian sporting federations and competed in Asian regional competitions. Political tensions between Arab and Muslim nations and Israel over the occupation of Arab lands, which only increased following the 1973 Arab-Israeli war, led to teams and athletes refusing to compete against Israel and eventually to its expulsion from the AFC in 1974, the Asian Games Federation in 1978, and ultimately all Asian sports federations. This is why Israel ended up a member of European sports bodies such as UEFA.

When the possibility of a sports boycott of Israel is raised, there are a number of common responses. One is that sports should instead be used as a tool to build bridges and strengthen co-existence between Israelis and Palestinians,[38] a stance supported by the Israeli state and international sporting bodies. Examples of this approach include FC Barcelona's 2013 "peace tour" of Israel and Palestine at the invitation of former Israeli president Shimon Peres and former FIFA president Sepp Blatter's proposal for a "peace match" between the Israeli and Palestinian national teams. Yet this glosses over the wider context of occupation, systematic racism, and oppression that characterizes the relationship between Israel and the Palestinians. As Dart's examination of a number of sport-for-peace schemes in Palestine-Israel found, "most sport-for-peace activity is little more than a smokescreen and propaganda tool for the Israeli government in their continued systematic subjection of the Palestinian people."[39] Palestinian footballers have also criticized such proposals as a "public-relations spectacle bringing no substantive change."[40] Another argument is that sports are not important enough to Israel and Israelis for a sports boycott to have any real impact.[41] International sports are certainly not as important as they were in apartheid South Africa, whose teams were far more successful in their preferred sports codes—cricket and rugby—than Israel is in football. But as Galily and Ben-Porat highlight above, it still matters to Israelis, even those not interested in sports, because it is read as a measure of international prestige. Denying Israel the ability to compete internationally would serve as a powerful symbol of international intolerance for its treatment of the Palestinians.

One of the strongest arguments used by opponents of a sports boycott is that Palestinian citizens of Israel are not excluded from playing for Israeli football teams in the same way that black people were excluded from South African teams in the early decades of apartheid.[42] Indeed, it was the systematic racial discrimination in South African sports that provided the initial justification for the sports boycott. However, as outlined earlier, the focus was soon broadened to explicit opposition to the whole apartheid system. By contrast, discussions of racism in Israeli football are often limited to the notorious club Beitar Jerusalem and its hardcore group of supporters, "La Familia." Beitar—originally founded by the youth wing of the "Revisionist" Zionist movement, of which former Israeli prime minister Benjamin Netanyahu's Likud is the party-political arm—is the only Israeli club not to have signed an Arab player. Beitar is also one of the most popular clubs in Israel. At least at one point it could count an estimated one-fifth of all Israeli football fans as its supporters, including members of Israel's political establishment such as Netanyahu.[43] Despite attempts by authorities to crack down on La Familia's anti-Arab racism and attempts by various owners to reform the club, the violent and racist behavior of La Familia has not changed, and the club is still yet to sign an Arab player. In late 2020, the announcement that Emirati royal Sheikh Hamad bin Khalifa al-Nahyan was set to purchase a 50 percent stake in Beitar prompted a backlash from fans angry at Arab ownership of the club.[44] This followed the normalization of relations between Israel and the United Arab Emirates (which was also accompanied by a football cooperation agreement), a move strongly condemned by Palestinians who saw the Arab state as having abandoned the Palestinian cause.[45] Beyond Beitar, racism is hardly absent in the rest of Israeli football.[46] Yet Haim Kaufman and Galily, among others, have claimed that "in terms of representative teams, it can be justifiably argued that the sports field is practically the only place where the State of Israel can be defined as a state of all its citizens."[47] It is true that Palestinian citizens of Israel can feature and have featured prominently in Israeli club and national football teams. But the above claim arguably says more about the systematic level of discrimination in the rest of Israeli society than it does about the lack of it in Israeli football. Furthermore, it only reveals part of the picture. To succeed in Israel, Arab-Palestinian players are "expected to swallow their pride and tolerate racist taunts."[48]

According to Tamir Sorek, football functions as an "integrative enclave" in which Palestinian citizens of Israel can achieve a measure of integration and acceptance within Jewish-Israeli society, including long-term involvement at all levels of competition that is not available to them elsewhere.[49] Yet Sorek goes on to point out that this has not led to wider acceptance of Palestinian citizens within Israeli society or to a change in the discriminatory nature of the Israeli state. In addition, Eran Shor and Yuval Yonay have highlighted the censure that Palestinian footballers in Israel face if they attempt to make any critical comments about the political situation, as opposed to the positive reaction if they speak favorably about Israel.[50] In contrast, they argue Jewish athletes are largely given free rein by the media and sports fans. Ilan Tamir and Alina Bernstein have also shown that despite the narrative of integration and broad representation in Israeli football, most Jewish fans consistently downplay the contributions of Palestinian footballers and oppose their very presence.[51] The result is an environment in which the participation of Palestinian footballers is seemingly either simply tolerated while their achievements are downplayed, and they themselves are depoliticized, or their presence and the veneer of diversity and inclusiveness that it provides are used as a propaganda tool by those seeking to deflect criticism of Israel. As Shor and Yonay argue, the "participation of Arab athletes and teams in Israeli sports, is exploited to boost a desirable political image of Israel as an egalitarian society."[52] Given the discrimination and oppression that characterize the political system in Palestine-Israel, Sorek contends that "by depoliticizing the Arab–Jewish encounter, sport joins other uncommon isolated enclaves in Israel ... in which the Jewish political advantage is suspended and replaced only temporarily by an egalitarian interaction based on commercial, professional, or sportive criteria."[53] The broader nature of the Palestinian-Jewish relationship is left unchanged. As Palestinian footballer Iyad Abu Gharqoud notes, it is only when the injustices of the existing system are confronted and dismantled, as the BDS movement seeks to pressure Israel into doing, that sports can truly be used as a means for reconciliation and bridge-building.[54]

The issue for the BDS movement is not simply Israel's treatment of its Palestinian citizens but its treatment of Palestinians more broadly. Despite the rhetoric regarding a two-state solution, what effectively exists is a binational state throughout Palestine and Israel under a system of Israeli apartheid rule privileging Jews over Palestinians.[55] The Israeli apartheid regime exercises ultimate control over the lives of both its Palestinian citizens and the roughly five million Palestinians in the occupied territories of East Jerusalem, the West Bank, and Gaza. While Israel and Palestine have separate football competitions and are separate members of FIFA, the Israeli occupation still has a significant impact on Palestinian football. Israeli restrictions on the movement of people in and out of Gaza have regularly and arbitrarily prevented players from taking part in the FIFA-recognized Palestine Cup between the champions of the West Bank and Gaza football leagues and have often prevented the cup from taking place altogether.[56] Palestinian footballers are frequently subjected to restrictions on their freedom of movement that hinders their ability to train and compete, and have been attacked, detained, and even killed by Israeli authorities.[57] The case of Mahmoud Sarsak, a Palestinian footballer who went on a hunger strike during the three years he was detained by Israel without charge or trial, attracted widespread international attention in 2012. Meanwhile, Palestine's sporting infrastructure and resources have also been affected through the bombing of stadiums and the disruption of the movement of equipment.[58] So while Israeli and Palestinian football may be technically separate in that they have their own clubs and national teams, and are independently members of international football bodies, the nature of the Israeli occupation means that Israel has a significant and destructive influence over Palestinian football. In addition, there are six Israeli football clubs located in West Bank settlements that are illegal under international law, while a seventh club plays some of its games in a settlement. The presence of the clubs constitutes a violation of FIFA statutes, which state that a national association can only operate clubs in the territory of another national association with its consent, something the Palestine Football Association (PFA) has not granted. A report by Human Rights Watch in 2016 argued that by allowing the IFA to base clubs in the illegal settlements and by giving financial contributions to the IFA, FIFA is actively supporting the illegal settlements, and is contradicting the human rights commitments it has affirmed.[59]

The limitations of the claim that Israeli football represents an inclusive sphere, the reality of Israel's treatment of Palestinian footballers and football infrastructure, and the presence of Israeli club teams in illegal settlements all form an important part of the case for a sports boycott of Israel. Indeed, they have been the basis of calls by the BDS movement and the PFA for FIFA to suspend or even expel Israel. But the sports boycott of South Africa had a broader focus. It was not simply concerned with protesting racial discrimination in South African sports or the exclusion of athletes of color from teams playing South Africa, even if it was initially articulated that way. It was also about demonstrating opposition to

213

the whole system of apartheid and to those who represented or supported it. Kaufman and Galily argue that sports in the early years of the State of Israel had a "functional use for the new state's foreign needs: forging friendly ties, cooperation with other nations, spreading propaganda, and gaining respect and prestige" and that though international sporting success was hard to come by, Israel's "participation and opportunity to carry the national flag as an equal to all other nations was perceived as more important."[60] Kaufman and Galily claim that the enthusiasm surrounding seeing the Israeli flag fly as an equal in international sporting competition has faded, that spreading national propaganda is no longer the objective of Israeli national teams, and that they now include Palestinian and other non-Jewish citizens of Israel. Despite this, the reality is not so convenient. Israeli football teams still function as a form of propaganda on the international stage. They convey both the idea that Israel is a nation like any other and that it does not discriminate against its Palestinian citizens. Sorek argues that sports are an "effective vehicle for Israel to rehabilitate its image with the international community" because they provide an "ideal opportunity for Israel to present itself as a normal country."[61] Dart highlights how Israel uses sporting events, such as the men's 2013 UEFA European Under-21 Championship, as part of its broader soft power strategy to bolster its international image, with sports providing cover for "the legitimisation of the status quo and unequal power relations."[62] International football offers a high-profile stage for the production and expression of national identity and can play a key role in influencing how nations are perceived. The sight of Israeli football teams competing regularly in Europe, the Israeli flag being flown and the anthem being played alongside those of other nations, Israeli athletes walking in the Olympic opening ceremony alongside athletes from around the world, athletes going to Israel to compete in international tournaments, and Israel's membership in international sporting bodies all serve to make Israel's participation on the world stage quotidian and unremarkable. In these moments Israel is not seen as a nation engaged in a violent, decades-long occupation, or one that is responsible for egregious and ongoing violations of international law and Palestinian human rights. Instead, it is seen as just another competitor—imperfect, perhaps, but no better or worse than the nations it is competing against, playing sport like everyone else. Because of the powerful legitimizing and normalizing role that international and European club football plays for Israel, disrupting its access to this function could prove to have a significant symbolic and reputational impact.

Football in the BDS Movement

As noted earlier, football has been central to the BDS sports boycott. UEFA's decision in 2011 to award Israel hosting rights for the 2013 UEFA European Under-21 Championship football tournament was significant in that the tournament represented "the most high-profile international sporting event held in the country since the 1968 Paralympic Games" and offered "a significant opportunity for the state to promote itself on the international stage."[63] It was also significant in that the subsequent campaign against the decision—which involved BDS groups; Palestinian football clubs, players, and officials; and international footballers, including former Sevilla star Frédéric Kanouté—"marked a shift in the Palestinian BDS campaign" and appeared "to be the first coordinated BDS attempt to address a multilateral sports event."[64] Although the tournament (as well as the women's UEFA European Under-19 Championship) went ahead in Israel, the campaign showed that football, and sports in general, provides a powerful means for shining a spotlight on the realities of the Israeli occupation and disrupting its ability to sportswash its international image. A similar campaign launched in 2014 against Israel's bid to host part of the men's 2020 UEFA European Football Championship again brought together BDS groups, Palestinian NGOs and sports clubs, and Kanouté in criticism of the bid. The criticism gained strength in the wake of Israel's 2014 war on Gaza, and Israel's bid was ultimately unsuccessful, with the BDS movement claiming that its campaign "undoubtedly played a role" in UEFA's decision.[65] These campaigns helped to increase the momentum and profile of the BDS sports boycott. The highest-profile action in the sports boycott to date has been the campaign to have Israel sanctioned by FIFA. Since at least

2013, there have been calls by both the BDS movement and the PFA for FIFA to suspend or even expel Israel.[66]

Although these efforts have been led institutionally by the PFA as Palestine's official representative in FIFA, the parallel activism of the BDS movement has helped to generate further publicity and increase the pressure on FIFA and Israel. The campaign has centered on Israeli restrictions on freedom of movement of Palestinian players and officials, disruption of the import of football equipment, interference in the construction of football facilities, the clubs based in the illegal settlements, and racism in Israeli football. Since the BDS movement and the PFA began calling for FIFA to sanction Israel, the story has largely been one of PFA president Jibril Rajoub repeatedly backing down from threats to call a vote in FIFA's annual congress on Israeli membership and compromises resulting in the creation of toothless monitoring committees designed to resolve issues relating to Israeli restrictions on Palestinian football. Along the way, FIFA has avoided taking action on the above issues (the most prominent being the status of the settlement clubs). All of this has been accompanied by intense Israeli lobbying to avoid any sanction. Eventually, in 2017, FIFA decided not to do anything about the settlement clubs. As I wrote at the time, while FIFA said it must remain neutral on political matters, it in fact made a political decision not to sanction Israel.[67] In doing so, it effectively legitimized the settlements and ignored previous precedent in opting not to apply its own rules when it was politically inconvenient to do so. The PFA appealed FIFA's decision to the Court of Arbitration for Sport but the appeal was dismissed in 2018. Nevertheless, the campaign generated sustained international attention on Israeli settlements and the occupation more broadly. This is unlikely to be the end of the issue, with no real sign of Israel making changes to address its destructive impact on Palestinian football, the status of the settlement clubs, or its violations of international law and Palestinian human rights more broadly.

The campaign against Israel's FIFA membership has helped to spur further action and significantly raised the profile of the BDS sports boycott. In 2018, Adidas ended its sponsorship of the IFA following a successful campaign by the BDS movement centered around the presence of the clubs in the illegal Israeli settlements.[68] Since then, a similar campaign has targeted new IFA sponsor Puma. The biggest success in the sports boycott to date has been the cancellation of a 2018 friendly match between the Argentine and Israeli national football teams in Israel. This followed a campaign launched by the BDS movement, and later joined by the PFA. Originally planned for Haifa, the match was moved to Jerusalem and was set to be played in Beitar Jerusalem's stadium, built on land once home to a Palestinian village later destroyed by Israeli forces in 1948.[69] The BDS campaign called on the Argentine national team not to play Israel "until Palestinians' human rights are respected."[70] Argentina eventually withdrew from the match as pressure mounted on its players and its football association. A subsequent campaign against another friendly football match between Argentina and Uruguay in Israel was unsuccessful in 2019. In addition, throughout the past decade there have also been regular pro-Palestinian demonstrations by football fans, predominantly in Europe. Most notably, fans of the Scottish club Glasgow Celtic raised over £170,000 for Palestinian charities after being fined by UEFA for flying Palestinian flags en masse to raise awareness of the BDS movement during a 2016 UEFA Champions League qualifier against Israeli club Hapoel Be'er Sheva.[71]

The Future of the BDS Sports Boycott

The strength of the Israeli reaction to the highest-profile action (the campaign for FIFA sanction) and the biggest success (the cancellation of the game against Argentina) in the BDS sports boycott shows how seriously Israel takes the threat of exclusion from international football. The reaction to the threat of expulsion from FIFA was labelled "almost hysteric," given the significance of the possible consequences.[72] The extensive diplomatic efforts included lobbying sports ministers and foreign ministries as well as the heads of football associations and Olympic committees from around the world, getting famous Israeli athletes and high-profile Jews to use their networks to influence association heads, and even allegedly enlisting the White House to put pressure on FIFA Council members, as well as trying to promote Israel's case in the media.[73] The negative publicity caused by the cancellation of the Argentina match also prompted Netanyahu to unsuccessfully lobby then Argentine president Mauricio Macri to get it reinstated.[74] The problem for Israel is that in being forced to engage with BDS campaigns it has already partly lost the public relations battle. When Israel responds "with panic and outrage to any BDS advance, however small, Israel is repeatedly affirming that yes, BDS is working, and working really well."[75] The debate and publicity engendered by BDS is damaging in itself, regardless of whether the action is successful. And as diplomatic cables have shown, Israeli officials are aware of the effectiveness of the sports boycott in generating attention for the BDS movement.[76]

The sports boycott was part of the campaign against apartheid South Africa from the beginning, whereas it is only in the past decade that it has become a growing aspect of the BDS movement. Early victories in the South African case helped to raise the profile of the boycott. The same level of success (such as having Israel suspended or expelled from international sporting institutions) has so far eluded the BDS movement in the sporting sphere but it is gaining traction. Going forward, a key tension the movement will have to navigate is between itself and the Palestinian establishment. As MacLean points out, "the groups calling for BDS are not national liberation movements similar to those in South Africa but civil society institutions that are often critical of the 'official' national liberation groups, now dominated by those gathered around Fatah and around Hamas."[77] In addition, the fractured nature of Palestinian politics also means that there is no single unified political leadership that provides representative political support to the BDS movement. Even the Palestinian establishment (in the form of the Palestine Liberation Organization and the Palestinian Authority), with the former internationally recognized as the representative of the Palestinian people, does not officially support the BDS movement. This complicates things for the BDS movement, particularly because advancing the sports boycott at the level of international sporting bodies requires the support of the national institutional leadership which appoints the delegates that represent Palestine's interests internationally. While the interests of the BDS movement and the Palestinian establishment may align at times, this is not always the case. The establishment can at once be both more conservative in its efforts to challenge the Israeli occupation and more inflammatory in its rhetoric. The BDS movement was critical of the PFA for repeatedly backing down from promises to call for a vote on Israel's FIFA membership and for not taking the issue far enough.[78] In addition, controversies such as Rajoub's threatening call for Palestinian football fans to burn Argentine star Lionel Messi's jerseys if the game against Israel went ahead could also serve to undermine the nonviolent BDS campaigns. However, the lack of establishment support is not necessary for the BDS movement to function and grow, and in some respects allows it to be more flexible, progressive, and forthright in its campaigns. And, as Nathan Thrall has noted, the movement is increasingly "encroaching on [the Palestine Liberation Organization's] position as the internationally recognised advocate and representative of Palestinians worldwide."[79]

The current geopolitical context is important when considering the prospects for the sports boycott. The United States continues its unconditional support for Israel; European and other Western nations are reluctant to push too hard in sanctioning or criticizing Israel; the relationship between Israel and China, India, and countries across the African continent grows; and Gulf states are continuing to warm to Israel. This makes it unlikely that individual states will express explicit support for a sports boycott, or BDS more broadly, and also severely limits the prospect of UN declarations or Commonwealth agreements in support of a sports boycott. International sporting organizations such as FIFA are unlikely to take decisive action to suspend or expel Israel unless pressure grows significantly due to a combination of factors, including Israeli lobbying and a deep-seated reluctance to be seen to be mixing sports and politics. While they have always been mixed, a sports boycott of Israel is seen as the *wrong* sort of politics for those who subscribe to this mantra. All of which highlights the fact that the pressure will have to continue to come from civil society.

The BDS movement has frequently highlighted the South African precedent across its sports boycott campaigns. As outlined earlier, in the South African case, the sports boycott shifted from a focus on racial discrimination in sports to apartheid more broadly. Yet most of the focus of the BDS sports boycott so far has been on highlighting football-related issues. While it has done so, to an extent, to ensure the growth and longevity of the sports boycott, the BDS movement may need to more explicitly expand its justification for it beyond this to encompass a broader focus on the Israeli occupation and the role of sports in normalizing it. The importance of doing so is exemplified by South Africa where, under growing international pressure, the apartheid regime made token racial selection changes or relaxed racial selection demands for touring teams in an effort to weaken support for the boycott. While the systematic racial discrimination and oppression in South African society remained unchanged, this made it easier for people to argue that a sports boycott was not necessary.

Israel's participation in international sports reinforces the notion that it is a normal state and projects a positive image of it competing alongside other nations as an equal. Yet this soft power strategy is somewhat limited. James M. Dorsey argues that football's "potential as a tool of public diplomacy ... is considerable," but harnessing this power "takes a mix of policies that address both domestic and foreign concerns, an efficient public relations and communications policy, and a measure of transparency and accountability."[80] Instead of the above, Israel has only further entrenched its occupation and tried to whitewash it through public propaganda. While international sporting competition still plays an important normalizing role for Israel, its soft power strategy remains hollow. This vulnerability provides a useful opportunity for activists to exploit by spotlighting Israel's policies through sports boycott campaigns.

Conclusion

The impact of BDS is primarily psychological and reputational, disrupting Israel's international image by drawing attention to its treatment of the Palestinians. The challenge to Israel posed by BDS is clearly being taken seriously. Senior Israeli politicians have labelled the movement "an 'existential' or 'strategic' threat,"[81] while the Israeli government and its supporters have invested millions of dollars and significant effort and resources in trying to combat it.[82] Only months after the BDS call was issued, Israel launched a "Brand Israel" public relations campaign designed to re-brand itself as a relevant, modern nation rather than one defined by the conflict with the Palestinians. At the heart of this is the idea that, as the then deputy director-general for media and public affairs in the Israeli Foreign Ministry put it, images presented in the media "have a much greater and immediate impact on what the public abroad feels about Israel, than the arguments Israel presents."[83] The biggest and most important success of the BDS movement has been its ability to generate continued publicity regarding the Israeli occupation.

Key to the impact of the sports boycott has been, and will be, its ability to force people to confront and question Israeli policies, educating them about the reality of life for Palestinians under occupation. Given that so many people around the world watch, support, and participate in a wide variety of sports, there exists a large captive audience for efforts to draw attention to Israel's violations of international law and Palestinian human rights, and to mobilize support for the BDS movement. Attempts to build a sports boycott will face further setbacks and obstacles. It may only ever play a small part in the BDS movement compared to its significance in the South African case. But as was the case with South Africa, Israel does not need to be completely isolated from international competition in order for sports to play a significant role in helping to shift the conversation regarding its policies and increase international pressure on it. Ultimately, a sports boycott of Israel may not achieve the same prominence that the sports boycott of South Africa did. But if it continues to draw attention to Israeli apartheid, just as it did to South African apartheid, and energizes the wider BDS movement then a sports boycott can still form a significant and effective part of the Palestinian struggle.

It is not always possible to identify a singular cause for a decision, and organizations and companies are reluctant to admit to being influenced by activist pressure. Nevertheless, between UEFA deciding not to name Israel as a host for the 2020 European Football Championship, Argentina withdrawing from its match against Israel, and Adidas ending its sponsorship of the IFA, the costs of associating with Israel in the sporting sphere are becoming increasingly high. There will be a cumulative psychological and reputational toll on Israel if the sports boycott results in protests every time Israeli teams compete; disruptive campaigns against any Israeli attempts to host tournaments, events, or matches; continued efforts to suspend or even expel Israel from football institutions; and repeated pressure on companies not to sponsor the IFA. Until Israel ceases its violations of international law and Palestinian human rights, a sports boycott constitutes an effective and legitimate response. By limiting Israel's access to international competition and Israelis' ability to see their teams and players compete abroad, it will function as a powerful symbol of growing displeasure and disapproval with Israel and act as counter to normalization efforts.

9

QATAR, THE WORLD CUP, AND THE GLOBAL CAMPAIGN FOR MIGRANT WORKERS' RIGHTS

Zahra Babar

Introduction

When it was announced on December 2, 2010 that Qatar had been awarded the rights to host the 2022 Fédération Internationale de Football Association (FIFA) World Cup, the news was greeted by those who resided within the state's borders with both euphoria and incredulity. For many, it was hard to grasp that this small country of less than 2 million inhabitants would be holding one of the world's largest sporting events within just a few years. By joining the elite ranks of seventeen countries that have hosted the World Cup, and becoming only the third Asian country and the first Arab and Muslim state to do so, Qatar had certainly arrived on the global sporting stage. As soon as the news was announced, the machinery of the state redirected its focus to everything that would need to be done to turn what had so far just been an imagined possibility into a functional reality. Over the course of the

223

next twelve years, Qatar would need to embark on a herculean effort, devote massive resources, and marshal multiple branches of state and society to pull off its commitment.

Just days after the bid announcement, *The Guardian*, a British newspaper widely known for its progressive viewpoints, launched the first missile of what would become a seemingly endless journalistic barrage. Authored by Human Rights Watch's Nicholas McGeehan, the headline was stark and left absolutely no ambivalence in the mind of the reader as to its central message: "Let Qatar 2022 not be built on brutality."[1] This was to be the first of many similarly critical articles published by media outlets in the months and years that followed, each drawing additional attention to Qatar's dismal track record of protecting the rights of its large migrant worker population.

International sporting competitions such as the World Cup typically rely on the labor contribution of migrant workers, regardless of where they are held.[2] These events always involve investment in massive infrastructural development, such as the construction of new stadiums and other sporting facilities. Given the nature of the construction industry, with its complex labor supply chain, and the transient nature of the work, such projects invariably depend on the labor of temporary migrants drawn from elsewhere.[3] Workers on such building projects are normally sub-contracted and work under the relentless pressure of deadlines. The very time-bound nature of these projects can cause a host of challenges for workers, leading to many violations of their labor rights, as they may be expected to work very long hours and have limited time off. The diffuse and complicated sub-contracting arrangements under which they are hired mean that duty of care for worker well-being is frequently passed further down the chain of command.

From the initial stages, human rights and migrants' rights practitioners drew a direct causal link between the awarding of the World Cup hosting rights to Qatar and the expansion of difficult, if not unendurable, working and living conditions for migrant workers. In order to host the games, Qatar would have to spend around US $100 billion on infrastructural development. Out of that figure, only about US $8–10 billion were ear-marked for the construction of the eight enormous stadiums where the World Cup football matches would be played, as well as for specific football infrastructure, such as practice fields and training facilities.[4] In addition to the arenas where the games would be played and watched, Qatar would need to invest heavily in the abundance of supportive infrastructure, without which hosting a mega sporting event would not be remotely possible. These would include the building of a new airport, expanding the country's roads and transport networks, and erecting dozens of new hotels and recreational facilities. In 2011, when Qatar had a total of 10,000 hotel rooms, the national tourism authority stated that it aimed to increase this to 70,000 by 2022.[5] This massive amount of new construction would depend on the labor of an army of workers, most of whom would come from the developing world.

Migrants rights' advocates and international human rights organizations pointed to the extensive academic and policy literature that had scrutinized, documented, and publicized the precarious lived reality of labor migrants in Qatar.[6] As the state had done little of substance to address the extensive criticism it received in the years prior to being awarded the bid, campaigners argued, it was entirely feasible that workers directly associated with World Cup projects would endure a continuation of the same deprivation of their basic human and labor rights. One of the most effective elements of the international campaign was its success in promoting this central message all around the world: unless something was done in Qatar, football infrastructures and the very hosting of the tournament risked becoming an arena for the exploitation of migrants' rights.

This chapter discusses the impact that the awarding of the FIFA 2022 bid has had on Qatar's labor migration governance system. It reviews the evolution of significant labor reforms that began in Qatar before the bid, and that have been reinforced since 2015 and are currently underway. The chapter is built around three central arguments. The first is that labor reforms that have occurred in Qatar have not been solely due to the global human rights campaign around the World Cup. Qatar's decision and ability to undertake comprehensive reforms have been a result of a far more complex set of factors, and have been influenced by domestic as well as international conditions. One of the most significant of these was the geopolitical crisis that Qatar confronted in May 2017, when several of its closest neighbors severed ties, imposed a regional blockade, and began a relentless, global campaign to discredit and isolate the small state.[7]

The chapter's second argument contends that despite the state's undertaking of these labor reform efforts, their current trajectory, and their long-term potential to guarantee greater protection of labor rights, it is disingenuous to assume that lower income migrants' lives will be radically transformed. The root causes of vulnerabilities and exposures of labor migrants are transnational, multidimensional, and driven by factors tied to the global political economy.[8] While it is critically important that migrant-receiving states adopt enhanced labor protections for those on their territory, one cannot dismiss how conditions in sending states or the pressures of the globalization of production shape migration dynamics in the Gulf. Without global commitment to addressing the broader structural factors that have accelerated poverty and inequality, migrant workers will continue to have their rights impinged.

The third and final contention of this chapter is that Qatar 2022 represents a missed opportunity for global human rights organizations and journalists who spearheaded the campaign. By focusing attention solely on the conditions of migrant workers as a discrete and separate category of concern, and by adopting a myopic lens that does not seek connective tissue to broader local and regional demands for labor rights and human rights, the campaign not only dilutes its potential to galvanize demands for enduring change, but it also continues to do something deeply problematic: to introduce and reproduce the Gulf to the global public as an Orientalized, exceptional space.

Background and Context

Global campaigns galvanizing support to address adverse human rights conditions in countries hosting mega sporting events have become a common occurrence over the recent past. The damaging exposure that Qatar has received over the past years is not unique. Brazil faced similar reactions when it hosted the Summer Olympic Games in 2016. It received intense criticism from global as well as national media when entire lower-income neighborhoods were demolished to make way for stadiums and other games-related infrastructure.[9] The 2014 FIFA World Cup also drew negative international media attention to Brazil, but this was primarily through a series of articles that focused on local Brazilian mobilization efforts to address domestic social justice issues and exclusions under the banner of the "Our Cup is on the Street" protests.[10] Ahead of the World Cup in 2018, Russia also received its fair share of negative global media scrutiny that, among other things, threw a spotlight on the challenges of fan safety, racism, and LGBTQ issues in Russia.

International sports tournaments, globally branded museums, and any large public events that capture the world's attention in a particular geography for a limited period of time now serve as potential sites for human rights mobilization around a particular rights issue. Transnational human rights activists are quick to identify potential venues and occasions that can be leveraged to get maximum exposure and momentum around a particular cause. These bodies use their extensive networks to research rights violations, engage the media, publicize findings, and influence policymakers. Gone are the days when a state could hope to benefit solely from the positive attention that comes with hosting a global event and assume that its domestic politics and internal affairs would be of little interest. The media glare will highlight the bad as much as the good.

The criticism of Qatar that suddenly erupted in 2010 was not new in the sense that the country (along with its five Gulf neighbors) had a history of being on the receiving end of censure for its treatment of migrant workers. A decade of policy and academic work had already provided substantial evidence of the extreme labor rights violations experienced by lower-income migrants not just in Qatar but across the six monarchies of the Persian Gulf. What was new was the speed, intensity, and duration of the bad press that Qatar attracted following the bid announcement. Migrants' advocacy organizations were not only able to amplify their message significantly at that immediate point, correctly identifying the bid's announcement as one made for exerting maximum media pressure. They were also able to sustain global interest in Qatar and its migration reform efforts for the years that followed. And it certainly was not European media that did this on their own; the bid announcement brought together multiple actors to mobilize resources and to collaborate effectively so that their efforts translated into a consolidated and focused campaign.[11]

Media disclosures on migrants' past experiences of contending with terrible violations of their labor and civil rights constructed a narrative of what could be expected in the years to come: hundreds of thousands of migrants laboring outdoors in the Doha heat to construct lavish, air-conditioned stadiums for the World Cup. The visa sponsorship or *kafala* system, and the vulnerability and precarity it engendered, became synonymous with modern-day slavery or unfree labor in Qatar.[12] Gaining global traction was the underlying message: it would go completely against the spirit of the game if football's signature event were to be played in a country that engaged in systematically mistreating and abusing its foreign workforce. It was not just human rights actors and journalists, but also sports pundits, football fans, and even political figures who started publicly condemning Qatar for its poor track record on migrant labor governance and urging the state to take proactive measures to improve conditions for workers associated with World Cup projects.[13] Migrants rights activists, international labor unions, assorted United Nations agencies, senior European government officials, a host of human rights-based advocacy organizations like Amnesty International and Human Rights Watch, along with both traditional and social media, participated in what would become a sustained, years-long campaign. For over a decade, this campaign has succeeded in dimming much of the world's interest in Qatar for its football ambitions and achievements and for how it is preparing itself to serve as a host to the biggest game of all. However, it has certainly succeeded in amplifying global interest in Qatar's labor migration governance.

QATAR, THE WORLD CUP, AND THE GLOBAL CAMPAIGN

Qatar was clearly caught off guard in 2010 when *The Guardian* article was published. The country struggled to launch an immediate and effective response. One can only assume that the leadership or those in charge of the bid thought that if left alone the story would die a natural death. Perhaps concerned that engaging in a debate might prolong the media interest and provoke further negative attention, the state chose to remain largely silent in the face of the media onslaught. The initial strategy of not mounting a strong response and hoping the situation would resolve itself was clearly a strategic failure in the long run, as the barrage of negative attention did not diminish but rather gained further momentum.[14] Given both its own history of being on the receiving end of criticism for migrant labor issues, as well as the past experiences of other countries hosting mega sporting events, the senior Qatari leadership should have anticipated this kind of activism arising in relation to the World Cup, and attempted to pre-empt it by drawing attention to its ongoing efforts to address migrants rights and its intention to do so more robustly. Certainly, they should have prepared a better strategy for communicating on the subject.

Qatar's deliberate efforts to engage and invest in the domain of international sports and sporting events are tied to a larger determination to expand its soft power and build brand recognition for the country. These efforts are closely linked to the country's strategic political, economic, and social considerations as a small state.[15] Being suddenly on the receiving end of a focused global media campaign seeking to discredit the country for its treatment of workers was an unanticipated obstacle to achieving core foreign policy objectives. During the initial stages of the campaign, Qatar was unable to organize and launch a strong response, and its weak capacity to engage and communicate with international media demonstrated this as a glaring deficiency. Unable to swiftly roll out a coherent, centralized message to address growing international concern on how it was protecting migrant workers, through the latter part of 2010 and early 2011, it was largely left up to different state entities involved with the awarding of the games, primarily the Supreme Committee for Delivery and Legacy, to devise appropriate responses.[16] Without the full force of the state behind them, these initial responses appeared both tentative and defensive.

Given the nature and pace of labor reforms Qatar has undertaken since it won the right to host the FIFA World Cup, and in particular the intensification of the reform process from 2017 to 2022, international media and international organizations can reasonably argue that their efforts have not proven fruitless. The bid and the World Cup have provided an opportunity to push the state to focus greater attention to amending the most problematic features of its labor law, and recent policy efforts indicate that progress has been made. That the labor migration system in Qatar certainly looks different in 2022 to how it did in 2010 is a testament to both institutional and individual actions, as well as policy documentation and scholarship that has raised awareness of the exposure of migrant workers to exploitation and abuse. However, the success of the international campaign has been enabled and facilitated by additional challenges that Qatar has encountered, such as efforts by its neighbors to isolate it and turn it into a pariah state, as well as domestic conditions which enabled processes of labor reform to unfold.

Qatar's Labor Migration System and Its Reform

For decades, the governments of the six Gulf monarchies adopted a hands-off, limited role in the day-to-day lives of their large migrant worker population.[17] Private actors, businesses, and companies have determined the priority labor requirements to keep the economy moving, and then adopted means to source and maintain their workforces. The state's role has been to vet labor requests on a project-by-project basis, ensuring that the contracts employers provide to their foreign workers adhere to the *kafala* or worker sponsorship system, and that generally the terms and conditions under which foreign labor is hired are in compliance with national labor law. In all other ways, it was left largely up to employers and companies to manage their foreign workforces. Well before 2010, this region-wide sponsorship system was receiving increased scrutiny and critique by both scholars and international migrants' rights advocates for its inherent imbalance in favor of employers and the limited capacity or interest of governments in protecting migrant workers' rights.[18] Given that the *kafala* ties foreign workers to specific employers who sponsor their visas, there is vast potential for its abuse.[19] Migrants contending with violations of their labor rights risk losing both their job contracts as well as their legal status should they seek redress from their employer and risk being punished with dismissal and potential deportation.

Due to the "privatization of migration governance,"[20] and an overall governance structure that relies excessively on ineffectual legal frameworks that are half-heartedly enforced, protections for migrants have been considered weak region-wide. The Gulf states have frequently deflected criticism levied at them both by international organizations and migrant-sending states for not safeguarding migrants' rights by shifting the blame to employers and sponsors for not adhering to the requirements of labor law or the *kafala*. Despite these protestations, and the fact that the protective apparatus of the state might feel visibly absent to Gulf migrants in their daily lives, it is undeniable that the state is very much present through its central configuration in labor migration governance. Firstly, there is no clear line partitioning the public and private sectors in the Gulf, as the state and its subsidiaries make up a large component of what operates as the "business" sector in the region. The largest infrastructural projects in Qatar that require labor input from migrants are state-led. Many sectors, from real estate to retail, are dominated by a few large Qatari holding companies whose senior leadership has multiple connections to the government.[21] With such an intense blurring of boundaries between "state" and "business," it is disingenuous for the state to posit that it is not accountable for labor violations that occur.

Secondly, the *kafala*, rather than being a vestigial remnant of a localized and "traditional" understanding of migration and mobility, has been a strategic and deliberate tool deployed by the Gulf states both to support and sustain their modernization efforts, as well as to maintain dominant political control over their populations. The problematic features of the *kafala* as well as Qatar's unusual demography, where over 80 percent of its population is non-citizen, arise out of structural features of the rentier state's welfare arrangements, which make it next to impossible for citizens to actively contribute to a range of jobs in the lowest tiers of the labor market. Both subtly and overtly, the *kafala* has served to reinforce Gulf rulers' capacity to control and discipline both their citizen and non-citizen populations.[22] Combined with various restrictive controls over migrants' social, political, and economic participation, it has allowed Gulf states to navigate their development agendas in partnership with business elites, while marginalizing their own citizen workers and diminishing prospects for citizens to actualize their labor rights.

Multiple scholarly and policy reports have drawn attention to the problematic features of the *kafala*,[23] and, by the early 2000s, several Gulf states began to acknowledge that the system failed to provide protections for migrant workers.[24] In Qatar, reforms of the labor migration system, and, in particular, addressing the most problematic features of the *kafala*, commenced in earnest around 2009. Over the next decade, however, the pace and scope of intervention significantly increased. Law No. 4 of 2009—"Regulating the Entry and Exit of Expatriates in Qatar and their Residence and Sponsorship"—was one of the earlier efforts at reform, and enhanced the Qatari state's capacity to enforce its national labor law and to ensure employers were meeting their contractual obligations to their sponsored workers.[25] Without attempting to dismantle any central features of the *kafala* itself, Law No. 4 allowed the state to reinforce measures to ensure that employers were abiding by the labor rights that migrant workers were given under labor law and via their employment contracts.[26] The establishment of the new law was supported by various amendments to national labor law, the issuance of new emiri decrees, and a variety of policy interventions, through which the state has sought to align national labor law with international standards, to address core issues around wages and contracts, and to enhance migrants' rights to mobility (both into and out of the country, as well as within the labor market).[27]

Many lower-skilled migrants in Qatar contend with challenging living and working conditions, as well as with limited financial and social resources to improve their experiences.[28] As a result of the low wages that they earn, these migrants endure ongoing financial anxieties both in sustaining themselves while in the host state and in supporting their families at home who rely on their remittances. The delayed payment of wages, not being paid contractually agreed-upon amounts, and salary withholding have consistently served as the primary source for provoking workers' grievances against their employers.[29] On an annual basis, thousands of workers in Qatar have lodged complaints of wage denial, delayed wages, or receiving wages that do not match contractually promised amounts.[30] Beyond wage issues, contracts in general have proved problematic, as there is extensive evidence of recruiters and employers habitually engaging in the practice of contract switching.[31] This occurs when the documents that migrants have reviewed and signed (usually in the offices of labor brokers and recruiters) prior to departure from their country of origin do not match up to the contracts they receive once they arrive in Qatar. Gulf receiving states have long contended that contract switching occurs due to the unethical behavior of private transnational recruiters located at both ends of the migration corridor, in both sending and receiving states. Qatar established new processes to enhance and monitor the activities of private labor recruiters, one of which was to electronically validate work contracts in the sending country so that contract substitution could not occur once workers arrived.[32] Steps were also taken to enforce laws around the illegal withholding of workers' passports by employers, to address migrants working excessive hours and working outdoors in particularly hot temperatures, and to ensure that standards of workers' accommodation are being met by employers who were providing housing to their sponsored workers. Additional policy interventions to uphold health and safety in the workplace have occurred. The ministry's capacity to enforce labor law by increasing the number of labor inspectors from the Ministry of Administration, Labor and Social Affairs (MADLSA) who are deputized to carry out labor inspections of worksites and workers' accommodations has also increased.

In 2011, Qatar launched the wage protection system, mandating that all workers' salaries are transferred electronically to bank accounts, which are tracked by the Central Bank and the MADLSA.[33] In 2015, Law No. 21, the first comprehensive effort by Qatar to dismantle the *kafala*, was announced. Under the new law, and with the government's permission instead of their employer's, workers are allowed to switch employers either after completing five years of service or else completing their contract—whichever comes first. Workers could appeal to the MADLSA for an earlier release from their contract. In that case, however, they would need to first obtain their employer's approval in addition to the approval of the Ministry of Interior and Ministry of Labor. Law 21 also removed employers' control over their sponsored workers' exit visas, making the Ministry of Interior responsible for approving requests to exit the country rather than employers themselves.

Complementing the official reforms announced at the state level and implementation of these by various ministries and branches of government have been the initiatives by key Qatari actors directly involved in the hosting of the 2022 FIFA World Cup. Qatar's Supreme Committee for Delivery and Legacy (SC) is the primary body accountable for all aspects of the 2022 FIFA World Cup. Among other things, the SC has been responsible for overseeing the building of all the World Cup stadiums, and from early on has come under intense international scrutiny for how it is managing the thousands of migrant construction workers involved in these projects. Under its Worker Welfare Standards, the SC has committed to a range of labor protections for those migrants involved in World Cup projects, including workers who are not directly hired by the SC but employed under sub-contracted arrangements.[34] The SC has also mandated that representational bodies for migrant workers known as Workers' Welfare Forums are established at all SC worksites. While not operating precisely as labor unions, the Welfare Forums are meant to raise workers' concerns with management. They also serve to draw attention to any issues or problems being encountered by workers. The SC has committed itself, among other things, to protecting migrants from paying illegal recruitment fees to the labor agents through which they acquired their Qatar job contracts. Many migrants arrive in the Gulf laden with debt that they take on to finance the costs of their migration. By the end of 2020, the SC stated that approximately

50,000 of its workers had paid around US $31 million in recruitment fees, which the organization had paid back to the workers, either directly or by contracting companies.[35]

Despite the various efforts at reform that unfolded over several years and in incremental stages, Qatar mostly continued to draw fundamental criticism from many international actors.[36] Reports in the media suggested that most of the state's efforts were directed at crafting cosmetic and superficial modifications that served to camouflage the fact that there was no effort to systematically address the root cause of temporary migrants' vulnerabilities.[37] Advocates for migrants' rights stressed the need to address the deep inequality built into the *kafala*, which perpetually left sponsored migrants heavily dependent on their employer-sponsors and thus lacking any capacity to negotiate against poor working conditions.[38] Human Rights Watch, Amnesty International, and the International Trade Union Confederation (among others) demanded that Qatar engage in a rapid process of completely dismantling the *kafala*, as any other reforms would consistently fall short of meeting standards of protection for workers.[39] There has long been political and social resistance among the Qatari population to completely overhauling the migration governance system, out of the fear that without it foreigners will overwhelm the country.[40] Key business leaders and industry stakeholders have had a vested interest in maintaining the status quo around the sponsorship system, and public opinion surveys further demonstrate that many average Qataris also regard migration reform as an immediate threat to themselves and the country's economic and social priorities.

Post-Blockade Reforms: 2017–21

The most dramatic reforms to the labor migration system were witnessed in 2017–18, after the crisis that led to the rupture in relations between Qatar and its neighbors amid the Saudi and UAE-led blockade. Within a few months of the blockade against Qatar, the state began a process of dismantling many of the most problematic features of the *kafala* hitherto resisted. Among other things, the reforms stipulated that employers had to lodge their workers' contracts with the government; a minimum wage of $200 a month was mandated; employers no longer had any control over workers' exit permits; and—even more importantly—employers were no longer in charge of issuing or extending their sponsored workers' Qatari IDs and residency permits. The state also mandated the formation of workers' committees in almost every workplace and established a special dispute resolution authority. Most surprisingly was that on August 22, 2017, the emir of Qatar, Sheikh Tamim bin Hamad Al-Thani, ratified Law No. 15 on service workers in the home.[41] The law of 2017 was the first domestic worker law ever established in Qatar, guaranteeing domestic workers a maximum 10-hour workday, a weekly rest day, three weeks of annual leave, an end-of-service payment, and healthcare benefits. On October 26, 2017, Qatar also committed to further extending reforms to the *kafala* system, and pledged to: establish a nondiscriminatory minimum wage; improve its capacity to enforce the timely payment of wages; end the illegal practice of passport confiscation through reinforcing disciplinary mechanisms against it; enhance its labor inspection capacity; and improve occupational safety and health standards, including by introducing a targeted heat mitigation strategy for migrants working outdoors. An additional goal was to develop a far more focused strategy of controlling labor recruitment procedures to protect migrants from paying any illegal fees to recruiters.

In early 2018, the International Labor Organization (ILO) Project Office was opened in Qatar, a significant sign of Qatar's commitment to seriously addressing international concerns over its labor issues. Through its technical cooperation agreement with Qatar, the ILO committed to working with the state between January 2018 and January 2021 to support it in carrying out extensive reforms of the *kafala*.[42] Among other things, the agreement identified specific actions to be undertaken within the three-year period: to improve the timely payment of workers' wages; to establish a nondiscriminatory minimum wage; to end the practice of employers' withholding of workers' documents; to strengthen labor inspection capacity; and to address labor recruitment issues.

QATAR, THE WORLD CUP, AND THE GLOBAL CAMPAIGN

The ILO began working closely with the Qatari government to ensure that concrete steps were taken to enhance protections for migrant workers through a focused effort at dismantling the *kafala*. Later in 2018, through Cabinet Resolution No. 6 of 2018, the MADLSA established a centralized Labor Disputes Resolution Committee located at the ministry's headquarters, while also increasing the number of complaints offices through which migrants could lodge work issues.[43] The goal was to create a more rapid mechanism by which workers can have their cases legally addressed. This centralization allows for labor complaints to be directly linked to the courts, and has reinforced mechanisms for judicial intervention in cases where workers' labor rights are being violated. The government also passed a law establishing the Workers' Support and Insurance Fund, designed to ensure workers receive their due wages in cases where the Labor Disputes Resolution Committees rules in their favor but their company or employer cannot (or will not) pay them what they are owed. Additionally, in order to further enhance Qatar's control over the transnational recruitment process, and primarily to ensure that potential migrants are not made to pay excessive fees for obtaining job contracts in Qatar to middlemen and labor brokers, twenty Qatar Visa Centers were established in the primary migrant-sending countries.

Qatar's heightened efforts to push through labor reforms while still in the midst of a geopolitical crisis were driven by several factors. For the Qatari leadership, the Gulf crisis presented an important opportunity to address a skeptical global audience, particularly in the face of the Saudi and Emirati determination to discredit and isolate Qatar at every level. For Qatar, mitigating the effects of the Saudi and Emirati efforts to discredit it was not just a question of demonstrating ideational or aspirational commitment. For such a small state, viability depends on a supportive international sphere where allies and alliances guarantee its territorial integrity. In the face of its neighbors' efforts to cast Qatar as a malign force in the region and beyond, and with fears of potential military invasion not seeming completely unrealistic, Qatar pressed back against this narrative by demonstrating an active engagement on labor rights and human rights.

237

On the domestic front, the crisis also allowed the state and its rulers to push forward with labor reforms which had previously faced resistance from key domestic constituencies as well as the Qatari public at large. Core facets of Qatari society have long been alarmed by the idea of expanding rights to foreign workers, seeing this as a threat to their economic well-being as well as to social stability. Pushing labor reforms through the Qatar Chamber of Commerce had frequently proved difficult. For the Qatari leadership, the Gulf Cooperation Council (GCC) crisis allowed for the cultivation of national support and the circumvention of resistance. Crises such as external attacks or wars are moments that allow governments to reshape policies towards their own preferences and also heighten sentiments of civic citizenship and support of publics for their leadership.[44] Following the blockade and geopolitical tension, patriotism was high and local stakeholders had to demonstrate their loyalty, thus diminishing their capacity to adopt positions seen as confrontational towards or critical of the state.[45] Additionally, local media seemed to suggest the blockade imposed on Qatar created at least brief and passing solidarities between citizens and foreigners, and that during the year after the blockade was imposed there was a greater sense of unity among the entire population.[46] However, it is hard to say at this stage that sentiments of camaraderie towards foreign residents generated greater public acceptance amongst Qataris for the labor reform processes. It is more likely that citizens had greater trust in the state. While Gengler's analysis of public survey data suggests that there are indications that post-blockade Qatari citizens' trust of Western expatriates increased, data do not show any increase of affinities or trust between citizens and South Asian worker populations.[47]

In September 2020, through "Ministerial Decision No. 25 of 2020 On the Establishment of the Minimum Wage for Workers and Domestic Workers," and through "Ministry of Interior Decree No 51 Amending the Entry, Exit and Residence of Expatriates," Qatar simultaneously announced a nondiscriminatory minimum wage and a removal of some of the critical controls sponsors have over employees under the *kafala* system, namely removing the need for sponsored workers to seek their employer's approval for switching jobs.[48] Under the new mandatory minimum wage, which came into full effect from March 2021, workers are to be paid at least QR 1,000 (US $275) per month, and an additional monthly allowance of QR 800 (US $220) in cases where housing and food are not provided by the employer. While the monthly minimum wage amount is still very low, according to ILO estimates, approximately 400,000 migrant workers in Qatar will see their salaries increase as a result of it.[49] Setting and sustaining minimum wages demonstrates the state's commitment to protecting vulnerable categories of workers, and these reforms were duly acknowledged as being more comprehensive.[50] Ongoing monitoring as well as data gathering will be necessary to determine the effectiveness of the removal of employers' control over sponsored workers when it comes to their capacity to change jobs, as this will be the most critical factor in improving working conditions for migrants in the country. Between September 2020 and March 2022, over 240,000 migrant workers were able to successfully transfer their sponsorship, but reports indicate that many migrants are still facing difficulties in moving to a new job.[51]

Whether conditions for migrants are significantly improved in the coming years will depend not only on the state's will to implement and enforce the reforms once the spotlight of 2022 has been removed, but also on how effective the reforms are at addressing core issues of vulnerability to which migrants are exposed. While the improvement of legal protections for migrants' labor rights is a critical necessity, a decade of scholarship, and particularly ethnographic studies on the Gulf's migrant population, has indicated that their exposures are a result of broader economic and social marginalization and exclusion that occur as a result of their "temporary status."[52] Migrant workers in Qatar live in a perpetual state of non-belonging due to weak capacity to actualize their citizenship rights at home and a lack of citizenship or rights to permanent settlement in the Gulf.[53]

There is recognition by both international actors as well as sending states that there is a limit to the demands that can be made on Qatar. While current reforms continue to receive criticism from some international human rights organizations that believe they have not gone far enough, from a realist perspective, even limited and bounded protections for migrants can be considered a win. This is relevant not only in Qatar but in many other parts of the world to which temporary labor migrants gravitate for employment, and where legal systems alone are not enough to protect them from exploitation and vulnerability. The extent of the reforms that can or should be sought is frequently underpinned by the recognition that pushing for an all or nothing sweeping reform of the labor migration system could lead Qatar (and other GCC host states) to seek alternate means of addressing labor needs, and to reduce their dependency on foreign workers over time. Even the successful reforms and the changing legal and economic rights that strengthen the financial rights of migrants in Qatar may well change the nature of employment patterns in the country. As other scholars have pointed out in relation to global migration trends, for potential migrants (and their sending states) there is a trade-off between equal rights and numbers admitted.[54] States that provide labor market access to large numbers of temporary migrants tend to do so with the provision of a very limited set of social, economic, and political rights. The primary benefit is access to employment and wages and to the combined density of remittance flows between the host and sending states. On the other hand, states that aim to maximize equality of rights between their citizens and foreign workers tend to provide far fewer numbers of migrants entry and access to the labor market in the first place.[55] As scholars have suggested when reviewing existing approaches to migration governance in comparative perspective: "the choice, in reality, is between few legal openings for migrant workers with the promise of equal citizenship and many openings for migrant workers without the promise of citizenship."[56] Northern European states and Scandinavia offer some of the highest sets of economic rights to lower skill workers, but take in very few of them on an annual basis.[57] For example, during 2020, Sweden granted just over 15,000 work permits to foreigners, and by early 2021 had a total Indian migrant population of about 30,000, while Qatar's labor market gives entry to thousands of new migrants each year, and currently employs about 700,000

Indians.[58] Particularly in 2021, with increasing job insecurity after the global economic impact of the COVID-19 pandemic, sending states in South Asia are anxious to retain labor market access for their citizens in the Gulf and to maintain the flow of remittances. The critical dependency on jobs in the Gulf means that for many sending states, protecting access for their citizens to regional labor markets is balanced against protecting their citizens' rights.[59] The enhancement of conditions for lower income migrants in the Gulf will depend on sustaining transnational commitments to addressing the complex challenges and pressures that they contend with at multiple stages of the migration process.

Unpacking the Campaign

There has been little analysis on the strategies adopted by international activists to galvanize and mobilize efforts for migrant labor reform around Qatar 2022, nor has there been a deconstruction of the tools and techniques that were applied. This is unsurprising given that the campaign is still underway, the games in Qatar have not yet been held, and the future consequences are as yet unknown. Still, given that the previous section of this chapter discussed the reforms, this section is an attempt—admittedly premature, and thus fairly limited in scope—to examine the campaign on its own merits.

Literature on human rights campaigns stresses that there are a few basic guidelines that need to be adhered to by transnational activists if a campaign is to succeed in its objectives.[60] The very first of these is that activists recognize the environment in which they are launching their campaign and, in particular, acknowledge the sociocultural context of the communities they are targeting.[61] While human rights are assumed to be universal and guaranteed for all people everywhere, it is understood that messaging around rights must be rooted within a particular sociocultural and political context if they are to gain any traction. Campaigns must be designed to be motivational and indicate broad and integrated sets of future positive outcomes for the societies where they are being carried out. Human rights activists must avoid the use of shaming tactics that target specific groups in society as offenders or even societies as a whole, as these tactics serve to alienate rather than encourage broad support for rights agendas.[62] When examining the case of Qatar and the attention devoted to it by international activists over the past decade, it is difficult to see signs of these common guidelines being adopted.

The socioeconomic and historical contexts of Qatar were deployed strategically by journalists, most frequently as a means to highlight the contrast to conditions and experiences of migrant workers. Much of the campaign's success in gaining global support was in the story of Qatar that it told to the world: that Qatar is a highly exceptional, small state with a massive amount of natural wealth and a booming economy managed by a ruling Arab tribe, where a handful of citizens live lavishly, clinging to outdated behaviors (including slavery) and are normatively out of touch with accepted global values around equality and rights. There was little representation of the diversity and heterogeneity, both ethnically and economically, that has historically existed among the Qatari citizen population.

Media narratives on Qatar appeared to bind migration governance and the very real and modern problems arising out of the restrictive *kafala* system to early Gulf histories of slavery and subjugation, as though all of this was one seamless continuum. Pete Pattisson published his article titled "Revealed: Qatar's World Cup 'Slaves'" in *The Guardian* on September 25, 2013. A couple of years later, in May 2015, another *Guardian* article, by Marina Hyde, asked "How Many Slave Deaths in Qatar Can FIFA Put Up With?" With nearly 80 million online views per month, *The Guardian* has a global reach, and the newspaper itself reported that Pattisson's article had been shared over 100,000 times on social media within three months of its publication.[63] The reductionist messaging used by campaigners, and then amplified by others online, ignored what scholarship has long established, that cultural identity is pliable, porous, demonstrates multiple inconsistencies, and is constantly in flux. Social and cultural behavior in Qatar, like anywhere else, comprises a complex set of ideas, values, and practices that, while tied to local geography and history, is constantly evolving and deeply influenced by regional and international forces.

International human rights activism around global sporting events appear to exist as a moveable feast across time and countries, unmoored from any unifying logic that translates gains from one event to the next, with limited success in consolidating and building on previous experiences, or even maintaining a sustained momentum that can be carried beyond the life cycle of a single event. For a short time, the world's eye is drawn to a particular country, and then, it seems, it moves on. Activists and journalists who brought attention to the conditions of migrant workers in relation to Qatar 2022 could have built on the legacies and drawn on the knowledge learned from comparative rights campaigns around mega sporting events in other parts of the world. A broader strategic approach that placed the emirate as one of multiple global locations where sports, globalization, and capital accumulation collide to fundamentally undermine economic rights would have served to strengthen rather than dilute the importance of the core message: that workers, and particularly construction workers involved in massive builds anywhere in the world, need to have their well-being, health, and safety guaranteed.

When Brazil hosted the 2014 FIFA World Cup, activists across multiple sectors leveraged the occasion to draw attention to a host of workers' rights issues occurring in the construction sector around projects affiliated with the games.[64] In the Brazilian case, as Rombaldi states, local Brazilian actors worked closely with international organizations on setting the goals of the campaign, as well as determining its agenda and activities.

> Although the construction companies involved in the preparations for 2014 were Brazilian, mega-events such as the World Cup became opportunities to broaden union strategies in that they involved large numbers of workers, required mediation for negotiating with entities not traditionally approached by local unions such as the national and international organizing committees, facilitated the acquisition of expertise that might lend support to social organizations established in the host country, and finally, promoted coordination between national and international agendas with the aim of strengthening ties between the different levels of workers' associations.[65]

Not only did activism around the 2014 World Cup present an immediate opportunity to raise global awareness of and seek redress for workers associated with the games' infrastructures, but a longer-term success of the campaign was also in how it served to strengthen local activists and unionists within Brazil. Cooperation with international unions and campaigners during the 2014 campaign served to develop indigenous capacity for local Brazilian unions, labor rights activists, and even for workers themselves. Given the heightened media interest and domestic attention given to the games, local campaigners were able to broaden the social base for support of domestic labor rights among the Brazilian public and were also able to enhance their strategies for cooperation. The campaign deliberately developed mechanisms for collaboration so as to overcome traditional divisions within Brazilian unions, leading to a far more unified national agenda.[66] It is difficult to see whether there will be similar long-term benefits out of the 2022 campaign in terms of strengthening indigenous human rights capacity among the Qatari population so that citizens are able to address their state directly with demands for reform across multiple areas. The focus has been on strengthening the state's capacity, which, while critical in terms of developing appropriate law and protective measures, does little to change its authoritarian architecture.

As the literature points out when evaluating the outcomes of human rights campaigns, there are both intended and unintended consequences.[67] Research is still needed to comprehensively capture Qataris' responses to the effects of international media and activism around the Cup and the labor reforms Qatar has engaged in. It cannot be determined at this juncture whether the World Cup has enabled broad socialization of norms around migrant workers' rights amongst the Qatari citizen population. Past experience demonstrates that for this to materialize, transnational civil society organizations and human rights advocates needed to invest in developing solid, broad-based networking capacity in the local context. Efforts at addressing shortfalls in human rights elsewhere have demonstrated that the greatest chances of achieving long-term success entails the development of collaborative mechanisms for dialogue through working closely with citizens and locals, even in contexts where civil society may appear to be weak or absent.[68] Without the participations of insiders who can help

localize a movement, human rights agendas can appear as imposi-
tions of Western imperialism and will struggle to achieve momentum and long-term social change.[69] The Qatar 2022 campaign
messaging and approach was launched directly at the Qatari state
from external actors. There is little to indicate that international
activists attempted to build solidarities on the ground or support
meaningful dialogues with citizens or between citizens and
migrants on the issue of labor rights and protections. Global
human rights activists have had decades of experience advocating
for reforms and sensitive human rights agendas in environments
where civil society is absent and freedom of expression heavily
restricted, and have developed ample and creative means of overriding the structural limitations of engagement in authoritarian
contexts similar to Qatar's.[70] Activists in many other parts of the
world that are non-democratic and heavily controlled have used a
variety of techniques and strategies to challenge and change citizens' perceptions around particular rights issues.[71] Without the
involvement and inclusion of citizens in the reform process or in
deliberations on what the reforms should look like, the top-down
approach adopted in Qatar has served to reinforce the notion that
Qatari citizens are irrelevant to processes of governance. One of
the unintended consequences of this is that it has encouraged an
ongoing system where citizens and migrants are assumed to
cohabit the country as discrete and oppositional categories. It has
also strengthened the notion that only the authoritarian state can
serve as a neutral arbiter between the two communities. As
Gruffydd-Jones argues, authoritarian regimes can quite effectively
use international human rights agendas as a means to enhance or
strengthen the support of their population, while continuing to
suppress their citizens' own human rights.[72]

Migrant workers and their lack of rights have been reproduced
in media narratives as existing in stark contrast to citizens' access
to broad economic and social rights. The narratives implicitly stress
that the contrast between these two groups is so great that their
interests are too far removed from each other for possible solidarities to form. A lasting benefit of a successful campaign would have
been if it had generated social conditions that could enable both

citizens and residents in Qatar to collectively demand that the state enhance labor rights and participation, and perhaps even seed the ground for more organized forms of labor activism as well as human rights engagement in Qatar. A lingering consequence instead might be that the years of media attention on migrant worker abuse has served to deepen fissures and mistrust of locals towards international rights regimes as well as dampened enthusiasm for organized labor activism.

Historical studies of Arab leftists labor movements in the Gulf in the 1950s and 1960s demonstrate that the current status quo is not necessarily a legacy of past bifurcations, but rather, to the contrary, migrants have been an intrinsic component of earlier forms of labor activism that took place on the Peninsula.[73] During the era of pan-Arabism across the region, both skilled and less skilled migrants collaborated effectively with citizens to mobilize around a host of labor rights issues, established and participated in activist organizations, and contributed to local demands for greater participation and justice. While much of the migrant labor activism in the Gulf during that time was undertaken by non-Gulf Arabs, there was also participation from South Asian workers in terms of coordinated strike actions.[74]

While it is undeniable that migrant workers are a marginalized community in the Gulf, they are also endowed with human agency. Examples from across the region demonstrate that increasingly migrants are not only engaging in labor actions, but also seeking ways in which to engage in solidarity building. From 2012 onward, workers in Bahrain, the UAE, Qatar, and Saudi Arabia have engaged in strikes and work stoppages to address a variety of labor violations, and in many cases collective actions have resulted in workers winning concessions from their employers.[75] One of the primary challenges has been the capacity for migrants to find citizen collaborators and form alliances with citizen workers to support their demands for their labor rights. However, a few recent examples of organizations successfully transcending the migrant-foreigner divide are visible, and offer hope of the sorts of solidarities that could be formed and could serve as a platform towards greater cooperation between citizen and non-citizen communities.[76] In Kuwait, in 2010, Filipino women established the Sandigan Kuwait Domestic Workers Federation (SKDWF), bringing together over 5,000 domestic workers to engage in supporting other domestic workers through offering training, counselling, and other support services. While Sandigan has refrained from tackling labor right issues head on, or articulating labor rights for domestic workers as a stated goal, they have done considerable work to support a variety of social and economic needs and supporting domestic workers and other Filipinos in crisis. SKDWF has also been able to develop a collaborative relationship with the Kuwaiti Trade Union Federation (KUTF), working with them on targeted activities supporting domestic workers. Additionally, the KUTF, along with the principal trade union in Bahrain in 2012, signed official cooperative agreements with Nepal's General Federation of Trade Unions.[77] These efforts indicate that there are possibilities for bringing both citizens and foreigners in the Gulf together under the banner of worker solidarity. Such efforts allow for both migrant and citizen activists to identify common causes and consequences of economic and social dislocation and seek joint redress. As Boodrookas noted in 2018: "These quasi-official, transnational union connections are a significant innovation, crossing a citizen-noncitizen divide that is often thought of as an unbridgeable chasm. New coalitions seem to be on the cusp of coalescing—just as the space for dissenting politics is under immediate and unprecedented threat."[78] Innovative coalitions that cross national and class boundaries and channel group aspirations can have a transformative and long-term impact on the existing political and economic structures in the Gulf states. Strategies to support such efforts should have been a central focus for human rights activists engaged in the Qatar 2022 migrant reform campaign.

The sensationalist overreach of certain newspaper articles has not only diminished the credibility of certain media outlets but could potentially also desensitize the Qatari public and policymakers from factual and evidence-based data and analysis on the conditions of migrants. In February 2021, *The Guardian* published an article on migrant worker deaths in Qatar, stating that 6,500 had died since the country was awarded the FIFA Cup and suggesting that most of these deaths were tied to stadium builds.[79] While the article, with its designed-to-shock headline, was picked up by many other European media outlets, this time the Qatari state was able to muster a far firmer and more organized response. Through a written statement on February 24, 2021, Qatar's Government Communication Office pointed out the glaringly obvious, that over 1.5 million South Asian migrants live in Qatar, and work across multiple sectors and industries, and are also students and accompanying family members. The death rate per annum includes deaths from across all these categories and across all sectors. As many academics and analysts were also quick to point out, 6,500 deaths over 10 years among around 1.5 million migrant workers per year from five countries across multiple age groups is actually a fairly low average. Per annum adult mortality rates in most of the South Asian sending countries are far higher, and even if one is to account for age boundaries, as one academic on Twitter states, "Out of 1 million young men under the age of 25, 560 die each year in Germany, i.e. 5600 in ten years."[80]

While the loss of even a single migrant worker's life due to unsafe working conditions is not something to be glossed over, the deliberate manipulation and misrepresentation of data by outlets like *The Guardian* is deeply problematic. Because once an opposing message debunking the data is provided, not only is the credibility of the original communicator affected, but so too is the credibility of the message itself.[81] Playing fast and loose with numbers eroded not only the credibility of *The Guardian* and others publishing these articles, but has a damaging impact on those undertaking or planning to undertake focused research to collect evidence and objective data on the working and living experiences of migrants in the Gulf. The actions and behavior of media actors as well as certain human rights organizations that deploy similar tactics of deliberate manipulation of data or misinformation has the potential for blunting the policy impact of, and eroding public trust in, evidence-based findings.

National communities are seldom homogenous, but exhibit divisions and different interests. Some social groups are motivated to support social change, while others might be interested in safeguarding the status quo. Traditionally, human rights campaigners avoid treating a national group as a whole, preferring instead to examine potential divisions and different interest groups in local society so as to identify potential collaborators. External activists who campaigned to promote better conditions for migrant workers in Qatar made limited effort to reach out to other social actors in Qatar. For example, Qatari youth groups and university students who have already engaged in activism calling for greater inclusion of immigrant communities and the ending of racial stereotyping would certainly be receptive to messaging on migrant workers' rights.[82]

One of the campaign's glaring failures was its lack of inclusion of local voices, and its inability to foster solidarities in Qatar between social actors. Qatari citizens themselves were largely dismissed by the campaign, or at least by the most vocal global media and human rights communities, and were treated as if they had no relevance to the issue. It is almost as though by being the subjects of an authoritarian state they were considered completely irrelevant. Where the campaign could have been directly helpful would have been in nurturing an environment where a sustained discussion of migration could have taken place that included both the perspective of citizens as well as migrants. Forums that could have generated a reduction in citizens' disquiet and facilitated an atmosphere of greater cooperation between citizens and migrants could have led to a long-term environment where the partitions and divided blocks of Qatari society might have been less severe. Instead, the campaign has actually served to reinforce the divisions and false binaries that serve the authoritarian nature of the state, the divide and rule systems that provide the state with greater power and control over all who live on its territory.

Concluding Thoughts

It is understandable if Arabs living across the Middle East feel a degree of cynicism as to how international media and activists pick and choose the occasions to which they turn their attention, and which rights agendas gain the greatest global momentum.

International human rights campaigns, and the various stakeholders that participate in them, strategically target and deploy their resources towards those sporting events and rights issues that have the greatest chances of resonance among their own constituencies and with their audiences. Sports fans, sports bodies, and the global media appear to offer less condemnation to Middle Eastern regimes for their treatment of their own citizens over the recent past. The world's sporting elites returned to the Bahrain Grand Prix without any qualms during the Arab uprisings, despite the Bahraini regime's continuing brutal repression against its own citizenry since 2011. Many Bahrainis involved in the uprisings, and who were subsequently detained, arrested, and had their citizenship stripped, were protesting for improved economic conditions and an expansion of their labor rights. Yet global human rights activists and the media demonstrated limited interest in using the prestigious occasions of F1 racing as a venue for galvanizing global support for Bahraini citizens and their social and economic exclusion and oppression by the state. While European footballers have called for a boycott of Qatar 2022, there have been no similar sentiments expressed by these athletes or any European national teams to boycott football games played with or in Israel, despite ample evidence that the Israeli state adopts entrenched systems of discrimination against Palestinians, thousands of whom provide their temporary labor to Israeli worksites.[83]

While Qatar may end up as a landmark case of labor migration reform, and perhaps will be emulated by other Gulf states in the coming years, its citizens were marginalized from contributing to these processes of reform, and the top-down policy directives that have been adopted have ultimately strengthened the state's capacity. The Qatari regime has gained experience and exposure through the process of addressing its external critics. Ultimately, if the reforms are successful at alleviating international pressure, the state will have enhanced its international reputation, demonstrating both its commitment to modernization and capacity as a developmental state. Citizens remain sidelined and alienated from participation, as the state might be more responsive to external critics but appears less amenable to responding to its own domestic citizen constituencies, beyond reinforcing the welfare basket as needed.

QATAR, THE WORLD CUP, AND THE GLOBAL CAMPAIGN

No doubt human rights activism must determine at the outset what goals are desirable and feasible, and seldom would these be articulated as revolutionary attempts to upend an entire political and economic system. While the state-led labor reforms in Qatar are important and necessary, and will hopefully make lives better for lower income workers, broader discussions around rights, participation, inclusion, and possibly integration for migrants have not gained any traction. Those discussions could only occur if the population of Qatar, not just the state, was part of the conversation. As Qatar, like other states in the region, considers the multiple long-term economic and political challenges that will materialize when the rentier arrangements start to fray, the World Cup presented an opportunity to establish a trajectory that could have allowed for greater insertion of both citizen and migrant voices on important aspects on what the future of Qatar, and its demography, ought to look like.

10

GCC FOOTBALL FANS AND THEIR ENGAGEMENT

ESTABLISHING A RESEARCH AGENDA

Simon Chadwick

Introduction

With Qatar hosting the 2022 Fédération Internationale de Football Association (FIFA) World Cup, the world's attention has shifted towards the country and to football in the Middle East in general in recent years. Over the last decade, the tournament has been positioned as being regional—an acknowledgment of the significant position that the Middle East has come to occupy in world football as well as the passion that people across the six Gulf Cooperation Council (GCC) countries have for the sport.[1] Critics elsewhere in the world have repeatedly labelled GCC member states as being countries without a football culture, and thus ill-deserving of the right to host major football competitions.[2] Such views are at best naïve or perhaps ill-informed, but at worst they are patronizing, condescending, and reflect a troubling xenophobia.

Nevertheless, the case for staging international football competitions in GCC countries has not been helped by, for example, the problems associated with attracting spectators to events. The 2019 IAAF Athletics World Championship in Doha, for instance, received widespread criticism due to low attendance figures. Similarly, when Spain's Supercopa took place in Saudi Arabia in 2020, critics bemoaned the move, citing all manner of problems—ranging from accusations that the government in Riyadh was engaged in sportswashing (attempting to cleanse its reputation by investing in sport),[3] to condemnation that matches were being snatched away from Spanish fans by a foreign government.[4]

However, for every contentious episode, there is alternative and clear evidence of passionate football fandom across the GCC, involving successfully staged events, with positive attitudes and behaviors being displayed towards sport, and consumer spending by fans on products associated with football. To demonstrate this, one need look no further than the 2019 Asian Champions League Final, when Saudi Arabian club Al-Hilal defeated Japan's Urawa Red Diamonds over two legs. At the Riyadh leg of the tie, there were almost 25,000 fans in attendance. Shortly after this match, FIFA's Club World Cup took place in Doha, with Al-Hilal taking part along with top Qatari club Al-Sadd, and international champions, including Liverpool—a perennial favorite among football fans in the MENA region, partly the result of the club's Egyptian star winger Mohamed Salah. Earlier in 2019, Qatar triumphed in the Asian Nations Cup, which was held in the United Arab Emirates. Despite the GCC's diplomatic feud at the time, fans from Qatar still attended the event—not an easy feat, given the air blockade imposed by some of its GCC neighbors. Qatari fans travelled to the tournament via a circuitous route, mostly through Kuwait.

As such, fan engagement has become a primary consideration for decision-makers working for clubs and national associations in the GCC. The same is true for overseas clubs seeking to expand their fanbases among passionate fans in the region. As the above examples suggest, fandom is not necessarily an easy notion to conceptualize. Indeed, it continually occupies the minds of commercially oriented people in football across the world.[5] While fans in the GCC are sometimes fervent in their support of local clubs, in places such as Oman and Kuwait many are more likely to be transnationally engaged with the likes of Real Madrid or Bayern Munich. Other fans may prioritize supporting a national team—sometimes their own, but also those of other nations such as Brazil or Italy. When making the decision to support a particular team, a family member may be influential; once engaged, some fans may buy tickets to watch the team in a stadium, while others may prefer to use digital media as the main channel through which to engage. In other words, fans and fan engagement are notions, at least in commercial terms, that are complex and worthy of more detailed consideration, particularly from a GCC perspective.

It is on this basis that this chapter is written, with a particular emphasis being placed upon where and how a better understanding of GCC fan engagement may be established. In so doing, the reader should note that the chapter provides a business and marketing perspective of fandom; as such, there is no explicit reference to other literatures. Nevertheless, it is worth keeping in mind that notions and conceptions of heritage, tribe, and identity drawn from literatures such as those in cultural studies, history, and sociology may be of some relevance in adding depth and insight into the observations made here. Readers are therefore encouraged to seek out such studies as Tuastad's work on football in the Middle East.[6][7]

This chapter begins with a brief overview of the GCC, and the countries which it comprises. Thereafter, the chapter highlights some of the unique features and challenges associated with fan engagement in the GCC; in particular, issues of match attendance, and the predisposition of many fans in the region to engage with teams both domestically and internationally. What constitutes being a "fan" is subsequently examined, specifically through established literature in the field. This section notably highlights the paucity of marketing and business literature pertaining to fandom in the Gulf and across the Middle East in general. It is in this context that the chapter is written; hence, when reading this section, readers are invited to contemplate why this is an issue and what opportunities it creates for future research and analysis. Subsequently, the chapter moves on to explore the notion of engagement, with a focus on understanding the motives of fans who engage with sports. In this section, as well as throughout the chapter, reference is made to the preponderance of studies in the field that have been undertaken in either a North American or European setting. Notwithstanding commonalities in the motives, attitudes, and behaviors of humans, the dearth of studies examining fandom in the GCC is highlighted. Readers are thus asked to consider how the sociocultural embeddedness of football fandom impacts upon engagement. The chapter concludes in this vein, identifying opportunities for further research in a field that is currently poorly served by existing bodies of research and literature.

The Gulf Cooperation Council (GCC)

The GCC is a regional political and economic alliance consisting of six members: Bahrain, Kuwait, Oman, Qatar, Saudi Arabia, and the UAE. Established in 1981, the initial foundation of this alliance was a mutual desire to maintain security in the region following the Islamic Revolution in Iran and the subsequent Iran–Iraq War. While such security concerns remain, the GCC has more prominently sought to promote social and cultural cohesion, coordinate scientific and environmental activity, and ensure economic cooperation.[8] Members share several common features: notably, each is either an autocratic monarchy or sheikdom with limited (or no) political participation. In addition, the countries derive significant proportions of their national wealth from deposits of natural resources, specifically oil and gas. In terms of demography, each of the members has a population of less than 10 million people—the exception being Saudi Arabia, which has a population of 33.5 million. On average, the populations of GCC countries comprise 50 percent nationals and 50 percent non-nationals; although in the case of Qatar and the UAE, this non-national figure rises to almost 90 percent. Notably, the analysis contained in this chapter pertains to football fans who are nationals rather than non-nationals.[9]

Some scholars have traditionally examined GCC states through the lens of Rentier State Theory. "Rent" in this sense is not based upon an English definition; instead, it is derived from the French "*rente*"—meaning private income. Such states have social structures rooted in tribal relations, with ruling families governing on an autocratic basis—gathering incomes and determining expenditures. Rentier states thus operate as a form of patronage that guarantees the legitimacy and stability of the countries' rulers. Foreign investments also serve as a risk mitigation strategy practiced by the rentiers.[10] In this context, over the last two decades, GCC countries have envisioned a post-oil and gas future toward which they pursue industrial diversification, risk mitigation, the promotion of national well-being, a desire for internationally enhanced identities, and a more general pursuit of global legitimacy. Strategically, this has resulted in most of these countries investing in sport as one means through which to realize their visions. Football has become an intended driver of economic and industrial activity; a basis for achieving health, lifestyle, and community-based goals; and a vehicle for building international relations and projecting soft power. Dubai has compiled a high-profile portfolio of sponsorship properties via Emirates, its state airline, including deals with Spanish La Liga club Real Madrid, the English Premier League's Arsenal, and Italian Serie A's AC Milan. Qatar's strategy has largely been characterized by its pursuit of event-hosting rights, with the 2022 World Cup emblematic of the small nation's success in this field. Abu Dhabi acquired English club Manchester City, which has subsequently been used as the platform for creating a global sports and entertainment franchising network. Saudi Arabia has been rather slower than its regional neighbors to embrace the power of football, though plans are afoot for the country's leading clubs to be privatized, and a collaborative agreement has been signed with La Liga in Spain to develop some of its players. The Saudi government has also been linked to the acquisition of several overseas clubs.

Despite the diverse and growing investment of GCC countries in international football, the impact of this phenomenon on domestic football appears to have been limited. Although the likes of

Saudi Arabian clubs Al-Hilal and Al-Ittihad have enjoyed some success in the Asian Champions League, the GCC's other clubs have largely failed to challenge East Asian sides, such as South Korea's Pohang Steelers, or West Asian giants, such as Esteghlal of Iran, for continental superiority. Furthermore, the GCC countries' national teams continue to languish outside world governing body FIFA's top-50 nations rankings, even after Qatar's success in winning the 2019 AFC Asian Cup.

Table 10.1: Attendance and capacity at Saudi Professional League matches during 2018–19

Finishing position	Team	Stadium capacity	Total attendance	Average attendance	Average capacity utilization
1.	Al-Ittihad	62,241	365,128	33,193	53.3%
2.	Al-Ahli	62,242	253,178	21,098	33.9%
3.	Al-Hilal	25,000	210,903	21,090	84.4%
4.	Al-Nassr	67,000	146,542	14,654	21.9%
5.	Al-Wahda Mekka	38,000	75,915	7,592	20%
6.	Ohod Al-Medina	24,000	43,816	6,259	14.3%
7.	Al-Taawon	25,000	39,931	4,437	17.7%
8.	Al-Ettifaq	35,000	39,072	4,884	14%
9.	Al-Batin	6,000	36,369	3,031	50.5%
10.	Al-Raed	25,000	31,987	3,554	14.2%
11.	Al-Shabab Riyadh	67,000	31,752	2,887	4.3%
12.	Al Qadisiyah FC	11,800	27,658	2,766	23.4%
13.	Al-Fateh	20,000	26,289	2,921	14.6%
14.	Al-Hazm	3,000	18,997	2,375	79.2%
15.	Al-Feiha FC	7,000	17,381	1,931	27.6%
16.	Al-Faisaly Harmah	7,000	10,345	1,149	16.4%

The same picture is evident off the field as well; several media outlets have bemoaned how few people attend football matches in the region, while others continue to ponder how best to build fanbases.[11] A cursory glance at, say, the Emirati Pro League reveals the scale of the challenges facing the region's football administrators. During the 2018/19 season, Al-Ain recorded the season's highest match attendance at 18,103. However, given the club stadium's 25,000 seats, this marked only a 69.7 percent utilization of capacity. That season's lowest attendance in the Pro League was for a match between Dibba Al-Fujairah and Al-Dhafra; thirty-nine fans were present in a stadium with space for 10,000, meaning a capacity utilization of 0.39 percent.

In Saudi Arabia, a country whose population is more than three times larger than the UAE's, the picture is only marginally better. Notwithstanding the preeminent Al-Hilal's healthy matchday crowds, general attendance and stadium capacity utilization are also worryingly low (see Table 10.1). To provide some context, in Europe, clubs such as Manchester United, Real Madrid, and Bayern Munich invariably play home games in front of sell-out crowds with stadium capacity being fully utilized. Elsewhere in the region, the top teams of Turkey (see Table 10.2) and Iran (see Table 10.3) yield more impressive numbers for attendance and capacity utilization.

Table 10.2: Attendance and capacity at selected Turkish Süper Lig matches during 2018–19

Team	Stadium capacity	Total attendance	Average attendance	Average capacity utilization
Fenerbahce SK	47,834	311,200	38,900	81.3%
Galatasaray SK	52,223	288,889	36,111	69.1%
Beşiktaş SK	41,188	229,808	28,726	69.7%

Table 10.3: Attendance and capacity at selected Persian Gulf Pro League matches during 2018–19

Team	Stadium capacity	Total attendance	Average attendance	Average capacity utilization
Persepolis FC	80,000	570,500	38,033	47.5%
Tractor FC	66,833	551,441	45,953	68.8%

In simple terms, the poor utilization of capacity across the GCC constitutes the sub-optimal use of a physical asset, adversely impacting the investment returns from such an asset. In commercial terms, therefore, many of the GCC's clubs underperform, which potentially affects the stability and sustainability of these organizations. Such issues are problematic for other stakeholders such as media corporations and sponsors. Fans are widely seen as being a feature of the football product, generating noise and atmosphere that serve to differentiate football both from other sports and from other products. Without large numbers of fans inside stadiums, the product is undermined and therefore of less value to the likes of broadcasters. In turn, broadcasters are typically less predisposed toward paying for substandard content, which affects the rights fees they pay. Under-supported clubs, therefore, derive lower revenues than other, better-supported clubs. This is a problem for sponsors as well; small crowds and weak television coverage reduces the number of people who see the names and logos that are typically placed on the front of football shirts and on perimeter signage. If nothing else, empty stadiums are a problem for fans themselves; the experience of football is co-created, which is underpinned by the simultaneous consumption and production of a matchday atmosphere. As such, one can argue that small gatherings of fans beget small gatherings of fans—if people do not get what they are seeking from a product, then they limit or withdraw their consumption of it.

Problems of fan engagement in the GCC are not, however, solely the concern of individual clubs and fans. Governments across the region have a considerable stake in their football governing bodies, clubs, events and, indeed, in the sport's success (in its various forms). For instance, in the case of Saudi Arabia, its leading football clubs are state-owned, a status the government is trying to change by privatizing the clubs. The view is that subsidies and government intervention have made Saudi Arabian clubs dependent, inefficient, and introspective. By making them private organizations, clubs would have to professionalize and become more commercial. As a result, clubs would have to think more carefully about how to generate new or additional revenues from the likes of fans, necessitating a better understanding of their engagement. However, engaged fans are not simply a commercial or an economic imperative—there are also political dimensions to the phenomenon. Engaged football fandom can serve as a basis for creating collective identity, the benefits of which may include social cohesion or a stronger, shared sense of national (or regional) identity. This may also serve a political purpose, especially as large numbers of engaged fans may help to communicate an ideology or set of values. In turn, some would argue that such engagement is fundamental to the generation and projection of soft power. For a country like Qatar, this is a serious and significant issue, especially considering critics who claim that the country has no football culture and therefore should not be hosting the 2022 FIFA World Cup. Effective engagement of fans is therefore of paramount importance to the country's football administrators.

Policies over the last decade clearly show how investments in football remain consistent with the complex game plan of rentier states. This complex interplay of sporting, economic, social, and political issues marks out the notion of fandom in the GCC as being different to fandom in territories elsewhere in the world, especially those in Europe and the Americas, where more research has been undertaken. This complexity is underscored when one considers anecdotal evidence from populations in the Gulf who question why, for example, the Abu Dhabi United Group lavishes money on Manchester City, and why Qatar Sports Investments (a Qatari state investment vehicle) does the same at Paris Saint Germain (PSG), while each countries' domestic clubs languish. Building one's domestic football clubs and their business activities is surely more desirable than spending on teams abroad, so one argument goes.

Somewhat perversely, Manchester City and PSG appear to have become "local favorites" among some fans in Abu Dhabi and Qatar, who have elevated the teams above local clubs in their repertoires of fandom.[12] This provides an insight into the complexities of GCC football fandom; it is likely that most football fans from Bur Dubai, Doha, and Sharjah will probably never attend a game at the Etihad Stadium in Manchester or the Parc des Princes in Paris. Yet they will gather in local cafes to watch the games on television, talk about the clubs and players among family and friends, and access content via social media for the latest developments in England and France. These ways of being a GCC football fan also highlight the need for more and better fan engagement research to be undertaken in the region. Thus far, the balance of academic research has typically focused on fans and their engagement in North American and European settings. Whereas the likes of, say, Italian football fans often only support one club side for the entire duration of their lives (often accompanied by engagement with the Italian national team), existing evidence shows that fans in the GCC region sometimes support or follow multiple teams. In turn, for each of these teams—some of which may be domestic, some of which may be overseas—the affective, cognitive, and behavioral dimensions of engagement may be configured in a multiplicity of different ways.

It is also clear that fan engagement in the GCC is not simply just a matter of buying matchday tickets. The region's football administrators may yearn for packed stadiums across the Gulf, which always makes for an attractive spectacle that appeals to broadcasters and sponsors, yet fandom in the likes of Bahrain, Kuwait, and Oman seems to be more nuanced and distinctive than fandom in places like Naples, Rome, and Turin. Unlike those whose fandom is typically linked to locality, and for whom loyalty is unswerving, football fandom in the GCC countries comprises a more diverse and rich mix of consumption choices, sometimes accompanied by a degree of brand-switching—changes in team support—that may be less evident elsewhere.

Research undertaken by Deloitte on behalf of Qatar's Supreme Committee for Delivery and Legacy (SC),[13] provides some interesting insights into GCC football fan engagement. Of the respondents (n = 1,233) who participated in this study:

- 73 percent said that football is very important to them;
- 89 percent watched football regularly on television;
- 77.9 percent identified that they had both a favorite local team and a favorite overseas team;

- 78 percent of 18–24 year olds agreed that football is very important to them, although they preferred to follow overseas teams;
- 39 percent have been lifelong fans of their favorite local team, compared to 26 percent for international teams;
- 56.1 percent indicated that they had bought team-related merchandise during the previous twelve months.

While such industry consultant analyses are helpful, they are often undertaken as market research rather than rigorous studies based upon scientifically proven measurement scales. Nonetheless, there is a paucity of academic studies in the field of GCC football fans and their engagement. In one study, Theodorakis et al. undertake an analysis of the earlier Deloitte study,[14] observing that the Middle East should not be seen as a homogenous market as there are significant variations in attitudes and behaviors among football fans in the region. Furthermore, their findings indicated that football consumption largely takes place via television and sports-related online platforms, rather than through football match attendance. Fans from the GCC were identified in general as watching significantly less local football on television than international football. Crucially, a low frequency of match attendance across the region was reported.

These findings resonate with those reported by Binjwaied et al. who highlighted issues with the numbers of Saudi Arabians buying matchday tickets.[15] The authors noted that the profusion of broadcast content and a lack of commitment displayed across the local population to domestic teams are two causes of small crowd sizes (and poor capacity utilization). Interestingly, the authors concluded that due to the more positive associations that many football fans in Saudi Arabia have with overseas teams and leagues, collaborative relations between Saudi clubs and those in countries such as Spain might have helped to build attendances at matches. This perhaps partially explains why in 2018, the Saudi Arabian Football Association sent nine national team players on loan to nine different Spanish La Liga clubs. Then, in 2020, Spain's leading clubs played Supercopa de España games in Jeddah.

In both the Theodorakis et al. and Binjwaied et al. studies, it is evident that football fans in the GCC are enthusiastically engaged with Spanish football. The strength of this affiliation is confirmed in Al Gadineh and Good's study of Arab fans' team identification, fandom, and Spanish clubs.[16] In a later study, Al Gadineh and Good again reiterate the preferences that football fans in the Middle East have for clubs playing not only in Spain but in England and Italy as well. It is thought that people, by supporting such overseas clubs, can temporarily escape from the hardships of life and boost their self-esteem by supporting successful teams like Real Madrid, Juventus, and Liverpool. Somewhat counterintuitively, however, the same research identifies that higher income levels are likely to be a predictor of fan engagement in the region. This possibly implies that fans' decision to engage with teams may be driven by aspects of status and conspicuous consumption.

This small number of studies essentially constitutes the total number of English-language literature examining fan engagement in the GCC from a business or marketing perspective. Given the increasing prominence of GCC nations across world football, their growing investments in the sport, the region's population size (approximately 54 million people), and the undoubted passion of many people for football, this constitutes an extremely small body of work. Therefore this chapter is intended to prompt greater interest in the field and help stimulate future research, particularly from a Middle Eastern perspective, rather than simply relying upon adaptations of North American or European studies of fan engagement. While domestic football teams in the region may struggle to fill their stadiums, it is nevertheless clear that fans still buy team-related merchandise, watch matches on television, and engage with both domestic and international teams. To a certain extent, this differentiates GCC football fans from other fans elsewhere in the world; as such, this warrants closer analysis of affect, cognition, and behavior in a regional setting. What is therefore presented below is a specific and direct attempt to frame and analyze football fan engagement in a GCC context.

GCC FOOTBALL FANS AND THEIR ENGAGEMENT

What is a Fan?

People who maintain a relationship with football may either self-label or be described by others as being followers or supporters of a football club or team. However, football fans are not the same as followers and supporters; indeed, they display significantly different traits and characteristics. Followers and supporters have a casual, distant, or somewhat disengaged connection with their favorite team. They may occasionally attend a match or discuss a team with their friends. However, fans are typically affiliates of and advocates for a team; they think and act in a multiplicity of ways, including attending matches, watching games on television, posting and sharing news about their teams on social media, and discussing "their" team with others. They are often co-creators, both inside stadiums and via other channels.[17] They also engage in extra-role behaviors, such as spreading positive word of mouth, recruiting new fans, providing suggestions to teams and clubs, participating in new product development, and collaborating with other fans. As such, fans typically are very clear about their motives for supporting a team, what their attitudes are toward that team, and how they want to behave in their engagements with it.

In turn, according to Gladden and Funk,[18] fans possess a strong and intense emotional attachment to the teams they support. Park et al. observe that fans are closely associated with certain forms of intensity or affect, often bound up in their sense of self or of their social identity.[19] Abercrombie and Longhurst go so far as to say that some fans may even display attitudes and behaviors that are cultish,[20] while Cova et al. characterize such people as tribal.[21] Trail and James note that this means fans can therefore sometimes be persistent and resistant to change in their relationships with teams.[22] Fans also behave as consumers who exhibit clear loyalty behaviors, including their insistence on staying in a relationship. Indeed, Reysen and Branscombe note that fandom involves an emotional investment,[23] leading to regular and repeated consumption. Fiske identifies that fans are not only co-producers,[24] but are also creators of cultural objects.

Given the existing Western-centric literature, a simple question seems apparent. Who is a football fan in the GCC? As the evidence above highlights, football in the region enjoys a considerable fan base, although this fandom is not necessarily manifest in terms of stadium capacity utilization. Understanding this contradiction represents a pressing need for football marketers as gate receipts commonly contribute a significant proportion of a club's annual revenues. Otherwise, there is no doubt that certain human characteristics unite fans of LA Galaxy in the United States, Juventus in Italy, Al-Ain in Dubai, and Guangzhou Evergrande in China. Indeed, the need, for example, to congregate and gather is a fundamental trait that has been examined over time across a multitude of literatures.

What is largely unclear from existing research, both academic and practitioner, are two things: it remains unproven how these shared human traits configure in different settings, and it is unclear how they manifest themselves amongst football fans in the GCC. For instance, culturally specific factors are likely to motivate fans in different parts of the world, ensuring that conditioning, learning, and engagement are configured differently in, say, Manchester and Riyadh. To illustrate this, much Western fan engagement literature highlights the role that family members play in influencing the fandom of young people. Yet Westerners typically live in flatter, more nuclear families, where distances between younger and older family members are smaller, and liberal values pervade. By comparison, families in the GCC are typically hierarchical, patriarchal, and extended. Therefore the established body of work in this field seems ill-equipped to address the specific contexts within which GCC populations become engaged with football. More work is required in such contexts if we are ever to effectively understand the true nature of fandom across the GCC. Indeed, one is struck by the failure of Western researchers to successfully address the conundrum of low attendance at matches in countries such as Saudi Arabia. Perhaps this failure contains a hidden message: that the defined cultural parameters within which fan research takes place should be dictated by those from, or located within, the territories being researched.

Fandom in the GCC also appears to be a more nuanced and complex phenomenon than one might typically observe in, for example, the United States or Great Britain. Literature on sports fandom and fan engagement in sports such as baseball and American football is deeply culturally embedded, to the extent that one must question its relevance and applicability to football in, say, Kuwait or Oman. Furthermore, even in more broadly appealing sports, such as basketball, fandom exists against the backdrop of a franchise system where teams can and do move to other parts of a country. The organization of football leagues in the GCC is undertaken on a completely different basis, with clubs garnering support according to what would seem a unique basis. For instance, Saudi Arabia's elite professional football teams are state-owned, often with explicit links to institutions such as the police or military. Similarly, Qatar's Al-Sadd has considerable and significant links to the country's ruling family, which dictates that fans engage with the team for very different reasons to those that routinely appear in the established literature.

In much the same vein, for more than a century, British football fandom has been framed and driven by the industrial development of cities. Most professional clubs were the product of urban living, and fans engaged with them to escape the pressures of work. Later, teams such as Chelsea, Manchester City, and Newcastle United became the means through which fans could assert their geographic identity, sometimes manifesting itself through violence. Perhaps there are some generic parallels that can be drawn with the likes of Al-Rayyan of the Qatar Stars League: the club is a historical representation of location, tribe, and an increasingly distant past way of life. The role of nostalgia in sports marketing and football fandom is not an alien concept; in fact, it seems highly pertinent in this context. However, fan research undertaken in working-class British cities appears inappropriately positioned to generate meaningful insights into the fans of a team formerly located in the desert.

We also know that people in the GCC are not simply—or typically—linear fans, whereby they engage with a team and remain loyal to it for the duration of their lifetimes (as happens in countries like Great Britain). Research findings presented above alert us to the reality that Bahrainis, Saudis, and Emiratis may be engaged fans of more than one team. This suggests that something akin to parallel fandom exists in the region, whereby a single individual could support a local club team, their national team, an overseas club team, and an overseas national team. Tapp and Clowes have previously studied repertoire fans—people who support more than one club,[25] often for a multitude of reasons—though again, in the context of English football, where the football consumption environment is significantly different to that in the GCC. The small number of published studies examining fandom in the region means that scant attention has been paid to this unique portfolio of consumption alternatives with which GCC fans engage. On what basis such fan portfolios are constructed, how they are developed and managed, and the apportioning of one's engagement to each of the clubs in the portfolio represent compelling research opportunities, though also a necessity if sports marketers are to better understand the GCC market.

In this context, it is also worth addressing the growing list of investments being made by GCC nations in football elsewhere in the world. The Abu Dhabi government owns the City Football Group, a growing global franchise network that consists of—among others—England's Manchester City, Girona in Spain, and Sichuan Juniu of China. Reports indicate that some fans in the emirate increasingly see Manchester City as their local club,[26] which adds a further layer to the fan engagement landscape. Qatar Sports Investments' acquisition of PSG has resulted in similar fan behavior being exhibited by fans in Doha and elsewhere in the small Gulf nation. The apparent dichotomy between local and global implies an opportunity in the region to analyze fan engagement as a "glocal" phenomenon. As an extension of this, while it is not unusual for PSG to visit Qatar for training camps or exhibition matches (the same with Manchester City in Abu Dhabi), the transnational remoteness of respective Qatari, Emirati, and other GCC fans dictates that their engagement is established and sustained by club retail outlets, and by mobile devices. With existing studies of fan engagement effectively premised upon the possibility of physically attending games, a new body of work in the GCC needs to emerge in which the underlying tenets of engagement are different.

Adding to the already complex fan landscape, it is important to note that the notion of a fan is not a uniform one. Indeed, rather than being a homogenous mass, fans are often significantly distinct from one another. This has led researchers in the field of business to identify typologies of fans. Stewart and Smith highlighted five types: "Aficionados"—fans who seek a great team performance but are not intensely loyal to that team; "Theatre Goers"—fans who want to be entertained, specifically in a dramatic way; "Passionate Partisans"—fans who identify with a team and want that team to win; "Champ Followers"—fans who switch between teams depending upon who is winning at the time; and "Reclusive Partisans"—fans who identify strongly with a team but rarely attend matches.[27] Tapp and Clowes differentiated between casual fans, regulars, and fanatics.[28] Fanatics were identified as living and breathing football, having strong engagement with their chosen team (often based upon community ties) and a strong desire for their team to win. Regulars are less engaged with the teams of which they are fans; indeed, football is likely to be less important to them than it is to fanatics. Furthermore, some may even go so far as to label Regulars as "glory hunters" because being the fan of a winning team is most important to them. Casual fans typically have low engagement with a team, preferring instead to watch entertaining teams. Consequently, such people are sometimes characterized as being professional wanderers.

In other typologies, a distinction is broadly made between temporary fans, devoted fans, and fanatical fans. Among temporary fans, there is little evidence that such people self-identify as football fans, suggesting that neither a team nor the sport are part of their self-identity. Furthermore, the temporary fan's team engagement is time-constrained, indicating that once they have achieved their consumption goals, they return to their other, more normal consumption behaviors. Some commentators, notably Caldini et al., highlighted the role that "BIRGing" (Basking-In-Reflected-Glory) plays in the consumption habits of temporary fans.[29] That is, these people simply internalize the success of a team for their own purpose, and then desist once the success dissipates.

Devoted fans are not short-termers. Indeed, they remain engaged with a specific team beyond the initial event that led to a connection being made between them. Some have characterized this as being a form of attachment (for example, Kwon et al.) often linked to a person's sense of self,[30] which in turn is bound up in identity and the actualization of whom one seeks to be. The greater a team contributes to a person's identity, the more they are likely to display protective behaviors towards it. Such devoted fans often struggle to separate themselves from the teams they support, hence match wins induce happiness, and in some cases even euphoria.[31] Conversely, these fans will experience loss as something deeply personal, challenging who they are and how they see themselves.

Taking the intensity of attachment to an even deeper level, the loyalty of some fans marks them as being fanatical. Observers of engagement sometimes go so far as to express fanaticism as a genetic phenomenon that is bound up in one's DNA.[32] More commonly, the longevity of this form of engagement is characterized as being fanatical fandom, borne of psychological conditioning manifest in family, peer, and community groupings. This helps explain why football teams often target their marketing activities at children, as they learn to accept values, goals, beliefs, attitudes, and norms that effectively lock them into team fandom. So embedded can values and goals become in the psyche of an individual that they become lifetime fans. In financial terms, this can mean that a fanatical fan can be the source of significant revenues for a team throughout the duration of their lives.

Fanaticism is a unique form of loyalty characterized by strong and intense levels of commitment, allegiance, devotion, passion, emotional attachment, enthusiasm, and involvement.[33] Furthermore, fanatical fans voluntarily engage in behaviors that they believe protect their teams and ensure their existence and legacy.[34] Fanatical consumers exhibit a deep love that remains despite poor performances.[35] They also display a devotion, passion, and enthusiasm for teams that is considered infectious. Fanatics go to great personal and financial lengths to support a team, such as by joining and actively participating in brand communities (groups of people who consume the same brands).[36] In some ways, fanatics are no different to devoted fans—they are not bound by time or distance, and both construct their sense of self in the context of their engagement with a team. Nevertheless, fanatics display attitudes and behaviors that demonstrate greater levels of knowledge, and more anxiety and arousal watching their team compete.[37] Devoted fans may go to every home match, but fanatical fans may go to every single match, home and away, season after season.[38]

The narrative around different fan types is intriguing, and notions of fanaticism are seductive. Indeed, there can be no doubt about their relevance for analyses of fans and fan engagement in the GCC. For instance, Saudi football fans have been identified as being just as active as others elsewhere in the world.[39] Existing literature in the field is therefore clearly resonant, warranting further consideration of how it can be applied in a GCC setting. However, there are some clear differences between sports in the Gulf and sports in, say, North America (from where much of the established fan engagement literature originates). In the United States, tailgating is a feature of the fan landscape, whereas in Europe the use of, for example, flares and banners is synonymous with engagement. Although not commonly addressed as a variable in fan studies in the sports marketing literature, violence is often associated with fandom and engagement in some countries. However, each of these instances is not necessarily a characteristic of fans and their engagement in the GCC, indicating that there are some significant differences between continents, regions, and perhaps even countries that are part of the same region. Given a paucity of business and marketing literature pertaining to the GCC, understanding the similarities, differences, specifics, and peculiarities of fandom in the region should be a priority.

In the same vein, it is worth noting that a large proportion of the existing body of work in the field has typically been undertaken in a stadium environment, specifically in the context of match attendance. The top clubs in Saudi Arabia aside, we have already established that match attendance at stadiums across the GCC is an issue for both researchers and practitioners to address. Furthermore, existing research clearly shows that different degrees of fandom exist, which are based upon, among other things, the number of away games a fan attends. For researchers focusing on fan engagement in the GCC, this presents a problem, as few people travel to away games. Instead, the online nature of fandom in the region, the connections people have with teams abroad, and the way in which fans maintain a portfolio of clubs they support, indicate that engagement is different to Kuwait, Oman, Bahrain, and elsewhere in the GCC. This suggests the intriguing possibility that, for example, one might be a fanatical fan of Al-Ain in Abu Dhabi, a devoted fan of the Emirati national team, but also a passionate fan of a club such as Italy's Juventus. Understanding the configuration of such portfolios is therefore both an opportunity and a significant research challenge.

Indeed, such is the paucity of research in the field of GCC football fandom that it demands further work. With many of the GCC nations employing sport as a policy instrument to enable the pursuit of national visions—with the intention of fostering a stronger sense of national identity—fan research seems of paramount importance across the region. Football has come to occupy an important part of the policy landscape. Hence, determining the contribution that being engaged with a football team makes to individual and group notions of national identity is vital. Furthermore, understanding how engaged fandom can bring about improvements in perceptions of and attitudes towards national well-being is also important.

Equally, understanding how the Western framing and labelling of fans applies in the context of, say, Qatar or Saudi Arabia is also worth exploring. For instance, when the Spanish Super Cup Final was staged in Saudi Arabia in early 2020, more than 59,000 people attended the match in Jeddah, delivering stadium capacity utilization of 95 percent. Most fans in the venue were local, with less than one thousand traveling fans from Spain present, implying that a significant proportion of the attendees were "Aficionados" or instead were perhaps "Theatre Goers." Later, between January and March 2020, the popular Winter Wonderland attraction staged in Riyadh hosted Real Madrid as the only football club to have a presence at the fairground. At the same time, there are several Real Madrid retail outlets across the GCC, including in Doha, where one can also find the world's very first Spanish La Liga lounge. Notwithstanding the fractious politics of Spanish football, the prominence of Spain in the landscape of GCC football fandom strongly indicates that a much better understanding of engagement is needed. While some teams from GCC countries struggle to utilize their stadium capacities, the profusion of Spanish investment into the region is an illustration of how strong GCC football fandom is. The question is: What form(s) does it take?

A final point to note about much of the business and marketing literature pertaining to football fandom is that there is a profusion of studies that are focused on men's football and on male-dominated sample populations. There have been some recent studies of female football (and others sports) fans,[40] though these remain relatively scarce in number. Hence, there is a clear need for a commitment to studying female fandom, though this appears specifically to be a more pressing issue in the GCC. Indeed, with Saudi Arabia recently having permitted women to attend football matches for the first time, and with Qatar set to stage global football's biggest mega-event, understanding female fans and their engagement with the sport is an especially pressing issue. It is therefore anticipated that this chapter will not only provoke further discussion about fandom in general, but also stimulate studies examining female football fandom in a GCC setting.

What is Engagement?

In business and marketing, definitions of customer engagement emphasize deep and intimate connections between consumers and products (or brands) that endure over time, which in turn drive conversations and purchase decisions.[41] Engaged relationships have been variously characterized as being mutually beneficial, co-creative, experiential, and emotional.[42] Typically, engagement is framed as a multidimensional concept consisting of affective, cognitive, and behavioral dimensions. As such, consumer engagement is a three-stage process that is initially driven by consumption motives, which then leads to attitude formation, and subsequently drives both intended and actual purchase behavior. The process is commonly modelled and then tested using multivariate data analysis techniques that establish significant relationships between vari-

FOOTBALL IN THE MIDDLE EAST

ables in a hypothesized model. However, research undertaken specifically within the field of sports marketing and football fandom is much less developed. It is largely focused on examining affect, generally fails to establish behavioral outcomes, conflates the complexities of attitude formation with team loyalty, and inadequately explores the causal relationships between hypothesized relationships. This is inevitably a constraint upon fan engagement research in general, though it specifically places limits upon the extent to which existing literature can be applied within a GCC context. Nevertheless, this helps to identify an interesting challenge for multivariate researchers: to formulate and statistically test models that examine fan engagement as a multidimensional process.

One issue that engagement researchers must contend with is in deciding upon direction of causality. While watching a favorite team on television might typically be considered as a behavioral outcome of fandom, being exposed to watching a team on television might actually be the point at which initial engagement takes place. This is something that marketers refer to as a "touchpoint."[43] Establishing the precise direction of influence is therefore of considerable importance. Across the process of affect, distinguishing between touchpoints and motives is also important; although the two are different, these differences are subtle. Nevertheless, when a person, who may ultimately become a fan, deliberately or consciously seeks further engagement, they are likely to be motivated by a number of factors. Among the most common motives are:

- Vicarious achievement—the need for social prestige, self-esteem, and the sense of empowerment that an individual may receive from their association with a team;[44]
- Escape—the need to find a diversion from work and the normal, sometimes mundane, activities of everyday life;[45]
- Family—the opportunity to spend time with one's family doing something everyone enjoys;[46]
- Attractiveness of participants—appreciation of the physical appearance of a team and/or its players;[47]
- Skill of participants—appreciation of the physical skill of a team and/or its players.[48]

As previously stated, the majority of work in this area has been undertaken in other geographical and sociocultural settings, raising questions about the prevailing literature's applicability to GCC fandom. Nevertheless, there is sufficient breadth in the existing body of work to suggest some interesting research possibilities for those examining the GCC's football fans. Without necessarily being exhaustive in addressing the range and depth of influences, presented below are some considerations for researchers working in (or seeking to work in) this field.

Vicarious Achievement

One of the core features of the sports product is the way in which it deeply resonates with human emotions. The need for survival and the consequent competition for resources and power this evokes leads to a desire among people to succeed in their quest. It is from such basic motives that sports fandom is born; indeed, football provides an opportunity to fulfill basic needs vicariously. Hence, football fans in the GCC are fundamentally the same as fans elsewhere, engaging with a team that brings social prestige, self-esteem, and a sense of empowerment. In a similar way, vicarious achievement may enable individuals who perceive themselves as being otherwise unsuccessful to realize whatever personal goals they may set themselves. This could lead to people engaging with teams that have a strong record of success, though it may also encompass elements of, for example, status and glamour. Vicarious achievement might also be correlated with conspicuous consumption and, similarly, with "BIRGing" and with "CORFing" (Cutting-Off Reflected Failure) too.[49] This is likely to explain the predisposition of significant numbers of GCC fans towards teams such as Al-Sadd and Al-Wahda; that is, top teams in their respective countries. It may also help to explain wider engagements with the likes of club teams such as Real Madrid and Liverpool, or with national teams such as Brazil and Argentina. This is, however, conjecture, as some key research questions remain: On what basis and in which terms do football fans in the GCC frame achievement, and how do they vicariously engage? Put another way: What is the process of affect? Then, in turn, how does this play out in terms of attitudes and behaviors?

Escape

If one examines the history of European professional sports, most notably football, their growth was bound in industrial and socio-cultural developments. Football and support for a team were a means through which to escape the labor hardships and urban blight that afflicted many people in areas where the sport developed. The growth of sports in the United States during the twentieth century was somewhat different, in the sense that they were strategically developed on a commercial basis. Sports as a commodity and as an entertainment product has thus been a prevailing North American view that has often dominated the sports marketing literature on fandom. Even within this context, however, the view has nevertheless prevailed that sports provide an experience that enables one to escape the challenges of everyday life.

Escapism is important to many fans and one would seem justified in claiming that the same arguments about the role and purpose that football serves elsewhere today also hold in the GCC. Football is a way of getting away from the sheer mundanity of everyday life, and one can therefore extrapolate that this is also true for fans who are engaged or potentially may engage with football teams in the GCC. However, this does raise an interesting question regarding the aspects of daily life from which people are presumably escaping. Notions of industrial blight and suffering seem far less fitting when considering countries that feature some of the highest standards of living in the world. This implies that notions of escapism should be explored specifically within a GCC setting.

Family

In most cultures, the role of family members is central to the process through which fans initially engage with a football team. This is often prompted by someone such as a parent or a relative taking young family members to a match or encouraging them to watch a game on television. Based on such an initial stimulus, a lifetime of fandom can be built with some individuals who are likely to be unswerving in their loyalty for a team, and who remain engaged with it in some cases until they die. This raises an important question about the nature of family influence that is not explored in a detailed or wholly convincing way by the existing literature. It largely generalizes, making no distinctions between males and females or between older and younger family members, while failing to address the dynamics of the relationships between them. In the GCC, these are important considerations in the development of fan engagement. Whereas family structures in Western societies are commonly flat and based around a small nucleus, Arab families are more likely to be hierarchical and extended.[50] In addition, gender plays an important role in the development of engagement, not least in countries where there are issues pertaining to equality and social cohesion. All of this suggests that older males in the GCC are likely to be at the heart of driving football fan engagement, with grandfathers, fathers, and other senior male figures often being enablers and moderators of family support for specific teams.

Attractiveness of Participants

Attractiveness is a concept that is commonly examined in the marketing literature; unsurprisingly, it is a basic human driver of choice and, thus, engagement. In the broader literature, attractiveness is commonly associated with product features, functional benefits, and design aesthetics. However, specifically within the sports marketing literature, attractiveness is conceived in a rather narrower, stark way. Attractiveness is seen as being an entirely physical phenomenon—at one level, bound up in notions of athleticism but, at another level, linked with perceptions of sexuality. Both together and separately, athleticism and sex have become cornerstones in, for example, examining athletes as brands. In liberal societies, the prevailing fan engagement literature focuses on physical attraction, which is arguably warranted. However, such a focus seems not only inappropriate to analyses of fan engagement in the GCC but may even be considered insensitive. Whether or not this is the case is perhaps worthy of further exploration by researchers from the region. In addition to the physical, sexual framing of athletes, attractiveness is sometimes also connected with, for instance, hairstyles and tattoos. To some observers in the Gulf, such trivial detail might be seen as facile and inadequate in explaining how fans engage with either football players or teams. Instead, one suspects that, for example, religious devotion, tribal ties, or commitment to family might be much more significant affective determinants of engagement. In which case, new studies may seek to develop and test new measurement scales of attractiveness.

Skill of Participants

As was noted at the beginning of this chapter, domestic football matches in the GCC can sometimes be poorly attended, although engagement is, of course, often manifest in other ways. However, it could be that the general quality of players and teams in the GCC may be a determinant of the extent to which local fans engage with a team. To help illustrate this point, it is worth considering that in November 2010, within twenty-four hours of each other, two international games were played in Doha. The first involved a friendly match between the national teams of Brazil and Argentina at Khalifa Stadium; the second, played at the same venue, took place the next day between Haiti and Qatar. For the former, all tickets for the 40,000-capacity stadium were sold out; for the latter, barely 5,000 people attended. Significantly, the South American teams' starting line-ups were populated by the likes of Lionel Messi and Neymar Jr. One interpretation of this dichotomy is that GCC football fans engage in different ways and to different extents with the teams they support. Another interpretation is that the skill of players for the likes of Argentina and Brazil (and, for that matter, Real Madrid and Juventus) is a more enticing prospect for fans in the region than the domestic talent appearing for club and national teams across the Gulf. That said, some of the region's leading club teams are awash with global talent, yet they still do not necessarily draw a crowd. This implies once more that there is a peculiarity in the distinctions the region's fans make between their engagement with domestic teams and with teams from elsewhere in the world. This may be due to issues of "BIRGing", of self-actualization, or of appropriating status for one's own ends. However, as is the recurrent theme of this chapter, existing literature in the field focuses on sports in the West and not the GCC. Understanding how skillful participants (that is, players) engage Saudis, Bahrainis, and others is therefore necessary.

Conclusions and Recommendations

In the GCC, some traditional sports still maintain a hold over the imagination and self-image of people—falconry and camel racing being two examples. Equally, there are other sports that embody the zeitgeist, in which there is growing interest—esports epitomizing this. However, there remain some grounds for arguing that one sport transcends all in the region: football. While attendance at matches across the region continues to be somewhat unevenly spread, there is no doubt that significant numbers of people in each of the six GCC member countries are engaged with the sport. Some will buy tickets to watch games of various types, others will follow a team on television or via social media, and fans often buy merchandise. In many ways therefore, fandom mirrors that which one finds elsewhere in the world and that is reflected in established literature in the field.

In simple, human terms, the football fans of Saudi Arabia, Oman, and Kuwait engage with football and football teams due to affect variables. Similarly, those found in Qatar, Bahrain, and the UAE form attitudes and establish behaviors that one can also observe in Europe, South America, and other places where football is popular. However, fandom and fan engagement in the GCC is distinct from elsewhere in the world; this is the result of a multitude of factors, ranging from the role that one's family circumstances and religion might play in influencing fandom through to the teams with which fans engage. As such, the existing literature in the fields of business and marketing is helpful to researchers, and might even be necessary preconditions for a more detailed understanding of GCC football fandom to emerge. However, this body of work is insufficiently diverse in its foundation and focus, as it fails to account for the distinctiveness of engagement across the region. On this basis, this chapter aims to promote research possibilities and stimulate responses from researchers in the field. Understanding engagement—affect, attitudes, behaviors—should be central to the research agenda. One hopes that both a new generation of researchers from within the GCC, as well as others from outside the region, can help push fan research to the fore over the coming decade.

11

TO SEE AND BE SEEN

FOOTBALL, MEDIA, AND SOCIAL CHANGE IN IRAN

Niki Akhavan

Introduction

That football is often politicized in the Middle East almost goes
without saying; and much has been written about football as a lit-
eral and figurative arena for asserting both people power and the
power of the state.[1] Iran is no exception in this regard, and both
the popularity and politicization of the sport has continued steadily
since the late 1990s. The reasons for this can be attributed to several factors often cited in explaining shifts in the political and social
landscape of Iran at the turn of the millennium: the rise (and fall)
of the reform movement, the bulging youth population, and the
appearance of alternative media outlets and digital media. While
all of these are relevant, perhaps the most important factor is the
obvious one: the Iranian national football team became a competitive and entertaining team to watch, placing third at the 1996 Asian

Football Confederation (AFC) Asian Cup and qualifying for the 1998 World Cup, during which it managed its first World Cup victory in a much anticipated game against the United States.

The success of national teams and even domestic league clubs offers golden opportunities for states to ride the waves of nationalist and group sentiments in order to legitimize their rule and use football victories as an affirmation of policies, even when there are no apparent links to the sport. Similarly, the role of football in nation-building and/or consensus-building has been noted in countries with vastly differing circumstances such as Fascist Italy, post-colonial countries, sub-Saharan African states, and contemporary China. Martin Simon has examined how the Fascist state rode the victories of the national soccer team—two world cups and the Olympics between 1934 and 1938—to make a case for the state's organizational commitments. He also points out how both national and domestic football allowed the state to reach all strata of society.[2] In an empirical study conducted between 2002 and 2015 in sub-Saharan African nations, Depetris-Chauvin et al. found that following the victories of national teams, participants were less likely to identify primarily with their ethnic group and more likely to have positive views of other ethnic groups from their country. The study found this effect particularly following victories of what they called "high stakes" matches such as World Cup qualifiers and the Africa Cup of Nations, noting a pronounced impact when national teams faced traditional rivals.[3] Noting the historical place of sports in building state legitimacy in post-Communist China, Sullivan et al. highlight how the state has emphasized "the special role of football in satisfying the spiritual and cultural demands of the Chinese people,"[4] and used the sport as a means of maintaining and exercising its symbolic power.

Despite being highly factionalized and known for infighting, the Iranian state and officials are no exception in attempting to politicize football for their own agendas. Yet the state finds itself increasingly challenged in this pursuit, as football has become a platform for magnifying criticism of the state. The increasing number of foreign-funded Persian language broadcasts, well-connected and active social media platforms, and Iranian activists who have become more outward looking in involving foreign organizations and sports governing bodies all mean that the state is facing a formidable rival in the struggle to define Iranian football, and, by extension, Iranian social and political mores. No place is this more evident than in the case of restrictions on women watching football. Iran is not alone in the way that football and the spaces associated with it are male-dominated. Looking at Yemen, for example, Stevenson and Alaug points to the function of football "as an expression of male dominance or hegemony,"[5] and Archetti examines how the nationalist discourses around Argentinian football became a "mechanism through which male cultural power is established."[6] What is unique to Iran is that it has both an active women's movement and has barred women from entering football stadiums. As will be further examined below, activists and ordinary football fans have managed to push the stadium ban to the forefront of a national conversation, both about the ban itself and as an allegory for the greater discrimination women face.

Unlike other recreational venues such as cinemas, live theaters, concerts, and parks, which are not gender segregated and where populations from different social strata, ages, and genders may intermix, football matches in Iran offer women a stage for publicly asserting themselves in male dominated spaces. One Iranian study examining women's desires to attend in-person football matches posits that the stadium allows women to show their agency in a public space, as opposed to the passivity that is implied when one watches the games on television.[7] International games and broadcasts magnify this opportunity, disrupting the state's ability to control the discourses around women's presence in the stadiums. With social media giving individual attendees the opportunity to broadcast themselves to local and international audiences, the state's ability to mobilize the sport toward fostering feelings of national unity and consensus is further undermined. As such, state sanctioned television and media coverage become even more important because they can allow for some mitigation of these challenges to government policies and politics. Yet mirroring its difficulties in other arenas, such as politics and cultural production more generally, the Iranian state has not been successful in its various efforts to mobilize domestic broadcasting against pressures from opposition media or digital outlets. This is despite the fact that the state has a monopoly over broadcasting and that domestic television has an extensive reach throughout the country. Put another way, football is a powerful lens for seeing the intersections and divergences of Iranian media and social policies. For these reasons, any discussion of the intersections of football, women's rights, and politics in Iran requires an examination of the post-revolutionary developments pertaining to watching football, be it from home or in the stadium.

In this regard, two moments in football and spectatorship stand out in the first decade of the Islamic Republic of Iran. The first is the banning of women from stadiums in 1981, and the second is the 1987 change in media policy allowing sports to be broadcast. As Chehabi has observed, in the strict environment of the early post-revolutionary period, attending public football matches "was one of the few leisure activities for young men."[8] Chehabi also implies that the 1981 ban on women in the audience exacerbated the charged atmosphere of the stadiums, "where the presence of tens of thousands of frenzied young males occasionally led to riots."[9] Indeed, the "vulgar" atmosphere of the stadiums is a recurring theme in the state's paternalistic defense of the stadium ban. Needless to say, the differences between the public spaces of the football stadium and the private spaces where Iranians watch football broadcasts are many. The increasing resonance of football as a site where multiple challenges may be posed to social policies explains the state's investment in both spaces.

To examine more closely how this has been the case, this chapter first reviews Iranian stadium attendance policies and efforts to bring about equity in sports spectatorship. In doing so, it will highlight the political and cultural developments that have made football the frontlines of the fight for gender equality in Iran. This is followed by an overview of the sports broadcasting landscape in Iran. Drawing from scholarly and mainstream discourses inside Iran, the study sketches some of the main topics of debate around sports broadcasting with a focus on women as both participants in sports and as audience for it. This section also captures the state's dilemmas regarding football broadcasting—dilemmas that are also mirrored in relation to stadium games. Live football games and sports broadcasting are double-edged swords that, on the one hand, serve as a pressure release valve for a young populace and draw audiences otherwise lost to opposition media and social media platforms. On the other hand, fanning the flames of football fandom strengthens its potential for becoming an effective locus for individual and communal action.

Against this background, the chapter will then examine two important events from 2019 that exemplify how football in contemporary Iran has become a central site for political action and social change enacted by the state, activists, and ordinary citizens. The first is the tragic self-immolation of Esteghlal Club supporter Sahar Khodayari and the second is the 2022 Fédération Internationale de Football Association (FIFA) World Cup qualifying match between Iran and Cambodia, where thousands of women were allowed to watch the game. An examination of both events and how they were framed and circulated in domestic, international, and social media platforms reflect the complex layers at play in the highly politicized landscape of contemporary Iranian football. While the power plays around the game continue, it is clear that football has emerged as one of the few arenas where citizens have successfully pushed for the enactment of tangible changes toward chipping away at codified forms of inequality in Iran.

Stadium Football: Structuring Public Spaces, Shifting Public Outreach

The 1981 ban on women in stadiums is coextensive with the post-revolutionary policies of creating gender segregated spaces, about which much has been written.[10] For nearly two decades, the challenges to the stadium ban were few and far between and did not garner significant attention. These include the example of a persistent female student from Tehran University in 1984, who was admitted to Shiroudi Stadium and allowed to watch the game from a VIP section. There was also a case of a showdown in 1996 between security forces and a woman attempting to enter the stadium disguised as a man. In an interview with *Shargh* newspaper, the current head of the Iranian Football Federation's financial department, Sadeq Doroodgar, recalled the incident and claimed that the confrontation was filmed by an Islamic Republic of Iran Broadcasting (IRIB) reporter who was later told by security forces that he could not air the footage.[11]

It was not until the early 2000s that women's attendance at stadiums emerged as a major social and political issue.[12] This is reflected in popular culture and films, the uptick in women's rights campaigns focused on women's exclusion from stadiums, and even in the state's own actions. Indeed, football-linked activism expanded from local efforts to more international-facing actions, including attempts to involve football's governing bodies. New possibilities afforded by social media platforms and international broadcasters also facilitated international attention and interest, placing the Iranian state under more pressure to change or justify its football-related policies. Before the June 2005 Iran–Bahrain World Cup qualifying match, for example, a group of women football fans gathered outside the stadium to protest the prohibition on women's entrance into the game. In response to the protests, Sports Minister Mohsen Mehralizadeh relented and allowed a group of women to watch the game from a VIP section. As this small victory occurred at the height of the Iranian blogosphere's popularity, women who had taken part in the protest were able to narrate their own experiences. In some cases, this included a critique of what some saw as a co-optation of their activism by Mehralizadeh and others.[13] This indicates a subtle but important shift in the dynamics around football and the state where the asymmetrical power of the state to politicize the sport to its benefit is challenged from multiple vectors online and off.

In the spring of the following year, then President Mahmoud Ahmadinejad lifted the ban on women's attendance at football matches. Turning on its head the often-repeated argument that women would be harmed by the vulgar atmosphere of stadiums, Ahmadinejad claimed in a letter to the head of Iran's national Physical Education Organization that women's presence in the stadium would bring "morality" and "chastity." Within days, however, Iran's clerical establishment expressed their opposition to Ahmadinejad's order on religious grounds, citing both the corrupting nature of the environment as well as the sinfulness of a woman looking at a man's body.[14] Even parliamentarians from Ahmadinejad's "principalist" faction similarly objected to the order,[15] using familiar arguments about the nature of the stadium atmosphere.[16] In another sign of a struggle within the establishment that same year over the question of whether women could be part of live audiences, the Tehran municipality announced its intention to screen football matches publicly on large LCD screens, but then cancelled this without any explanation.[17]

On the cultural front, films like Jafar Panahi's 2006 *Offside* captured the phenomena of girls and women sneaking into stadiums by dressing as boys. Although shot on location in Iran with state-issued permits for filming, the film itself did not receive permission to screen. Despite—or perhaps due to—being banned in Iran, the film was received well in international festivals. A realist comedy, it captured some of the absurd consequences of the ban as well as the collective joys of football. The first decade of the millennium saw increased attention to the intersection of social issues and football in documentary films as well; Bahari's 2001 film *Football, Iranian Style* is one such work.[18] In looking at the politicization of football, the film also draws attention to sports spectatorship both in stadiums and via broadcasts. Assman and Najafi's 2008 *Football Under Cover* told the story of a game between the Iranian women's soccer team and a local amateur team from Berlin.[19] In showing all the obstacles that had to be overcome for the game to happen, the film sheds light on a range of social and political restrictions in Iran. In short, all of these films show how football and football spectatorship become sites where the state apparatus has to contend with the social consequences of its policies. Furthermore, the fact that all these films were screened internationally once again highlights that the state can no longer contain these social negotiations within its borders or on its own terms.

Activists' letters to FIFA and the AFC mark another shift in the boundaries within which football becomes grounds for social and political negotiations. These appeals to football's governing bodies received a boost in 2013 in conjunction with the visit to Iran by then FIFA President Sepp Blatter and FIFA Executive Committee member Moya Dodd, both of whom urged Iranian officials to revise their stadium policies. An Iranian group calling itself the Open Stadiums movement was also a player in promoting the involvement of international sports bodies. The Open Stadiums movement includes women who have been working on the stadium access issue since the early 2000s, and while there are specific activists who have been visible on the issue, as well as women journalists who have covered women's unequal access to watching live sports, it is also an amorphous movement in that it does not claim a singular leader and is inclusive of many efforts on the part of ordinary people who support the campaign.[20] Open Stadiums credits the advocacy of Dodd and others connected with international bodies for raising the profile of the campaign to end gender discrimination in football games.[21] Activists with the Open Stadiums campaign also used the occasion of the 2018 FIFA World Cup in Russia to attend all Iran games prepared with placards and slogans. Photos of traveling female fans holding their signs at the games in Russia were then disseminated on various social media platforms. All the above set the stage for pushing the state to allow women to attend FIFA qualifiers in 2019.

Before continuing on to an examination of that FIFA qualifying game and the tragic football-linked death of Sahar Khodayari that preceded it by one month, it is necessary to pivot back to the domestic landscape to consider football and spectatorship in their mediated forms, with a focus on broadcasting. As noted earlier, there are several important reasons for looking at Iranian sports media and the debates around it. For one, an examination of the broadcasting landscape inside Iran will show that football dominates sports programming. Looking at the debates and discourses around sports broadcasting also indicates the ambiguities within the state in relation to how football can mobilize audiences, including female ones. Just as there are fissures within the state in relation to the game and whether or how to allow women to participate as live audiences for football, similar tensions are apparent when it comes to broadcasting. With its monopoly on domestic broadcasts, state-owned television has access to a large audience and can wield control over content creation and dissemination. While there seems to be an understanding in Iran that sports broadcasting has much potential to shape public opinions and private spaces, the self-imposed restrictions placed on content and on how female audiences are engaged has meant that broadcasting has in some senses worsened the state's position vis-à-vis women.[22] That is to say, the focus on football heightens the passion for the sport but does not provide a satisfactory alternative for equity in sports spectatorship and sports participation.

Football on the Screen: Public Airways and the Shaping of Private Spaces

The policy of sports broadcasting has been fraught, criticized for both its international and domestic content. In 1994, newspapers complained that Iranian coverage of the World Cup was a de facto propaganda opportunity for the US, who was hosting the games that year.[23] On less politicized grounds, scholars and observers have noted that not only in terms of games broadcast but sports news coverage is also largely dedicated to football, with more attention given to international games than domestic ones.[24] Similarly, the domestic broadcasts focus more on the Iranian professional league and tend to be Tehran-centered at the expense of local clubs and smaller leagues. The IRIB's own internal analysis has also highlighted the focus on football over other sports.[25] As such, critics have contended that sports broadcasting in Iran needs to enhance its local community- and culture-building functions, something which it is failing to do because of the outsized focus on football and professional games.[26]

The popularity of football, however, presents a dilemma, as it is guaranteed to draw in audiences, prompting even channels with an entirely different focus to include football programming in a bid to attract new viewers.[27] In recognition of the popularity of sports broadcasting and as part of broader attempts to invigorate state programming, the Islamic Republic of Iran Broadcasting (IRIB) established a sports channel—IRIB Varzesh, Channel 3 (IRIB 3)—

in 2012. In 1997, IRIB's own polls showed that 48 percent of citizens surveyed did not express any interest in sports programming.[28] In the fifteen years between that poll and the establishment of IRIB 3, the appetite for sports has steadily increased. The channel's range of programming includes live and pre-recorded shows covering domestic leagues and European club matches, sports comedy, and home exercise instructions. As was the case prior to the channel's establishment, most of the shows on IRIB 3 are dedicated to football, and it is those shows that have proven the most popular. These include Football 120, a live show dedicated to news and analysis of soccer (with a focus on European games), *Shabhay-e Footballi* ("Football Nights"), a live show that provides analysis and commentary on Iranian football matches, and *Lezat-e Football* ("The Pleasure of Football"), another live show that broadcasts and analyzes European games. Alongside IRIB 3's exclusive sports programming, other IRIB channels such as 1, 2, 5, and 6 run sports shows as well. Regional IRIB channels also cover local sports. In addition to sports news and sports shows, featured programming is also dedicated to football. The IRIB documentary channel, for example, ran a multi-part documentary series called *Football-e Irani* about the national team at the 2018 World Cup and the AFC Asian cup.[29] Whether on football or not, sports coverage is also almost exclusively for men's sports. One review of local IRIB sports broadcasts of 327 different programs revealed that women's sports received no coverage at all.[30] A similar lack of women's sports coverage has been noted on the national Channel 3 as well.[31]

One factor explaining the absence of women's sports broadcasting may be traced to debates about the appearance of women on IRIB channels more generally. Anyone watching IRIB for the first time will soon come to notice that while there are women without hijab present in entertainment programming or news coverage, Iranian women without hijab are not among them. In other words, while the IRIB allows for foreign women to be shown uncovered (e.g., in the case of western movies, or news segments about foreign leaders or countries), Iranian women on screen must adhere to strict dress codes, regardless of what role they are playing in an Iranian show or Iranian film. The same standard applies to Iranian women anchors, program hosts, and even guests. While veiling has been a legal requirement for all women and girls of age since the Iranian Revolution, the parameters of what constitutes hijab and "modest" clothing has greatly expanded since the zealous early years of the Islamic Republic. Women working or conducting business in state institutions are subject to rules requiring the full coverage of hair as well as over-garments (in the form of manteaux, or full chador) that go to one's knees or beyond. This is not to say that women's appearance on IRIB has been static for the last forty years; there too, there is evidence of some loosening of codes, allowing, for example, for more colorful and varied forms of hijab. Nonetheless, the hijab and manner of dress of Iranian women on IRIB is not at all representative of the range of looks evident within Iranian society. Even though the IRIB requires adherence to stricter dress codes for Iranian women on screen, more conservative elements of the state have consistently critiqued the broadcaster for how Iranian women appear on its channels.[32]

It is beyond the scope of this chapter to capture the range of struggles and discourses around the post-revolutionary participation of women in sports. However, a brief overview of major developments is useful background for understanding the current state of Iranian sports broadcasting. Faezeh Rafsanjani, the daughter of the former president, and a former parliamentarian herself, is credited for paving the way for Iranian women to return to sports after the revolution. Noting the importance of sports to mental and physical wellness and underlining its compatibility with Islam, Rafsanjani managed to procure government buy-in for women's post-revolutionary participation in sports. In large part due to her efforts, Iran hosted the first Islamic Countries Women's Sports Congress in 1991. In 1998, Rafsanjani claimed that about 2 million Iranian women were active in sports, as compared to 400,000 only two years earlier.[33] While women's sports continued in the first years of the new millennium, administrative and political changes following the 2005 election of Mahmoud Ahmadinejad which continued through his second term led to setbacks and difficulties for women athletes. In 2006, the merging of the women's and men's sports organization meant that women and women's sports had less representation in the new administrative body governing sports. On the field, already restrictive rules for how female athletes could dress and how they could interact with their male coaches and trainers were further tightened.[34]

Sadly, women athletes were not only subject to clothing restrictions in Iran, but were also punished by international sports bodies for following the rules set by their government: in what was seen by many as a politically motivated ruling in 2011, FIFA barred the Iranian women's football team from playing the final qualifying match for the 2012 London Olympics on the grounds that Iran's hijab rule for players was in contravention of the association's dress codes.[35] Despite the ongoing politicization of Iranian women in sports both inside Iran and internationally, Iranian women athletes have continued to make some significant strides, and the state, too, has made some important concessions. In 2017, for example, the Iranian Weightlifting Federation established a women's committee and announced that women would be able to compete in international competitions, something that was previously never allowed.[36] In May 2018, the Iranian women's futsal team won the AFC Women's Futsal Championship. Yet politics and debate has also tainted women's victories in sports. Iran's only female Olympic medalist, Taekwondo athlete Kimia Alizadeh, left Iran in 2017, citing the mandatory hijab rules and sexism among the reasons for her decision to pursue the sport outside the country.[37] It is worth noting that Taekwondo is one of the rare women's sports that does get broadcast on Iranian airwaves because the sports' uniform provides full body coverage.

In short, the debates and restrictions around the appearance of women on IRIB—whether as on-air personalities, actors, or athletes—explain the lack of coverage women's sports receive. To put it another way, the near absence of women's athletics on air appears to be a feature, rather than a bug in the Islamic Republic broadcasting services.

Returning to Iranian discourses and scholarship on sports broadcasting, it is important to note that the focus has not been merely on the programming side. Indeed, mirroring discussions about the impact of the stadium and live sports on attendees, the audience of sports broadcast has also been an object of scrutiny. Some have argued that sports broadcasting has made Iranians mere spectators rather than participants in sports and exercise.[38] Yet much of the discussion remains positive, with sports broadcasting praised for stirring values of sportsmanship, fairness, and community in viewers.

Given that sports programming is almost exclusively focused on male sports, it is noteworthy that women are not entirely ignored as an existing or potential audience for televised sports. Speaking specifically with housewives who watched Channel 3 in one district in Tehran, for example, a 2017 study examined which social factors played a role in audience viewing habits and the extent to which they internalized messaging about sports and exercise. The study attempted to measure whether the then newly established sports channel was meeting the mandate to encourage exercise among the population.[39] Other studies have examined whether there is a link between women's interest (or lack thereof) in televised sports and their desire (or lack thereof) to attend games in stadiums. In a survey of women across colleges in Tehran, for example, Ghyasvand and Rezazahdeh found that over 70 percent of college women seldom or never watched televised football, but also found that the majority supported women's ability to watch football at stadiums, with 27 percent stating that they would certainly attend stadium games if given the chance.[40]

In terms of sports broadcasting, both the scholarship and mainstream discussions around sports broadcasting and sports attendance are cognizant of women's desire to engage with sports as live audience members on the one hand, and of the cultural building and political potential of sports, and football in particular on the other. Ideally, from the perspective of the state and the clerical establishment, sports can be mobilized toward the broader goals of governance and governmentality: that is to say, toward meeting goals such as providing safe entertainment and distractions for citizens, promoting values of health and self-care, and stirring feelings of patriotism and national unity when convenient for the ruling powers. However, these goals are complicated—if not thwarted—when the audience makes its own demands (such as women's demands for entry into stadiums) and when the state is competing with other broadcasters and sources of soccer content.

In short, sports broadcasting and football broadcasting in particular can draw a large audience, thus giving the state some room to frame the social and political issues that arise around the sport. To limit football broadcasts would risk losing a coveted youthful audience and—more dangerously for the state—it would mean ceding ground to foreign-funded international broadcasters to politicize the game without competition. At the same time, a national broadcaster that does not fully interpellate its female audience—either by sufficiently airing women's sports or adequately addressing them as an audience with agency—is a poor substitute for in-person attendance at football matches. The continued political and social contestation centered on football games further discussed below captures the position in which the state finds itself: caught between the benefits of football for engaging the population and allowing the state to legitimize its policies and the downside of football as a site where demands are made on the state.

Two very different recent events best illustrate this tension: the tragic self-immolation of "the blue girl" in September 2019 as well as the October 2019 World Cup qualifier between Iran and Cambodia, historic for setting aside 3,500 tickets for women who wanted to attend the game. The former took place in the context of domestic club teams, while the occasion for the latter was an international game with the national team. Women's attendance was at the center of both: in the first case, the state played its prohibitive role, whereas in the second, it had loosened its own rules to allow women to attend. Both cases received significant attention outside Iran, engaging both the diaspora and international press and pushing the boundaries beyond what the Iranian state could control with its own messaging.

Dying to Watch: "The Blue Girl," Football Fandom, and Change in Policies

In September 2019, Sahar Khodayari self-immolated in front of an Iranian courthouse. In March of the same year, Khodayari, who was a diehard fan of Tehran's Esteghlal Football Club, had dressed in male disguise to sneak into a match between her team and Abu Dhabi's Al-Ain Football Club. Suspecting she was a woman, security forces confronted and detained her. On the day she set herself on fire, Khodayari had shown up to court to face charges related to what transpired in March. The news of her self-immolation immediately spread within social media and media networks outside Iran. Dubbed "the blue girl" after her team colors, she became an instant and tragic symbol of discrimination against women in Iran, and football was at the center of it all. The initial flurry of media activity around Khodayari, the subsequent contestations of what really led to her self-immolation, and the developments in football that followed—including the involvement of international bodies like FIFA—all indicate how powerfully and quickly football can become a site for social and political upheaval and change. Furthermore, the sad case of Khodayari is notable because of the element of female fandom.

Kohdayari was literally a true-blue fan, and her undisputable devotion to the game and the team is crucial. She was attempting to enter the stadium because she truly wanted to watch the game. As Nasrin Afzali has acknowledged, women's activism around the stadium issue is not necessarily always about the sport itself, but rather an opportunity to shine a light on women's exclusion.[41] Opponents of stadium access may be able to use this against activists, critiquing them of cynically exploiting the matter of football spectatorship to push a broader political agenda. But Khodayari's case highlights the existence of dedicated female fans who simply want to watch the game. She was a real-life example of the kinds of girls and women depicted in Panahi's *Offside*. In a country filled with diehard fans of football and domestic football clubs, her obsession with her team and the sport explains her relatability and the resonance of her case.

Initial social media accounts of Khodayari's self-immolation claimed that she had taken such extreme measures out of devastation in the face of a six-month prison sentence for attempting to breach the ban. As will be discussed further below, this does not appear to have been an accurate account. Nonetheless, it cannot be disputed that the ban on stadium attendance was central to the tragic events that unfolded, and, as such, social media platforms exploded with anger in the face of this discriminatory policy. Hashtags of "blue girl" in both Persian and English dominated the social media platforms most used by Iranians such as Instagram and Twitter.

To stem the flow of criticism about its role in bringing about the tragedy, Iranian officials quickly announced that the court never convened due to the judge being absent. The judiciary also announced that Khodayari was facing charges of "harming public decency and insulting officers."[42] In short, they claimed the charges were related to how Khodayari conducted herself after being confronted rather than for the act of attempting to sneak into the stadium. In an attempt to further distance itself from responsibility, state-sanctioned media outlets inside the country were also swift in offering alternative reasons for the tragedy and foregrounded her history of mental health issues. They also disseminated an interview with her father, wherein he confirmed the state narrative and spoke out against those who "use what happened to Sahar as an excuse to speak against the country."[43]

While the information war dynamic is a familiar one in contemporary Iran, several aspects of this case stand out. One is the swiftness with which Iranian officials and media responded to the widespread reactions to Khodayari's self-immolation. The fact that state and state-sanctioned voices inside Iran worked to disassociate Khodayari's case from football and football policies is particularly noteworthy. Khodayari was not the first to set herself publicly aflame in an ostensible act of protest in post-revolutionary Iran, and sadly she was not the last. But the link to football meant that her case appealed to a broader intersection of Iranians inside and outside the country. Khodayari's desire to see her favorite team and the dismay at not being allowed to do so is legible to a broad spectrum of Iranians and cannot be dismissed by the state or critics as a cynical play by an activist. The aspect of fandom and her unmet desire to simply watch the game also made her relatable to the non-Iranian football world. This was seen, for example, in a tweet by the official account of FC Barcelona offering condolences for her death: "Football is a game for everyone—men AND women, and everyone should be able to enjoy the beautiful game together in stadiums."[44] Professional players abroad also appealed to the universality of football in mourning the death of Khodayari. Bayern Munich's Jerome Boateng, for example, tweeted "Something like that should never ever happen again! Football is for everyone. Rest in peace Sahar Khodayari."[45]

Home Game, Transnational Audience: The Football Stadium as a Site of Social Change

The Iran-Cambodia game that took place with the presence of women spectators in October of 2019 seemed to be the ostensible result of Khodayari's self-immolation and the responses it generated. However, as noted previously, pressure had already been mounting on the Iranian state to change its football policies well before her tragic death. In a June 2019 letter to the head of the Iranian Football Federation, FIFA President Gianni Infantio requested a statement regarding the concrete steps the Iranian authorities would be taking to ensure entry for Iranian and foreign women to Qatar 2022 qualifiers. In other words, allowing women to attend the Cambodia-Iran qualifier was an explicit pre-condition set by FIFA.

Similarly, in its July 2019 report, the UN Special Rapporteur on Cultural Rights specifically cited the Iranian stadium issue and the importance of equity in shared public spaces.[46] Nonetheless, the close proximity of the two events, and the fact that many attending and writing about the historic day referred back to the case of Khodayari, further imbricated the two events. It also prevented the state from taking full credit for the change in the policy on women's attendance. An occasion that would have been ripe for the state to make claims about its legitimacy and to rile up nationalist sentiment could now be claimed by a range of other actors, including, but not limited to, those critical of, or in outright opposition to, the state.

In October 2019, what might have otherwise been an unremarkable game between the Iranian national team and the much weaker Cambodian team became a historic game where close to three thousand seats were taken up by Iranian women. Both before and during the game, the state found itself under the gaze of local and international actors closely watching how Iran would deliver its promises about women's attendance. Iranian officials had reserved a limited number of tickets in advance, resulting in pushback from activists and human rights organizations who critiqued the low number of tickets set aside for women—a few thousand tickets for a stadium seating 80,000. A week prior, for example, Human Rights Watch issued a statement condemning the ticket cap, arguing that "the effective five percent quota on seats for women contravenes FIFA's constitution, statutes, and its human rights policy."[47] FIFA also sent representatives to ensure that the Iranian authorities abided by their promise to allow women to attend. Women lamented the quota on Twitter and other social networks and shared the challenges they faced in obtaining the tickets. State officials once accustomed to wielding control over the manner in which audiences viewed football in stadiums and via national broadcasts now found themselves under observation by international sports bodies, human rights organizations, activists, and ordinary people.

Similarly, the actions of the women in attendance also made it difficult for the state to control the narrative about the day. Not only did photos circulate on social media showing women holding signs commemorating "the blue girl," but so did accounts of attempts to silence the women in the stadium. For example, a photo of a woman holding a sign saying "Dokhtar-e Abi Iran, Esm-e to Javidan" ("Blue Girl of Iran, your name will be immortal") was juxtaposed with another showing a woman working with the Iranian Football Federation ripping that same sign, presumably in an attempt to prevent any references to Khodayari.[48] Women also reported being heavily policed in the stadium, not simply for holding up banners with messages about "the blue girl" but also for actions such as smoking or being too loud when cheering—acts that men could do unhindered.[49] Foreign state-funded Persian broadcasters, such as the US government-funded Voice of America, ran extensive commentary on these issues. The show Tablet—

hosted by opposition figures—ridiculed women's presence in the stadium as merely a "performance of freedom."

Despite the pushback from international organizations, ordinary citizens, and foreign-funded Persian language stations, state officials and media outlets worked to frame women's attendance as a win. Minister of Sports and Youth Masoud Soltanifar celebrated the event and claimed that women's presence multiplied the joy of the team's victory.[50] IRIB broadcasts highlighted the presence of women and included clips showing the players walking toward the women's section at the conclusion of the game and applauding them. Other clips included interviews with the players, who stated that women's presence at the game had made it particularly special. The front pages of several newspapers printed photos of women in attendance at the game, again linking the team's victory with the victory of women's presence at Azadi Stadium. Playing on the meaning of Azadi as freedom in Persian, the *Hamdeli* newspaper ran the headline "Women Reach Azadi," while *Arman-e Melli* stated that "Azadi Smiles at Women."

Of course, not all papers featured positive cover stories of the game. Even though hardline outlet *Kayhan* featured photos of the women at the game on its front pages,[51] the newspaper juxtaposed photos of women football fans—dressed in colorful team colors and regalia, some tooting horns—with photos of women and young girls, mostly dressed from head to toe in black, appearing to be en route in pilgrimage. The faces of the former were blurred and they were tagged with the heading *"Ghorbaniyan-e Azadi"* ("victims of freedom")—again playing on the meaning of the name of the stadium—while the latter appeared with their faces clearly visible and were labeled as *"Rahiyan-e Azadegi"* ("on the path to freedom"). This framing of the issue of women's attendance at stadiums, and in fact women's freedom more broadly, is reflective of a bigger culture war that undergirds the ideological and political divides inside the Iranian political apparatus and within Iranian society as whole. Known as the mouthpiece of the most conservative elements of the Iranian state, *Kayhan* here articulates two interrelated assertions about the stakes of allowing women into stadiums: the first is to dispute the notion that the freedom to enter the stadiums represents true freedom, and that, therefore, those who buy into this false notion of freedom are victims; second, true and permanent freedom comes through the path of religion, a path from which the women at the stadium have strayed. In short, the *Kayhan* headline brings into sharp relief the stakes for the conservative and most powerful elements of the ruling state. The stadium issue is a women's rights issue, which in turn is at the heart of the post-revolutionary project and the ongoing contestations of that project since its earliest days. This juxtaposition of the two "freedoms" is about a clash of values and a fear of foreign influence, which has ramifications far beyond the debates about game attendance.

The internal opposition to women attending games adds another layer complicating the state's ability to claim the football game as an unvitiated victory. In fact, the dynamics around Iran's football policies are an iteration of a pattern seen in other arenas, up to and including Iran's foreign and nuclear policy. Divided within and pushed from the outside, state actors must at once consider the demands and threats of international bodies and activists as well as the reactions of domestic constituents and rivals: forced to negotiate, the state nonetheless does not want to appear as though it has given in to pressure. In the case of football, this has manifested as a game of give and take where the state makes concessions but at the same attempts to assert itself. Thus, the state allowed women to enter stadiums in the Iran-Cambodia match, for example, but it set quotas for entrance, and attempted to micromanage women's behavior in the stands.

Conclusion

The Iran-Cambodia game has not put an end to the contestations around the stadium issue. Since the World Cup qualifying games, attention has turned back to domestic league games, where women still are not given seats. Women activists such as those working with the Open Stadiums movement have continued to use social media platforms to bring attention to this exclusion. In February, 2020, when the two rival Tehran teams of Esteghlal and Persepolis faced off in the biggest domestic game of the year, activists used the occasion to bring attention to the fact that women were given no seats for this game. Similarly, international bodies have also kept up the pressure. According to a report in *Hamshahri* newspaper, FIFA's latest letter to the Iranian authorities had not only asked that women be allowed seats for upcoming international games, such as the AFC Championships and the Persian Gulf Pro League Games, but also stated that women should be allowed to attend domestic league games by June 2020.[52] It is noteworthy that within the Iranian state, some have welcomed the involvement of football's international governing body. In an interview published in February 2020, Parvaneh Salahshouri, Tehran's representative to parliament, said: "I hope with the help of FIFA this problem will be forever solved, and we will no longer witness resistance to women's presence in the stadiums."[53] As Salahshouri's comment once again indicates, the state itself is not unified in its stance toward the stadium issue.

What impact the COVID-19 crisis has on games and stadium attendance, and whether and to what extent the Iranian state will meet the demands set by FIFA for 2020 and beyond, is yet to be fully tested. However, with the next World Cup in sight, and with many other international cups and domestic derbies played until then, occasions abound for relaunching the momentum around football and social change. What is certain is that Iranian football is now both a game and a political theater, both in terms of the performance of politics but also as a physical space for asserting individual and communal rights. Yet while the state does not go unchallenged in using football and the passions stirred by it to assert its own legitimacy, neither is it ready to cede control. As such, football is likely to remain a volatile site for intense political and social contestation for the foreseeable future in Iran.

12

QATAR'S BEIN SPORTS AND FOOTBALL BROADCASTING IN THE MIDDLE EAST

INTERNATIONAL INFLUENCE AND REGIONAL RANCOR

Craig L LaMay

Introduction

Of the many Arab Gulf state investments in international football, none has had the global reach or the regional impact of Qatar's BeIN Sports network. Since it became independent of Al Jazeera Sport in 2013 and through its acquisition of top-tier sports rights, BeIN has become a major plank of Qatar's efforts to brand itself as a global and regional power in the world of sports.[1] The company broadcasts independently or with partners in Europe, North America, Australia, and Asia,[2] but is far and away the dominant sports broadcaster in the Middle East and North Africa (MENA), where it has more than 50 percent of the market and the rights to most top-tier sports events in the twenty-three countries it counts in its MENA portfolio.[3] That market dominance was aggressively challenged in 2017, when BeIN suddenly found itself in a fight for its life with BeoutQ, an industrial-scale piracy operation based in Saudi Arabia that roiled international sports broadcasting. The story of that battle and what it means for football broadcasting in the Middle East is the focus of this chapter.[4]

BeIN's reach in MENA extends across multiple platforms—pay television (PTV), Internet Protocol Television (IPTV), and Over-the-Top (OTT) services—and the company lists forty-six sports channels: twenty-one of its own; eight more from Qatari sports broadcaster Al Kass; and other regional sports channels from Dubai, Abu Dhabi, and Kuwait.[5] In 2016, the company acquired Turkish broadcaster Digiturk, along with its sports channels, its Turkish Super Lig rights, and a domestic and diaspora viewership estimated at 3.5 million.[6]

For all that, BeIN is not particularly well-liked in the region. In MENA states where there is a long tradition of state-run free-to-air (FTA) sports channels, BeIN's subscription model simultaneously demanded the loyalty and invited the animosity of fans, leagues, and even governments. As a result, BeIN has endured repeated pirating operations—including state-sponsored ones during major football tournaments—but until 2017, with the sudden blockade of Qatar led by Saudi Arabia (KSA) and the United Arab Emirates (UAE), the broadcaster faced no challenge as threatening as BeoutQ, a Riyadh-based bootlegging operation that was able to steal BeIN's entire encrypted feed and distribute it on the Arabsat satellite, which is principally owned by Saudi Arabia. Eventually, sports broadcasters and rights-holders everywhere came to understand BeoutQ as an existential threat to their business model. With their support in 2020, Qatar brought a successful claim of intellectual property theft against Saudi Arabia at the World Trade Organization (WTO), although it is too soon to judge the practical effect of that victory, if any.[7] The WTO's only enforcement mechanisms are the good faith of its member states and the authorization of trade sanctions.[8] While KSA has been named and shamed by the WTO and trade authorities in the United States and Europe, it has nonetheless characterized the WTO decision as a victory, has never acknowledged its involvement in BeoutQ, and, in July 2020, officially banned BeIN from the kingdom.[9]

Indeed, given the stated goals of the blockading countries to knock BeIN from its position of dominance in MENA, KSA can view BeoutQ as a success. Its three-year raid severed or damaged relationships BeIN had with several key rights partners, from Formula 1 to the Tour de France, but also with important football leagues in Europe and with the Asian Football Confederation, of which Qatar is a member. Citing losses of well more than $1 billion from piracy and the loss of key Gulf markets, in 2019 and 2020 BeIN laid off almost half of its Doha staff—only two years before Qatar will host the World Cup, to which BeIN holds the MENA broadcast rights. What damage piracy did not do, the COVID-19 pandemic did, forcing the cancellation or postponement of sports events around the world in 2020 and 2021.

As noted, this chapter's focus on BeIN reflects the current state of football broadcasting in the Middle East, but it is important to note that there are articles yet to be written about football broadcasting in the region before the age of PTV sports. The history of state sports channels in the Arab world has received almost no attention in the scholarly literature and, as this chapter describes, the sudden transition to PTV sports over a decade ago made many of those channels irrelevant to football fans.[10] Though the number of FTA channels in the region has nearly doubled over the last twenty years, and many of them do show domestic football competitions, fans who want to watch their teams play in continental or international competitions usually require either BeIN or, as discussed below, a pirate stream of BeIN. In large part because of that piracy, football broadcasting in the Middle East is in a state of flux. Some of the world's premier football properties are struggling to maintain their value in the region. BeIN itself is beset by financial losses and has been slow to innovate.[11] Qatar presumably will remain invested in sports broadcasting as part of its 2030 national development plan, but there are new and potentially well-financed competitors on the horizon in MENA, and the industry will remain a proxy for political influence.[12] Finally, the sports broadcasting industry everywhere faces continuing uncertainty caused by the pandemic.

Football and the MENA Sports Broadcasting Market

In terms of rights valuation, MENA is the third-fastest growing sports media market in the world and the seventh largest, pushing into the top ten for the first time in 2019. MENA comprises 2.4 percent of the $51 billion annual sports market, about the same as the Indian Subcontinent and Latin America without Brazil. By comparison, the United States is 43.6 percent of the annual sports market, the United Kingdom 9.4 percent.[13]

Several factors account for that growth, but none is more important than Qatar's willingness to pay premium prices for sports rights and especially for football, which is by far the most popular sport to watch or attend among nationals in the Middle East.[14] Football is unique for its worldwide appeal, and the world's most valuable sport, valued in 2019 at $20.7 billion annually, or 41 percent of the global sports market. The European leagues, especially, have a wide international following, and generate significant revenue by selling their rights in international markets. The English Premier League (EPL), for example, generates just under half of its revenue from the international sale of its rights, and MENA is the league's fourth most lucrative international market after Sub-Saharan Africa, China, and the United States.[15]

The MENA sports market is also unique in that it is the only one whose most valuable property—UEFA Champions and Europa League, which generated $278 million in the region in 2019—is not domestically based. UEFA saw a huge increase in regional value in 2017 when, almost immediately after the blockade of Qatar began, BeIN tripled its existing contract, making UEFA worth 22 percent of the market and almost twice the value of the second-ranked property in the market, the EPL.[16] The most valuable domestic property in the region is the Saudi Professional League, which, with an annual value of $141 million in 2019, is six times more valuable than the second largest domestic league, the UAE Arabian Gulf League, but still slightly less than the EPL was worth the same year ($149 million).[17]

At the time of writing, BeIN owns the MENA rights to three of the five major European leagues (the EPL, Spain's La Liga, and France's Ligue 1), the UEFA Champions League, Europa League, the FA Cup, the English Football League, the Scottish Professional Football League, the Fédération Internationale de Football Association (FIFA) men's and women's World Cups, Nations League, the Turkish Super Lig, the Confederation of African Football (CAF), Copa Libertadores, Copa America,[18] and, domestically, the Qatar Stars League.[19] Until 2020, BeIN also had regional rights to Italy's Serie A and Germany's Bundesliga, and to the Asian Football Confederation (AFC), but BeoutQ put an end to those relationships, as discussed below. BeIN's first major deals, in 2015, were its wresting away of EPL and UEFA rights from rival Abu Dhabi Media—in the case of EPL, by paying 30 percent more than the previous contract.[20] BeIN renewed its EPL deal in 2019, through 2022, at an 8 percent increase, and then renewed it again in December 2020 during the COVID-19 pandemic, but at the same value as the existing contract. That deal runs through 2025 and includes Saudi Arabia as part of the rights package.[21]

Smaller PTV providers in MENA like Orbit Showtime Network (OSN), Abu Dhabi Media, and Dubai Sports have competed for second- and third-tier sports rights and distinctive audiences. Abu Dhabi Sports (AD Sports) has mostly regional sports rights; major football rights it once held, including to the EPL and to the Arabian Gulf Cup, are now held by BeIN.[22] In February 2021, Dubai Sports picked up Japan's J.League football competition for the MENA region.[23] Until recently, OSN focused on cricket for the large South Asian expat market in the region, but after BeIN acquired rights to the coveted Indian Premier League in 2018, OSN closed five of its six sports channels and the next year dropped OSN Cricket, its only remaining sports channel, citing BeIN's "aggressiveness," the widespread availability of "illegal streaming sites," and "pirate IPTV decoders" in its territory.[24]

Over-the-Top (OTT) sports media that bypass traditional providers like satellite or terrestrial broadcast are growing in the Middle East and are expected to challenge PTV for consumers in the coming decade, particularly in the Gulf states with their overwhelmingly young populations, high connectivity rates, extensive mobile penetration, and wide availability of banking and payment cards. BeIN launched its OTT service BeIN Connect in 2014, though like many such services it offers no added value or unique content for the subscriber. It simply streams BeIN's PTV sports and entertainment channels. Other OTT football products to have entered the market include UK-based Dugout, a consortium of some seventy international football clubs, that streams free and exclusive Arabic-language content, game highlights, interviews, and behind-the-scenes features, but no live matches.

The Politics of Football Broadcasting in the Middle East

The value of PTV in many markets around the world was largely built on the back of sports investments, and thus made PTV sports a political issue practically from the industry's beginnings.[25] In many countries, certain national and international competitions are required to be free-to-air, or, as in MENA, there is a historic expectation that sports are free to watch.[26] As sports, and particularly football, became the primary competitive battlefield for all forms of television in MENA, the acquisition of rights by companies backed by sovereign wealth funds pushed up the price of rights and thus upended the expectation that football broadcasting should be free. With the absence of a regulatory framework for managing that transition, PTV sports in MENA spurred both political conflict and piracy.

If there was a bellwether year for football broadcasting in MENA it was 2006, when free access to World Cup matches in the region came to an abrupt end. That year, KSA-based Arab Radio and Television (ART) bought the rights to the 2006, 2010, and 2014 World Cups for $220 million, then offered only highlights sublicensing deals to state-owned TV channels.[27] The change was hugely unpopular, and, for the first time, made football broadcasting a regional political issue requiring the involvement of governments and even religious authorities.[28] Governments in the region found themselves compelled to subsidize the purchase of ART subscriptions, to negotiate deals for their public channels, or to provide public venues for viewing the matches. What ensued was a vibrant piracy market that continues to this day.

In 2009, Al Jazeera Sport bought ART and its six sport channels for $2 billion, the biggest media takeover in the history of the Middle East. With the purchase came not only World Cup rights for 2010 and 2014, but rights to the African Cup of Nations from 2010 to 2016.[29] Once again, viewers in the region found themselves either unable to watch matches they were accustomed to seeing for free or required to purchase expensive upgrades on their Al Jazeera subscriptions. In 2010, resentment over the withdrawal of World Cup matches from public television led to calls for boycotts of Al Jazeera, the promotion of alternative German or French channels on satellite, and countless illegal internet streams.[30]

Al Jazeera eventually broadcast select matches for free to the MENA region, but still found itself the object of attack. On the first day of the 2010 World Cup matches, the broadcaster's satellite signal was repeatedly jammed by a source later identified to be in Jordan, forcing Al Jazeera to find alternative frequencies for its broadcast.[31] The jamming extended to Al Jazeera's news channel because of the company's extensive and unwelcome coverage of political unrest in Tunisia, Egypt, Libya, Yemen, and Syria. Three years later, state broadcasters in both Egypt and Algeria pirated streams of World Cup qualifying matches played by their national teams abroad.[32] Al Jazeera complained, leading the CAF to fine the Egyptian Football Association $2 million.[33] Algerian National TV had used footage of the Algeria-Burkina Faso match from Burkina Faso TV and blurred the Al Jazeera logo. In response to Al Jazeera's complaint, Algeria said it had been forced "to protect the right of Algerian viewers to watch the national team playing outside of Algeria."[34] In 2017, FTA broadcasters in Algeria, Tunisia, Morocco, and Tunisia criticized BeIN for asking "astronomical" licensing fees for the Africa Cup of Nations, leaving viewers in those countries unable to watch the tournament.[35] In 2018, BeIN acceded to pressure from the five MENA countries playing in the World Cup (among them Saudi Arabia and Egypt) and from FIFA to make twenty-two matches available in the region via its FTA channels.[36]

The 2017 Blockade of Qatar and the Threat of BeoutQ

The piracy of live and recorded television sports broadcasts has been an issue from the earliest days of television.[37] With the arrival of PTV and then digital transmission across multiple devices, a growing literature has recognized a concurrent increase in pirated live sports streams around the globe, the practical and legal difficulties of containing those streams, and the financial cost to rights holders from lost revenues and diluted rights values.[38] But none of those sources identify industrial-scale, state-sponsored, commercial privacy. That ended in 2017, when Riyadh-based Arabsat began to distribute BeoutQ, a wholly pirated stream of Doha-based BeIN's entire portfolio of sports channels, across the MENA region.[39]

BeoutQ was the result of the blockade of Qatar that began on June 5, 2017, when KSA, the UAE, Bahrain, and Egypt abruptly severed all ties with Qatar, expelling Qatari nationals and cutting off land, sea, and air travel to the country. The boycotting countries accused Qatar of supporting terrorism and issued a list of thirteen demands for lifting the blockade—among them, that Qatar close Al Jazeera, the Doha-based international news network. Almost immediately, Saudi authorities told BeIN that it no longer had the legal right to operate in the country, offering neither a regulatory justification for the claim nor a remedy for it. The BeIN website was blocked, and it was no longer possible for BeIN to collect payment from any KSA-registered credit card or money transfer service. Saudi authorities confiscated BeIN boxes from distributors and shut down licensed BeIN viewing locations. BeIN employees in the country were harassed or detained and deported.[40] Qatar, as would be the case for other affected rights holders, was unable to find any law firm in Saudi Arabia willing to represent its interests.[41]

Several prominent Saudi nationals, including the legal counsel for the Saudi Royal Courts, tweeted in support of the shutdown, criticized BeIN for its regional "monopoly" and its "political bulletins," and hinted that "alternative solutions" to BeIN would be forthcoming.[42] In August, several tweets from the general manager of *Al Riyadh* newspaper identified and promoted BeoutQ by name as a pirate of BeIN channels. Several news sources covering the region quoted Muflih Al Haftaa, the chairman of Saudi Media City, about the imminent creation of PBS Sports, a free service with eleven sports channels to be produced by Egypt, financed by Saudi Arabia, and available on the Nilesat satellite that would "end the monopoly" of BeIN.[43]

In August 2017, BeoutQ appeared—initially web-only and geo-blocked to KSA. Though the UAE had at first blocked BeIN's channels, it bowed to domestic political pressure and football demand and reinstated them after six weeks to both Du and Etisalat, the two UAE-based telecom providers.[44] Faced with the same problem, KSA evidently realized that any effort to compete with BeIN was impossible in the short term, as BeIN had virtually all of the most valuable rights locked up for the foreseeable future. The only way to get those rights was to steal them and then to use that leverage to disrupt the relationships BeIN had with its rights holders.

From the outset, Arabsat and KSA denied any involvement with BeoutQ, which KSA claimed was a Colombian-Cuban entity despite the channels' Arabic content.[45] A month later, BeoutQ began to be distributed on Arabsat, which while nominally owned by the Gulf League countries is 36.7 percent owned by KSA and 45 percent owned by the blockading countries as a group.[46] As several news and industry sources noted, what was unique about BeoutQ was its scale and sophistication, with a Chinese-made set-top box emblazoned with the BeoutQ logo and presented as a legitimate service. BeoutQ added its own production by layering its commentaries over those from the BeIN broadcast.[47] It sold advertising, both to Saudi companies and, through agencies, to unwitting international ones.[48] Speaking to *SportBusiness* in 2018, BeIN's Executive Director of Content Dan Markham said, "This is not piracy happening in someone's house, it's not Justin.tv, it's not the guy in his bedroom who's making money from Google ads, it's not the standard one the Premier League closes down week-in, week-out. This undermines the very model that sport is funded on."[49] The greatest harm from BeoutQ, another BeIN executive told the author, would not fall on elite sports but lesser ones: "We'll never drop EPL, of course, but BeoutQ will destroy our ability to do rights deals for all the little sports. The major leagues and properties will be okay, but the knock-on effect for other sports is huge. Teams and leagues will no longer be able to buy the best players, not buy the best coaches. Ticket prices will go up. Women's sports will be hit hard. It's just a downward spiral."[50]

In 2018, while World Cup play was underway, FIFA announced its intention to take legal action against KSA.[51] Dubai-based *Al Arabiya*'s confused messaging reported that KSA "welcomed" the move and, in the same article, promoted BeoutQ as an "alternative to BeIN in MENA and accused Qatar of engaging in a "smear campaign."[52] A month later, BeIN released a report it had commissioned from three different security firms, all of whom confirmed that Arabsat was the distributor of BeoutQ.[53] Almost a year later, after trying and failing to secure legal representation in Saudi Arabia, FIFA, UEFA, and Europe's top five football leagues together released a report prepared by the software and security firm MarkMonitor, which also identified Arabsat as the transmitter of BeoutQ.[54] Never before, the report said, had there been piracy of so many encrypted channels on a major satellite operator. In response to the report, Arabsat denied any connection to BeoutQ and branded the report "irresponsible" and "disgraceful."[55]

A critical but little-publicized turn in the case came on November 2, 2018, when Qatari authorities arrested three BeIN employees and charged them with supplying KSA intelligence officials with the coordinates and encryption codes for BeIN satellite feeds. Two of the men were Egyptian and one Lebanese; all three were eventually prosecuted and all are presumably now in prison in Qatar, though there is no public information to confirm that. But for an Al Jazeera documentary about the arrests, the incident received little news coverage in Qatar or elsewhere in the region, and none in the sports industry trade press.[56]

About a month before the men's September 2019 prosecution, on August 7, 2019, the Arabsat satellite feed was shut off, after which BeoutQ became an IPTV service only. Long before then, however, the IPTV service had been carrying pirated feeds of virtually every sport broadcaster in the world, including Sky Sports and ESPN, US network television sports and college cable networks, Telemundo, public sport channels across Europe, and hundreds of movie and entertainment channels.[57] By September 2019, BeIN's monitoring facility at its Doha studios was tracking more than 1,300 channels available worldwide through the service, including more than 160 European and US sports channels.[58] By then, too, BeoutQ was itself beset by pirates, and vendors across North Africa were selling hacked set-top boxes and becoming an even bigger problem in MENA than BeoutQ itself.[59]

In 2018, BeIN estimated its subscription revenue losses from piracy at $1 billion, most of that from lost subscribers in Saudi Arabia—its largest market—but also in Egypt and Bahrain. BeIN lost about 45 percent of its subscription base as a result of the blockade and, between the beginning of the blockade in June 2017 to the end of 2018, more than $600 million in subscriber revenue.[60] In July 2019, BeIN cut 18 percent of its Doha staff—nearly 300 people, layoffs the company said affected its Middle East operations only.[61] At a sports industry summit in London two months later, BeIN CEO Yousef Al-Obaidly told his colleagues that his problem was their problem and warned,

> If you don't get your house in order and quickly, the sports rights market will disintegrate beyond recognition. And I can tell you that as the largest buyer of sports rights in the world, because of BeoutQ in MENA and piracy generally, we now regard all sports rights as non-exclusive and our commercial offers will reflect that. I am also convinced that other broadcasters will make similar devaluations, while many once-premium rights will remain unsold.[62]

If a goal of BeoutQ was to end BeIN's "monopoly" in MENA by throwing the rights market into turmoil, it had some success—particularly as regards international football. Early on, BeIN pressured all its rights partners to bring pressure on KSA by protesting publicly, lobbying regulators and national governments, taking legal action against BeoutQ and Arabsat, and avoiding any future sports deals with KSA. The pressure at first yielded mixed results. No rights holders were able to find legal representation in KSA, and several had conflicting interests and even other obligations to negotiate.[63] BeIN urged FIFA to take legal action against Arabsat in May 2018, for example, about the same time that FIFA President Gianni

Infantino was reported to be in negotiations with mystery investors in support of his vision of an enlarged Club World Cup. One of the investors was thought to be Saudi Arabia.[64]

Italy's Serie A incurred BeIN's wrath when it chose to honor a deal it had signed in 2018 to play three Supercoppa matches over the next five years in Riyadh, the first of them in January 2018. BeIN threatened to cancel its contract with the league. In June 2019, Serie A finally condemned BeoutQ and promised unspecified legal action against Arabsat.[65] Not satisfied, BeIN in June 2020 blocked Serie A broadcasts across its networks worldwide, restoring them only when Serie A agreed to accept a 30 percent reduction on its current deal—compensation, BeIN said, for lost broadcast exclusivity.[66] In January 2021, Serie A announced it would tender its MENA rights both in a region-wide package and in individual countries. The league made clear that its existing Supercoppa deal with KSA would remain in place; BeIN declined to bid, preferring a region-wide process only.[67] For Serie A the decision was a gamble, as BeIN at the time provided nearly 50 percent of the league's total broadcast revenue.[68]

The Asian Football Confederation (AFC)—which the Qatari national team won in February 2019—announced in May 2019 that it would re-tender its 2021–4 rights for the MENA region, even though BeIN owned them. Two months earlier, the AFC made its Champions League matches available in KSA by broadcasting them on its geo-blocked Facebook and YouTube channels, a breach of contract for which BeIN said it would sue for damages.[69] In June 2020, AFC began to sell its MENA rights on a country-by-country basis.[70] The Saudi Football Federation then urged other football leagues to follow the AFC's example. At about the same time, reports surfaced that KSA was negotiating with Bundesliga, whose rights agreement in MENA with BeIN was soon to end.[71] In April 2021, Saudi Sports Company acquired KSA rights for AFC competitions—including the Asian qualifiers for the World Cup, the AFC Champions League, and the 2023 Asian Cup in China—in the 2021–4 cycle. Saudi Sports Company will begin AFC coverage on its OTT service GSA Live, then move to broadcast channels in late 2021.[72] As of the time of writing, the AFC has no other broadcast partner in MENA.[73]

The WTO and International Law in the BeoutQ Case

If the conflict between Qatar and KSA was political and regional, the implications for the case were global and the applicable international law straightforward. Both Qatar and KSA are signatories to the 1994 Trade-Related Aspects of Intellectual Property (TRIPS) agreement of the General Agreement on Tariffs and Trade (GATT), administered by the WTO since 1994. TRIPS says a country cannot discriminate against foreigners and must provide "no less favorable" treatment to nationals of other WTO members.[74] In the BeIN case, Qatar accused KSA of multiple violations of TRIPS, including failing to protect copyrights, failing to provide national treatment, and failing to provide adequate enforcement options.[75]

In an interview with the author, the US regional trade official acknowledged the scope of the problem, saying, "When the entire population of the region sees a pirate as a genuine place to access content, that changes the entire dynamic to something that we have never actually seen before ever in the history of IP piracy."[76] The US Trade Representative (USTR) had listed KSA on its international trade watch list in 2018 because of issues in its pharmaceutical sector, but the BeoutQ case resulted in KSA appearing on the priority watch list in 2019 and 2020. At the time, no other country had publicly called out KSA in this way. The US went further and identified BeoutQ as a KSA operation in its 2019 "notorious markets" list, and KSA itself as a notorious market in its 2020 report.[77] In January 2020, the European Commission also added Saudi Arabia to its piracy priority list.[78] A year later, in January 2021, the International Olympic Committee urged the USTR to keep KSA on its priority watch list and "consider further steps," noting that BeIN owns the MENA broadcast rights to the Games until 2024.

Qatar brought a formal complaint against Saudi Arabia to the WTO in October 2018, saying that KSA was both blocking BeIN and refusing to take action against BeoutQ.[79] When KSA refused to enter into consultation, Qatar, with support of several WTO member states, requested a formal investigation of the case.[80] KSA responded to Qatar's complaint by asserting the national security exception contained in both GATT and TRIPS but which in the history of international trade law had been rarely invoked, never denied, and its scope largely undefined.[81] At issue in KSA's defense was whether the security exception is self-judging, meaning effectively outside the scope of WTO authority. In principle, the security exception is to be balanced by the expectation that it is used in good faith, but complicating Qatar's case was that the United States had also asserted the security exception in relation to tariffs the Trump administration had imposed on steel and aluminum the same year. The United States argued the exception to be non-justiciable, that the WTO could only recognize the security invocation and make no further findings, threatening not just Qatar's case but the very legitimacy of the WTO.[82] The WTO rejected the claim that the exception is non-justiciable in a separate dispute between Russia and Ukraine a year later.[83]

On June 16, 2020, a three-judge WTO dispute panel issued a 125-page report agreeing with Qatar that Saudi Arabia had violated multiple provisions of the TRIPS Agreement. The panel rejected KSA's national security defense—the first time in the 73-year history of multilateral trade rules that the WTO had done so—declared BeoutQ to be a KSA-based operation that Saudi had made no effort to shut down, and found KSA in violation of the TRIPS agreement for preventing Qatar from enforcing its rights in the country.[84] Of particular interest to the sports industry, the panel considered questions of first impression regarding the scope of the Berne Convention and TRIPS Agreement as they apply to copyright protection for live sports broadcasts.[85]

KSA appealed the panel's findings and Qatar counter-proposed arbitration.[86] As of the time of writing, there has been no further action in the case, which Saudi news sources reported as a victory for the kingdom,[87] and in July 2020, KSA permanently banned BeIN from the country.[88] The WTO decision, combined with KSA's decision to ban BeIN, proved fatal to KSA's bid to buy Newcastle United in the English Premier League (EPL). Had the Newcastle deal been approved, the EPL would have had a known pirate as an owner, and the team's new fans in KSA would have had no legal way to watch their team play on television.[89] Reportedly, during negotiations, Saudi Crown Prince Mohammed bin Salman called on UK Prime Minister Boris Johnson to intervene in the Newcastle deal,[90] and, as recently as March 2021, Newcastle owner Mike Ashley publicly reaffirmed his commitment to push the deal through.[91]

PTV, Politics, Piracy, and the Pandemic: The Future of Middle East Football Broadcasting

At a meeting of Gulf rulers in early January 2021, Saudi Arabia agreed to end its blockade of Qatar and to reopen borders and airspace, ending the diplomatic crisis as abruptly as it began. Over the course of the next twelve months, the relationship between the two countries was publicly patched up, with news media in both countries celebrating the "historical bonds of affection" between the two states,[92] and a cascade of football détentes that concluded November 2021 with BeIN's last-minute acquisition of the regional broadcast rights to the first FIFA Arab Cup, held in December of the same year.[93] In mid-January 2021, Reuters reported that BeIN was again available in Saudi Arabia, but almost certainly because Saudi residents were able to enter Qatar and secure subscriptions. Only 10 months later, in October, did KSA officially lift its ban on BeIN and offer to settle Qatar's $1 billion WTO claim, though there is no confirmation from either government that any settlement has been paid.[94] That same month, the Saudis finally succeeded in acquiring an 80 percent stake in the EPL's Newcastle United club for £352 million, reportedly after the favorable intervention of BeIN and European Club Association Chairman Nasser Al-Khelaifi and assurances from EPL leadership that "the Kingdom of Saudi Arabia will not control" the club.[95]

The thaw between the Qataris and the Saudis will doubtlessly ease the instability caused by BeoutQ, but the MENA football broadcast market has been reset, and though the new one has yet to take shape it will probably not end the enmity that attends BeIN's regional "monopoly" or curtail piracy in the region. Though BeIN has regained its license in Saudi Arabia, it will face new competition in the country's PTV market, and possibly regionally; it is unlikely ever to recoup its estimated $4 billion in piracy losses; and, most important, the company's rights investments will never return to pre-blockade levels. Some former rights partners, notably Serie A and Bundesliga, appear to have permanently ended their relationship with BeIN, and others key to BeIN's regional strategy, like UEFA, have been forced to concede on their rights value. Finally, cheap IPTV boxes and bootlegging software are plentiful in MENA—and especially in Saudi Arabia, the region's most valuable market—and piracy will remain a threat to sports properties and sports broadcasters both in the region and, as BeIN CEO Al-Obaidly has repeatedly warned, to the sports industry worldwide. It will be interesting to watch BeIN's future acquisitions in a market where its CEO has declared rights "non-exclusive."

Just as important to BeIN's future will be whether and how the company transitions from a PTV service, reliant on subscription fees, to a more digital business that incorporates ecommerce, streaming, ticketing, sponsorship, membership, and loyalty.[96] Despite the low PTV penetration rate in MENA compared to Europe, the price of licensing premium content is significantly higher, and industry analysts do not believe it sustainable. *DigitalTVResearch* estimated in 2018 BeIN's annual $1 billion outlay for sports rights to be well in excess of its subscription revenues.[97] In 2016, Banque Francais weighed BeIN's expanded rights portfolio against revenues and estimated the company's annual loss at €200 million.[98] No credible source thinks BeIN will become profitable any time soon, and how much longer the company will be allowed to operate with losses depends in part on the changing sports broadcasting rights market, discussed below, but presumably also on the Qatari government's judgment of the company's effectiveness as an instrument of diplomacy.

The COVID-19 pandemic has further complicated the picture by flattening sports rights. According to *Sportbusiness'* 2020 *Global Media Report*, the global value of sports media rights—$44.6 billion in 2020—fell by just over 12 percent from 2019. Some markets were hit by the pandemic harder than others—particularly the UK and the MENA region, neither of which is expected to return to pre-pandemic values until at least 2023, if then.[99] In a

2020 survey of sport executives by consultancies Mailman and Seven League, a large majority said rights valuations had peaked and that the COVID-19 crisis had accelerated a trend in which rights holders will need to diversify revenue streams.[100] The recession-reduced spending power of consumers, a sharp drop in revenues caused by the loss of matches or entire seasons, weak viewership, and gate revenue for matches played in empty stadiums, all contributed to dim growth expectations for rights values. Throughout 2020, rights deals around the world had to be renegotiated or terminated, with some leagues paying substantial rebates to broadcasters.[101] The European Club Association predicted in November 2020 that COVID-19 would cost Europe's top football clubs at least €5 billion between 2019 and 2021,[102] and, five months later, UEFA reported a 21 percent drop in revenues for the year, a loss of €819 million.[103] Figures from EPL clubs indicate the league's losses over the same period to be approximately £1 billion.[104] Such losses almost certainly gave impetus to the announcement of a European Super League in April 2021, an opportunity for Europe's richest clubs to consolidate their market dominance. Criticism of the idea was quick, fierce, and widespread.[105] The six English clubs withdrew from the project within days, but the fact that the long-discussed league got as far as it did suggests that FIFA could seize the opportunity to expand the Club World Cup, as Gianni Infantino has urged. Qatar hosted the Club World Cup in 2019 and 2020.

There is also the possibility of new regional competition for BeIN. In August 2020, Egypt announced Ontime Sports, an FTA channel to be carried on Nilesat and Arabsat. In December 2020, Ontime signaled its intention to compete in the region when it acquired the MENA rights to the 2021 Men's Handball World Championship, a hugely popular competition previously owned by BeIN.[106] In late 2020, Saudi Arabia confirmed that it would create a rights-acquisition platform, Saudi Sports Company, to secure rights within KSA and not for the whole of the MENA region.[107] So far, the Kingdom has not pursued European football and has not bid for the regional rights for any competition. However, that could change, simply because KSA is the biggest piece of the MENA market.[108]

But if any story best captures BeIN's beleaguered position at the center of MENA football broadcasting, it is one that came out of nowhere in early 2021, when a conspiracy theory arose among Fenerbahce football fans in Turkey who convinced themselves that BeIN was engaged in a covert campaign to undermine their team.[109] Fenerbahce is one of Turkey's most storied football clubs, with the Super Lig the sixth largest in Europe by value of broadcasting rights, and Turkey a major football market in the MENA region.[110] The anti-BeIN sentiment among Fenerbahce fans grew so heated that it forced the network to change how it broadcast the club's matches, in which angry fans and players bedecked themselves and their stadium with logos reading "BeFair." BeIN sued to enjoin the logos as a trademark infringement, leading fans to come up with new and angrier protests and Fenerbahce's president, the billionaire Ali Koc, to threaten a boycott against the company.[111]

It is not the first skirmish BeIN has had with Turkish football. In 2020, the company's Digiturk subsidiary and the Turkish Football Federation (TFF) repeatedly quarreled over rights fees. The dispute found its way to the pitch, where protesting players in multiple games refused to play for a full minute after the game whistle during several matches. Part of the issue has been that BeIN's payments are in US dollars, and currency fluctuations between the Turkish lira and the dollar have resulted in disputes over payments. Further complicating relations are payments BeIN withheld in 2020, when the Super Lig postponed matches because of COVID-19.[112]

But an important subtext in the Fenerbahce story is, again, regional politics: Qatar is associated in Turkey with its political and financial support for President Recep Tayyip Erdoğan, and Fenerbahce, like other clubs in the TFF, is heavily in debt, so BeIN's financial investment in Turkish football looks increasingly like a foreign takeover of the people's game.[113] BeIN's global rights deal with the Turkish Football Federation ends in 2022, and, in April 2021, Digiturk announced that it would not bid to renew its Turkish rights for UEFA Champions League or Europa League, citing both piracy and the downturn in the value of premium rights packages.[114]

Explaining Fenerbahce's theory of BeIN's skullduggery to the *New York Times*, club General Secretary Burak Kizilhan captured the current confused state of Middle East football broadcasting perfectly: "If our arguments are considered individually they would not make much sense," he wrote. "But seeing them as parts of a puzzle, it shows the big picture clearly."[115]

NOTES

INTRODUCTION

1. Jim Hart, "A Hot Night in Java: How Iraq Won the Asian Cup While War Raged at Home," *These Football Times*, March 8, 2017, https://thesefootballtimes.co/2017/03/08/a-hot-night-in-java-how-iraq-won-the-asian-cup-while-war-raged-at-home.

2. Aidan Williams, "How Iraq's Unlikely 2007 Asian Cup Victory United a Troubled Nation," *Footy Analyst*, January 19, 2019, https://footyanalyst.com/how-iraqs-unlikely-2007-asian-cup-victory-united-a-troubled-nation.

3. Stephen Farrell and Peter Gelling, "With Eyes Fixed on a Distant Soccer Field, Iraqis Leap at a Reason to Celebrate," *New York Times*, July 30, 2007, www.nytimes.com/2007/07/30/world/middleeast/30iraq.html; Julian Linden, "Iraq's Asian Cup Win Transcends Sport," *Reuters*, July 30, 2007, www.reuters.com/article/us-soccer-asia/iraqs-asian-cup-win-transcends-sport-idUSSYD28314920070730.

4. FIFA.com, "M. al-Thani: Qatar is the Right Choice," December 2, 2010, www.fifa.com/worldcup/news/thani-qatar-the-right-choice-1345006.

5. Regan E. Doherty, "2022 World Cup Presents Challenge for Tiny Qatar," *Reuters*, December 15, 2010, www.reuters.com/article/us-worldcup-qatar/2022-world-cup-presents-challenge-for-tiny-qatar-idUSTRE6BE31N20101215.

6. Ian Rodgers, "What Were FIFA Thinking When They Awarded Finals to Qatar for 2022?" *Bleacher Report*, March 21, 2013, https://bleacherreport.com/articles/1575977-world-cup-what-were-fifa-thinking-when-they-awarded-finals-to-qatar-for-2022.

7. Brian Homewood, "Qatar World Cup a Potential Health Risk: FIFA," *Reuters*, November 17, 2010, www.reuters.com/article/us-soccer-fifa-world/qatar-world-cup-a-potential-health-risk-fifa-idUSTRE6AG2JJ20101117.

8. Doherty, "2022 World Cup Presents Challenge for Tiny Qatar."

9. Matt Scott, "Millions Paid in Bribes for Qatar's 2022 World Cup Votes, Report Claims," *The Guardian*, May 10, 2011.

10. Nicholas McGeehan, "Let Qatar 2022 Not Be Built on Brutality," *The Guardian*,

December 6, 2010, www.theguardian.com/football/2011/may/10/millions-bribes-qatar-2022-world-cup-claims.

11. Human Rights Watch, "Building a Better World Cup: Protecting Migrant Workers in Qatar Ahead of FIFA 2022," June 12, 2012, www.hrw.org/report/2012/06/12/building-better-world-cup/protecting-migrant-workers-qatar-ahead-fifa-2022.

12. James Montague, "Egypt's Revolutionary Soccer Ultras: How Football Fans Toppled Mubarak," *CNN*, June 29, 2011, http://edition.cnn.com/2011/SPORT/football/06/29/football.ultras.zamalek.ahly/index.html.

13. Karim Zidan, "Ultras in Mourning: How a Massacre, Revolutionary Aftermath, and Politics Killed Egyptian Football," *Open Democracy*, December 12, 2016, www.opendemocracy.net/en/north-africa-west-asia/ultras-in-mourning-how-massacre-revolutionary-aftermath-and-politics-kill.

14. "Egypt Allows Football Fans—but Not Ultras—Back into Stadiums," *Middle East Eye*, September 18, 2018, www.middleeasteye.net/news/egypt-allows-football-fans-not-ultras-back-stadiums.

15. Rashid Khalidi, "The 'Middle East' as a Framework of Analysis: Re-mapping a Region in the Era of Globalization," *Comparative Studies of South Asia, Africa and the Middle East* 18, no. 1 (1998): 74–80.

16. Khalidi, "The 'Middle East' as a Framework of Analysis," 78.

17. Wilson Chacko Jacob, *Working Out Egypt: Effendi Masculinity and Subject Formation in Colonial Modernity, 1870–1940* (Durham, NC: Duke University Press, 2011), 47.

18. Ibid. 127–9.

19. Tamir Sorek, *Arab Soccer in a Jewish State: The Integrative Enclave* (Cambridge, UK: Cambridge University Press, 2007), 16–19.

20. Joseph Massad, *Colonial Effects: The Making of National Identity in Jordan* (New York, NY: Columbia University Press, 2001), 254–5; Heather J. Sharkey, *Living with Colonialism: Nationalism and Culture in the Anglo-Egyptian Sudan* (Berkeley, CA: University of California Press, 2003), 46–7.

21. Mahfoud Amara and Youcef Bouandel, "Algeria," in *The Palgrave International Handbook of Football and Politics*, eds. Jean-Michael De Waele, Suzan Gibril, Ekaterina Gloriozova, and Ramón Spaaij (Cham, Switzerland: Palgrave Macmillan, 2018), 332.

22. Larbi Sadiki and Layla Saleh, "Playing Ball: Crowd and 'Contra-Crowd' in the Politics of Egyptian and Tunisian Football," in *The Routledge Handbook of Sport in Asia*, eds. Fan Hong and Lu Zhouxiang (New York, NY: Routledge, 2021), 478–9.

23. Sadiki and Saleh, "Playing Ball," 479.

24. Houchang E. Chehabi, "The Politics of Football in Iran," *Soccer & Society* 7, nos. 2–3 (2006): 243.

25. Peter Hough, "'Make Goals not War': The Contribution of International Football to World Peace," *The International Journal of the History of Sport* 25, no. 10 (2008): 1288–99.

26. Houchang E. Chehabi, "Sport Diplomacy between the United States and Iran," *Diplomacy & Statecraft* 12, no. 1 (2001): 89–106.

27. Franklin Foer, *How Soccer Explains the World: An Unlikely Theory of Globalization* (New York, NY: HarperCollins, 2004), 221–3.

28. Osvaldo Croci and Julian Ammirante, "Soccer in the Age of Globalization," *Peace Review* 11, no. 4 (1999): 499–500.

29. Richard Giulianotti and Roland Robertson, *Globalization and Football* (London: Sage, 2009), 165.

30. Giulianotti and Robertson, *Globalization and Football*, xiv.

31. Scott Waalkes, "Does Soccer Explain the World or Does the World Explain Soccer? Soccer and Globalization," *Soccer & Society* 18, nos. 2–3 (2017): 2.

32. Salma Thani and Tom Heenan, "The Ball May Be Round but Football Is Becoming Increasingly Arabic: Oil Money and the Rise of the New Football Order," *Soccer & Society* 18, no. 7 (2016): 1016–18.

33. Sonia Benghida, "World Cup Football in International Relations: The 2009 Algerian-Egyptian Football Conflict," *International Journal of Innovation and Applied Studies* 9, no. 1 (2014): 234–8.

34. See, for example: Robbert Woltering, "'Ultras' as Political Actors in the Egyptian Revolution," *Arab Studies Quarterly* 35, no. 3 (2013): 290–304; Yağmur Nuhrat, "Fair to Swear? Gendered Formulations of Fairness in Football in Turkey," *Journal of Middle East Women's Studies* 13, no. 1 (2017): 25–46; Babak Fozooni, "Iranian Women and Football," *Cultural Studies* 22, no. 1 (2008): 114–33.

35. "Qatar Spending $500m a Week on World Cup Infrastructure Projects," *BBC News*, February 8, 2017, www.bbc.com/news/world-middle-east-38905510.

36. See, for example: James M. Dorsey, "The Turbulent World of Middle East Soccer," mideastsoccer.blogspot.com and the book of the same title; Ronnie Close, *Cairo's Ultras: Resistance and Revolution in Egypt's Football Culture* (Cairo: American University of Cairo Press, 2019); "Soccer in the Middle East," special issue of *Soccer & Society*, 13, nos. 5–6 (2012); "Football in the Middle East," research initiative, Center for International and Regional Studies, Georgetown University in Qatar, 2019, https://cirs.qatar.georgetown.edu/research/research-initiatives/football-middle-east.

1. THE POLITICAL GAME: A GENEALOGY OF THE EGYPTIAN LEAGUE

I thank former Ahly's CEO Mohamed Morgan, former Ahly Television Channel Director Mohamed El-Adl, and Madame Omneya from the club's secretariat for their hospitality and support that made this research possible.

1. International Olympic Committee, "Olympic Charter," September 2019, https://stillmed.olympic.org/media/Document%20Library/OlympicOrg/General/EN-Olympic-Charter.pdf#_ga=2.134274610.275388483.1583855387-165357441.1574291712.

2. FIFA, "Laws of the Game 2015/2016," May 2015, https://img.fifa.com/image/upload/datdz0pms85gbnqy4j3k.pdf.

3. George Orwell, "The Sporting Spirit," *Tribune*, December 14, 1945, www.orwell-foundation.com/the-orwell-foundation/orwell/essays-and-other-works/the-sporting-spirit.

4. Carl Schmitt famously defines politics as a warlike practice; a space reducible to the existential distinction between friend and enemy. See Carl Schmitt, *The Concept of the Political* (Chicago: University of Chicago Press, 1996).

5. See, for example, Shawki E. El-Zatmah, "Āhā Gūn!: A Social and Cultural History of Soccer in Egypt" (PhD diss., UCLA, 2011), 70–1.

6. See, for example, Michel Raspaud and Monia Lachheb, "A Centennial Rivalry, Ahly vs Zamalek: Identity and Society in Modern Egypt," in *Identity and Nation in African Football: Fans, Community, and Clubs*, eds. Chuka Onwumechili and Gerard Akindes (New York, NY: Palgrave, 2014), 99–115.

7. This "overlap" argument seems to be the standard narrative in the study of sports and politics. El-Zatmah's otherwise compelling study of the social and cultural history of Egyptian football, for example, suggests that "the history of soccer in Egypt overlaps with and has been affected by major political, economic, social and cultural transformations of Egypt," see El-Zatmah, "A Social and Cultural History of Soccer in Egypt," 1. Politics, that is to say, is external to sports: it belongs in formal political institutions, and political actors directly operating within these institutions. Professional football is, at best, a platform on which this politics plays out. My proposition, on the other hand, is that the very professionalization of football is political.

8. Christopher Ferraro, "The Bulldog, the Pharaoh, and the Football: British Imperialism and Egypt's National Sport and Identity, 1882–1934," in *Sports in African History, Politics, and Identity Formation*, eds. Michael J. Gennaro and Saheed Aderinto (New York, NY: Routledge, 2019), 184–6.

9. See, for example Luṭfi Aḥmad Naṣṣār, *Wasāʾil al-Tarfīh fī ʿAṣr Salāṭīn al-Mamālīk fī Miṣr* [Means of Leisure in the Age of Mamluk Sultans in Egypt] (Cairo: Al-Hayʾa Al-Miṣriyya al-ʿĀammah lil-Kitāb, 1999); Moḥammad ʿĀdel Khaṭṭāb, *Al-Alʿāb al-Rīfiyya al-Shaʿbiyya* [Popular Games in the Countryside] (Cairo: Maktabat Al-Anglo Al-Miṣriyya, 1961).

10. For more on calling the masses' game *awlād al-balad* football, see El-Zatmah, "A Social and Cultural History of Soccer in Egypt," 14.

11. Yāsir Ayūb, *Miṣr wa-Kurat al-Qadam: al-Tārīkh al-Ḥaqīqī—Ayna wa-Kayfa Badaʾat al-Ḥikāyah* [Egypt and Football: The Real History—Where and How the Story Began] (Cairo: Al-Dār Al-Miṣrīyah Al-Lubnānīyah, 2018), 32.

12. Ibid., 27.

13. Al-Sayyid Farag, *Abṭāl Baladnā* [Our nation's heroes] (Cairo: Akhbār Al-Yawm, 1978), 20–1.

14. Shaun Lopez, "Football as National Allegory: *Al-Ahram* and the Olympics in 1920s Egypt," *History Compass* 7 (2009): 282–305. At 286.

15. Partha Chatterjee, *The Black Hole of Empire: History of a Global Practice of Power* (Princeton, NJ: Princeton University Press, 2012), 292.

16. Wilson Chacko Jacob, *Working Out Egypt: Effendi Masculinity and Subject Formation in Colonial Modernity, 1870–1940* (Durham: Duke University Press, 2011), 65.

17. Ayūb, *Miṣr wa-Kurat al-Qadam*, 49–52.

18. David Graeber, *The Utopia of Rules: On Technology, Stupidity, and the Secret Joys of Bureaucracy* (New York, NY: Melville House Publishing, 2015), 190–1.

19. Jacob, *Working Out Egypt*, 72.

20. Playing football outside the enclosed spaces designated for the effendi game oftentimes resulted in fights with others, especially for children. See El-Zatmah, "A Social and Cultural History of Soccer in Egypt," 40. Effendi parents did not therefore bar their children from playing street football, which also had unfavorable (working) class associations.

21. Ferraro, "The Bulldog, the Pharaoh, and the Football," 186.

22. Farag, *Abṭāl*, 24.

23. Mounah Abdallah Khouri, *Poetry and the Making of Modern Egypt: 1882–1922* (Leiden: Brill, 1971), 71.

24. Ḥassan Al-Mistikāwī, *Al-Nādī Al-Ahlī 1907–1997: Qiṣṣat al-Riyāḍa wa-l-Waṭaniyya* [Ahly Club 1907–1997: The Story of Sports and Patriotism] (Cairo: Dār Al-Shoruk, 1997), 22–3.

25. Jacob, *Working Out Egypt*, 86.

26. At least 119 foreign joint stock companies were registered in Egypt between 1905 and 1907, a numbed unparalleled in any previous period. See Al-Mistikāwī, *Al-Nādī*, 18.

27. Alongside Ahly, Luṭfī contributed to the foundation of agricultural cooperatives— corporations aimed at empowering farmers with less than five fiddans (acres).

28. Other accounts suggest that the Alexandrian Club, *Al-Nadī Al-Aulimbī* (The Olympic Club) was founded before Ahly.

29. Ahly Sporting Club Archives, *Maḥāḍir al-Jam'iyya al-'Umūmiyya Li-l-Nādī Al-Ahlī, 1907–1938* (hereafter, *MJU* followed by the date), January 19, 1916.

30. Ibid.

31. *MJU*, March 31, 1918. Ahly's documents in general make clear that membership was restricted to high school students and graduates. Middle school graduates were denied membership. See Ahly Sporting Club Archives, *Maḥāḍir Majlis al-Idāra, 1913–1919* (hereafter *MMI* followed by the date), March 15, 1914.

32. *MJU*, December 28, 1923.

33. *MJU*, November 7, 1924.

34. *MJU*, January 19, 1916.

35. Raspaud and Lachheb, "A Centennial Rivalry, Ahly vs Zamalek," 103.

36. *MJU*, January 19, 1916.

37. Etienne Balibar, "The Nation Form: History and Ideology," in *Race, Nation, Class: Ambiguous Identities*, eds. Etienne Balibar and Immanuel Wallerstein (New York, NY: Verso, 1998), 89.

38. Jacob, *Working Out Egypt*, 72.

39. *MJU*, December 3, 1920.

40. Al-Mistikāwī, *Al-Nādī*, 159.

41. Ferraro, "The Bulldog, the Pharaoh, and the Football," 189.

42. Al-Mistikāwī, *Al-Nādī*, 159.

43. Ferraro, "The Bulldog, the Pharaoh, and the Football," 189.

44. See, for example, 'Umar Ṭāhir, *Zamalkāwī: Albūm Mi'awiyyat al-Jumhūr* [A Zamalek Fan: The Fans' Centenary Album], (Cairo: Atlas, 2011), 60–1.

45. Juhayna, "Al-Al'āb Al-Riyāḍiyya: Iftitāḥ Al-Nādī Al-Mukhtalaṭ Bi-l-Zamālek," [Physical Games: Opening of Al-Mukhtalat Club in Zamalek], *Ahrām*, February 12, 1927, 6.

46. Ṭāhir, *Zamalkāwī*, 65–6.

47. Jacob, *Working Out Egypt*, 93.

48. Yūsuf Moḥammad, "Al-Al'āb Al-Riyāḍiyya," [Physical Games], *Ahrām*, October 3, 1921, 3.

49. El-Zatmah, "A Social and Cultural History of Soccer in Egypt," 25.

50. In 1917, for example, only 6.8 percent of the Egyptian population were literate. See Ziad Fahmy, *Ordinary Egyptians: Creating the Modern Nation Through Popular Culture* (Stanford, CA: Stanford University Press, 2011), 6.

51. Lopez, "Football as National Allegory," 288.

52. Ibid., 287–9.

53. Benedict Anderson, *Imagined Communities: Reflections on the Origin and Spread of Nationalism* (New York, NY: Verso, 2006), 36.

54. Joshua Barkan, *Corporate Sovereignty: Law and Government Under Capitalism* (Minneapolis, MN: University of Minnesota Press, 2013), 20.

55. Michel Foucault, *The Birth of Biopolitics: Lectures at the Collège de France, 1978–1979*, trans. Graham Burchell (New York, NY: Picador, 2008), 13–15.

56. *Al-Abṭāl*, "Al-Andiya al-Riyaḍiyya fī Miṣr wa-Oūrobba," [Sports Clubs in Egypt and Europe], January 21, 1933, 3.

57. El-Zatmah, "A Social and Cultural History of Soccer in Egypt," 62.

58. *Al-Abṭāl*, "Al-Andiya al-Riyaḍiyya."

59. *MMI*, January 21, 1916.

60. There is significant disagreement over his birth year. Some accounts claim it is 1891. Al-Mistikāwī claims however that he was born in 1880. This is less likely, because he played football until the early 1930s, which would make him over 50 years old when he retired. A 1933 profile of Ḥegāzī in Al-Abṭāl sports magazine however states that he was born in 1889. See *Al-Abṭāl*, "Abṭāluna: Ḥussein Ḥegāzī Baṭal Kurat al-Qadam," January 21, 1933, 7.

61. Several accounts, including those of Al-Mistikāwī and Farag, claim that Ḥegāzī played for the "British/English National Team." This is inaccurate, however. Not only because there was no British team at the time, but also because the contemporaneous accounts, notably the aforementioned Al-Abṭāl profile, suggests that he played for the Wanderers Club team, which "borrowed" Ḥegāzī during its European tour, the same way Egyptian teams borrowed players for other clubs when playing against foreign teams.

62. "Trial Game at Cambridge," *The Times*, October 23, 1913, 12.

63. "Freshmen's Match at Cambridge," *The Times*, October 18, 1913, 13.

64. "Association Football: Cambridge University v. United Hospitals," *The Times*, December 4, 1913, 15.

65. El-Zatmah, "A Social and Cultural History of Soccer in Egypt," 34.

66. *MMI*, December 1, 1914.

67. *Al-Abṭāl*, "Abṭāluna: Ḥussein Ḥegāzī."

68. *MMI*, November 28, 1916.

69. Al-Mistikāwī, *Al-Nādī*, 161.

70. *MJU*, April 17, 1928.

71. Raspaud and Lachheb, "Centennial Rivalry," 102.

72. *MJU*, General assembly meeting, 1923.

73. Farag, *Abṭāl*, 87–101.

74. *MMI*, November 18, 1913.

75. *MMI*, December 9, 1913.

76. *MMI*, June 8, 1915.

77. *MMI*, January 26, 1916.

78. *MMI*, March 10, 1918.

79. *Al-Abṭāl*, "Abṭāluna: Ḥussein Ḥegāzī."

80. *Al-Ahrām*, "Al-Alʿāb Al-Riyāḍiyya: Qarārāt al-Ittiḥād al-Miṣrī li-Kurat al-Qadam," May 11, 1929, 8.

81. Ayūb, *Miṣr wa-Kurat al-Qadam*, 177.

82. *Al-Ahrām*, "Kurat al-Qadam," [Football], January 6, 1935, 8.

83. Partha Chatterjee, *Nationalist Thought and the Colonial World: A Derivative Discourse* (London: Zed Books, 1986), 51.

84. El-Zatmah, "A Social and Cultural History of Soccer in Egypt," 99–105.

85. Ibid., 103.

86. *Al-Abṭāl*, "Al-Andiya al-Riyaḍiyya," 3.

87. El-Zatmah, "A Social and Cultural History of Soccer in Egypt," 42.

88. See, for example, Fahmy, *Ordinary Egyptians*, 104–7.

89. See, for example, Fakhrī Adel-Nūr, *Mudhakkirāt Fakhrī Adel-Nūr: Thawrat 1919 wa-dawr Saʿd Zaghlūl wa-l-wafd fi al-ḥaraka al-waṭaniyya* (Cairo: Dar al-Shorouk, 1992), 45–6.

90. *MMI*.

91. Jacob, *Working Out Egypt*, 79.

92. Murat Yıldız, "Mapping the 'Sports Nahḍa': Toward a History of Sports in the Modern Middle East," in *Sport, Politics, and Society in the Middle East*, eds. Danyel Reiche and Tamir Sorek (New York, NY: Oxford University Press, 2019), 19.

93. *MJU*, December 13, 1907.

94. *MJU*, December 28, 1923.

95. *MJU*, General Assembly meeting, 1924.

96. Ayūb, *Miṣr wa-Kurat al-Qadam*, 178.

97. *MJU*, January 12, 1918.

98. *MMI*, January 20, 1918.

99. *Al-Ahrām*, "Al-Alʿāb Al-Riyāḍiyya."

100. *MJU*, General Assembly meeting, 1924.

101. Naguib Mahfouz, the famous Egyptian novelist, for example, notes that three voices

made the radio popular: Rif'at (a Quran reciter), Umm Kulthūm (the famous singer), and Latīf, a football commentator (quoted in el El-Zatmah, 111).

102. Fahmy, *Ordinary Egyptians*, 15.

103. Al-Mistikāwī, *Al-Nādī*, 182.

104. "Kurat al-Qadam," *Al-Ahrām*, January 6, 1935, 8.

105. Chatterjee, *Nationalist Thought*, 51.

106. Richard Giulianotti and Roland Robertson, *Globalization and Football* (London: Sage Publications, 2009), 23.

107. Al-Mistikāwī, *Al-Nādī*, 162.

108. Raspaud and Lachheb, "Centennial Rivalry," 105.

109. Al-Mistikāwī, *Al-Nādī*, 70.

110. Victor D. Cha, "Theory of Sport and Politics," *The International Journal of the History of Sport* 26, no. 11 (2009): 1583.

111. Philip Stern, *The Company-State: Corporate Sovereignty and the Early Modern Foundations of the British Empire in India* (Oxford: Oxford University Press, 2011), 6.

112. James M. Dorsey, *Shifting Sands, Essays on Sports and Politics in the Middle East and North Africa* (New Jersey: World Scientific, 2017), 380.

2. BEYOND SOFT POWER: FOOTBALL AS A FORM OF REGIME LEGITIMATION

1. Will Magee, "How the African Cup of Nations Became a Powerful Propaganda Tool," *Vice News*, January 13, 2017, www.vice.com/en_au/article/yp8b7b/how-the-africa-cup-of-nations-became-a-powerful-propaganda-tool.

2. Amin Salih and Ahmad Arafa, "Tarikh al-riyadha al-masriya fi 'alam korat-al-qadam al-ifriqiya" [The history of Egyptian leadership in the world of African football], *al-Yawm al-Sabi'*, June 16, 2019, https://bit.ly/Youm7EgyptianFootball.

3. Peter Alegi, *African Soccerscapes: How a Continent Changed the World's Game* (Ohio, OH: Ohio University Press, 2010), 64.

4. Michel Raspaud and Monia Lachheb, "A Centennial Rivalry, Ahly vs Zamalek: Identity and Society in Modern Egypt," in *Identity and Nation in African Football: Fans, Community, and Clubs*, eds. Chuka Onwumechili and Gerard Akindes (London: Palgrave Macmillan, 2014), 104.

5. David Goldblatt, *The Ball is Round: A Global History of Soccer* (New York, NY: Riverhead Books, 2008), 495.

6. Salah Essa, "Football Hysteria," *Egypt Independent*, November 14, 2009, https://egypt-independent.com/football-hysteria.

7. 'Adel al-Sanhouri, "Qisat zawaj al-siyasa bi-korat-al-qadam al-ifriqiya" [The story of the marriage between politics and African football], *Sawt al-Ummah*, June 21, 2019, https://bit.ly/SoutAlOmmaFootball.

8. In defining the nation's post-revolutionary place in the world, Nasser positioned Egypt within three circles: Arab, African, and Islamic. Gamal Abdel Nasser, *The Philosophy of the Revolution* (Cairo: Mondiale Press, 1955), 69.

9. See, for example, Sean Brown and Souvik Naha, eds., "Soccer in the Middle East," Special Issue of *Soccer & Society* 13, nos. 5–6 (2012). See also a number of related chapters in the recent volume: Danyel Reiche and Tamir Sorek, eds., *Sport, Politics, and Society in the Middle East* (New York, NY: Oxford University Press, 2019).

10. Alon Raab, "Soccer in the Middle East: An Introduction," *Soccer & Society* 13, nos. 5–6 (2012): 623.

11. Joseph S. Nye Jr., *Soft Power: The Means to Success in World Politics* (New York, NY: Public Affairs, 2004), x.

12. Derek Shearer, "To Play Ball, Not Make War: Sports, Diplomacy and Soft Power," *Harvard International Review*, 36, no. 1 (2014): 53–7.

13. Rene Slama, "Qatar Hits Back at Rivals with Neymar Soft Power Play," *Daily Sabah*, August 4, 2017, www.dailysabah.com/economy/2017/08/03/qatar-hits-back-at-gulf-rivals-with-high-profile-neymar-soft-power-play. For more on the role of transfer policies as an extension of diplomacy, see: T. B. James, "Soft Power and the 2022 World Cup in Qatar," *Tajseer* 3, no. 2 (2021), Special issue on "Culture as a Tool of Soft Power."

14. Rene Slama, "UAE and Qatar Stake Billions in 'Soft Power' Showdown," *Naharnet*, November 6, 2017, www.naharnet.com/stories/237820-uae-and-qatar-stake-billions-in-soft-power-showdown/print. For more on kit sponsorships as an example of soft power, see: John S. Krzyzaniak, "The Soft Power Strategy of Soccer Sponsorships," *Soccer & Society* 19, no. 4 (2016): 498–515.

15. Motez Bishara, "European Soccer Feels Force of PSG and Qatar's 'Soft Power,'" *CNN*, August 29, 2017, https://edition.cnn.com/2017/09/01/football/soft-power-and-football-mega-transfers-psg-neymar-mbappe-qatar/index.html. For more on Gulf state investment in European football, see: Salma Thani and Tom Heenan, "The Ball may Be Round but Football Is Becoming Increasingly Arabic: Oil Money and the Rise of the New Football Order," *Soccer & Society* (2016): 1012–26.

16. Andrew England and Murad Ahmed, "Why the Gulf States Are Betting on Sport," *Financial Times*, November 26, 2019, www.ft.com/content/15bc48b6–0c8c-11ea-b2d6–9bf4d1957a67. For other examples of the 2022 World Cup examined through the lens of soft power, see: Paul Michael Brannagan and Richard Giulianotti, "Soft Power and Soft Disempowerment: Qatar, Global Sport and Football's 2022 World Cup Finals," *Leisure Studies* 34, no. 6 (2014): 703–19. See also: Jonathan Grix and Donna Lee, "Soft Power, Sports Mega-Events and Emerging States: The Lure of the Politics of Attraction," *Global Society* 27, no. 4 (2013): 521–36.

17. Alexander Dukalskis and Johannes Gerschewski, "What Autocracies Say (and What Citizens Hear): Proposing Four Mechanisms of Autocratic Legitimation," *Contemporary Politics* 23, no. 3 (2017): 253.

18. Ibid., 259.

19. Lisa Wedeen, *Ambiguities of Domination: Politics, Rhetoric, and Symbols in Contemporary Syria* (Chicago, IL: University of Chicago Press, 1999), 6, quoted in Dukalskis and Gerschewski, "What Autocracies Say (and What Citizens Hear)," 259.

20. Dukalskis and Gerschewski, "What Autocracies Say," 259.

21. David Beetham, "The Contradictions of Democratization by Force: The Case of Iraq," *Democratization* 16, no. 3 (2009): 448. For more on the question of democratic legitimacy and the invasion of Iraq, see: Steven Wheatley, "The Security Council, Democratic Legitimacy, and Regime Change in Iraq," *European Journal of International Law* 17, no. 3 (2006): 531–51. See also: Richard B. Miller, "Justifications of the Iraq War Examined," *Ethics & International Affairs* 22, no. 1 (2008): 43–67; Rick Fawn and Raymond Hinnebusch, eds., *The Iraq War: Causes and Consequences* (Boulder, CO: Lynne Reiner, 2006).

22. "Securitization" here refers to the identification or construction of a perceived threat that is then referred to for urgent policy action that often exceeds standard security policy and methods. See: Holger Stritzel, "Toward a Theory of Securitization: Copenhagen and Beyond," *European Journal of International Relations* 13, no. 3 (2007): 357–83. The discussion of securitization in this example is informed by the field of Critical Security Studies, and in particular the recent calls by regional specialists to shift the focal points of the field in its exploration of the Middle East and North Africa regions. See: Columba Peoples and Nick Vaughan-Williams, eds., *Critical Security Studies: An Introduction* (New York, NY: Routledge, 2015). See also: Samer Abboud et al., "Towards a Beirut School of Critical Security Studies," *Critical Studies on Security* 6, no. 3 (2018): 273–95.

23. Michał Marcin Kobierecki and Piotr Strożek, "Sports Mega-Events and Shaping the International Image of States: How Hosting the Olympic Games and FIFA World Cups Affects Interest in Host Nations," *International Politics* (2020): 4.

24. Qatar Olympic Committee, *Sports Sector Strategy 2011–2016* (Qatar: Qatar Olympic Committee, 2011), www.yumpu.com/en/document/read/9498710/qatars-sports-sector-strategy-aspire, quoted in Danyel Reiche, "Investing in Sporting Success as a Domestic and Foreign Policy Tool: The Case of Qatar," *International Journal of Sport Policy and Politics* 7, no. 4 (2014): 498.

25. Reiche, "Investing in Sporting Success," 10–11.

26. Kobierecki and Piotr Strożek, "Sports Mega-Events," 3.

27. Natalie Koch, "Sport and Soft Authoritarian Nation-Building," *Political Geography* 32 (2013): 42–51.

28. Eva Bellin, "The Robustness of Authoritarianism in the Middle East," *Comparative Politics* 36, no. 2 (2004): 139–57.

29. For more on the subject of sectarianization in Iraq, see Bassel F. Salloukh, "The Sectarianization of Geopolitics in the Middle East," in *Sectarianization: Mapping the New Politics of the Middle East*, eds. Nader Hashemi and Danny Postel (New York, NY: Oxford University Press, 2017), 35–52; Fanar Haddad, "Sectarian Relations before 'Sectarianization' in Pre-2003 Iraq," in *Sectarianization: Mapping the New Politics of the Middle East*, eds. Nader Hashemi and Danny Postel (New York, NY: Oxford University Press, 2017), 101–22.

30. David E. Sanger, "President Says Military Phase in Iraq Has Ended," *New York Times*, May 2, 2003.

31. Tracy Wilkinson, "Iraq Olympians Say Bush is Not on Their Team," *Los Angeles Times*,

August 24, 2004, www.latimes.com/archives/la-xpm-2004-aug-24-fg-iraqiteam24-story.html.

32. George Vecsey, "Sports of The Times; Game is Half the Battle for the Iraqi Team," *The New York Times*, August 25, 2004, www.nytimes.com/2004/08/25/sports/sports-of-the-times-game-is-half-the-battle-for-the-iraqi-team.html.

33. Sally Jenkins, "In Iraq, No Gold Medals for Trying," *Washington Post*, August 25, 2004, www.washingtonpost.com/archive/sports/2004/08/25/in-iraq-no-gold-medals-for-trying/217d65fe-78e0-4d5a-b1de-c0738aff313b.

34. Shane Clapper, *Shooting Straight: How the American Led Coalition is Winning the War in Iraq* (Oklahoma, OK: Tate Publishers, 2007), 139.

35. Jeffrey Donovan, "Iraq: Olympic Soccer Team Inspires Nation, Rebuffs Bush," *Radio Free Europe*, August 24, 2004, www.rferl.org/a/1054468.html.

36. Ibid. See also: Donovan, "Iraq: Olympic Soccer Team Inspires Nation."

37. Wilkinson, "Iraq Olympians Say Bush is not on Their Team."

38. Ibid.

39. For examples of Bush's position on nation-building, see: *The New York Times*, "The 2000 Campaign; 2nd Presidential Debate Between Gov. Bush and Vice President Gore," October 12, 2000, www.nytimes.com/2000/10/12/us/2000-campaign-2nd-presidential-debate-between-gov-bush-vice-president-gore.html.

40. Raymond Hinnebusch, "Authoritarian Persistence, Democratization Theory and the Middle East: An Overview and Critique," *Democratization* 13, no. 3 (2006): 374.

41. Clapper, *Shooting Straight*, 135.

42. Stefan Talmon, *The Occupation of Iraq, Volume 2: The Official Documents of the Coalition Provisional Authority and the Iraqi Governing Council* (Oxford: Hart Publishing, 2013), 1468 and 1103.

43. Jenkins, "In Iraq, No Gold Medals for Trying."

44. Dave Zirin, "Iraq Soccer Team Give Bush the Boot," *CounterPunch*, August 21, 2004, www.counterpunch.org/2004/08/21/iraq-soccer-team-give-bush-the-boot.

45. Ibid.

46. Ibid.

47. *BBC News*, "Egypt's President Mubarak Enters Algeria Football Row," November 21, 2009, http://news.bbc.co.uk/2/hi/8372202.stm.

48. Jack Shenker, "Mubarak Adds Fuel to Fire as Football Riots Spread," *The Guardian*, November 21, 2009, www.theguardian.com/world/2009/nov/22/mubarak-adds-fuel-to-fire.

49. Ursula Lindsey, "The Soccer Wars," *Foreign Policy*, December 3, 2009, https://foreignpolicy.com/2009/12/03/the-soccer-wars.

50. James Montague, "Egypt Against Algeria Revives Some Bitter Memories," *World Soccer*, November 17, 2009, https://web.archive.org/web/20091117201441/http://www.worldsoccer.com/features/egypt_against_algeria_revives_some_bitter_memories_part_one_by_james_montague_features_290898.html.

51. Lindsey, "The Soccer Wars."

52. Mohamed El Dahshan, "Egypt's Football Party Gets Out of Hand," *The Guardian*,

November 16, 2009, www.theguardian.com/commentisfree/2009/nov/16/egypt-algeria-football-qualifier.

53. Sarah A. Topol, "Egypt-Algeria World Cup Violence Used to Rally Support for Mubarak Regime," *The Christian Science Monitor*, November 25, 2009, www.csmonitor.com/World/Middle-East/2009/1125/p06s20-wome.html; Lindsey, "The Soccer Wars."

54. Ibid.

55. Lindsey, "The Soccer Wars."

56. Heba Helmy, "Writers Decry Egypt-Algeria 'Football War,'" *Egypt Independent*, November 24, 2009, https://egyptindependent.com/writers-decry-egypt-algeria-football-war; Joseph Mayton, "Feeble Excuses for Egypt's Football Riots," *The Guardian*, November 24, 2009, www.theguardian.com/commentisfree/2009/nov/24/egypt-cairo-football-riots.

57. Topol, "Egypt-Algeria World Cup Violence."

58. Michael Slackman, "This Time, Egyptian Riot Over Soccer, Not Bread," *The New York Times*, November 20, 2009, www.nytimes.com/2009/11/21/world/africa/21egypt.html.

59. Ibid.

60. Topol, "Egypt-Algeria World Cup Violence."

61. *BBC News*, "Mubarak Enters Algeria Football Row."

62. El Dahshan, "Egypt's Football Party."

63. Michael Slackman, "A Nation's Shaken Ego Seen in a Soccer Loss," *The New York Times*, December 9, 2009, www.nytimes.com/2009/12/10/world/middleeast/10egypt.html?ref=todayspaper.

64. Christian von Haldenwang, "The Relevance of Legitimation—A New Framework for Analysis," *Contemporary Politics* 23, no. 3 (2017): 274.

65. Lindsey, "The Soccer Wars."

66. Slackman, "A Nation's Shaken Ego."

67. Patrick Kingsley, "Egypt Massacre Was Premeditated, Says Human Rights Watch," *The Guardian*, August 12, 2014.

68. "How Sisi's Egypt Hands Out Justice," *Reuters*, July 31, 2019.

69. Alessandro Accorsi and Max Spiegelbaum, "Banning Fandom: Football and Revolution in Egypt," *Middle East Eye*, June 12, 2015.

70. Brian Rohan, "Egypt Puts Soccer Stat Aboutrika on No-fly, Terror List," *Associated Press (AP)*, January 18, 2017, https://apnews.com/7ae41d1ee8024c248cacbe851bd64487/Egypt-puts-soccer-star-Aboutrika-on-no-fly,-terror-list.

71. Karim Zidan, "How Egypt's Strongman Is Turning Sports into Propaganda," *Deadspin*, March 6, 2018, https://deadspin.com/how-egypts-strongman-is-turning-sports-into-propaganda-1823075979.

72. Zidan, "Egypt's Strongman."

73. *KingFut*, "Legal Letters Explain Dispute Between Mohamed Salah and Egyptian FA," April 25, 2018, www.kingfut.com/2018/04/25/mohamed-salah-egyptian-fa-exclusive.

74. Abdullah Al-Arian, "Why the Muslim Brotherhood Was Blamed for Egypt's World

Cup Woes," *Al Jazeera*, July 20, 2018, www.aljazeera.com/indepth/opinion/sisi-salah-egypt-failed-world-cup-180719080842364.html.

75. *Masr al-Yawm*, "Masadir takshif asbab insihab Salah wa rafdh al-la'b amam al-Sa'udiya" [Sources reveal reasons for Salah's withdrawal and refusal to play against Saudi Arabia], June 20, 2018, https://bit.ly/MasrAlYawmSalah.

76. Andrew Roth, "Mohamed Salah 'Honoured' with Gift of Citizenship from Chechen Leader," *The Guardian*, June 23, 2018, www.theguardian.com/football/2018/jun/23/mo-salah-egypt-liverpool-ramzan-kadyrov-chechnya-russia-world-cup.

77. Jack Austin, "Mohamed Salah Considering Egypt Future Over Political Controversy with Chechnya Leader," *Independent*, June 24, 2018, www.independent.co.uk/sport/football/world-cup/mohamed-salah-egypt-quit-retire-liverpool-fc-chechnya-leader-photo-video-watch-a8414626.html.

78. Ruth Michaelson, "Mohamed Salah Blames Egypt's FA for World Cup Disruptions," *The Guardian*, August 28, 2018, www.theguardian.com/football/2018/aug/28/mohamed-salah-egypt-fa-hampering-world-cup-russia.

79. Robert Springborg, "Egypt's World Cup: A Spectacular Own Goal for Sisi's Regime," *The New Arab*, July 3, 2018, https://english.alaraby.co.uk/english/comment/2018/7/3/egypts-world-cup-an-own-goal-for-sisi-regime.

80. *The New Arab*, "Egypt FA Blames Muslim Brotherhood for Poor World Cup Performance, Mo Salah Crisis," July 6, 2018, https://english.alaraby.co.uk/english/news/2018/7/5/egypt-blames-muslim-brotherhood-for-poor-world-cup-performance.

81. *The New Arab*, "Egypt's Election Produces Surprise Runner-up: Mohamed Salah," April 3, 2018, https://english.alaraby.co.uk/english/news/2018/4/3/egypts-election-produces-surprise-runner-up-mohamed-salah.

82. David Conn, "Qatar Cash Is Stirring French Football Revolution at Paris St-Germain," *The Guardian*, November 22, 2011.

83. "Barca to Have Qatar Airways as Shirt Sponsor Next Season," *Reuters*, November 16, 2012. Prior to that, during the 2011–12 season, Barcelona's shirt featured the Qatar Foundation as its sponsor.

84. Steven Price, "Report Says Qatar World Cup is 'Risky' But Firms Already Know That," *Forbes*, October 7, 2017, www.forbes.com/sites/steveprice/2017/10/07/report-says-qatar-world-cup-is-risky-but-firms-already-know-that/#684d06807e8f.

85. Patrick Wintour, "Donald Trump Tweets Support for Blockade Imposed on Qatar," *The Guardian*, June 6, 2017, www.theguardian.com/world/2017/jun/06/qatar-panic-buying-as-shoppers-stockpile-food-due-to-saudi-blockade.

86. Simeon Kerr, "Qatar Attempts to Build its Way Out of a Blockade," *Financial Times*, May 16, 2018, www.ft.com/content/a39cd232-5517-11e8-b24e-cad6aa67e23e.

87. Tim Adams, "From Qatar's Blockade, a Bold, Unexpected New Vision Is Emerging," *The Guardian*, May 6, 2018, www.theguardian.com/world/2018/may/06/qatar-blockade-unexpected-new-vision-isolation.

88. Simon Chadwick, "Qatar, PSG and the Real Reason Neymar Could Sell for a Record £198m," *The Conversation*, August 1, 2017, https://theconversation.com/qatar-psg-and-the-real-reason-neymar-could-sell-for-a-record-198m-81859.

89. *Associated Press (AP)*, "The Latest: France Spokesman Links Neymar Deal to Qatar," August 4, 2017, https://apnews.com/27d58ddd4c854ec7b6ac2902360c2b64/The-Latest:-France-spokesman-links-Neymar-deal-to-Qatar.

90. See, for example: Slama, "Qatar Hits Back."

91. Bishara, "European Soccer."

92. See: Paul MacInnes, "How Can PSG Pay £200m for Neymar? What Happened to Financial Fair Play?," *The Guardian*, August 2, 2017, www.theguardian.com/football/2017/aug/02/psg-200m-neymar-barcelona-financial-fair-play. See also: Tariq Panja, "Qatar Faces a Tight Squeeze for Its Compact World Cup," *The New York Times*, November 14, 2019, www.nytimes.com/2019/11/14/sports/qatar-world-cup-visitors.html. See also: Tariq Panja, "Soccer's New Rich Leave the Old Guard Looking Beleaguered," *The New York Times*, September 2, 2021, www.nytimes.com/2021/09/02/sports/soccer/soccer-transfer-market-lionel-messi.html.

93. David D. Kirkpatrick, "The Most Powerful Arab Ruler Isn't M.B.S. It's M.B.Z.," *The New York Times*, June 2, 2019, www.nytimes.com/2019/06/02/world/middleeast/crown-prince-mohammed-bin-zayed.html.

94. David D. Kirkpatrick, "Recordings Suggest Emirates and Egyptian Military Pushed Ousting of Morsi," *The New York Times*, March 1, 2015, www.nytimes.com/2015/03/02/world/middleeast/recordings-suggest-emirates-and-egyptian-military-pushed-ousting-of-morsi.html.

95. Jason Burke and Patrick Wintour, "Suspected Military Supplies Pour into Libya as UN Flounders," *The Guardian*, March 11, 2020, www.theguardian.com/world/2020/mar/11/suspected-military-supplies-libya-un-cargo; Samuel Ramani, "Saudi Arabia and the UAE Reboot Their Partnership in Yemen," *Carnegie Endowment for International Peace*, September 26, 2019, https://carnegieendowment.org/sada/79925.

96. Jonathan Fenton-Harvey, "Can Tunisia Survive Foreign Attempts to Derail its Democracy?," *The New Arab*, October 4, 2019, https://english.alaraby.co.uk/english/comment/2019/10/4/can-tunisia-survive-attempts-to-derail-its-democracy. See also: Richard Spencer, "UAE Was Behind Tunisian Power Grab, Claims Speaker," *The Times*, July 31, 2021, www.thetimes.co.uk/article/uae-was-behind-tunisian-power-grab-claims-speaker-cf2xzbbjp

97. Robert F. Worth, "Mohammed bin Zayed's Dark Vision of the Middle East's Future," *The New York Times*, January 9, 2020, www.nytimes.com/2020/01/09/magazine/united-arab-emirates-mohammed-bin-zayed.html.

98. Randeep Ramesh, "UAE Told UK: Crack Down on Muslim Brotherhood or Lose Arms Deals," *The Guardian*, November 6, 2015, www.theguardian.com/world/2015/nov/06/uae-told-uk-crack-down-on-muslim-brotherhood-or-lose-arms-deals.

99. Worth, "Mohammed bin Zayed's Dark Vision."

100. Ramesh, "Crack Down on Muslim Brotherhood."

101. Ibid.

102. Peter Oborne and David Hearst, "UK Intelligence Had Warned Against 'Fruitless'

Probe of Muslim Brotherhood," *Middle East Eye*, December 17, 2015, www.middleeasteye.net/fr/news/uk-intelligence-had-warned-against-fruitless-probe-muslim-brotherhood-1121433450.

103. Kristian Coates Ulrichsen, *The United Arab Emirates: Power, Politics and Policy-Making* (New York, NY: Routledge, 2017), 168.

104. Ibid.

105. David Conn, "Abu Dhabi Accused of 'Using Manchester City to Launder Image,'" *The Guardian*, July 30, 2013, www.theguardian.com/football/2013/jul/30/manchester-city-human-rights-accusations.

106. Rori Donaghy, "UAE Paid PR Firm Millions to Brief UK Journalists on Qatar, Brotherhood Attacks," *Middle East Eye*, January 19, 2016, www.middleeasteye.net/news/uae-paid-pr-firm-millions-brief-uk-journalists-qatar-brotherhood-attacks.

107. James Montague and Tariq Panja, "Ahead of Qatar World Cup, a Gulf Feud Plays Out in the Shadows," *The New York Times*, February 1, 2019, www.nytimes.com/2019/02/01/sports/world-cup-2022-qatar.html.

108. James Montague, "Political Football: How Warring Gulf States are Playing out Their Rivalries on the Pitch," *Delayed Gratification*, August 3, 2017, www.slow-journalism.com/from-the-archive/political-football-how-warring-gulf-states-are-playing-out-their-rivalries-on-the-pitch.

109. Ibid.

110. Will Hersey, "Remembering Argentina 1978: The Dirtiest World Cup of All Time," *Esquire*, June 14, 2018, www.esquire.com/uk/culture/a21454856/argentina-1978-world-cup.

111. James Montague, "Saudi Stars Arrive in Spain, With One Eye on Russia," *The New York Times*, February 8, 2018, www.nytimes.com/2018/02/08/sports/soccer/saudi-soccer-la-liga.html.

112. Ivana Kottasova and Chandler Thornton, "Saudi Arabia Launches a Soccer League for Women," *CNN*, February 27, 2020, https://edition.cnn.com/2020/02/25/football/saudi-arabia-football-league-women-rights-intl/index.html.

113. Tariq Panja, "Adviser to Manchester City Owner Has Role in Newcastle Sale," *The New York Times*, June 15, 2020, www.nytimes.com/2020/06/15/sports/soccer/newcastle-premier-league.html.

114. Liam Killingstad, "A Closer Look at Newcastle's $409 Million Sale to Saudi Arabia's Wealth Fund," *Front Office Sports*, October 24, 2021, https://frontofficesports.com/a-closer-look-at-newcastles-409m-sale-to-saudi-arabias-wealth-fund/.

115. David D. Kirkpatrick, "Yemen Has Been a Saudi Prince's War. Now it's His Quagmire," *The New York Times*, July 18, 2019, www.nytimes.com/2019/07/18/world/middleeast/saudi-prince-yemen-emirates.html.

116. Ben Hubbard et al., "Saudis Said to Use Coercion and Abuse to Seize Billions," *The New York Times*, March 11, 2018, www.nytimes.com/2018/03/11/world/middleeast/saudi-arabia-corruption-mohammed-bin-salman.html.

117. *RT*, "Inside the Vast Web of PR Firms Popularizing the Saudi Crown Prince," March 31, 2018, www.rt.com/news/422858-saudi-pr-firms-yemen-terrorism.

118. Jeanne Whalen and Justin Wm. Moyer, "Western Walkout of Saudi 'Davos in the Desert' Conference over Jamal Khashoggi Undermines Kingdom's Modernization Plans," *The Washington Post*, October 12, 2018, www.washingtonpost.com/business/2018/10/12/western-walkout-saudi-davos-desert-conference-over-jamal-khashoggi-undermines-kingdoms-modernization-plans.

119. Rory Smith, "Saudi Arabia, Newcastle, and Soccer's Worship of Money," *The New York Times*, October 8, 2021, www.nytimes.com/2021/10/08/sports/soccer/newcastle-saudi-arabia-premier-league.html.

120. Dermot Corrigan, "Why Spanish Football Federation's Lucrative Revamp of Supercopa is Proving More Hassle Than It's Worth," *Independent*, October 14, 2019, www.independent.co.uk/sport/football/european/real-madrid-barcelona-atletico-valencia-spanish-super-cup-rubiales-rfef-a9155086.html.

121. Tariq Panja, "La Liga Chief Claims Saudi Arabia Is Using Sports to 'Whitewash' Reputation," *The New York Times*, January 20, 2020, www.nytimes.com/2020/01/20/sports/soccer/spain-soccer-saudi-arabia.html.

122. Corrigan, "Spanish Football Federation's Lucrative Revamp."

123. Sean Ingle, "Saudi TV Piracy Ruling Puts Newcastle Takeover Under Renewed Scrutiny," *The Guardian*, June 16, 2020, www.theguardian.com/football/2020/jun/16/newcastle-takeover-latest-saudi-arabia-tv-piracy-ruling-released-by-wto-premier-league-pressure.

124. Nicholas Brookes and Peter Osborne, "Football: Second Religion of the Middle East," *Middle East Eye*, July 18, 2018, www.middleeasteye.net/big-story/football-second-religion-middle-east.

3. A STUDY OF FOOTBALL CHANTS AS POLITICAL EXPRESSION IN THE ALGERIAN HIRAK

1. Mourad Hachid, "Six ans après l'assassinat de Guermah Massinissa" [Six years after the assassination of Guermah Massinissa], *El Watan*, April 19, 2007, www.elwatan.com/archives/actualites/six-ans-apres-lassassinat-de-guermah-massinissa-19-04-2007.

2. Nabia Lahchi, "En un an, la révolte algérienne du Hirak est passée de l'espoir à la désillusion" [In one year, the Algerian Hirak revolt has turned from hope to disillusion], *Le Figaro*, February 19, 2020, www.lefigaro.fr/international/en-un-an-la-revolte-algerienne-du-hirak-est-passee-de-l-espoir-a-la-desillusion-20200219.

3. Mouh Milano, "Y'en a marre | Official Audio," YouTube, October 23, 2018, www.youtube.com/watch?v=EA-pVOEVzoI.

4. *Le Matin d'Algérie*, "Encore une histoire de cadre de Bouteflika!!!" [Another Bouteflika portrait story!!!], June 12, 2018, www.lematindalgerie.com/encore-une-histoire-de-cadre-de-bouteflika.

5. Hocine Lamriben, "Meeting du FLN à la Coupole pour le 5e mandat: Le show de l'absent" [FLN meeting at the La Couple for the 5th mandate: The absent's show], *El Watan*, February 10, 2019, www.elwatan.com/a-la-une/meeting-du-fln-a-la-coupole-pour-le-5e-mandat-le-show-de-labsent-10-02-2019.

6. Mahfoud Amara, "Football Sub-Culture and Youth Politics in Algeria," *Mediterranean Politics* 17, no. 1 (2012): 41–58. Mahfoud Amara, "Soccer, Post-Colonial and Post-conflict Discourses in Algeria: Algérie-France, 6 Octobre 2001," *International Review of Modern Sociology*, 32, No. 2 (Autumn) 2006: 217–38.

7. Youcef Fates, "Les mots du stade: Modalité inédite d'expression politique de la jeunesse algérienne?" [Words from the stadium: An unprecedented form of political expression of Algerian youth?], in *Les espaces publics au Maghreb* [Public spaces in the Maghreb], eds. Hassan Remaoun and Abdelhamid Henia (Oran: CRASC, 2013), 199–221.

8. *ElDjazair365*, "Le 7 août 1921, le Mouloudia Club d'Alger voit le jour" [August 7, 1921, Algiers' Mouloudia Club is created], August 7, 2016, https://eldjazair365.com/fr/le-7-aout-1921-le-mouloudia-club-dalger-voit-le-jour.

9. *Sebbar.kazeo*, "Abderrahmane Aouf: 'Le père spirituel du Mouloudia'" [Abderrahmane Aouf: "The spiritual father of Mouloudia"], December 22, 2006, http://sebbar.kazeo.com/aouf-abderrahmane-a120165444.

10. Lucas Alves Murillo, "Le Mouloudia, un monument algérien" [Mouloudia, an Algerian monument], *Mediapart*, February 2, 2019, https://blogs.mediapart.fr/edition/folk-football/article/300119/le-mouloudia-un-monument-algerien.

11. Lucas Alves Murillo, "Le football de la liberté en Algérie" [Freedom football in Algeria], *LeCorner*, July 23, 2019, www.lecorner.org/le-football-de-la-liberte-en-algerie.

12. Ahmed Rouaba, "L'incroyable histoire des 'dribbleurs de l'indépendance' de l'Algérie" [The incredible story of Algeria's "independence dribblers"], *BBC Afrique*, May 8, 2019, www.bbc.com/afrique/sports-44039897.

13. Nadia Kerraz, "La légendaire équipe de football du FLN: Une fabuleuse épopée" [FLN's legendary football team: A fabulous epic], *El Moudjahid*, October 31, 2011, www.elmoudjahid.com/fr/mobile/detail-article/id/19048.

14. The Kabyle people are a Berber people indigenous to northern Algeria. Approximately 10 percent of the Algerian population (3–4 million) lives in the Kabyle region of Algeria, just east of Algiers.

15. *El Watan*, "Boumediène et la décolonisation linguistique" [Boumediène and the linguistic decolonization], December 27, 2008, www.elwatan.com/archives/numero-special/boumediene-et-la-decolonisation-linguistique-27-12-2008.

16. Ilyes A., "Iboud: 'La Finale de 1977 était une occasion pour les supporters de déclencher la revendication berbère'" [Iboud: "The 1977 final was an opportunity for supporters to trigger the Berber claim"], *Le Buteur*, April 27, 2014, www.lebuteur.com/interview/detail?id=62&titre=iboud-la-finale-de-1977-etait-une-occasion-pour-les-supporters-de-declencher-la-revendication-berbere.

17. The Berber Spring of 1980 refers to a series of protests asking for the recognition of Berber identity and language in the Kabyle region and in Algiers. It is considered the first protest movement in Algerian history post-independence.

18. Mahfoud Amara, "Football Sub-Culture and Youth Politics in Algeria," *Mediterranean Politics* 17, no. 1 (2012): 41–58.

19. Adlène Meddi, "Algérie: 30 ans après, les leçons (non apprises) du 5 octobre 1988" [Algeria: 30 years later, the (not learned) lessons of October 5, 1988], *Middle East Eye*, October 5, 2018, www.middleeasteye.net/fr/opinion-fr/algerie-30-ans-apres-les-lecons-non-apprises-du-5-octobre-1988.

20. Fates, "Les mots du stade."

21. Ibid.

22. Peter Speetjens, "Remembering Algeria 1992: The First Arab Spring that Never Became a Summer," *Middle East Eye*, January 14, 2017, www.middleeasteye.net/opinion/remembering-algeria-1992-first-arab-spring-never-became-summer.

23. Amara, "Football Sub-Culture and Youth Politics," 41–58.

24. Peter Kenyon, "Chaabi: The 'People's Music' of North Africa," *NPR*, August 11, 2008, www.npr.org/templates/story/story.php?storyId=93502483.

25. Abdelkrim Tazaroute, "El hadj M'hamed El Anka, l'éternelle référence" [El hadj M'hamed El Anka, the eternal reference], *El Moudjahid*, November 24, 2010, www.elmoudjahid.com/fr/actualites/5788.

26. Ibid.

27. Youcef Fates, "Du café maure au 'café des sports'" [From Moorish cafes to "sports cafes"], in *Générations engagées et mouvements nationaux: Le Xxème siècle au Maghreb* [Engaged generations and national movements: The 20th century in the Maghreb], eds. Ouanassa Siari-Tengour and Aissa Kadri (Oran: CRASC, 2012), 269–86.

28. Ibid.

29. *El Watan*, "Pause-Café. Les Lieux d'El Anka" [Coffee break. Places of El Anka], May 17, 2007, www.elwatan.com/archives/arts-et-lettres-archives/pause-cafe-les-lieux-d-el-anka-17-05-2007.

30. Chris Silver, "Saoud l'Oranais—Gheniet U.S.M.O.—Polyphon, 1934," *Gharamophone Blog* April 10, 2019, https://gharamophone.com/2019/04/10/saoud-loranais-gheniet-u-s-m-o-polyphon-1934.

31. Safinez Bousbia, *El Gusto* (Quidam Productions, 2011).

32. Ah. A. "USM Alger: Les Rouge et Noir rendent hommage à Amar Ezzahi" [USM Alger: The Red and Blacks pay homage to Amar Ezzahi], *Le Soir d'Algérie*, December 11, 2016, https://lesoirdalgerie.com/articles/2016/12/11/article.php?sid=206044&cid=5.

33. Mickaël Correia, "The Soccer Fans That Toppled a Government," *The Nation*, May 15, 2019, www.thenation.com/article/archive/algeria-bouteflika-fans-protests.

34. Ibid.

35. Meziane Abane, "Je n'ai connu que Bouteflika comme président. Je veux que ça change" [I only knew Bouteflika as president. I want that to change], *El Watan*, March 1, 2019, www.elwatan.com/edition/actualite/je-nai-connu-que-bouteflika-comme-president-je-veux-que-ca-change-01-03-2019.

36. Mark Doidge, "The *Ultras*," in *Football Italia: Italian Football in an Age of Globalization* (London: Bloomsbury Academic, 2015), 142.

37. Correia, "The Soccer Fans That Toppled a Government."

38. Ibid.

39. Aida Alami, "The Soccer Politics of Morocco," *The New York Review of Books*, December 20, 2018, www.nybooks.com/daily/2018/12/20/the-soccer-politics-of-morocco.

40. Gruppo Aquile, "Fbladi Dalmoni," YouTube, October 11, 2018, www.youtube.com/watch?v=7ivFYHMIJr4.

41. *Mosaique FM*, "Une nouvelle chanson du Club africain: Out of foot (Vidéos)" [A new song from Club Africain: Out of foot (videos)], December 24, 2019, www.mosaiquefm.net/fr/actualites-sport-tunisie/660218/une-nouvelle-chanson-du-club-africain-out-of-foot.

42. Dag Tuastad, "From Football Riot to Revolution: The Political Role of Football in the Arab World," *Soccer & Society* 15 no. 3 (2014): 376–88.

43. James M. Dorsey, "Egypt's Banning of Ultras Constitutes Effort to Outlaw Legitimate Opposition," *Huff Post*, September 6, 2014, www.huffpost.com/entry/egypts-banning-of-ultras_b_5776282.

44. Ibid.

45. Omar Kabbadj, "À Tétouan, les ultras du MAT en porte-voix de la colère après la mort de Hayat Belkacem" [In Tétouan, the MAT ultras speaking out in anger after the death of Hayat Belkacem], *Telquel*, September 29, 2018, https://telquel.ma/2018/09/29/a-tetouan-les-ultras-du-mat-en-porte-voix-de-la-colere-apres-la-mort-de-hayat-belkacem_1612366.

46. Ibid.

47. El Mehdi Berrada and Hicham Oulmouddane, "Les Ultras, totems et baston" [The ultras, totems and fighting], *Le Desk*, March 27, 2016, https://ledesk.ma/grandangle/les-ultras-totems-et-baston.

48. *Le Parisien*, "Bouteflika, le fantôme d'Alger" [Bouteflika, the ghost of Algiers], February 22, 2014, www.leparisien.fr/international/bouteflika-le-fantome-d-alger-22–02–2014-3615061.php.

49. Dey Boys, "'Nostra Eredita' #bladna mel bekri mekhdou3a," YouTube, March 7, 2016, www.youtube.com/watch?v=5dZLmUTwxHg.

50. Correia, "The Soccer Fans That Toppled a Government."

51. Kheireddine Batache, "Dix ans de prison requis contre 'El Bouchi,' deux ans contre Tebboune Khaled" [Ten years in prison required against 'El Bouchi,' two years against Tebboune Khaled], *Maghreb Emergent*, February 26, 2020, https://maghrebemergent.info/dix-ans-de-prison-requis-contre-el-bouchi-deux-ans-contre-tebboune-khaled.

52. Mouh Milano, "Y'en a marre | Official Audio."

53. Caroline Delabroy, "Bouteflika Wins Option to Run for Third Mandate," *France 24*, November 12, 2008, www.france24.com/en/20081112-bouteflika-wins-option-run-third-mandate-algeria.

54. *Le Parisien*, "Bouteflika, le fantôme d'Alger" [Bouteflika, the ghost of Algiers], February 22, 2014, www.leparisien.fr/international/bouteflika-le-fantome-d-alger-22–02–2014-3615061.php.

55. *Le Monde Afrique*, "Algérie: manifestation à Kherrata, berceau du Hirak, un an après

la première marche" [Algeria: Demonstrations at Kherrata, cradle of the Hirka, one year after the first march], February 17, 2020, www.lemonde.fr/afrique/article/2020/02/17/algerie-manifestation-a-kherrata-berceau-du-hirak-un-an-apres-la-premiere-marche_6029820_3212.html.

56. Islam Amine Derradji and Amel Gherbi, "Le *Hirak* algérien: un laboratoire de citoyenneté" [The Algerian *Hirak*: A citizenship laboratory], *Métropolitiques*, July 12, 2019, www.metropolitiques.eu/IMG/pdf/pdfmet-derradji-gherbi.pdf.

57. Citoyen Algérien, Twitter, June 8, 2019, https://twitter.com/CitAlgr/status/1137148135845879808?s=20.

58. Correia, "The Soccer Fans That Toppled a Government."

59. Ouled El Bahdja, "La Casa Del Mouradia," YouTube, April 14, 2018, www.youtube.com/watch?v=kHZviPhZQxs, translation by author.

60. Charlotte Bozonnet, "En Algérie, Bouteflika a ramené la paix, pas la réconciliation" [In Algeria, Bouteflika brought peace, but not reconciliation], *Le Monde*, April 3, 2019, www.lemonde.fr/international/article/2019/04/03/en-algerie-bouteflika-a-ramene-la-paix-pas-la-reconciliation_5445290_3210.html.

61. Correia, "The Soccer Fans That Toppled a Government."

62. Groupe Diamant Noir and Amarilo Negro, "Chkoun Sbabna [Doula] Usmh," YouTube, June 30, 2018, www.youtube.com/watch?v=jLHo9qtDYq8, translation by author.

63. Marie Poussel, "'Liberté' de Soolking devient l'hymne de la jeunesse algérienne" ['Liberty' by Soolking becomes the anthem of Algerian youth], *Le Parisien*, March 21, 2019, www.leparisien.fr/international/liberte-de-soolking-devient-l-hymne-de-la-jeunesse-algerienne-21–03–2019–8036535.php.

64. Ouled El Bahdja, "Ultima Verba," YouTube, February 17, 2019, www.youtube.com/watch?v=l_oFC5isVR8, translation by author.

65. *France 24*, "Algeria Jails Bouteflika-Era Tycoon Ali Haddad," June 17, 2019, www.france24.com/en/20190617-algeria-jails-bouteflika-era-tycoon-ali-haddad.

66. *Algérie Presse Service*, "La Cour suprême ordonne le réexamen de l'affaire de l'autoroute Est-Ouest" [Supreme Court orders a reconsideration of the East-West highway case], June 19, 2019, www.aps.dz/algerie/90860-la-cour-supreme-ordonne-le-reexamen-de-l-affaire-de-l-autoroute-est-ouest.

67. *France 24*, "Algeria Jails Bouteflika-Era Tycoon Ali Haddad."

68. Maher Mezahi, "In Algeria's Bordj Bou Arreridj, Political Art Takes Centre Stage," *Al Jazeera*, April 28, 2019, www.aljazeera.com/news/2019/04/algeria-bordj-bou-arreridj-political-art-takes-centre-stage-190428055122476.html.

69. Ibid.

70. Ibid.

71. Doidge, "The *Ultras*," 143.

72. *Le Matin D'Algérie*, "Qui osera juger le vénérable moudjahid Lakhdar Bouregaâ?" [Who will dare to judge the venerable moudjahid Lakhdar Bouregaâ?], July 10, 2019, www.lematindalgerie.com/qui-osera-juger-le-venerable-commandant-bouregaa.

73. Mustapha Benfodil, "45e vendredi du mouvement populaire: Le vibrant hommage

du hirak à Abane" [45th Friday of the popular movement: The Hirak's vibrant tribute to Abane], *El Watan* December 28, 2019, www.elwatan.com/a-la-une/45e-vendredi-du-mouvement-populaire-le-vibrant-hommage-du-hirak-a-abane-28-12-2019.

4. THE TRIVIALIZATION OF WOMEN'S FOOTBALL IN TURKEY

1. Lindsey Meân, "Identity and Discursive Practice: Doing Gender on the Football Pitch," *Discourse & Society* 12, no. 6 (2001): 789–815; Gertrud Pfister, "Assessing the Sociology of Sport: On Women and Football," *International Review for the Sociology of Sport* 50, nos. 4–5 (2015): 563–9; R. W. Connell, *Gender and Power* (Stanford: Stanford University Press, 1987).

2. *The Guardian*, "US Women's Team Sues US Soccer Over 'Institutionalized Gender Discrimination,'" March 8, 2019, www.theguardian.com/football/2019/mar/08/usa-womens-team-sues-us-soccer-pay-equality. Also see Rachel Allison, *Kicking Center: Gender and the Selling of Women's Professional Soccer* (New Brunswick: Rutgers University Press, 2018).

3. Pınar Öztürk and Canan Koca, "The Women in the Football: Analysis of a Women's Football Team as a Social Field," *Türkiye Klinikleri* 10, no. 3 (2018): 150–63; Jack Black and Beth Fielding-Lloyd, "Re-establishing the 'Outsiders': English Press Coverage of the 2015 FIFA Women's World Cup," *International Review for the Sociology of Sport* 54, no. 3 (2019): 282–301.

4. Jayne Caudwell, "Women's Football in the United Kingdom: Theorizing Gender and Unpacking the Butch Lesbian Image," *Journal of Sport and Social Issues* 23, no. 4 (1999): 390–402; Leda Maria da Costa, "Beauty, Effort and Talent: A Brief History of Brazilian Women's Soccer in Press Discourse," *Soccer & Society* 15, no. 1 (2014): 81–92; and Caitlin Fisher and Jane Dennehy, "Body Projects: Making, Remaking, and Inhabiting the Woman's Futebol Body in Brazil," *Sport in Society* 18, no. 8 (2015): 995–1008.

5. Barbara Cox and Richard Pringle, "Gaining a Foothold in Football: A Genealogical Analysis of the Emergence of the Female Footballer in New Zealand," *International Review for the Sociology of Sport* 47, no. 2 (2011): 217–34.

6. Jonny Hjelm, "The Bad Female Football Player: Women's Football in Sweden," *Soccer & Society* 12, no. 2 (2011): 143–58.

7. I was able to follow up with some of my interlocutors at the end of 2021 to better understand some of the changes in women's football around this time; I describe and interpret these changes throughout the chapter.

8. Much of my earlier work has focused on football fans. For this research, I deliberately sought to gain insight from other actors, mainly players.

9. Cem Tınaz, Emir Güney, Deniz Nihan Aktan, Elzem Seren Dinç, İlknur Hacısoftaoğlu, Sarp Samuray and Hazal Bayazıt helped me reach key contacts for this research at various points. I thank them for their help and guidance. Also, Kerem Tokel assisted with this research; I thank them for thinking through some of the issues here and particularly their observations at the game we attended together. I also thank Burkal Efe, the cofounder and co-chair of Fan Rights Association based in Izmir, for welcoming me

NOTES

there and helping me to get in touch with people at the Izmir team. Finally, I thank the participants of the working group at Georgetown University Qatar for their insightful feedback at various stages of research and writing.

10. Murat Toklucu, "Futbol Kadını Bozar Mı?" [Does football corrupt women?], *5 Harfliler*, April 4, 2016, www.5harfliler.com/futbol-kadini-bozar-mi. Also regarding astroturfs and football culture around them see Kadir Engil. "Men and Masculinities at Play: The Halı Saha Football in Istanbul," (MA thesis, Boğaziçi University, 2019).

11. *Cumhuriyet*, "Hanım Futbolcular Eşlerinden Veya Babalarından İzin Alacaklar" [Lady footballers will seek permission from their husbands or fathers], March 23, 1968, www.cumhuriyetarsivi.com/katalog/192/sayfa/1968/3/23/8.xhtml.

12. *Ataşehir ekspres*, "Kırmızı Beyazlıların Parolası: Şampiyonluk" [The red and whites aim for championship], October 20, 2016, http://edergi.atasehir.bel.tr/102016/mobile/index.html#p=22. See the following for the corresponding social context especially concerning women's movements and feminism in Turkey: Nükhet Sirman, "Feminism in Turkey: A Short History," *New Perspectives on Turkey* 3 (1989): 1–34.

13. Pınar Öztürk and Canan Koca, "Women, the 'Other' of Football Write Fotonovela, the 'Other' of Photography," *Moment Dergi* 2, no. 2 (2015): 157–183.

14. Toklucu, "Futbol Kadını Bozar Mı?"

15. Lale Orta, "Women and Football in Turkey," *International Journal of Humanities and Social Sciences* 4, no. 7 (2014): 85–93.

16. "Bayan" is a contested word in Turkish because it is used as a "more polite" alternative to "woman," associated with sexuality. See Pinar Arpinar-Avsar, Serkan Girgin, and Nefise Bulgu, "Lady or Woman? The Debate on Lexical Choice for Describing Females in Sport in the Turkish Language," *International Review for the Sociology of Sport* 51, no. 2 (2014): 178–200.

17. The women's game was eighty minutes long and had other rule differences from men's football until the 1995 FIFA Women's World Cup. The reasoning was that ninety minutes could have been too exhausting for women—mocked by some players at the time. See Barry Glendenning, "Women's World Cup: Game-Changing Moment No 3: China in 1991," *The Guardian*, June 18, 2019, www.theguardian.com/football/2019/jun/18/womens-world-cup-game-changing-moments-no-3-china-in-1991.

18. İlhan Özgen, "Bir Dinarsu Vardı, N'oldu?" [What happened to Dinarsu?], *Toprak Saha*, March 2014, http://topraksaha.net/03/2014/bir-dinarsu-vardi-noldu; Öztürk and Koca, "Women, the 'Other' of Football."

19. There are varying explanations for this suspension in the literature as well as in my interview notes. The issues and accounts surrounding the suspension are topic for another paper in and of themselves. See Alp Çolak, İlkay Barboros and Merve Yenidünya, "Türkiye'de Kadın Futbolunun Var Olma Mücadelesi," ["Women's Football Struggles to Exist in Turkey"], *Maçkolik*, June 8, 2019, www.mackolik.com/futbol/haber/oezel-dosya-1-boeluem-tuerkiyede-kadin-futbolunun-var-olma-muecadelesi/195rbco5cs3u81pgwky7hqnb32; Orta, "Women and Football in Turkey."

20. I received this figure from TFF; there are no formal or published statistics or data regarding these figures and no updates were available when I spoke to my interlocutors at the end of 2021.

21. My research is mainly focused on club football although I do include some references to the national team.

22. Turkey has an ongoing conflict-ridden relationship with the Kurdish minority. Some of this has transpired in the relations between sports teams from Kurdish regions and the authorities. For more on this, see Mesut Yeğen, "Turkish Nationalism and the Kurdish Question," *Ethnic and Racial Studies* 30, no. 1 (2007): 119–51. In specific relation to Amed as a sports club see: Dağhan Irak, "Kurdish Identity and Sports in Turkey: The Case of Amedspor," *Society Register* 2, no. 1 (2018): 59–76. "Amed" is the Kurdish name for what is officially "Diyarbakır;" for a news story on the name reversal demand see: *Birgün*, "Kayyum Amedspor'un İsminin Değiştirilmesini İstemiş" [Government-appointed official demands name change for Amed], February 19, 2017, www.birgun.net/haber/kayyum-amedspor-un-isminin-degistirilmesini-istemis-147450.

23. All interlocutor names are pseudonyms for privacy purposes.

24. Personal interview with footballer, Istanbul, December 2019. Interview was conducted in Turkish and translated by the author.

25. Personal interview with footballer, Istanbul, December 2019. Interview was conducted in Turkish and translated by the author.

26. For a discussion on women footballers' career paths in Sweden and how education figures into their plans and lives, see: Rebecca Andersson and Natalie Barker-Ruchti, "Career Paths of Swedish Top-Level Women Soccer Players," *Soccer & Society* 20, no. 6 (2019): 857–71.

27. Louise Stirling and John B. Schulz. "Women's Football: Still in the Hands of Men," *International Sport Management Journal* 7, no. 2 (2011): 53–78; Mustafa Şahin Karaçam and Canan Koca, "Men's Resistance to Gender Equality in Sports Governance," in *Gender Diversity in European Sport Governance*, eds. Agnes Elling, Jorid Hovden, and Annelies Knoppers (Oxon: Routledge, 2019).

28. Gertrud Pfister and Ilknur Hacısoftaoğlu, "Women's Sport as a Symbol of Modernity: A Case Study in Turkey," *The International Journal of the History of Sport* 33, no. 13 (2016): 1470–82.

29. Pınar Öztürk, "Kadın Futbolcuların Futbol Alanındaki Deneyimleri" [Experiences of women footballers in the football field] (PhD diss., Hacettepe University, 2017).

30. Gertrud Pfister, "Sportswomen in the German Popular Press: A Study Carried Out in the Context of the 2011 Women's Football World Cup," *Soccer & Society* 16, nos. 5–6 (2015): 639–56; Barbara Ravel and Marc Gareau, "'French Football Needs More Women Like Adriana'? Examining the Media Coverage of France's Women's National Football Team for the 2011 World Cup and the 2012 Olympic Games," *International Review for the Sociology of Sport* 51, no. 7 (2016): 833–47.

31. Roxane Coche, "Promoting Women's Soccer through Social Media: How the US Federation Used Twitter for the 2011 World Cup," *Soccer & Society* 17, no. 1 (2016): 90–108.

32. Judith Butler, *Gender Trouble: Feminism and the Subversion of Identity* (New York, NY: Routledge, 1990); Sheila Scraton et al., "It's Still a Man's Game?: The Experiences of Top-Level European Footballers," *International Review for the Sociology of Sport* 34, no. 2 (1999): 99–111; Jonathan Magee, Jayne Caudwell, Katie Liston and Sheila Scraton. *Women, Football and Europe: Histories, Equity and Experience.* (Berkshire: Meyer & Meyer Sport, 2007).

33. Fisher and Dennehy, "Body Projects"; John Harris, "The Image Problem in Women's Football," *Journal of Sport & Social Issues* 29, no. 2 (2005): 184–97; Rens Peeters, Agnes Elling, and Jacco Van Sterkenburg, "WEURO 2017 as Catalyst? The Narratives of Two Female Pioneers in the Dutch Women's Football Media Complex," *Soccer & Society* 20, nos. 7–8 (2019): 1095–107; Cynthia Fabrizio Pelak, "Negotiating Gender/Race/Class Constraints in the New South Africa: A Case Study of Women's Soccer," *International Review for the Sociology of Sport* 40, no. 1 (2005): 53–70; Tamir Bar-On, *Beyond Soccer: International Relations and Politics as Seen through the Beautiful Game* (Lanham: Rowman & Littlefiel, 2017).

34. Amir Ben Porat, "Cosi (non) Fan Tutte: Women's Football 'Made in Israel,'" *Soccer & Society* 21, no. 1 (2020): 39–49; Kelly Knez, Tansin Benn, and Sara Alkhaldi, "World Cup Football as a Catalyst for Change: Exploring the Lives of Women in Qatar's First National Football Team—A Case Study," *The International Journal of the History of Sport* 31, no. 14 (2014): 1755–1773; Geoff Harkness, "Spring Forward: Female Muslim Soccer Players in Iraqi Kurdistan," *Soccer & Society* 13, nos. 5–6 (2012): 720–38; Charlotte Lysa, "Football Femininities: Lessons from the Gulf," *International Journal of Middle East Studies* 51, no. 3 (2019): 479–81; and Shenhav Perets, Moshe Levy, and Yair Galily, "National and Gender Identity Perceptions among Female Football Players in Israel," *Soccer & Society* 12, no. 2 (2011): 228–48; Babak Fozooni, "Iranian Women and Football," *Cultural Studies* 22, no. 1 (2008): 114–33.

35. For a series of newspaper articles on this issue published during the writing of this chapter, please see Erdem Göktürk, "Kadın Futboluna Dair 7: O Zaman Ne Yapmalı?" ["On Women's Football 7: What Shall be Done?"] *Gazete Duvar*, June 24, 2020, www.gazeteduvar.com.tr/spor/2020/06/24/kadin-futboluna-dair-7-o-zaman-ne-yapmali.

36. There have been significant changes regarding these dynamics after my research. Some of Turkey's most prominent clubs founded or reinaugurated women's football branches in 2021; new sponsorship deals were signed for first division women's football (called the "Super League" as of 2021) and some of the teams. I revisit these developments in the section entitled "Potential for Change."

37. BeIN Sports, "Gelenek Devam Edecek! Futbol 5 Yıl Daha Evinde!" [Tradition continues! Football is at home for another 5 years], 2016, https://tr.beinsports.com/haber/turk-futbolunda-tarihi-gun.

38. Personal interview with footballer, Istanbul, December 2019. Interview was conducted in Turkish and translated by the author.

39. Personal interview with footballer, Istanbul, November 2019. Interview was conducted in Turkish and translated by the author.

40. Personal interview with footballer, Istanbul, January 2020. Interview was conducted in Turkish and translated by the author.

41. Kenda R. Stewart, "A Hobby or Hobbling? Playing Palestinian Women's Soccer in Israel," *Soccer & Society* 13, nos. 5–6 (2012): 739–63.

42. Jessaca B. Leinaweaver, *The Circulation of Children: Kinship, Adoption, and Morality in Andean Peru* (Durham, NC: Duke University Press, 2008).

43. Personal interview with footballer, Istanbul, December 2019. Interview was conducted in Turkish and translated by the author.

44. Jørgen Bagger Kjær and Sine Agergaard, "Understanding Women's Professional Soccer: The Case of Denmark and Sweden," *Soccer & Society* 14, no. 6 (2013): 822; Alfred Archer and Martine Prange, "'Equal Play, Equal Pay': Moral Grounds for Equal Pay in Football," *Journal of the Philosophy of Sport* 46, no. 3 (2019): 416–36.

45. Personal interview with footballer, Istanbul, February 2020. Interview was conducted in Turkish and translated by the author.

46. I don't know about any specific examples regarding retribution for being outspoken. My understanding is that the women felt a general sense of unease and hesitation because they weren't sure of their position or their ability to mobilize any resources.

47. Personal phone interview with former footballer, January 2020. Interview was conducted in English.

48. Pınar Öztürk and Erdem Göktürk. *Kadın Futbol Çalıştayı Raporu [Women's Football Workshop Report]*, April 26, 2018, www.kasfad.org/?p=2662.

49. Even though they were not overtly referenced, these mobilizations, taken together with the kinds of developments referenced in the section describing generational differences, can be interpreted to explain the changing attitude with the new generation.

50. Personal interview with footballer, Istanbul, January 2020. Interview was conducted in Turkish and translated by the author.

51. See: Aksu Bora, "Eşitlik, 100 Metre, Fıtrat Gibi Şeyler…" [Equality, 100 meters, things like natural disposition], *Birikim*, March 24, 2019, www.birikimdergisi. com/haftalik/9417/esitlik-100-metre-fitrat-gibi-seyler#.XlepnBMza01; Tutku Ayhan, "KADEM's 'Gender Justice' or the Momentum of Anti-Genderism in Turkey," *London School of Economics Blog*, April 29, 2019, https://blogs.lse.ac.uk/ gender/2019/04/29/kadems-gender-justice-in-turkey. Please also note that the discussion around gender equality can often represent gender as a binary, I largely recycle that assumption here even though the binary does not represent many people. But the everyday categories of "man" and "woman" continue to implicate people's lives as well as those of footballers, including their experiences and struggle of equality.

5. HOMELAND: NATIONAL IDENTITY PERFORMANCE IN THE QATAR NATIONAL TEAM

1. Kristian Coates Ulrichsen, *Qatar and the Arab Spring* (New York, NY: Oxford University Press, 2014), 111.

2. For a more detailed account of the Blockade and the events that led to it, see Kristian Coates Ulrichsen, *Qatar and the Gulf Crisis* (London: Hurst, 2020).

3. Alan Bairner, *Sport, Nationalism, and Globalization: European and North American Perspectives* (Albany, NY: State University of New York Press, 2001), 17.

4. Three of the most discussed cases have been the propensity of Qatar, Bahrain, and most recently Turkey to recruit athletes from East Africa with little or no previous ties to the country. For a comprehensive and balanced overview this issue, see Joost Jansen, "Who Can Represent the Nation? Migration, Citizenship, and Nationhood in the Olympic Games" (PhD diss., Erasmus Universiteit Rotterdam, 2020).

5. This figure was calculated cross-referencing player information from Player Contact, 2020, www.playercontact.com, Transfer Markt, 2020, www.transfermarkt.com, and Qatar Football Live, https://twitter.com/QFootLive?ref_src=twsrc%5Egoog le%7Ctwcamp%5Eserp%7Ctwgr%5Eauthor.

6. Examples of such over-simplification include the headline in *Egypt Today*, "Qatari National Team Has Only 4 Qataris," July 4, 2017, www.egypttoday.com/Article/ 8/10072/Qatari-national-team-has-only-4-Qataris.

7. A detailed overview of France's successful 2018 team can be found at Paul Pradier, "Diverse French Team Brings Home World Cup Championship," *ABC News*, July 16, 2018, https://abcnews.go.com/International/diverse-french-team-brings-home-world-cup-championship/story?id=56619062.

8. Similar accounts of the 1998 team can be found at Ramy Allahoum, "Is France's Ethnically Diverse Team a Symbol of Multiculturalism?" *Al Jazeera*, July 10, 2018, www.aljazeera.com/indepth/features/france-ethnically-diverse-team-symbol-multi-culturalism-180709224535038.html; Adam White, "Liberté, Égalité, Diversity: How France Won the World Cup," *The Guardian*, July 17, 2018, www.theguardian.com/ football/2018/jul/17/france-win-world-cup-didier-deschamps-diversity.

9. Figures as per Jure Snoj, "Population of Qatar by Nationality—2019 Report," Priya DSouza Communications, August 15, 2019, https://priyadsouza.com/population-of-qatar-by-nationality-in-2017; Government of Qatar, Planning and Statistics Authority, "Monthly Figures on Total Population," June 30, 2020, www.psa.gov. qa/en/statistics1/StatisticsSite/pages/population.aspx?p=2.

10. For a comprehensive insight into the composition of the migrant workforce of the Gulf and the issues they face, see Zahra R. Babar, ed., *Arab Migrant Communities in the GCC* (New York: Oxford University Press, 2017).

11. For further information on the stratification of Qatar society and its citizenship laws, please refer to the following: A. Hadi Alshawi and Andrew Gardner, "Tribalism, Identity, and Citizenship in Contemporary Qatar," *Anthropology of the Middle East* 8, no. 2 (2013): 46–59; and Zahra R. Babar, "The Cost of Belonging: Citizenship Construction in the State of Qatar," *Middle East Journal* 68, no. 3 (2014): 403–20.

12. Noah, "The Privilege of a Normal Life," Migrant-Rights.org, August 16 2020, www. migrant-rights.org/2020/08/the-privilege-of-a-normal-life.

13. Gijsbert Oonk, "Who Are We Actually Cheering On? Sport, Migration, and National Identity in a World-Historical Perspective," Erasmus University Rotterdam, October 18, 2019, https://repub.eur.nl/pub/123010.

14. For a more detailed account of Law 38 on the acquisition of Qatari nationality, see State of Qatar, "Law No. 38 of 2005 on the Acquisition of Qatari Nationality," 2005, www.almeezan.qa/ClarificationsNoteDetails.aspx?id=7870&language=en.

15. Norbert Elias, *The Society of Individuals* (Dublin: University College Dublin Press, 2010), 183.

16. Benedict Anderson, *Imagined Communities: Reflections on the Origin and Spread of Nationalism* (London: Verso, 2016), 6–7.

17. Qatar does not have a women's team as per FIFA's current rankings. FIFA, "Women's Ranking," June 26, 2020, www.fifa.com/fifa-world-ranking/ranking-table/women. According to FIFA criteria, teams that have not played more than five matches against officially ranked teams or that have been inactive for more than 18 months do not appear on the table.

18. Nida Ahmad, "Sportswomen's Use of Social Media in the Middle East and North Africa (MENA)," in *Sports, Politics, and Society in the Middle East*, eds. Danyel Reiche and Tamir Sorek (New York, NY: Oxford University Press, 2019), 95–6.

19. Brett Hutchins, "The Acceleration of Media Sport Culture: Twitter, Telepresence and Online Messaging," *Information, Communication & Society* 14, no. 2 (2011): 238.

20. Michael Billig, *Banal Nationalism* (London: Sage, 1995), 6.

21. Ibid., 8.

22. Ibid., 103.

23. Ibid.

24. Ibid., 7.

25. Ibid., 44.

26. James G. Kellas, *The Politics of Nationalism and Ethnicity* (New York, NY: St. Martin's Press: 1991), 51–2.

27. Norbert Elias and John L. Scotson, *The Established and the Outsiders* (Dublin: University College Dublin Press, 2008), 20.

28. Ross Griffin, "Qatar Carves National Identity out of Saudi-Led Blockade," *Middle East Eye*, June 20, 2018, www.middleeasteye.net/opinion/qatar-carves-national-identity-out-saudi-led-blockade.

29. The Path Qatar, "Episode 1—Hassan Al-Haydos," *YouTube*, June 2, 2019, www.youtube.com/watch?v=1vUOSJT-3ms.

30. Matthew Gray, *Qatar: Politics and the Challenges of Development* (London: Lynne Rienner, 2013), 227.

31. David Storey, "National Allegiance and Sporting Citizenship: Identity Choices of 'African' Footballers," *Sport in Society* 23, no. 1 (2019): 129–41.

32. "Fawaz," Interview with the author, 2020, Doha, Qatar.

33. "Ahmed," Interview with the author, 2020, Doha, Qatar.

34. Miriam Cooke, *Tribal Modern: Branding New Nations in the Arab Gulf* (Los Angeles, CA: University of California Press, 2014), 124.

35. Ibid., 126–7.

36. Anh Nga Longva, *Walls Built on Sand: Migration, Exclusion, and Society in Kuwait* (Boulder, CO: Westview Press, 1997), 44.

37. Ibid., 114.

38. For a more detailed account of Law 38 on the acquisition of Qatari nationality, see State of Qatar, "Law No. 38 of 2005 on the Acquisition of Qatari Nationality."

39. Babar, "The Cost of Belonging," 413.

40. Stephen Castles and Alastair Davidson, *Citizenship and Migration: Globalization and the Politics of Belonging* (London: Macmillan, 2000), 94.

41. Basam Al-Rawi, Twitter post, January 22, 2019, https://twitter.com/basam_97/status/1087779302576410624.

42. "Khaled," Interview with the author, 2020, Doha, Qatar.

43. Ibid.

44. "Abdullah," Interview with the author, 2020, Doha, Qatar.

45. Desde la Grada, "Entrevista a Ali Almoez, Delantro de la CyD Leonesa," *YouTube*, April 12, 2016, www.youtube.com/watch?v=188XnUGJSM8.

46. *Al Jazeera*, "Qatar's Bassam Certain He Will Get a Final Chance to Shine in UAE," January 26, 2019, www.aljazeera.com/news/2019/01/qatar-bassam-final-chance-shine-uae-190126102631092.html.

47. Irene Bloemraad, "Who Claims Dual Citizenship? The Limits of Postnationalism, the Possibilities of Transnationalism, and the Persistence of Traditional Citizenship," *International Migration Review* 38, no. 2 (2004): 393.

48. Abdulkarim Hassan, Twitter post, April 15 2020, https://twitter.com/ABDULKARIM_QAT/status/1250455663018479627.

49. Abdulkarim Hassan, Twitter post, March 23 2020, https://twitter.com/ABDULKARIM_QAT/status/1242046469257023488.

50. Rommel Al-Samarrie, Twitter post, January 23 2020, https://twitter.com/RommelALsamarri/status/1088044398888316928; Karam, Twitter post, January 23 2020, https://twitter.com/mesopodentia/status/1088035660055932928.

51. Jason Tuck and Joseph Maguire, "Making Sense of Global Patriot Games: Rugby Players' Perceptions of National Identity Politics," *Football Studies* 2, no. 1 (1999): 38–9.

52. Qatar's National Anthem, "As-Salam al-Amiri," 2018, https://2018.qatar.qa/en/qatar/the-national-anthem.

53. Translated from Arabic into English by Ms Reem Abdulaziz and Ms Fatema Ahmed.

54. The video of the Qatar players singing "Shoomilah Shoomilah" quickly went viral on social media. Fatma Alzahraa, Twitter post, February 1, 2019, https://twitter.com/Fatalzaa/status/1091364018651127808.

55. "Fawaz," Interview with the author, 2020, Doha, Qatar.

56. Ibid.

57. "Ahmed," Interview with the author, 2020, Doha, Qatar.

58. "Khaled," Interview with the author, 2020, Doha, Qatar.

59. Ibid.

60. Four different categories of full citizen, as well as an arduous naturalization process, has seen an increase in the number of "Qatarized non-Qataris" who, despite being citizens of the state, are also frequently identified in terms of other identity markers.

6. PLAYING IN THE TRIPLE PERIPHERY: EXCLUSIONARY POLICIES
   TOWARDS PALESTINIAN FOOTBALL IN LEBANON

1. Gabriel Almond et al., *Comparative Politics Today: A World View*, 9th ed. (New York, NY: Pearson, 2010), 28.

2. Fateh Azzam, "Palestinian (Non)Citizenship," *The Middle East Journal* 73, no. 4 (2019): 574.

3. Tamir Sorek, *Arab Soccer in a Jewish State: The Integrative Enclave* (Cambridge: Cambridge University Press, 2007), 2 and 5.

4. Ibid., 150.

5. Ibid., 102.

6. Ibid., 49

7. Ibid., 50.

8. Eran Shor and Yuval Yonay, "'Play and Shut Up': The Silencing of Palestinian Athletes in Israeli Media," *Ethnic and Racial Studies* 34, no. 2 (2011): 244.

9. Ibid., 242.

10. Daoud Kuttab, "Palestinians Cry Foul at FIFA Decision," *Al-Monitor*, November 2, 2017, www.al-monitor.com/pulse/originals/2017/11/palestine-fifa-continue-israel-settlment-clubs-soccer.html.

11. Jodi Rudoren, "Palestinian Soccer Association Drops Effort to Suspend Israel From FIFA," *The New York Times*, May 29, 2015, www.nytimes.com/2015/05/30/world/middleeast/palestine-palestinian-fa-soccer-israel-fifa.html?searchResultPosition=6.

12. "Israel Bans Gaza Football Team From Playing Palestine Cup Final, Again," *TeleSur*, September 23, 2019, www.telesurenglish.net/news/Israel-Bans-Gaza-Football-Team-From-Playing-Palestine-Cup-Final-20190923–0017.html.

13. Azzam, "Palestinian (Non)Citizenship," 574.

14. As'ad Ghanem, "Palestinian Nationalism: An Overview," *Israel Studies* 18, no. 2 (2013): 11.

15. By Tuesday, January 7, 2020, the population of the State of Palestine was 5,043,144, according to www.worldometers.info/world-population/state-of-palestine-population.

16. In addition, there is one associate member association according to the Asian Football Confederation, 2017, www.the-afc.com/afc-home/about-afc/overview.

17. Glen M. E. Duerr, "Playing for Identity and Independence: The Issue of Palestinian Statehood and the Role of FIFA," *Soccer & Society* 13, nos. 5–6 (2012): 653.

18. Jon Dart, "Palestinian Football and National Identity under Occupation," *Managing Sport and Leisure* 25, nos. 1–2 (2019): 21.

19. Azzam, "Palestinian (Non)Citizenship," 574.

20. Dag Tuastad, "Football's Role in How Societies Remember: The Symbolic Wars of Jordanian–Palestinian Football," in *Sport, Politics, and Society in the Middle East*, eds. Danyel Reiche and Tamir Sorek (New York, NY: Oxford University Press, 2019), 44.

21. Ibid., 54.

22. Roy Arad, "Meet the Chilestinians, the Largest Palestinian Community Outside the

Middle East," *Haaretz*, October 31, 2018, www.haaretz.com/middle-east-news/palestinians/.premium.MAGAZINE-the-largest-palestinian-community-outside-the-mideast-thrives-in-chile-1.6613371.

23. Santiago born Roberto Bishara from Club Deportivo Palestino, for example, played 27 matches for Palestine from 2002–2011 while Luiz Jimenez played 26 matches for Chile from 2004–2011. National Football Teams, "Roberto Bishara," 2020, www.national-football-teams.com/player/5030/Roberto_Bishara_Adauy.html; National Football Teams, "Luiz Jiménez," 2020, www.national-football-teams.com/player/8187/Luis_Jimenez.html.

24. Kiran Moodley, "The Chilean Football Club that's Huge in Palestine," *The Independent*, March 19, 2015, www.independent.co.uk/news/world/americas/the-chilean-football-club-thats-huge-in-palestine-10119622.html.

25. Siri Schwabe, "Resistance in Representation: The Diasporic Politics of Club Deportivo Palestino," *Soccer & Society* 20, no. 4 (2019): 696.

26. Ibid., 699.

27. Jack Bell, "Chilean League Fines Club for Map of Palestine on Jersey," *The New York Times*, January 22, 2014, www.nytimes.com/2014/01/23/sports/soccer/chilean-league-fines-club-for-map-of-palestine-on-jersey.html?_r=0.

28. United Nations Relief and Works Agency (UNRWA), "Where We Work," 2019, www.unrwa.org/where-we-work/lebanon.

29. *The Jordan Times*, "Lebanon Conducts First-Ever Census of Palestinian Refugees," December 21, 2017, www.jordantimes.com/news/region/lebanon-conducts-first-ever-census-palestinian-refugees.

30. Sorek, *Arab Soccer in a Jewish State*, 185.

31. Uzi Dann, "With Israelis on the Squad, Palestine's Soccer Team Storms the Asia Cup," *Haaretz*, January 6, 2019, www.haaretz.com/middle-east-news/palestinians/.premium-palestine-s-soccer-team-ready-to-take-asia-cup-by-storm-with-players-from-all-over-1.6810442.

32. Stuart Winer, "Palestinian national soccer team star booted for signing with Israeli squad," *Times of Israel*, May 25, 2020, www.timesofisrael.com/palestinian-national-soccer-team-star-booted-for-signing-with-israeli-squad/#gs.fjqpqc.

33. Barrie Houlihan, "Politics and Sport," in *Handbook of Sports Studies*, eds. Jay Coakley and Eric Dunning (London: Sage, 2000), 213–27.

34. Schwabe, "Resistance in Representation"; Shor and Yonay, "Play and Shut Up"; Sorek, *Arab Soccer in a Jewish State*; Tuastad, "Football's Role in How Societies Remember"; Dart, "Palestinian Football and National Identity"; and Duerr, "Playing for Identity and Independence."

35. Kenda Stewart, "A Hobby or Hobbling? Playing Palestinian Women's Soccer in Israel," *Soccer & Society* 13, nos. 5–6 (2012): 741.

36. See, for example, Sawsan Abdulrahim and Marwan Khawaja, "The Cost of Being Palestinian in Lebanon," *Journal of Ethnic and Migration Studies* 37, no. 1 (2011): 151–66; Sari Hanafi, "Enclaves and Fortressed Archipelago: Violence and Governance in Lebanon's Palestinian Refugee Camps," in *Lebanon: After the Cedar Revolution*, eds.

Are Knudsen and Michael Kerr (London: Hurst, 2012), 105–21; Sari Hanafi, Jad Chaaban, and Karin Seyfert, "Social Exclusion of Palestinian Refugees in Lebanon: Reflections on the Mechanisms that Cement their Persistent Poverty," *Refugee Survey Quarterly* 31, no. 1 (2012): 34–53.

37. United Nations Relief and Works Agency (UNRWA), "Burj Barajneh Camp," 2020, www.unrwa.org/where-we-work/lebanon/burj-barajneh-camp.

38. Stefano Fogliata, "Who Does not Know How to Go Back Home? Overlapping Spatio-Temporalities of Exile in Lebanon's Palestinian Camps" (PhD diss., University of Bergamo, academic year 2015–2016).

39. Ibid., 266–7.

40. Alain Bryman, *Social Research Methods* (New York, NY: Oxford University Press, 2012), 470.

41. Hanafi, "Enclaves and Fortressed Archipelago," 106.

42. United Nations Relief and Works Agency (UNRWA), "Palestinian Refugees Living in Lebanon," *Protection Brief*, June 2018, www.unrwa.org/sites/default/files/unrwa_lebanon_protection_context_brief_june_2018.pdf.

43. Hanafi, Chaaban, and Seyfert, "Social Exclusion of Palestinian Refugees in Lebanon," 51.

44. Abdulrahim and Khawaja, "The Cost of Being Palestinian in Lebanon," 153.

45. United Nations Relief and Works Agency (UNRWA), "Palestinian Refugees Living in Lebanon."

46. Anies Al-Hroub, "Perspectives of School Dropouts' Dilemma in Palestinian Refugee Camps in Lebanon: An Ethnographic Study," *International Journal of Educational Development* 35 (2014): 53–66.

47. Hanafi, Chaaban, and Seyfert, "Social Exclusion of Palestinian Refugees in Lebanon," 42.

48. Fogliata, "Who Does not Know How to Go Back Home?," 223.

49. Ibid., 227.

50. Author's interview with the press officer of the Lebanese Football Association, Wadih Abdelnour, Beirut, June 30, 2020.

51. The season was cancelled in January 2020 because of the political and economic crisis in the country. For more information: *The New Arab*, "Lebanon's Football Association Announce League Suspension 'Due to Protests,' Others Say it's Lack of Money," January 21, 2020, www.alaraby.co.uk/english/news/2020/1/21/lebanese-premier-league-suspended-amid-deepening-economic-crisis.

52. Author's interview with the press officer of the Lebanese Football Association, Wadih Abdelnour, Beirut, December 16, 2019.

53. This converts to 33.17 USD instead of 13.27 USD, according to OANDA Currency Converter, 2019, www1.oanda.com/currency/converter.

54. Author's interview with former Homenmen player Aram Papazian, November 18, 2019.

55. Author's interview with the press officer of the Lebanese Football Association, Wadih Abdelnour, Beirut, October 24, 2019.

56. FIFA, "FIFA/Coca-Cola World Ranking," December 24, 2019, www.fifa.com/fifa-world-ranking/ranking-table/men/#AFC.

57. FIFA World Ranking—Table & Charts, "FIFA-Ranking Table and Transition Chart of 17 November 1999," November 17, 1999, http://fifa-ranking.free-data.net/fifa-ranking/1999-11-fifa_ranking_chart.

58. See Transfer Market, "Mehdi Khalil," 2020, www.transfermarkt.com/mehdi-khalil/profil/spieler/192855; Transfer Market, "Abbas Hassan," 2020, www.transfermarkt.com/abbas-hassan/profil/spieler/30395.

59. The main reason for the geographic divisions is to save on transportation costs.

60. Fogliata, "Who Does not Know How to Go Back Home?," 26.

61. Author's interview with the coach of the Palestinian national team in Lebanon, Jamal Khatib, Beirut, November 17, 2019.

62. Maria Rada-Soto, "League Brings Palestinian Camps Together," *The Daily Star*, November 20, 2017, www.dailystar.com.lb/Life/Lubnan/2017/Nov-20/427094-league-brings-palestinian-camp-teams-together.ashx.

63. UNRWA, "Where We Work."

64. Fogliata, "Who Does not Know How to Go Back Home?"

65. Tuastad, "Football's Role in How Societies Remember," 44.

66. Danyel Reiche, "War Minus the Shooting? The Politics of Sport in Lebanon as a Unique Case in Comparative Politics," *Third World Quarterly* 32, no. 2 (2011): 264.

67. Abbas Shiblak, "Stateless Palestinians," *Forced Migration Review* 26, no. 8 (2006): 8–9.

68. Lizzie Porter, "In Lebanon, Rage for Jerusalem but Not for Palestinians at Home," *The Arab Weekly*, December 17, 2017, https://thearabweekly.com/lebanon-rage-jerusalem-not-palestinians-home.

69. Hind Ghandour, "Naturalised Palestinians in Lebanon: Experiences of Belonging, Identity and Citizenship" (PhD diss., Swinburne University of Technology, 2017), 9.

70. Ibid., 66.

71. Ibid.

72. Sari Hanafi, "Stop Humiliating Palestinian Refugees," *The Daily Star*, March 16, 2012, www.dailystar.com.lb/Opinion/Commentary/2012/Mar-16/166826-stop-humiliating-palestinian-refugees.ashx.

73. Ahmed Moor, "Why Palestinians are Second Class Citizens in Lebanon," *The Guardian*, January 24, 2010, www.theguardian.com/commentisfree/2010/jun/24/middleeast-palestinian-territories.

74. Author's interview with the chair of the Palestinian rugby league federation, Rabih El Masri, Beirut, July 11, 2019.

75. Author's interview with the coach of the Palestinian national team in Lebanon, Jamal Khatib, Beirut, November 17, 2019.

76. For more information on the naturalization of athletes in Qatar: Danyel Reiche and Cem Tinaz, "Policies for Naturalisation of Foreign-Born Athletes: Qatar and Turkey in Comparison," *International Journal of Sport Policy and Politics* 11, no. 1 (2019): 153–171.

77. Porter, "In Lebanon, Rage for Jerusalem but Not for Palestinians at Home."

78. Moor, "Why Palestinians are Second Class Citizens in Lebanon."

79. Imad Harb, "Lebanon's Confessionalism: Problems and Prospects," United States Institute of Peace (USIP), March 30, 2006, www.usip.org/publications/2006/03/lebanons-confessionalism-problems-and-prospects.

80. *Middle East Eye*, "Palestinian Refugees Allegedly Banned from AFC Cup Match in Lebanon," May 1, 2019, www.middleeasteye.net/news/palestinian-refugees-allegedly-banned-afc-cup-match-lebanon.

81. Ibid.

82. Stewart, "A Hobby or Hobbling?," 759.

83. Ibid., 750.

84. Ibid., 755.

85. Ibid.

86. Les Roopanarine, "'Football is Forbidden': How Girls in a Lebanon Refugee Camp Kicked Back," *The Guardian*, October 11, 2019, www.theguardian.com/global-development/2019/oct/11/football-is-forbidden-how-girls-in-a-lebanon-refugee-camp-kicked-back.

87. Matthew Engel, "Delight is a Cricket Pitch in Beirut's Shatila Refugee Camp," *The Guardian*, March 9, 2019, www.theguardian.com/sport/2019/mar/09/cricket-beirut-shatila-refugee-camp-children.

88. United Nations Relief and Works Agency (UNRWA), "UNRWA Launches the Eleventh Edition of Palestiniadi in Lebanon with EU Support," July 5, 2019, www.unrwa.org/newsroom/press-releases/unrwa-launches-eleventh-edition-palestiniadi-lebanon-eu-support-0.

89. Azzam, "Palestinian (Non)Citizenship," 586.

90. *The Jerusalem Post*, Palestinian Passports Rejected by Citizens," July 4, 2013, www.jpost.com/middle-east/palestinian-passports-rejected-by-citizens-318799.

91. Passport Index, "Palestinian Territories," 2019, www.passportindex.org/compare-byPassport.php?p1=ps&fl=&s=yes.

92. Shiblak, "Stateless Palestinians," 8.

93. Azzam, "Palestinian (Non)Citizenship," 573.

94. United Nations High Commissioner for Refugees (UNHCR), "Global Trends: Forced Displacement in 2017," 2018, www.unhcr.org/5b27be547.pdf.

95. This aspect is elaborated in more detail in: Danyel Reiche, "National Representation Without Citizenship: The Special Case of Rugby," *Politics in Central Europe* 17, no. 3 (2021): 501–23.

96. FIFA, "FIFA Statutes: Regulations Governing the Application of the Statutes, Standing Orders of the Congress," August 2018, https://resources.fifa.com/image/upload/the-fifa-statutes-2018.pdf?cloudid=whhncbdzio03cuhmwfxa.

97. International Olympic Committee, "Olympic Charter," September 2019, 77, https://stillmed.olympic.org/media/Document%20Library/OlympicOrg/General/EN-Olympic-Charter.pdf#_ga=2.227061471.314482763.1542921705–5662 41420.1542921705.

98. *Football Palestine*, "Rapid Reaction: Lebanon 1:1 Palestine (International Friendly)," November 10, 2016, www.footballpalestine.com/2016/11/rapid-reaction-lebanon-palestine.html.

99. Duerr, "Playing for Identity and Independence," 661.

100. Khaled Abu Toameh, "PA Urges All EU Members to Recognize Palestinian State," *Jerusalem Post*, December 1, 2019, www.jpost.com/Middle-East/Palestinian-Authority-urges-all-EU-members-to-recognize-Palestinian-state-609464.

101. Duerr, "Playing for Identity and Independence," 660.

102. FIFA, "Palestinian Football Set for the Future with Refreshed Stadium and New Modern Facilities," March 5, 2019, www.fifa.com/about-fifa/who-we-are/news/palestinian-football-set-for-the-future-with-refreshed-stadium-and-new-modern-fa.

103. Dart, "Palestinian Football and National Identity," 5.

104. Duerr, "Playing for Identity and Independence," 657.

105. Transfer Market, "Palestine," 2020, www.transfermarkt.com/palastina/bilanz/verein/17758.

106. Hossam Ezzedine and Anne Levasseur, "With Help from Diaspora, Palestinians Hope for Asian Cup Soccer Surprise," *Times of Israel*, January 5, 2019, www.timesofisrael.com/with-help-from-diaspora-palestinians-hope-for-asian-cup-soccer-surprise.

107. Duerr, "Playing for Identity and Independence," 654.

108. An exception, which I learned in an interview with the operator of the social media platform *FA Lebanon*, is goalkeeper Kanaan Kanaan from the Lebanese Ghobeiry Futsal Club. He represented the Palestinian national futsal team in October 2019 in Bahrain for the 2020 AFC Futsal Championship qualification. Palestine lost all matches in this indoor football competition and did not qualify for the 2020 AFC Futsal Championship in Turkmenistan. Since this research looks at football (and not futsal), I did not look into details of this case.

109. Duerr, "Playing for Identity and Independence," 659.

110. For more information on Lebanon's boycott of Israel and its effects particularly on sport: Danyel Reiche, "Not Allowed to Win: Lebanon's Sporting Boycott of Israel," *The Middle East Journal* 72, no. 1 (2018): 28–47.

111. Author's interview with the Palestinian football player Wassim Abdul Hadi, Beirut, November 26, 2019.

112. Dart, "Palestinian Football and National Identity," 6.

113. Nadim Nassif, "Developing a National Elite Sport Policy in an Arab Country: The Case of Lebanon," in *Sport, Politics, and Society in the Middle East*, eds. Danyel Reiche and Tamir Sorek (New York, NY: Oxford University Press, 2019), 148.

114. For example, three out of ten Lebanese athletes at the 2012 Summer Olympic Games in London were from the United States. See for more information Danyel Reiche, "Why Developing Countries are Just Spectators in the 'Gold War': The Case of Lebanon at the Olympic Games," *Third World Quarterly* 38, no. 4 (2017): 1001.

115. Worldometer, "Countries in the World by Population," 2020, www.worldometers.info/world-population/population-by-country.

116. Worldometer, "Current World Population," 2020, www.worldometers.info/world-population.

117. World Vision, "Rohingya Refugee Crisis: Facts, FAQs, and How to Help," 2020, www.worldvision.org/refugees-news-stories/rohingya-refugees-bangladesh-facts.

118. Danyel Reiche and Axel Maugendre, "Struggling for Recognition: Developing Rugby Union in Lebanon," in *Rugby in Global Perspective: Playing on the Periphery*, eds. John Harris and Nicholas Wise (New York, NY: Routledge, 2019), 58 and 60.

119. *BBC*, "Rio Olympics 2016: Refugee Olympic Team Competed as 'Equal Human Beings,'" August 21, 2016, www.bbc.com/sport/olympics/37037273.

120. International Olympic Committee, "Olympic Charter," 11.

7. REFUGEES AND FOOTBALL IN THE GLOBAL AND MIDDLE EAST CONTEXTS

1. Ramón Spaaij et al., "Sport, Refugees, and Forced Migration: A Critical Review of the Literature," *Frontiers in Sports and Active Living* 1, no. 47 (2019): 1–18.

2. United Nations High Commissioner for Refugees (UNHCR), "Global Trends: Forced Displacement in 2018," *Global Trends Report*, 2019, https://unhcrsharedmedia. s3.amazonaws.com/2019/Global-Trends-19-June–2019/2019–06–18_Global_ Trends_2018_WEB_(4)_embargo-cover.pdf.

3. Ibid.

4. Hein de Haas, Stephen Castles, and Mark J. Miller, *The Age of Migration: International Population Movements in the Modern World*, 6th ed. (New York, NY: Guilford Press, 2020).

5. Caitlin Nunn et al., "Navigating Precarious Terrains: Reconceptualizing Refugee-Youth Settlement," *Refuge* 33, no. 2 (2017): 45–55.

6. Natasha Saunders and Faye Donnelly, "The Refugee Olympic Team at Rio 2016: Rallying around Which Flag?" *Open Democracy*, March 10, 2017, www.opendemoc-racy.net/en/refugee-olympic-team-at-rio-2016-rallying-around-which-flag.

7. UNHCR, IOC and Terre des hommes organization, *Sport for Protection Toolkit: Programming with Young People in Forced Displacement Settings* (Geneva: UNHCR, IOC and Terre des hommes, 2018).

8. UNHCR, "Sporting World Pledge Support for Refugees, Ahead of Next Week's Global Refugee Forum," Press Release, December 10, 2019, www.unhcr.org/ en-au/news/press/2019/12/5dee28304/sporting-world-pledge-support-refugees-ahead-next-weeks-global-refugee.html.

9. UNHCR, "Sport Programmes and Partnerships," 2020, www.unhcr.org/en-au/ sport-partnerships/html.

10. Quoted in Gerard Meagher, "From Helplessness to Hope: Inspirational Tales of the Refugee Olympic Team," *The Guardian*, August 5, 2016, www.theguardian.com/ sport/2016/aug/05/helplessness-rio-hope-olympic-refugee-team.

11. Roger Cohen, "The World Loves Refugees, When They're Olympians," *The New York Times*, August 8, 2016, www.nytimes.com/2016/08/09/opinion/the-world-loves-refugees-when-theyre-olympians.html.

12. Uri Friedman, "Rio 2016: Where Refugees Are Finally Being Recognized," *The*

Atlantic, August 10, 2016, www.theatlantic.com/international/archive/2016/08/refugee-olympic-team-rio/494969.

13. Yusra Mardini, *Butterfly: From Refugee to Olympian, My Story of Rescue, Hope and Triumph* (London: Bluebird, 2018).

14. Jon Schuppe and Kelly Cobiella, "How Yusra Mardini Survived a 25-Day Trek from Syria And Became an Olympian," *NBC News*, August 6, 2016, www.nbcnews.com/storyline/team-refugees/how-yusra-mardini-survived-25-day-trek-syria-became-olympian-n601946.

15. Yusra Mardini, "Story," 2017, www.yusra-mardini.com/?anchor=/life.

16. Yusra Mardini quoted in Gerard Meagher, "From Helplessness to Hope."

17. Chris Stone, "Utopian Community Football? Sport, Hope and Belongingness in the Lives of Refugees and Asylum Seekers," *Leisure Studies* 37, no. 2 (2018): 180.

18. Ramón Spaaij, Sarah Oxford, and Ruth Jeanes, "Transforming Communities through Sport? Critical Pedagogy and Sport for Development," *Sport, Education and Society* 21, no. 4 (2016): 570–87.

19. Ramón Spaaij, *Sport and Social Mobility: Crossing Boundaries* (London: Routledge, 2011), 145.

20. Spaaij et al., "Sport, Refugees, and Forced Migration"; Ramón Spaaij and Sarah Oxford, "SDP and Forced Displacement," in *Routledge Handbook of Sport for Development and Peace*, eds. Holly Collison et al. (London: Routledge, 2018), 385–95.

21. UNHCR, "Global Trends: Forced Displacement in 2018."

22. UNHCR, *Convention and Protocol Relating to the Status of Refugees* (Geneva: UNHCR, 2010), www.unhcr.org/protection/basic/3b66c2aa10/convention-protocol-relating-status-refugees.html.

23. Liisa Malkki, "Refugees and Exile: From 'Refugee Studies' to the National Order of Things," *Annual Review of Anthropology* 24, no. 1 (1995): 505; Roger Zetter, "More Labels, Fewer Refugees: Remaking the Refugee Label in an Era of Globalization," *Journal of Refugee Studies* 20, no. 2 (2007): 172–92.

24. Oliver Bakewell, "Research Beyond the Categories: The Importance of Policy Irrelevant Research into Forced Migration," *Journal of Refugee Studies* 21, no. 4 (2008): 432–53.

25. Malkki, "Refugees and Exile," 506.

26. Ibid.

27. Bakewell, "Research Beyond the Categories," 438.

28. The languages were: English, Croatian, Dutch, Farsi, French, German, Indonesian, Italian, Japanese, Portuguese, Slovenian, Spanish, Swedish, and Turkish. My co-authors were: Jora Broerse, Sarah Oxford, Carla Luguetti, Fiona McLachlan, Brent McDonald, Bojana Klepac, Lisa Lymbery, Jeffrey Bishara and Aurélie Pankowiak. Spaaij et al., "Sport, Refugees, and Forced Migration."

29. Journal articles, books, book chapters, peer-reviewed research reports, and published PhD and Master's theses were all included in the review.

30. The seven databases used were: Scopus, EBSCOhost, Web of Science, J-STAGE, CiNii, Open Access Theses and Dissertations (OATD), and Google Scholar.

31. Alan Bryman, *Social Research Methods*, 5th ed. (Oxford: Oxford University Press, 2016).

32. Spaaij et al., "Sport, Refugees, and Forced Migration."

33. UNHCR, "Global Trends: Forced Displacement in 2018."

34. Ibid.

35. Bakewell, "Research Beyond the Categories."

36. Darko Dukic, Brent McDonald, and Ramón Spaaij, "Being Able to Play: Experiences of Social Inclusion and Exclusion Within A Football Team of People Seeking Asylum," *Social Inclusion* 5 (2017): 108.

37. Ibid.

38. Clifton Evers, "Intimacy, Sport and Young Refugee Men," *Emotions Space and Society* 3, no. 1 (2010): 61.

39. Ibid., 57.

40. Ibid.

41. Spaaij et al., "Sport, Refugees, and Forced Migration."

42. Ibid.

43. Dukic, McDonald, and Spaaij, "Being Able to Play," 104–5.

44. Ibid., 107.

45. Ramón Spaaij and Hebe Schaillée, "Inside the Black Box: A Micro-Sociological Analysis of Sport for Development," *International Review for the Sociology of Sport* (2020); David Scott, "The Confidence Delusion: A Sociological Exploration of Participants' Confidence in Sport-For-Development," *International Review for the Sociology of Sport* 55, no. 4 (2020): 383–98.

46. Warren St. John, *Outcasts United: An American Town, a Refugee Team, and One Woman's Quest to Make a Difference* (London: Fourth Estate, 2009); Elizabeth Whitman, "Syrian Refugees Find Normalcy in Football," *Al Jazeera*, June 29, 2014, www.aljazeera. com/news/middleeast/2014/06/syrian-refugees-football-201462812734250415. html.

47. Brent McDonald, Ramón Spaaij, and Darko Dukic, "Moments of Social Inclusion: Asylum Seekers, Football and Solidarity," *Sport in Society* 22, no. 6 (2019): 935–49.

48. Stone, "Utopian Community Football? Sport, Hope and Belongingness in the Lives of Refugees and Asylum Seekers"; Ramón Spaaij, "Refugee Youth, Belonging and Community Sport," *Leisure Studies* 34, no. 3 (2015): 303–18.

49. Louise Olliff, "Playing for the Future: The Role of Sport and Recreation in Supporting Refugee Young People to 'Settle Well' in Australia," *Youth Studies Australia* 27, no. 1 (2008): 52–60; Meredith A. Whitley, Cassandra Coble, and Gem S. Jewell, "Evaluation of a Sport-Based Youth Development Programme for Refugees," *Leisure* 40, no. 2 (2016): 175–99; Guy J. Coffey et al., "The Meaning and Mental Health Consequences of Long-Term Immigration Detention for People Seeking Asylum," *Social Science & Medicine* 70, no. 12 (2010): 2070–9; Alison Baker-Lewton et al., "'I haven't Lost Hope of Reaching Out…': Exposing Racism in Sport by Elevating Counternarratives," *International Journal of Inclusive Education* 21, no. 11 (2017): 1097–112.

50. Malkki, "Refugees and Exile," 508.

51. Ramón Spaaij, "The Ambiguities of Sport and Community Engagement," *Ethos* 21, no. 2 (2013): 8–11.

52. UNHCR, IOC and Terre des hommes organization, *Sport for Protection Toolkit: Programming with Young People in Forced Displacement Settings*, 14.

53. Spaaij et al., "Sport, Refugees, and Forced Migration," 8.

54. Bruce Kidd, "A New Social Movement: Sport for Development and Peace," *Sport in Society* 11, no. 4 (2008): 370–80; Richard Giulianotti, "Sport, Peacemaking and Conflict Resolution: A Contextual Analysis and Modelling of the Sport, Development and Peace Sector," *Ethnic and Racial Studies* 34, no. 2 (2011): 207–28; Simon Darnell, *Sport for Development and Peace: A Critical Sociology* (London: Bloomsbury Academic, 2012).

55. Andrew M. Guest, "Thinking Both Critically and Positively About Development Through Sport," *Sport and Development International Bulletin* 4, no. 5 (2005): 1–5.

56. Ramón Spaaij and Ruth Jeanes, "Education for Social Change? A Freirean Critique of Sport for Development and Peace," *Physical Education and Sport Pedagogy* 18, no. 4 (2013): 448.

57. Joanna Macrae, "The Death of Humanitarianism?: An Anatomy of the Attack," *Disasters* 22, no. 4 (1998): 309–17.

58. For example: John Sugden and James Wallis, eds., *Football for Peace: Teaching and Playing Sport for Conflict Resolution in the Middle East* (Oxford: Meyer & Meyer, 2007); John Sugden, "Teaching and Playing Sport for Conflict Resolution and Co-Existence in Israel," *International Review for the Sociology of Sport* 41, no. 2 (2006): 221–40; John Sugden, "The Challenge of Using a Values-Based Approach to Coaching Sport and Community Relations in Multi-Cultural Settings: The Case of Football for Peace (F4P) in Israel," *European Journal for Sport and Society* 3, no. 1 (2006): 7–24.

59. Generation Amazing, "Generation Amazing Across the World," n.d., www.qatar2022.qa/en/opportunities/generation-amazing.

60. Valeria Kunz, "Sport as a Post-Disaster Psychosocial Intervention in Bam, Iran," *Sport in Society* 12, no. 9 (2009): 1148.

61. Ibid., 1155.

62. Spaaij and Oxford, "SDP and Forced Displacement;" International Platform for Sport and Development, www.sportanddev.org; and Beyond Sport, www.beyondsport.org.

63. United Nations Relief and Works Agency for Palestine Refugees (UNRWA), "UNRWA in Figures as of 1 Jan 2016," 2016, www.unrwa.org/sites/default/files/content/resources/unrwa_in_figures_2016.pdf.

64. Spaaij and Oxford, "SDP and Forced Displacement"; Ramón Spaaij, Jonathan Magee, and Ruth Jeanes, eds., "Sport for Development in the Global South," in *Sport and Social Exclusion in Global Society* (London: Routledge, 2014), 103–24.

65. Jimmy O'Gorman and Joel Rookwood, "Football and International Social Development," in *Routledge Handbook of Football Studies*, eds. John Hughson et al. (London: Routledge, 2016), 140–53.

66. Sean Hamil, Geoff Walters, and Lee Watson, "The Model of Governance at FC Barcelona: Balancing Member Democracy, Commercial Strategy, Corporate Social Responsibility and Sporting Performance," *Soccer & Society* 11, no. 4 (2010): 475–504.

67. International Platform for Sport and Development at www.sportanddev.org; and Beyond Sport at www.beyondsport.org.

68. Generations For Peace, "Sport For Peace," May 26, 2015, www.generationsfor-peace.org/en/sport-for-peace.

69. Fred Coalter, *A Wider Social Role for Sport: Who's Keeping the Score?* (Routledge: London, 2007); Spaaij, *Sport and Social Mobility: Crossing Boundaries*.

70. Bassam, quoted in Jonathan Wilson, "Football Becomes Mother to Syria's Traumatised Child Refugees," *The Guardian*, December 3, 2013, www.theguardian.com/football/blog/2013/dec/03/football-syria-zaatari-child-refugees.

71. UEFA Foundation, "UEFA Foundation for Children and the Turkish Football Federation Team Up to Help Refugees in Turkey," 2020, https://uefafoundation.org/news/uefa-foundation-for-children-and-the-turkish-football-federation-team-up-to-help-refugees-in-turkey.

72. Hannah Prytherch and K. Kraft, "The Psychosocial Impact of Capoeira for Refugee Children and Youth," Capoeira4Refugees and University of East London—Centre for Social Justice and Change, September 2015, https://repository.uel.ac.uk/item/854yx.

73. Margaret Whitehead, "Definition of Physical Literacy and Clarification of Related Issues," *Journal of the International Council of Sport Science and Physical Education* 65, nos. 1–2 (2013): 29.

74. Suzanne Wrack, "'We are Superhero Girls Here': How Football is Helping Refugees in Lebanon," *The Guardian*, April 2, 2019, www.theguardian.com/football/2019/apr/02/futbolnet-superhero-girls-barca-foundation-refugees-lebanon-syria.

75. World Vision, "Helping Syrian Refugee Women and Girls Kick Goals," 2019, www.worldvision.com.au/global-issues/world-emergencies/syrian-refugee-crisis/syria-refugee-football.

76. Martha Saavedra, "Dilemmas and Opportunities in Gender and Sport-In-Development," in *Sport and International Development*, eds. Roger Levermore and Aaron Beacom (New York, NY: Palgrave Macmillan, 2009), 127.

77. Megan Chawansky, "New Social Movements, Old Gender Games? Locating Girls in the Sport for Development and Peace Movement," in *Critical Aspects of Gender in Conflict Resolution, Peacebuilding, and Social Movements*, eds. Anna Christine Snyder and Stephanie Phetsamay Stobbe (Bingley, UK: Emerald, 2011), 121–34.

78. Megan Chawansky and Lyndsay Hayhurst, "Girls, International Development and the Politics of Sport: Introduction," *Sport in Society* 18 (2015): 877–81.

79. Sarah Oxford and Fiona McLachlan, "'You Have to Play Like a Man, But Still Be a Woman': Young Female Colombians Negotiating Gender through Participation in a Sport for Development Organization," *Sociology of Sport Journal* 35, no. 3 (2018): 258–67.

80. Lyndsay Hayhurst, "Girls as the 'New' Agents of Social Change? Exploring the 'Girl

Effect' Through Sport, Gender and Development Programs in Uganda," *Sociological Research Online* 18, no. 2 (2013), 8. Emphasis in original.

81. O'Gorman and Rookwood, "Football and International Social Development."

82. Richard Giulianotti, Hans Hognestad, and Ramón Spaaij, "Sport for Development and Peace: Power, Politics and Patronage," *Journal of Global Sport Management* 1, nos. 3–4 (2016): 129–41. For exceptions, see, e.g., Iain Lindsey and Alan Grattan, "An 'International Movement'? Decentring Sport-For-Development within Zambian Communities," *International Journal of Sport Policy and Politics* 4, no. 1 (2012): 91–110.

83. Giulianotti et al., "Sport for Development and Peace," 137.

84. Darnell, *Sport for Development and Peace*; Andrew M. Guest, "The Diffusion of Development-Through-Sport: Analysing the History and Practice of the Olympic Movement's Grassroots Outreach to Africa," *Sport in Society* 12, no. 10 (2009): 1336–52.

85. Oscar Mwaanga and Samantha Prince, "Negotiating a Liberative Pedagogy in Sport Development and Peace: Understanding Consciousness Raising Through the Go Sisters Programme in Zambia," *Sport, Education and Society* 21, no. 4 (2016): 588–604.

86. Spaaij and Jeanes, "Education for Social Change?," 442–57.

87. Giulianotti et al., "Sport for Development and Peace," 137.

88. Hamil et al., "The Model of Governance at FC Barcelona," 475–504.

89. UEFA Foundation, "A New Start for Refugee Kids in Lebanon," July 6, 2017, https://uefafoundation.org/action/a-new-start.

90. Kia Motors Corporation, "Numerous Young Refugees to Receive Football Boots from Donation Campaign by Kia Motors, UEFA Foundation for Children," *Newsmarket*, May 17, 2019, www.thenewsmarket.com/news/numerous-young-ref-ugees-to-receive-football-boots-from-donation-campaign-by-kia-motors—uefa-foundat/s/9729633b-0398–4585–9637–1f4f35ce870b.

91. Foreward by Ummul Choudhury in "The Psychosocial Impact of Capoeira for Refugee Children and Youth," 5.

92. Hayhurst, "Girls as the 'New' Agents of Social Change?

93. UNHCR, IOC and Terre des hommes organization, *Sport for Protection Toolkit: Programming with Young People in Forced Displacement Settings*.

8. MORE THAN JUST A GAME: FOOTBALL IN THE PALESTINIAN BOYCOTT, DIVESTMENT, SANCTIONS MOVEMENT

1. Palestinian BDS National Committee, "Palestinian Civil Society Call for BDS," BDS Movement, July 9, 2005, https://bdsmovement.net/call.

2. While the anti-apartheid campaign involved both sporting boycotts and sanctions against South Africa, for the sake of brevity I will use "sports boycott" throughout this chapter as a shorthand to refer to both in the case of South Africa and Israel.

3. See, for example, a documentary by Connie Fields, *Have You Heard From Johannesburg? Fair Play* (Clarity Films, 2010); Tony Karon, "As South Africa Proved, Sporting

Boycotts Work," *The National*, July 21, 2014, www.thenationalnews.com/opinion/
as-south-africa-proved-sporting-boycotts-work-1.254977; Rob Nixon, "Apartheid
on the Run: The South African Sports Boycott," *Transition* 58 (1992): 68–88; John
Nauright, *Sport, Cultures and Identities in South Africa* (London: Leicester University
Press, 1997); Malcolm MacLean, "Anti-Apartheid Boycotts and the Affective
Economies of Struggle: The Case of Aotearoa New Zealand," *Sport in Society* 13,
no. 1 (2010): 72–91, https://doi.org/10.1080/17430430903377870; Malcolm
MacLean, "Revisiting (and Revising?) Sports Boycotts: From Rugby against South
Africa to Soccer in Israel," *The International Journal of the History of Sport* 31, no. 15
(2014): 1832–51, https://doi.org/10.1080/09523367.2014.934680; Trevor
Richards, *Dancing on Our Bones: New Zealand, South Africa, Rugby and Racism*
(Wellington: Bridget Williams Books, 1999).

4. For a more detailed exploration of the comparison between South African and Israel
see, for example, Jon Soske and Sean Jacobs, eds., *Apartheid Israel: The Politics of an
Analogy* (Chicago: Haymarket Books, 2015).

5. Visualizing Palestine, "Collective Action Timeline," Visualizing Palestine, n.d.,
https://visualizingpalestine.org/collective-action-timeline#timeline.

6. See, for example, Palestine Solidarity Campaign, "Palestine News," Palestine
Solidarity Campaign, Summer 2007, https://palestinecampaign.org/wp-content/
uploads/2012/12/Palestine-News-2007-Summer.pdf; Boycott Israel Campaign,
"Sports Boycott of Israel," Innovative Minds, 2002, http://inminds.co.uk/sports-
boycott-of-israel.html.

7. Kevin Blackistone, "Of Sports Boycotts, South Africa and Israel," Palestinian
Campaign for the Academic and Cultural Boycott of Israel, June 9, 2010, www.
pacbi.org/etemplate.php?id=1268&key=sports+boycott.

8. Aubrey Bloomfield, "Sports and the Palestinian BDS Struggle (Part 3): Looking
Ahead," *Palestine Square* (blog), March 20, 2017, https://palestinesquare.
com/2017/03/20/sports-and-the-palestinian-bds-struggle-part-3-looking-ahead.

9. Richard Abraham, "Giro d'Italia's Start in Israel Provokes Accusations of 'Sport-
Washing,'" *The Observer*, September 24, 2017, www.theguardian.com/sport/2017/
sep/24/israel-giro-ditalia-race-conflict-2018-start-cycling.

10. Olivia Katbi Smith, "A BDS Campaign Tackles the Sports Industry in Portland—and
Wins," Truthout, November 22, 2019, https://truthout.org/articles/a-bds-
campaign-tackles-the-sports-industry-in-portland-and-wins.

11. MacLean, "Revisiting (and Revising?) Sports Boycotts"; Jon Dart, "Israel and a Sports
Boycott: Antisemitic? Anti-Zionist?," *International Review for the Sociology of Sport*,
2015, 1–25, https://doi.org/10.1177%2F1012690215583482; Jon Dart, "'Brand
Israel': Hasbara and Israeli Sport," *Sport in Society* 19, no. 10 (2016): 1402–18,
https://doi.org/10.1080/17430437.2015.1133595; Jon Dart, "Showing Israel the
Red Card: Activists Engaged in pro-Palestinian Sport-Related Campaigns,"
International Journal of Sport Policy and Politics 9, no. 3 (2017): 521–39, https://doi.
org/10.1080/19406940.2017.1292303; Francesco Belcastro, "Sport, Politics and
the Struggle over 'Normalization' in Post-Oslo Israel and Palestine," *Mediterranean
Politics* (2020), https://doi.org/10.1080/13629395.2020.1845938.

12. See, for example, Jonathan Cook, "Israeli Football, Racism and Politics: The Ugly Side of the Beautiful Game," *The National*, April 25, 2013, www.thenationalnews.com/world/mena/israeli-football-racism-and-politics-the-ugly-side-of-the-beautiful-game-1.286247; Karon, "As South Africa Proved, Sporting Boycotts Work"; Joseph Dana, "Sport is the Latest Theatre of Struggle in Palestine," *The National*, May 12, 2015, www.thenationalnews.com/opinion/sport-is-the-latest-theatre-of-struggle-in-palestine-1.128413.

13. These include Reut Ber, Moran Yarchi, and Yair Galily, "The Sporting Arena as a Public Diplomacy Battlefield: The Palestinian Attempt to Suspend Israel from FIFA," *The Journal of International Communication* 23, no. 2 (2017): 218–30, https://doi.org/10.1080/13216597.2017.1327449; Yair Galily, "From Terror to Public Diplomacy: Jibril Rajoub and the Palestinian Authorities' Uses of Sport in Fragmentary Israeli–Palestinian Conflict," *Middle Eastern Studies* 54, no. 4 (2018): 652–64, https://doi.org/10.1080/00263206.2018.1438272; Demetrios Xenakis and Nikos Lekakis, "From Hasbara to the Palestine-Israel Sport Conflict," *Diplomacy & Statecraft* 29, no. 2 (2018): 328–51, https://doi.org/10.1080/09592296.2018.1453984; Jon Dart, "Sport and Peacebuilding in Israel/Palestine," *Journal of Global Sport Management* (2019), https://doi.org/10.1080/24704067.2019.1604073; Jon Dart, "Palestinian Football and National Identity under Occupation," *Managing Sport and Leisure* 25, nos. 1–2 (2020): 21–36, https://doi.org/10.1080/23750472.2019.1641140.

14. MacLean, "Revisiting (and Revising?) Sports Boycotts," 1846.

15. Ramah Kudaimi, "This is a Game-Changer," *US Campaign for Palestinian Rights* (blog), February 21, 2017, https://uscpr.org/this-is-a-game-changer.

16. Mary Corrigall, "International Boycott of Apartheid Sport," *South African History Online*, 1971, www.sahistory.org.za/archive/international-boycott-apartheid-sport-mary-corrigall.

17. Bruce Kidd, "The Campaign against Sport in South Africa," *International Journal* 43, no. 4 (1988): 643–64.

18. Ibid.

19. Robin Kelley, "The Role of the International Sports Boycott in the Liberation of South Africa," *Ufahamu: A Journal of African Studies* 13, nos. 2–3 (1984): 26–38.

20. Kidd, "The Campaign against Sport in South Africa."

21. Corrigall, "International Boycott of Apartheid Sport."

22. Douglas Booth, "Hitting Apartheid for Six? The Politics of the South African Sports Boycott," *Journal of Contemporary History* 38, no. 3 (2003): 477–93, https://doi.org/10.1177%2F0022009403038003008.

23. See, for example, Nauright, *Sport, Cultures and Identities in South Africa*; Kidd, "The Campaign against Sport in South Africa."

24. Nixon, "Apartheid on the Run," 79.

25. The term "coloured," which is still used in South Africa today, refers to people classified as neither black nor white under apartheid's four racial categories and includes the descendants of former slaves, indigenous people, and the products of mixed unions.

26. Nixon, "Apartheid on the Run," 79.

27. MacLean, "Anti-Apartheid Boycotts and the Affective Economies of Struggle," 75.

28. Ibid.

29. Nauright, *Sport, Cultures and Identities in South Africa*, 153.

30. Nixon, "Apartheid on the Run," 75–6.

31. MacLean, "Anti-Apartheid Boycotts and the Affective Economies of Struggle," 72.

32. Nixon, "Apartheid on the Run," 70.

33. Fields, *Have You Heard From Johannesburg?*

34. Corrigall, "International Boycott of Apartheid Sport."

35. Kidd, "The Campaign against Sport in South Africa," 646.

36. Yair Galily and Amir Ben-Porat, "Introduction: Sport, Politics and Society in the Land of Israel," in *Sport, Politics and Society in the Land of Israel: Past and Present*, ed. Yair Galily and Amir Ben-Porat (Abingdon, Oxon: Routledge, 2009), 5.

37. Galily and Ben-Porat, "Introduction," 7.

38. See, for example, John Sugden, "Anyone for Football for Peace? The Challenges of Using Sport in the Service of Co-Existence in Israel," *Soccer & Society* 9, no. 3 (2008): 405–15, https://doi.org/10.1080/14660970802009023.

39. Dart, "Sport and Peacebuilding in Israel/Palestine," 16.

40. Iyad Abu Gharqoud, "FIFA Should Give Israel the Red Card," *The New York Times*, May 28, 2015, www.nytimes.com/2015/05/29/opinion/fifa-should-give-israel-the-red-card.html.

41. See, for example, Peter Foster, "Academia Split over Boycott of Israel," *The Telegraph*, May 16, 2002, www.telegraph.co.uk/news/worldnews/middleeast/israel/1394427/Academia-split-over-boycott-of-Israel.html; Iain M Banks, "Why I'm Supporting a Cultural Boycott of Israel," *The Guardian*, April 6, 2013, www.theguardian.com/books/2013/apr/05/iain-banks-cultural-boycott-israel; Jonathan Rosenhead, "A Boycott under a Lense," *New Scientist* 218, no. 2921 (2013): 28–9.

42. See, for example, MacLean, "Revisiting (and Revising?) Sports Boycotts."

43. James M. Dorsey, *The Turbulent World of Middle East Soccer* (London: Hurst & Co, 2016).

44. Oliver Holmes and Quique Kierszenbaum, "Far-Right Israeli Football Fans Rebel over Beitar Jerusalem's New Arab Owner," *The Observer*, December 27, 2020, www.theguardian.com/world/2020/dec/27/far-right-israeli-football-fans-rebel-over-beitar-jerusalems-new-arab-owner.

45. Ibrahim Husseini, "Palestinians Slam 'Traitor' UAE for Normalising Ties with Israel," *Al Jazeera*, August 15, 2020, www.aljazeera.com/news/2020/8/15/palestinians-slam-traitor-uae-for-normalising-ties-with-israel.

46. See, for example, Gideon Levy, "When a Soccer Game Reflects Israel's Ugly Nature," *Haaretz*, April 25, 2016, www.haaretz.com/opinion/.premium-when-a-soccer-game-reflects-israel-s-ugly-nature-1.5439497; Rami Younis, "Israel's Most Racist Soccer Club Isn't Shouting 'Death to Arabs,'" *+972 Magazine*, April 27, 2016, www.972mag.com/israels-most-racist-soccer-club-isnt-shouting-death-to-arabs/.

47. Haim Kaufman and Yair Galily, "Sport, Zionist Ideology and the State of Israel," *Sport*

in *Society: Cultures, Commerce, Media, Politics* 12, no. 8 (2009): 1025, https://doi.org/10.1080/17430430903076316.

48. Dorsey, *The Turbulent World of Middle East Soccer*, 158.

49. Tamir Sorek, *Arab Soccer in a Jewish State* (Cambridge: Cambridge University Press, 2007).

50. Eran Shor and Yuval Yonay, "'Play and Shut Up': The Silencing of Palestinian Athletes in Israeli Media," *Ethnic and Racial Studies* 34, no. 2 (2011): 229–47, https://doi.org/10.1080/01419870.2010.503811.

51. Ilan Tamir and Alina Bernstein, "Do they even Know the National Anthem? Minorities in Service of the Flag—Israeli Arabs in the National Football Team," *Soccer & Society* 16, nos. 5–6 (2015): 745–64, https://doi.org/10.1080/14660970.2014.963316.

52. Shor and Yonay, "'Play and Shut Up,'" 244.

53. Tamir Sorek, "Sport, Palestine, and Israel," in *A Companion to Sport*, ed. David L. Andrews and Ben Carrington (West Sussex, UK: Blackwell, 2013), 267.

54. Gharquod, "FIFA Should Give Israel the Red Card."

55. Although the term apartheid has a longer history of usage by Palestinians, South Africans, and Israelis to describe Israel's treatment of the Palestinian people, in the past decade its usage has become increasingly widespread, including by legal scholars, journalists, and human rights organizations. See, for example, John Dugard and John Reynolds, "Apartheid, International Law, and the Occupied Territory," *European Journal of International Law* 24, no. 3 (2013): 867–913, https://doi.org/10.1093/ejil/cht045; Richard Falk (Special Rapporteur), "Report of the Special Rapporteur on the situation of human rights in the Palestinian territories occupied since 1967," United Nations Human Rights Council, A/HRC/25/67, January 21, 2014, www.ohchr.org/EN/HRBodies/HRC/RegularSessions/Session25/Documents/A-HRC-25-67_en.doc; Soske and Jacobs, *Apartheid Israel*; Michael Sfard, "The Israeli Occupation of the West Bank and the Crime of Apartheid: Legal Opinion," Yesh Din, June 2020, www.yesh-din.org/en/the-occupation-of-the-west-bank-and-the-crime-of-apartheid-legal-opinion/; B'Tselem, "A Regime of Jewish Supremacy from the Jordan River to the Mediterranean Sea: This is Apartheid," B'Tselem, January 12, 2021, www.btselem.org/publications/fulltext/202101_this_is_apartheid; Nathan Thrall, "The Separate Regimes Delusion," *London Review of Books*, January 21, 2021, www.lrb.co.uk/the-paper/v43/n02/nathan-thrall/the-separate-regimes-delusion; Human Rights Watch, "A Threshold Crossed: Israeli Authorities and the Crimes of Apartheid and Persecution," April 27, 2021, /www.hrw.org/report/2021/04/27/threshold-crossed/israeli-authorities-and-crimes-apartheid-and-persecution; Amos Schocken, "A Lesson in Zionism for MK Amichai Chikli," *Haaretz*, December 8, 2021, www.haaretz.com/opinion/.premium-a-lesson-in-zionism-for-mk-amichai-chikli-1.10447900; Amnesty International, "Israel's Apartheid against Palestinians: Cruel System of Domination and Crime against Humanity," February 1, 2022, www.amnesty.org/en/documents/mde15/5141/2022/en/.

56. See, for example, Aubrey Bloomfield, "The Unique Challenges Faced by Clubs in

the Palestine Cup Final," *Howler Magazine*, August 15, 2017, www.whatahowler. com/unique-challenges-faced-clubs-palestine-cup-final; Dave Zirin, "Israel Canceled the FIFA Palestine Cup for No Apparent Reason," *The Nation*, September 26, 2019, www.thenation.com/article/archive/fifa-palestine-cup.

57. See, for example, Dave Zirin, "A Red Line for FIFA? Israel, Violence and What's Left of Palestinian Soccer," *The Nation*, March 10, 2014, www.thenation.com/article/archive/red-line-fifa-israel-violence-and-whats-left-of-palestinian-soccer; Mariabruna Jennings, "Israel Hinders Football in Occupied Palestine: 2008–2014" Nonviolence International and Palestine Football Association, June 10, 2014, http:// nonviolenceinternational.net/wp/ni-issues-report-on-how-israel-is-hindering-palestinian-football.

58. See, for example, Associated Press, "FIFA to Fund Gaza Soccer Field Repair," *Ynetnews*, November 4, 2006, www.ynetnews.com/articles/0,7340,L-3239176,00. html; International Paralympic Committee, "NPC Palestine Headquarters Destroyed," International Paralympic Committee, November 21, 2012, www.paralympic.org/news/npc-palestine-headquarters-destroyed; Kamel Hawwash, "Hey Israel, Give Palestinians a Sporting Chance," *Middle East Eye*, August 11, 2016, www. middleeasteye.net/opinion/hey-israel-give-palestinians-sporting-chance; Paul Nicholson, "Israel's Christmas Day Bombing in Palestine Delivers World Football a Political Reminder," *Inside World Football*, December 30, 2020, www.insideworld-football.com/2020/12/30/israels-christmas-day-bombing-palestine-delivers-world-football-political-reminder.

59. Human Rights Watch, "Israel/Palestine: FIFA Sponsoring Games on Seized Land," September 25, 2016, www.hrw.org/news/2016/09/25/israel/palestine-fifa-sponsoring-games-seized-land.

60. Kaufman and Galily, "Sport, Zionist Ideology and the State of Israel," 1022.

61. Cook, "Israeli Football, Racism and Politics."

62. Dart, "'Brand Israel,'" 13.

63. Dart, "Israel and a Sports Boycott," 7.

64. MacLean, "Revisiting (and Revising?) Sports Boycotts," 1842.

65. Palestinian BDS National Committee, "Victory for BDS Campaign as UEFA Decides against Jerusalem Tournament Bid," BDS Movement, September 19, 2014, https:// bdsmovement.net/news/victory-bds-campaign-uefa-decides-against-jerusalem-tournament-bid.

66. See Red Card Israeli Racism, "Settlement Clubs and FIFA," *Red Card Israeli Racism* (blog), n.d., https://rcir.org.uk/?page_id=527; Ali Sawafta, "Israel Must Ease Travel for Palestinian Players—Blatter," *Reuters*, July 8, 2013, https://uk.reuters. com/article/uk-soccer-palestinians-israel-idUKBRE9660KS20130707.

67. Aubrey Bloomfield, "Ignoring Its Own Rules and International Law, FIFA Opts to Support Israeli Settlements," *Palestine Square* (blog), November 8, 2017, www.palestine-studies.org/en/node/232115.

68. Aubrey Bloomfield, "Why Palestinians Are Calling for a Boycott of Puma," *Mondoweiss*, June 13, 2019, https://mondoweiss.net/2019/06/palestinians-calling-boycott.

69. "Argentina Urged to Cancel Football Match in Jerusalem," *Al Jazeera*, May 28, 2018, www.aljazeera.com/sports/2018/5/28/palestine-urges-argentina-to-cancel-foot-ball-match-in-jerusalem.

70. Palestinian Campaign for the Academic and Cultural Boycott of Israel, "Tell Argentina and Lionel Messi: There is #NothingFriendly About Israel Shooting Palestinian Footballers," BDS Movement, May 15, 2018, https://bdsmovement.net/nothing-friendly.

71. The Newsroom, "Celtic Fans Present £176k Cheque to Palestine Charities," *The Scotsman*, January 29, 2017, www.scotsman.com/sport/football/celtic-fans-pres-ent-aps176k-cheque-palestine-charities-1457288.

72. Meron Rapoport, "A Game of Fear: Israel, FIFA, and the Threat of Isolation," *Middle East Eye*, June 1, 2015, www.middleeasteye.net/opinion/game-fear-israel-fifa-and-threat-isolation.

73. See, for example, Barak Ravid, "Israel Steps up Diplomatic Action as Fears Grow over FIFA Suspension," *Haaretz*, May 14, 2015, www.haaretz.com/.premium-israeli-fears-grow-over-suspension-from-world-soccer-1.5361643; Galily, "From Terror to Public Diplomacy."

74. Belcastro, "Sport, Politics and the Struggle over 'Normalization' in Post-Oslo Israel and Palestine."

75. Dimi Reider, "BDS: Israel's Self-Fulfilling Prophecy," *Middle East Eye*, June 20, 2015, www.middleeasteye.net/opinion/bds-israels-self-fulfilling-prophecy.

76. Dana Somberg, "Diplomatic Cables Reveal Sharp Increase in Efforts to Boycott Israel," *The Jerusalem Post*, February 2, 2016, www.jpost.com/israel-news/politics-and-diplomacy/diplomatic-cables-reveal-sharp-increase-in-efforts-to-boycott-israel-443583.

77. MacLean, "Revisiting (and Revising?) Sports Boycotts," 1844.

78. See, for example, Rami Younis, "Interview: The Man behind the BDS Movement," *+972 Magazine*, June 14, 2015, www.972mag.com/interview-the-man-behind-the-bds-movement.

79. Nathan Thrall, "BDS: How a Controversial Non-Violent Movement Has Transformed the Israeli-Palestinian Debate," *The Guardian*, August 14, 2018, www.theguardian.com/news/2018/aug/14/bds-boycott-divestment-sanctions-movement-trans-formed-israeli-palestinian-debate.

80. James M. Dorsey, "A Study in Soft Power Strategy: Iceland 1, Qatar–1," *The Huffington Post*, October 10, 2016, www.huffpost.com/entry/a-study-in-soft-power-str_b_12425576.

81. Thrall, "BDS."

82. See, for example, Barak Ravid, "Military Intelligence Monitoring Foreign Left-Wing Organizations," *Haaretz*, March 21, 2011, www.haaretz.com/1.5139433; Jonathan Lis, "Israel Passes Law Banning Calls for Boycott," *Haaretz*, July 12, 2011, www.haaretz.com/1.5026309; Teresa Watanabe, "How a Casino Tycoon is Trying to Combat an Exploding Pro-Palestinian Movement on Campuses," *Los Angeles Times*, August 21, 2016, www.latimes.com/local/la-me-uc-israel-palestinian-adv-snap-story.html; Daniel Estrin, "Covertly, Israel Prepares to Fight Boycott Activists

Online," Associated Press, February 18, 2016, https://apnews.com/article/0601 a79f13e041b9b5b312ec73063c98; Ali Abunimah, "New Israeli Crackdown Aims to Root out, Expel BDS Activists," *The Electronic Intifada*, August 8, 2016, https://electronicintifada.net/blogs/ali-abunimah/new-israeli-crackdown-aims-root-out-expel-bds-activists; Jewish Telegraphic Agency, "Israel Approves $72 Million Anti-BDS Project," *The Jerusalem Post*, December 30, 2017, www.jpost.com/israel-news/israel-approves-72-million-anti-bds-project-521388; Itamar Benzaquen and The Seventh Eye, "Israeli Ministry Paying for Anti-BDS Propaganda in Major News Outlets," *+972 Magazine*, January 14, 2020, www.972mag.com/anti-bds-propaganda-ministry-media.

83. Gideon Meir, "What 'Hasbara' is Really all About," Israel Ministry of Foreign Affairs, May 24, 2005, https://mfa.gov.il/mfa/abouttheministry/pages/what%20hasbara%20is%20really%20all%20about%20-%20may%202005.aspx.

9. QATAR, THE WORLD CUP, AND THE GLOBAL CAMPAIGN FOR MIGRANT WORKERS' RIGHTS

1. Nicholas McGeehan, "Let Qatar 2022 not be Built on Brutality," *The Guardian*, December 6, 2010, www.theguardian.com/commentisfree/libertycentral/2010/dec/06/qatar-world-cup-human-rights.

2. Luana Gama Gato and Noel B. Salazar, "Constructing a City, Building A Life: Brazilian Construction Workers' Continuous Mobility as a Permanent Life Strategy," *Mobilities*, 13, no. 5 (2018): 733–45; Nick Bell, Colin Powell, and Peter Sykes, "Securing the Well-Being and Engagement of Construction Workers: An Initial Appraisal of the Evidence," in *Association of Researchers in Construction Management: Thirty-First Annual Conference 2015 September 7–9*, eds. Ani Raidén and Emmanuel Aboagye-Nimo (UK: Association of Researchers in Construction Management, 2015), 489–98.

3. Bell, Powell, and Sykes, "Securing the Well-Being and Engagement of Construction Workers," 490.

4. Yasmin Al Heialy, "Qatar's World Cup Stadiums to Cost $10 Billion, Official Says," *ArabianBusiness*, March 22, 2016, www.arabianbusiness.com/qatar-s-world-cup-stadiums-cost-10bn-official-says-632410.html.

5. Steven Humphrey, "Qatar Prepares for the 2022 World Cup," Oxford Business Group, 2015, https://oxfordbusinessgroup.com/analysis/qatar-prepares-2022-world-cup.

6. For a selection of some of this literature see: Andrew M. Gardner, "Engulfed: Indian Guest Workers, Bahraini Citizens, and the Structural Violence of the *Kafala* System," in *The Deportation Regime: Sovereignty, Space, and the Freedom of Movement*, eds. Nicholas De Genova and Nathalie Peutz (Durham, NC: Duke University Press, 2010), 196–223; Ray Jureidini, "Arab Gulf States: Recruitment of Asian Workers," *GLMM Explanatory Note* no. 3 (Gulf Labour Markets and Migration, 2014), https://cadmus.eui.eu/bitstream/handle/1814/32149/GLMM%20ExpNote_03–2014.pdf?sequence=1&isAllowed=y; Mehran Kamrava and Zahra Babar, eds. *Migrant Labor in the Persian Gulf* (London: Hurst, 2012); Abdulhadi Khalaf, Omar AlShehabi, and

Adam Hanieh, eds. *Transit States: Labour, Migration and Citizenship in the Gulf* (London: Pluto Press, 2015); Human Rights Watch, "*Building a Better World Cup: Protection Migrant Workers in Qatar Ahead of FIFA 2022,*" 2012, www.hrw.org/report/2012/06/12/building-better-world-cup/protecting-migrant-workers-qatar-ahead-fifa-2022.

7. See a collection of articles in David B. Roberts, guest ed., "The GCC Crisis: Qatar and its Neighbors," CIRS Special Issue of *Journal of Arabian Studies* 10, no. 2 (December 2020).

8. Gardner et al., "A Portrait of Low-Income Migrants in Contemporary Qatar," 15.

9. Abby Meaders Henderson, "Mega Sporting Events Procedures and Human Rights: Developing an Inclusive Framework," *American Indian Law Review* 41, no. 2 (2017): 374.

10. Simon Romero, "Soccer and Internal Discord, on Display for the World to See," *The New York Times*, June 12, 2014, www.nytimes.com/2014/06/13/world/americas/hundreds-of-brazilians-protest-outside-world-cup-stadiumin-sao-paulo.html; Sukari Ivester, "Culture, Resistance and Policies of Exclusion at World Cup 2014: The Case of the 'Baianas do Acarajé,'" *Journal of Policy Research in Tourism, Leisure and Events* 7, no. 3 (2015): 314–24; César Jiménez-Martínez, *Media and the Image of the Nation during Brazil's 2013 Protests* (London: Palgrave Macmillan 2020).

11. Kendall Baker, "The Secret Plan to Sabotage the 2022 World Cup," *Axios*, February 5, 2019, www.axios.com/qatar-world-cup-2022-saudi-arabia-sabotage-0511c195–6d81-4452-a168-09229a6f1790.html; Tom Pollitt, "Football's Proxy War: The Saudi Assault on Qatar 2022," *Inside Arabia*, October 9, 2020, www.insidearabia.com/footballs-proxy-war-the-saudi-assault-on-qatar-2022.

12. The *kafala* is the employer-sponsorship system that has been widely used across the six Gulf monarchies to manage temporary labor migration. This system provides foreign workers with residency visas along with fixed-term job contracts that bind them to particular employers. Migrant workers' right to residence exists as long as they are working for their *kafil*, who is both their employer as well as their visa sponsor.

13. See, for example, Robert Booth and Pete Pattisson, "Qatar World Cup Stadium Workers Earn as Little as 45p an Hour," *The Guardian*, July 29, 2014, www.theguardian.com/global-development/2014/jul/29/qatar-world-cup-stadium-workers-earn-45p-hour; Owen Gibson and Robert Booth, "World Cup 2022: Football Cannot Ignore Qatar Worker Deaths, says Sepp Blatter," *The Guardian*, October 4, 2013, www.theguardian.com/football/2013/oct/04/world-cup-2022-fifa-sepp-blatter-qatar-worker-deaths; Owen Gibson, "World Cup Sponsors should Pressurise Qatar 2022 Over Workers, Says MP," *The Guardian*, May 18, 2015, www.theguardian.com/football/2015/may/18/fifa-tory-mp-damian-collins-world-cup-qatar; and "Footballers Slam Qatar 2022 Labor Conditions," *Construction Weekly*, May 18, 2016, www.constructionweekonline.com/article-39095-footballers-slam-qatar-2022-labour-conditions.

14. Under a directive from the emir in 2015, Qatar's Government Communications office was established; the state entity is mandated to ensure that a centralized mes-

sage is issued during any crisis, and also that communication between different ministries in maintained is at least one outcome of the media campaign against Qatar.

15. Mehran Kamrava, *Qatar: Small State, Big Politics* (Ithaca, NY: Cornell University Press, 2013).

16. Qatar's Supreme Committee for Delivery & Legacy (SC) was established in 2011 and bears the overall responsibility for planning and operations associated with the 2022 World Cup.

17. Gardner et al., "A Portrait of Low-Income Migrants in Contemporary Qatar."

18. See, for example, E. J. A. M. Spaan, "Socio-Economic Conditions of Sri Lankan Migrant Workers in the Gulf States," in *Labour Migration to the Middle East: From Sri Lanka to the Gulf*, eds. F. Eelens, T. Schampers and Johan Dirk Speckmann (London: Kegan Paul International, 1992), 87–106; Anh Nga Longva, *Walls Built on Sand: Migration, Exclusion, and Society in Kuwait* (London and New York: Routledge, 1997); Anh Nga Longva, "Keeping Migrant Workers in Check: The *Kafala* System in the Gulf," *Middle East Report* no. 211 (1999): 20–2; Michelle Ruth Gamburd, *The Kitchen Spoon's Handle: Transnationalism and Sri Lanka's Migrant Housemaids* (Ithaca, NY, Cornell: 2000); Andrej Kapiszewski, *Nationals and Expatriates: Population and Labour Dilemmas of the Gulf Cooperation Council States* (Reading, Ithaca Press: 2001); Human Rights Watch, "Dubai: Migrant Workers at Risk," September 18, 2003, www.hrw. org/news/2003/09/18/dubai-migrant-workers-risk; Human Rights Watch, "Building Towers, Cheating Workers: Exploitation of Migrant Construction Workers in the United Arab Emirates," November 11, 2006, www.hrw.org/report/ 2006/11/11/building-towers-cheating-workers/exploitation-migrant-construction-workers-united; Human Rights Watch, "'The Island of Happiness:'" Exploitation of Migrant Workers on Saadiyat Island, Abu Dhabi," May 19, 2009, www.hrw.org/ report/2009/05/19/island-happiness/exploitation-migrant-workers-saadiyat-island-abu-dhabi.

19. Gardner, "Engulfed."

20. Zahra Babar and Andrew Gardner, "Circular Migration and the Gulf States," in *Impact of Circular Migration on Human, Political and Civil Rights: A Global Perspective*, eds. Carlota Solé, Sonia Parella, Teresa Sordé Martí, and Sonja Nita (Switzerland: Springer International Publishing, 2016), 51.

21. Mehran Kamrava, "State-Business Relations and Clientelism in Qatar," *Journal of Arabian Studies* 7, no. 1 (April 2017): 9–10.

22. Mohammed Dito, "Kafala: Foundations of Migrant Exclusion in GCC Labour Markets," in *Transit States: Labour, Migration and Citizenship in the Gulf*, eds. Abdulhadi Khalaf, Omar AlShehabi, and Adam Hanieh (London: Pluto Press, 2015), 79.

23. See, for example, Andrew Gardner, *City of Strangers: Gulf Migration and the Indian Community in Bahrain* (Ithaca, NY: Cornell University Press, 2010); Khalaf, AlShehabi, and Hanieh, *Transit States*; Kamrava and Babar, ed. *Migrant Labour in the Persian Gulf*; Zahra Babar, "Labor Migration in the Persian Gulf," in *Routledge Handbook of Persian Gulf Politics*, ed. Mehran Kamrava (London: Routledge, 2020), 216–31.

24. Susan F. Martin, "Protecting Migrants' Rights in the Gulf Cooperation Council," in

Migrant Labor in the Persian Gulf, eds. Mehran Kamrava and Zahra Babar (London: Hurst, 2012), 217–31.

25. International Labour Organization, "NATLEX Database of National Labour, Social Security and Related Human Rights Legislation," 2015, www.ilo.org/dyn/natlex/natlex4.detail?p_lang=en&p_isn=102231.

26. David Mednicoff, "The Legal Regulation of Migrant Workers, Politics and Identity in Qatar and the UAE," in *Migrant Labor in the Persian Gulf*, eds. Mehran Kamrava and Zahra Babar (London: Hurst, 2012), 206–8.

27. For further details on relevant legal amendments and ministerial decrees in Qatar between 2005 and 2021, see ILO, "NATLEX Database."

28. Gardner et al., "A Portrait of Low-Income Migrants in Contemporary Qatar," 6–7.

29. Gardner et al., "A Portrait of Low-Income Migrants in Contemporary Qatar," 9–10.

30. National Human Rights Committee, "Report of the National Human Rights Committee (NHRC) Regarding the Status of Human Rights in the State of Qatar and the Committee's Activities 2014," www.nhrc-qa.org/wp-content/uploads/2014/01/NHRC_Annual_Report_20141.pdf; Faras Ghani, "How Wage Abuse is Hurting Qatar's Migrant Workers," Al Jazeera, August 26, 2020, www.aljazeera.com/features/2020/8/26/how-wage-abuse-is-hurting-qatars-migrant-workers; Amnesty International, "Qatar: Despite Reform Promises, Migrant Workers Still Return Home Without Wages or Justice," September 19, 2019, www.amnesty.org/en/latest/news/2019/09/qatar-despite-reform-promises-migrant-workers-still-return-home-without-wages-or-justice.

31. Gardner et al., "A Portrait of Low-Income Migrants in Contemporary Qatar," 6–7; Ray Jureidini, "Migrant Labour Recruitment to Qatar," Report for Qatar Foundation Migrant Worker Welfare Initiative (Doha: Bloomsbury Qatar Foundation Publishing, 2014), 87–8.

32. Government of Qatar, Government Communications Office, "Labour Reform," 2021, www.gco.gov.qa/en/focus/labour-reform.

33. International Labour Organization, "Assessment of the Wage Protection System in Qatar," ILO Project Office for the State of Qatar, June 2019, www.ilo.org/wcmsp5/groups/public-arabstates-ro-beirut/documents/publication/wcms_726174.pdf; As a concrete example of the Wage Protection Unit's effectiveness, in January 2020, the WPS Unit reflagged 588 companies for wage violations and for disciplinary action. By June 2020, when COVID-19 restrictions took hold, the WPS Unit found 8,756 companies were in violation of the WPS, an immediate and visible sign of the impact that the virus had on economic conditions in the country.

34. Supreme Committee for Delivery and Legacy, "Workers Welfare Standards, Edition 2," 2016, www.qatar2022.qa/sites/default/files/docs/Workers%27-Welfare-Standards.pdf.

35. "Qatar World Cup: Workers Set to Receive Over $30 Million in Reimbursement," *GOAL*, March 12, 2020, www.goal.com/en/news/qatar-world-cup-workers-welfare-report/1eflit6qt4iv21ap2gb6bj9oew.

36. Human Rights Watch, "Qatar: New Reforms Won't Protect Migrant Workers,"

November 8, 2015, www.hrw.org/news/2015/11/08/qatar-new-reforms-wont-protect-migrant-workers; Amnesty International, "Qatar: Migrant Workers Still at Risk of Abuse Despite Reforms," December 12, 2016, www.amnesty.org/en/latest/news/2016/12/qatar-migrant-workers-still-at-risk-of-abuse-despite-reforms.

37. Amnesty International, "Qatar: Migrant Workers Still at Risk of Abuse Despite Reforms."

38. Amnesty International, "Qatar: Migrant Workers Still at Risk of Abuse Despite Reforms."

39. Human Rights Watch, "Qatar: New Reforms Won't Protect Migrant Workers;" Amnesty International, "Qatar: Migrant Workers Still at Risk of Abuse Despite Reforms."

40. Kaltham Al-Ghanim, "Kafala System Remains Resilient in the GCC," *Gulf Affairs* (Oxford Gulf and Arabian Peninsula Studies Forum, OxGAPS, September 26, 2015), www.oxgaps.org/files/analysis_al-ghanim.pdf; and Abdoulaye Diop, Mark Tessler, Kien Trung Le, Darwish Al-Emadi, and David Howell, "Attitudes Towards Migrant Workers in the GCC: Evidence from Qatar," *Journal of Arabian Studies* 2, no. 2 (2012):173–87.

41. "Qatar Law No. 15 of 22 August 2017 which Relates to Domestic Workers," International Labour Organization, www.ilo.org/dyn/natlex/docs/MONOGRAPH/105099/128416/F-1438071320/QAT105099 Eng.pdf.

42. International Labour Organization, "Technical Cooperation Programme Between the ILO and Qatar," 2021, www.ilo.org/beirut/projects/WCMS_620621/lang—en/index.htm.

43. Government of Qatar, Government Communications Office, "Labour Reform," 2021, www.gco.gov.qa/en/focus/labour-reform.

44. Justin Gengler, "Society and State in Post-Blockade Qatar: Lessons for the Arab Gulf Region," in David B. Roberts, guest ed., "The GCC Crisis: Qatar and its Neighbors," CIRS Special Issue of *Journal of Arabian Studies* 10, no. 2 (December 2020): 238–55; Jocelyn Sage Mitchell, "The Domestic Policy Opportunities of an International Blockade," in *The Gulf Crisis: The View from Qatar*, ed. Rory Miller (Doha, Qatar: HBKU Press, 2018): 58–68.

45. Mitchell, "The Domestic Policy Opportunities of an International Blockade," 61–63.

46. Saba Aziz, "Qatar 'Stronger, United' One Year after Blockade," *Al Jazeera*, June 4, 2018, www.aljazeera.com/news/2018/6/4/qatar-stronger-united-one-year-after-blockade.

47. Gengler, "Society and State in Post-Blockade Qatar."

48. The International Labour Organization provides translations of both decrees on its website: "ILO Project Office for the State of Qatar," 2021, www.ilo.org/beirut/projects/qatar-office/lang—en/index.htm.

49. "Qatar's Landmark Minimum Wage Comes into Force," *Al Jazeera*, March 19, 2021, www.aljazeera.com/news/2021/3/19/qatars-enforces-new-minimum-wage-legislation.

50. Peter Pattisson, "New Employment Law Effectively Ends Qatar's Exploitative Kafala System," *The Guardian*, September 1, 2020, www.theguardian.com/global-devel-

opment/2020/sep/01/new-employment-law-effectively-ends-qatars-exploitative-kafala-system; Amnesty International, "Qatar: New Laws to Protect Migrant Workers are a Step in the Right Direction," August 30, 2020, www.amnesty.org/en/latest/news/2020/08/qatar-annoucement-kafala-reforms; Human Rights Watch, "Qatar: Significant Labor and Kafala Reforms," September 24, 2020, www.hrw.org/news/2020/09/24/qatar-significant-labor-and-kafala-reforms.

51. Al Jazeera, "Qatar's Landmark Minimum Wage Comes into Force."

52. Abbie Taylor, Nada Soudy, and Susan Martin, "The Egyptian 'Invasion' of Kuwait: Navigating Possibilities among the Impossible," in *Arab Migrant Communities in the GCC*, ed. Zahra Babar (Oxford University Press/Hurst, 2017), 85–110; Noora Lori, *Offshore Citizens: Permanent Temporary Status in the Gulf* (Cambridge: Cambridge University Press, 2019).

53. Zahra R. Babar, "The Vagaries of the In-Between: Labor Citizenship in the Persian Gulf," *International Journal of Middle East Studies* 52, no. 4 (2020): 765–70.

54. Thomas Faist, "Cross-Border Migration and Social Inequalities," *Annual Review of Sociology* 42 (2016): 332.

55. Martin Ruhs, *The Price of Rights: Regulating International Labor Migration* (Princeton, NJ: Princeton University Press: 2013), 91–121 and 122–43.

56. Daniel A. Bell and Nicola Piper, "Justice for Migrant Workers? The Case of Foreign Domestic Workers in Hong Kong and Singapore," in *Multiculturalism in Asia*, eds. Will Kymlicka and Baogang He (Oxford: Oxford University Press, 2005), 209.

57. Martin Ruhs and Philip Martin, "Numbers vs. Rights: Trade-Offs and Guest Worker Programs," *The International Migration Review* 42, no. 1 (2008): 257–8.

58. Statista, "Number of Work Permits Granted in Sweden in 2020, by Citizenship," January 1, 2021, www.statista.com/statistics/1143215/number-of-work-permits-granted-in-sweden-by-citizenship; Priya D'Souza Communications, "Population of Qatar by Nationality—2019 Report," August 15, 2019, https://priyadsouza.com/population-of-qatar-by-nationality-in-2017.

59. S. Irudaya Rajan and Ginu Zacharia Oommen, "Asianization in the Gulf: A Fresh Look," in *Asianization of Migrant Workers in the Gulf Countries*, eds. S. Irudaya Rajan and Ginu Zacharia Oommen (Singapore, Springer: 2020), 6–8.

60. Elizabeth Heger Boyle et al., "Making Human Rights Campaigns Effective, While Limiting Unintended Consequences: Lessons from Recent Research," *USAID Research and Innovation Grants Working Paper*, September 2017, 1–3.

61. Elizabeth Heger Boyle et al., "Making Human Rights Campaigns Effective," 15–21.

62. Boyle et al., "Making Human Rights Campaigns Effective," 15–21.

63. Peter Millward, "World Cup 2022 and Qatar's Construction Projects: Relational Power in Networks and Relational Responsibilities to Migrant Workers," *Current Sociology* 65, no. 5 (2017): 756–76.

64. Mauricio Rombaldi, "The 2014 World Cup and the Construction Workers: Global Strategies, Local Mobilizations," *Latin American Perspectives* 46, no. 4 (2019): 53–65.

65. Rombaldi, "The 2014 World Cup and the Construction Workers," 57

66. Rombaldi, "The 2014 World Cup and the Construction Workers," 61.

67. Elizabeth Heger Boyle et al., "Making Human Rights Campaigns Effective," 27–8.

68. Joseph Yaw Asomah, "Cultural Rights Versus Human Rights: A Critical Analysis of the *Trokosi* Practice in Ghana and the Role of Civil Society," *African Human Rights Law Journal* 15 (2015): 142; Erica Chenoweth et al., "Struggles from Below: Literature Review on Human Rights Struggles by Domestic Actors," *USAID Research and Innovation Grants Working Papers* (2017): 23–9.

69. Asomah, "Cultural Rights Versus Human Rights," 147–8.

70. Freedom House, "Advocacy in Restricted Spaces: A Toolkit for Civil Society Organisations," 2020, https://freedomhouse.org/sites/default/files/2020-06/FINAL_COMPLETE_Lifeline_Toolkit_for_CSO_Advocacy_in_Restrictive%20Spaces_June_2020.pdf.

71. Freedom House, "Advocacy in Restricted Spaces."

72. Jamie J. Gruffydd-Jones, "Citizens and Condemnation: Strategic Uses of International Human Rights Pressure in Authoritarian States," *Comparative Political Studies* 52, no. 4 (2019): 579–612.

73. John Chalcraft, "Migration and Popular Protest in the Arabian Peninsula and the Gulf in the 1950s and 1960s," *International Labour and Working Class History* 79, no. 1 (2011): 28–47.

74. Chalcraft, "Migration and Popular Protest in the Arabian Peninsula and the Gulf in the 1950s and 1960s," 42.

75. Babar, The Vagaries of the In-Between," 766–8.

76. Rohan Advani, "A Realm Without Rights: Noncitizen Workers and Exclusive Citizenship in the Gulf," The Century Foundation, 2019, https://tcf.org/content/report/a-realm-without-rights/?agreed=1.

77. The International Trade Union Confederation (ITUC), "Kuwait and Bahrain Unions become first in the Gulf to Forget an Official Trade Union Relationship with Nepal," January 16, 2012, www.ituc-csi.org/kuwait-and-bahrain-unions-become.

78. Alex Boodrookas, "Crackdowns and Coalitions in Kuwait," Middle East Research and Information Project, January 18, 2018, https://merip.org/2018/06/crackdowns-and-coalitions-in-kuwait.

79. Pete Pattisson et al., "Revealed: 6,500 Migrant Workers Died in Qatar since World Cup Awarded," *The Guardian*, February 23, 2021, www.theguardian.com/global-development/2021/feb/23/revealed-migrant-worker-deaths-qatar-fifa-world-cup-2022.

80. Andreas Krieg (@andreas_krieg), Twitter, March 14, 2021, https://mobile.twitter.com/andreas_krieg/status/1371020257423396864.

81. Elizabeth Heger Boyle et al., "Making Human Rights Campaigns Effective," 19–21.

82. Danya Al-Saleh and Neha Vora, "Contestations of Imperial Citizenship: Student Protest and Organizing in Qatar's Education City," *International Journal of Middle East Studies* 52, no. 4 (2020): 726–32.

83. Human Rights Watch, "Israel/Palestine," 2021, www.hrw.org/middle-east/north-africa/israel/palestine.

10. GCC FOOTBALL FANS AND THEIR ENGAGEMENT: ESTABLISHING A
    RESEARCH AGENDA

1. James Montague, *When Friday Comes: Football in the War Zone* (Edinburgh: Mainstream Publishing, 2008).

2. Ed West, "Qatar Doesn't Deserve to Host the World Cup but Turkey Does," *The Spectator*, June 1, 2015, www.spectator.co.uk/article/qatar-doesn-t-deserve-to-host-the-2022-world-cup-but-turkey-does.

3. Simon Chadwick and Paul Widdop, "Saudi Arabia's Growing Sporting Influence," Asia and the Pacific Policy Forum, November 20, 2018, www.policyforum.net/saudi-arabias-growing-sporting-influence.

4. Richard Fitzpatrick, "Anger at Spanish Super Cup Held a Long Way from Home in Saudi Arabia," *Bleacher Report*, January 10, 2020, https://bleacherreport.com/articles/2870649-anger-at-spanish-super-cup-held-a-long-way-from-home-in-saudi-arabia.

5. Nielsen Sports, "World Football Report 2018," October 2018, https://nielsensports.com/wp-content/uploads/2014/12/Nielsen_World-Football-2018–6.11.18.pdf.

6. Amir Ben-Porat, "Cui Bono? Arabs, Football and State," *Soccer & Society* 17, no. 4 (2016): 496–511.

7. Dag Tuastad, "From Football Riot to Revolution: The Political Role of Football in the Arab World," *Soccer & Society* 15, no. 3 (2014): 376–88.

8. *Middle East Eye*, "What is the GCC?," April 8, 2014, www.middleeasteye.net/news/profile-what-gcc-18030284.

9. Gulf Labour Markets and Migration (GLMM), "GCC Total Population and Percentage of Nationals and Non-Nationals in GCC Countries," Demographic and Economic Database, January 2020, https://gulfmigration.org/gcc-total-population-and-percentage-of-nationals-and-non-nationals-in-gcc-countries-national-statistics-2017-2018-with-numbers.

10. Adam Hanieh, "Capital, Labor, and State: Rethinking the Political Economy of Oil in the Gulf," in *The Oxford Handbook of Contemporary Middle-Eastern and North African History*, eds. Amal Ghazan and Jens Hanssen (Oxford: Oxford University Press, 2015).

11. Burak Gurkan, "The Arabian Gulf League And It's Lack Of Attendance," *The Sports Journal*, October 13, 2017, www.sportsjournal.ae/arabian-gulf-league-lack-attendance.

12. Ali Khaled, "Manchester City's Loyal Middle East Fanbase Awaiting More Cup Success on Sunday," *Arab News*, February 27, 2020, www.arabnews.com/node/1634161/sport.

13. Josoor Institute and Deloitte, "Middle East Football Fan Engagement," January 2017, www.josoorinstitute.qa/content/middle-east-football-fan-engagement.

14. Nicholas D. Theodorakis et al., "Attitudes and Consumption Behaviors of Football Fans in the Middle East," *Journal of Sport Behavior* 42, no. 2 (2019): 225–50.

15. Mohammed Binjwaied, Ian Richards, and Lisa-Ann O'Keeffe, "The Factors

Influencing Fans' Attendance at Football Matches in the Kingdom of Saudi Arabia," *Athens Journal of Sports* 2, no. 2 (2015): 111–22.

16. Saeb Farhan Al Ganideh and Linda K. Good, "Cheering for Spanish Clubs: Team Identification and Fandom of Foreign Soccer Clubs (the Case of Arab Fans)," *International Journal of Sport Psychology* 46, no. 4 (2015): 348–68; Saeb Farhan Al Ganideh and Linda K. Good, "The Magic of Soccer: Transforming Animosity into Love (An Empirical Study of Arab Fans and Major European Soccer Leagues)," *International Journal of Sport and Exercise Psychology* 14, no. 2 (2016): 110–125.

17. Sebastian Uhrich, "Exploring Customer-To-Customer Value Co-Creation Platforms and Practices in Team Sports," *European Sport Management Quarterly* 14, no. 1 (2014): 25–49.

18. James M. Gladden and Daniel C. Funk, "Understanding Brand Loyalty in Professional Sport: Examining the Link Between Brand Associations and Brand Loyalty," *International Journal of Sports Marketing & Sponsorship* 3, no. 1 (2001): 67–95.

19. Seong-Hee Park, Daniel Mahony, and Yu Kyoum Kim, "The Role of Sport Fan Curiosity: A New Conceptual Approach to the Understanding of Sport Fan Behavior," *Journal of Sport Management* 25, no. 1 (2011): 46–56.

20. Nicholas Abercrombie and B. J. Longhurst, "Fans and Enthusiasts," in *The Fan Fiction Studies Reader*, eds. Karen Hellekson and Kristina Busse (Iowa City, IA: University of Iowa Press, 2014), 159–76.

21. Bernard Cova, Robert V. Kozinets, and Avi Shankar, eds., *Consumer Tribes* (Oxford: Butterworth-Heinemann, 2007).

22. Galen T. Trail and Jeffrey D. James, "The Motivation Scale for Sport Consumption: Assessment of the Scale's Psychometric Properties," *Journal of Sport Behavior* 24, no. 1 (2001): 108–127.

23. Stephen Reysen and Nyla R. Branscombe, "Fanship and Fandom: Comparisons Between Sport and Non-Sport Fans," *Journal of Sport Behavior* 33, no. 2 (2010): 176–193.

24. John Fiske, "The Cultural Economy of Fandom," in *The Adoring Audience: Fan Culture and Popular Media*, ed. Lisa A. Lewis (London: Routledge, 1992), 30–49.

25. Alan Tapp and Jeff Clowes, "From 'Carefree Casuals' to 'Professional Wanderers': Segmentation Possibilities for Football Supporters," *European Journal of Marketing* 36, nos. 11–12 (2002): 1248–69.

26. Khaled, "Manchester City's Loyal Middle East Fanbase."

27. Aaron C. T. Smith and Bob Stewart, "The Travelling Fan: Understanding the Mechanisms of Sport Fan Consumption in a Sport Tourism Setting," *Journal of Sport & Tourism* 12, nos. 3–4 (2007): 155–81.

28. Tapp and Clowes, "From 'Carefree Casuals' to 'Professional Wanderers.'"

29. Robert B. Cialdini et al., "Basking in Reflected Glory: Three (Football) Field Studies," *Journal of Personality and Social Psychology* 34, no. 3 (1976): 366–75.

30. Harry H. Kwon, Galen T. Trail, and Dean S. Anderson, "Are Multiple Points of Attachment Necessary to Predict Cognitive, Affective, Conative, or Behavioral Loyalty?," *Sport Management Review* 8, no. 3 (2005): 255–70.

31. Michele E. Capella, "Measuring Sports Fans' Involvement: The Fan Behavior Questionnaire," *Southern Business Review* 27, no. 2 (2002): 30–6.

32. Colin Shaw, *The DNA of Customer Experience: How Emotions Drive Value* (Hampshire and New York, NY: Palgrave Macmillan, 2007).

33. Daniel C. Funk and Jeff James, "The Psychological Continuum Model: A Conceptual Framework for Understanding an Individual's Psychological Connection to Sport," *Sport Management Review* 4, no. 2 (2001): 119–50.

34. Robert W. Pimentel and Kristy E. Reynolds, "A Model for Consumer Devotion: Affective Commitment with Proactive Sustaining Behaviors," *Academy of Marketing Science Review* 8, no. 7 (2004): 1–45.

35. Yun-Oh Whang et al., "Falling in Love with a Product: The Structure of a Romantic Consumer-Product Relationship," in *Advances in Consumer Research*, 31, eds. Barbara E. Kahn and Mary Frances Luce (Valdosta, GA: Association for Consumer Research, 2004), 320–7.

36. Albert M. Muniz and Thomas C. O'Guinn, "Brand Community," *Journal of Consumer Research* 27, no. 4 (2001): 412–32.

37. Todd D. Donavan, Brad D. Carlson, and Mickey Zimmerman, "The Influence of Personality Traits on Sports Fan Identification," *Sport Marketing Quarterly* 14, no. 1 (2005): 31–42.

38. Daniel L. Wann et al., "The Norelco Sport Fanatics Survey: Examining Behaviors of Sport Fans," *Psychological Reports* 92, no. 3 (2003): 930–6.

39. Thomas Aichner, "Football Clubs' Social Media Use and User Engagement," *Marketing Intelligence & Planning* 37, no. 3 (2019): 242–57.

40. Stacey Elizabeth Pope, "Female Fandom in an English 'Sports City': A Sociological Study of Female Spectating and Consumption around Sport" (PhD diss., University of Leicester, 2010).

41. Masayuki Yoshida et al., "Conceptualization and Measurement of Fan Engagement: Empirical Evidence from a Professional Sport Context," *Journal of Sport Management* 28, no. 4 (2014): 399–417.

42. Peter C. Verhoef, Werner J. Reinartz, and Manfred Krafft, "Customer Engagement as a New Perspective in Customer Management," *Journal of Service Research* 13, no. 3 (2010): 247–52.

43. Bernd Schmitt, *Experience Marketing: Concepts, Frameworks and Consumer Insights* (Hanover, MA: Now Publishers Inc, 2011), 21.

44. Shih-Hao Wu, Ching-Yi Daphne Tsai, and Chung-Chieh Hung, "Toward Team or Player? How Trust, Vicarious Achievement Motive, and Identification Affect Fan Loyalty," *Journal of Sport Management* 26, no. 2 (2012): 177–91.

45. Frederick W. Stander, "Escapism Motive for Sport Consumption as a Predictor of Meaning in Life," *Journal of Psychology in Africa* 26, no. 2 (2016): 113–18.

46. Kenneth A. Hunt, Terry Bristol, and R. Edward Bashaw, "A Conceptual Approach to Classifying Sports Fans," *Journal of Services Marketing* 13, no. 6 (1999): 439–52.

47. Janet S. Fink, Galen T. Trail, and Dean F. Anderson, "An Examination of Team Identification: Which Motives are Most Salient to its Existence?," *International Sports Journal* 6, no. 2 (2002): 195–207.

48. Galen T. Trail, Janet S. Fink, and Dean F. Anderson, "Sport Spectator Consumption Behavior," *Sport Marketing Quarterly* 12, no. 1 (2003): 8–17.

49. Angela Ware and Gregory S. Kowalski, "Sex Identification and the Love of Sports: BIRGing and CORFing among Sports Fans," *Journal of Sport Behavior* 35, no. 2 (2012): 223–37.

50. Halim Barakat, "The Arab Family and the Challenge of Social Transformation," *Al-Raida Journal* (1987): 6–7.

11. TO SEE AND BE SEEN: FOOTBALL, MEDIA, AND SOCIAL CHANGE IN IRAN

1. James M. Dorsey, *The Turbulent World of Middle East Soccer* (London: C Hurst & Company, 2016); Gabriel Kuhn, *Soccer vs. the State: Tackling Football and Radical Politics* (Oakland: PM Press, 2019); Alon Raab and Issam Khalidi, eds. *Soccer in the Middle East* (London: Routledge, 2016); Teresita Cruz-del Rosario and James M. Dorsey, "Street, Shrine, Square and Soccer Pitch: Comparative Protest Spaces in Asia and the Middle East," *RSIS Working Paper* no. 230 (Singapore: Nanyang Technological University, 2011).

2. Simon Martin, *Football and Fascism: The National Game under Mussolini* (Oxford, UK: Berg, 2004).

3. Emilio Depetris-Chauvin, Ruben Durante, and Filipe Campante, "Building Nations through Shared Experiences: Evidence from African Football," *American Economic Review* 110, no. 5 (2020): 1574.

4. Jonathan Sullivan et al., "China's Football Dream: Sport, Citizenship, Symbolic Power, and Civic Spaces," *Journal of Sport and Social Issues* 43, no. 6 (2019): 498.

5. Thomas B. Stevenson and Abdul Karim Alaug, "Football in Newly United Yemen: Rituals of Equity, Identity, and State Formation," *Journal of Anthropological Research* 56, no. 4 (2000): 461.

6. Eduardo Archetti, "Masculinity and Football: The Formation of National Identity in Argentina," in *Game Without Frontiers: Football, Identity And Modernity*, ed. Richard Giulianotti and John Williams (London and New York: Routledge,1994), 226.

7. Ahmad Ghyasvand and Ahmad Rezazahdeh-herati, "Gerayesh Dokhtaran be Tamashay-e Mosabeghat-e Footbal dar Varzeshgah va Avamel Moaser bar an" [women watching football in stadiums and the factors influencing it], *Masael-e Ejtemae-e Iran*10, no. 2 (2020): 212.

8. Houchang Chehabi, "The Politics of Football in Iran," *Soccer & Society* 7, nos. 2–3 (2006): 246.

9. Ibid.

10. See, for example, Reza Arjmand, *Public Urban Space, Gender and Segregation: Women-Only Urban Parks in Iran* (London and New York: Routledge, 2017); Nazgol Bagheri, "Tehran's Subway: Gender, Mobility, and the Adaptation of the 'Proper' Muslim Woman," *Social & Cultural Geography* 20, no. 3 (2019): 304–22; Nazanin Shahrokhi, "The Mothers' Paradise: Women-Only Parks and the Dynamics of State Power in

the Islamic Republic of Iran," *Journal of Middle East Women's Studies* 10, no. 3 (2014): 87–108.

11. *Shargh Daily*, "Tarikhche Mamnooiat Zanan az Varzeshgah-e Shiroudi ta Azadi" [The history of banning women from stadiums: from Shiroudi to Azadi], August 14, 2017, shorturl.at/qNORT.

12. Nasrin Afzali, "Gaze Reversed: Iranian Women's Campaign to be Football Spectators," in *Women's Sports as Politics in Muslim Contexts*, ed. Homa Hoodfar (London: Women living Under Muslim Laws, 2015), 167.

13. Sima Shakhsari, *Politics of Rightful Killing: Civil Society, Gender, and Sexuality in Weblogistan* (Durham, NC: Duke University Press, 2020), 84.

14. *BBC Persian*, "Mokhalefat-e Mavaje Mazhabi ba Hozoor-e Zanan dar Varzashgahhaye football" [The opposition of religious sources to the presence of women in soccer stadiums], April 26, 2006, www.bbc.com/persian/iran/story/2006/04/060426_ mf_footbal.shtml.

15. In English language discussions of Iran, the terms "hardliner" and "moderate" are often used broadly to refer to conservative and reformist wings of the political spectrum. Within this framework, the "principalist" (*osul-garayan*) fall into the former camp, with views that are in general continuity with the founders of the Islamic Republic. The self-identification as principalist, however, emerged relatively recently around the election of Mahmoud Ahmadinejad. In the lead up to his second presidential campaign and the campaign for the election of the 8th Majles in 2008, a number of different groups officially formed the United Principalist Front (*Jebh-e Motahed-e Osul garayan*).

16. *Deutsche Welle Persian*, "Zanan, Azadi va Osoolgarayee, Mokhalefat-e Shadeed-e Maraje Taghleed ba Hozoor-e Zanand dar Varzeshgaha" [Women, freedom and traditionalists, the strong opposition of the sources of emulation to women's presence in stadiums], April 27, 2006, shorturl.at/hlEKT.

17. Afzali, "Gaze Reversed," 166.

18. Maziar Bahari, *Football, Iranian Style* (Off-Centre Productions, 2001).

19. David Assmann and Ayat Najafi, *Football Under Cover* (Berlin, Germany: Flying Moon Filmproduktion, 2008); Assmann, Corinna, and Silke Gülker, "Football Under Cover in Tehran's Ararat Stadium," in *Stadium Worlds: Football, Space, and the Built Environment*, ed. Sybille Frank and Silke Steet (London and New York: Routledge, 2010), 213–26.

20. The Open Stadiums movement must itself be understood in the context of the contemporary iteration of the women's rights movement in Iran and can be traced to the era of Khatami's presidency (the history of the women's rights in Iran itself has a longer history going back to the Iranian Constitutional Revolution). During the early 2000s, a number of women's rights activities emerged, centering on issue specific campaigns. The One Million Signatures for the Repeal of Discriminatory Laws (sometimes called Change for Equality), Stop Stoning Forever, and burgeoning activism around the stadium issue all emerged in this period. It is important to note that like many other social movements that are described with the singular "movement" as I too have done here, the Iranian women's rights movement in Iran is diverse and

contested, even within a given side of the political spectrum. In addition, while there are specific activists identified with launching a particular campaign, ordinary supporters of women's rights issues may float in and out of a particular campaign.

21. Samantha Lewis, "Death of Blue Girl Shines Light on Women's Rights in Iran," *The Guardian*, September 20, 2019, www.theguardian.com/football/2019/sep/21/death-of-blue-girl-shines-light-on-womens-rights-in-iran.

22. Directly falling under the auspices of the Office of the Supreme Leader, the IRIB director has a broad purview to act and is not accountable to the government. As such, censorship decisions come from within the IRIB organization and are not imposed by external bodies. The imposition of arbitrary and inconsistent censorship and management decisions have long been a subject of criticism inside Iran across the spectrum of political allegiances. The absurd nature of some of these censorship decisions have also triggered ridicule within and outside Iran. One football related incident in 2018 captures this particularly well. In its live coverage of UEFA Champions League match between AS Roma and FC Barcelona, the broadcaster decided to blur AS Roma's logo of a wolf suckling her twins. For more on this incident and the criticism the IRIB incurred from both ends of the political spectrum, see Saeid Jafari, "Iran's TV Censors Draw Ridicule, Protests," *Al Monitor*, April 26, 2018, www.al-monitor.com/pulse/originals/2018/04/iran-irib-state-media-censorship-roma-khuzestan-parliament.html.

23. Chehabi, "The Politics," 246.

24. Rahnama cited in Fatemeh Azizabadi-Farhani, and Reza Dastani, "Vaziyat-e Farhangi-ye Barnamehay-e Varzeshi Shabake Varzeh ba Takeed bar Jahani Shodan" [the cultural situation of the sports programming of the sports channel with an emphasis on becoming global], *Majale Modeeriyat-e Farhangi* no. 28 (2016): 64.

25. Ebrahim Shokrani and Seyyed MehdiAghapour, "Barressi va Tahleel Mohtavay-e Barnamehay-e Varzeshi Simay-e Jomhoori Islami Iran" [Examination and content analysis of Islamic Republic broadcasting sports programming], *Pajoheshaye Modiriyat-e Varzeshi va Oloom-e Harakati* 4, no. 8 (2016): 90.

26. Mina Emami and Mina Mallaei, "Tahleel-e Mohtavaye-e Akhbar Varzeshi: Motaelle Moredi Shabak-e Sevom Sima," *Modiriyat-e Ertebatat dar resanehay-e varzeshi* [Content Analysis of Sports News Content: Case Study of Channel 3. Communication Management in Sports Media 1, no. 3 (2013): 17.

27. Khabaronline, "Pakhshe mosabeghe football az shabake Mostaned montafi shod" [Soccer broadcasting on the documentary channel cancelled], June, 10, 2012, shorturl.at/dwFZ3.

28. Shokrani and Aghapour, "Barressi va Tahleel Mohtavay-e Barnamehay-e Varzeshi Simay-e Jomhoori Islami Iran," 83.

29. The docuseries is available for streaming on DocTV, "Football Irani" [Iranian football], 2020, www.doctv.ir/program/156865.

30. Hamed Nazarveisi, "Rooykarde-Barnamahey-e Varzeshi Shabakehayi Ostani Montakheb Nesbat be Pooshesh Varzesh Banooan" [The approach of sports programming of selected province sports channels to covering women's sports]. *Faslnameh Elmi-Tarveeji Modiriyat-e Ertebatat dar Resanhay-e Varzeshi* (2013): 63–9.

31. Bahman Askari, Hamid Ghasemi, and Sarah Keshkhar, "Motaley-e Mohtavaye-e Barnamehay-e Varzeshi-ye Shabake-ye Varzesh va Javanan (shabake 3)" [content analysis of the sports programming of the sports and youth channel (channel 3)], *Pajhoheshhaye Ertebati* no. 18 (2011):135–51.

32. One recent manifestation of this came from the influential Mashad Friday prayer leader Ahmad Alamolhoda on May 30, 2020, when he called IRIB officials to task for giving airtime to a woman political analyst. Faulting her for "making her voice soft and thin," he asked "must political analysis be given by a young woman with those looks and that sound?" in *Tasnim News Agency*, "Ayatollah Alamolhoda: Nahi az Monker az Seda va Sima Daram: Hatman bayad yek zan-e javan ba on seda va zaher tahleelhay-e siyasi ra eraye dahad [Ayatollah Alamolhoda: I want to issue a warning against wrongdoing, must political analysis be given by a young woman with those looks and that sound?], May 30, 2020, shorturl.at/hFG56.

33. Jere Longman, "International Sports: Quiet Revolution: Iran, Beneath Coat and Scarf Women Discover the Freedom to Play," *New York Times*, May 26, 1998, www.nytimes.com/1998/05/26/sports/international-sports-quiet-revolution-iran-beneath-coat-scarf-women-discover.html.

34. Isobel Coleman, "The Bravery of Iran's Female Athletes," *The Atlantic*, January 21, 2012, www.theatlantic.com/international/archive/2012/01/the-bravery-of-irans-female-athletes/251753.

35. Thomas Erdbrink, "Olympics 2012: FIFA bans Headscarves for Iranian Women's Soccer Team," *Washington Post*, June 6, 2011, www.washingtonpost.com/sports/united/olympics-2012-fifa-bans-headscarves-for-irans-women-soccer-team/2011/06/06/AGzT1JKH_story.html.

36. *Radio Free Europe, Radio Liberty*, "Iran Allows Women Weightlifters to Compete Internationally," November 24, 2017, www.rferl.org/a/iran-sport/28873778.html.

37. *The Guardian*, "Iran's Only Olympic Medalist said She has Quit the Country," January 12, 2020, www.theguardian.com/world/2020/jan/12/irans-only-female-olympic-medallist-says-she-has-quit-country.

38. Hamid Ghasemi, Seyyed Amir-Ahmad Mozzafari, and Ali Mohammad Amirtash, "To'sey-e Varzesh az Tarigh-e Television dar Iran" [The growth of sports via television in Iran] *Pajhoesh dar Oloome varzeshi* (Research in Sports Science) 4, no. 17 (2006): 131–48; Farzad Ghaffouri, Hashem Kouzehchian, Mohammad Ehsani, Hossein Rahman-Seresht, "Motae'le va Bar-ressi Negaresh Motekhasessan Tarbiat Badani be naghshe resaneha-ye Jami (radio, television, va nashriyat) dar Geryaesh mardom be varzesh-e Ghahremani va Hamegani" (a study and investigation of the attitudes of physical education specialists about the role of mass media (radio, television, and print publications) on people's propensity for professional and public sports], no. 16 (2006): 57–78.

39. Azar Gholizadeh and Sepideh Seyyed-Salehi, "Naqsh-e Barnamehay-e Shabake Varzesh dar Erqa Farhang-e Varzeshi Zanan-e Khanedar Mantaghe Panj-e Tehran" [The role of sports channel programming in strengthening the culture of sports among housewives living in area 5 of Tehran), *Modiyaret-e Farhangi* 9, no. 28 (2015): 23–49.

40. Ghyasvand and Rezazahdeh-herati, "Gerayesh Dokhtaran be Tamashay-e Mosabeghat-e Footbal dar Varzeshgah va Avamel Moaser bar an," 205.

41. Afzali, "Gaze Reversed," 166.

42. *BBC Persian*, "Sahar-e Khodayari Keest? Dokhtari Abi ke Posht-e Estadium Azadi Mand" [Who is Sahar Khodayari? The Blue Girl who was left behind the gates of Azadi Stadium], September 14, 2019, www.bbc.com/persian/iran-features-49681697.

43. *Mehr News*, "Ham-e Cheez Darbarey-e Dokhtari ke Khodsoozi Kard/Enteshar-e soot-e pedar-e Sahar Khodayari" [Everything about the girl who set herself on fire/the voice of Sahar Khodayari's father], September 11, 2019, shorturl.at/bmsP6.

44. FC Barcelona, Twitter post, September 11, 2019, https://twitter.com/FCBarcelona/status/1171788631641661441.

45. Jérôme Boateng, Twitter post, September 12, 2019, https://twitter.com/JB17Official/status/1172057726396112896?s=20.

46. United Nations (UN), "Reports of the Special Rapporteur in the Field of Cultural Rights," 74th UN General Assembly, July 30, 2019, https://undocs.org/en/A/74/255.

47. Human Rights Watch, "Iran: Stadium Seating Cap Endangers Women," October 4, 2019, www.hrw.org/news/2019/10/04/iran-stadium-seating-cap-endangers-women.

48. Open Stadiums, Twitter post, October 17, 2019, https://twitter.com/openStadiums/status/1184906237303050240?s=20.

49. Ibid.; Macholand, *Tarikhche Talash-e Zanan Baraye Vorood be Varzeshgah, Bakhsh-e sevom* (History of women's struggle to enter the stadium, part 3), https://macholand.net/stad03. According to its "about us" website, Macholand was created by a group of Iranian activists and researchers as a "platform for anti-sexism activities." For more information, please see https://macholand.net/about.

50. *Aftab News*, "Vazir-e Varzesh: Hozoor-e Banooan dar Varzeshgah-e Azadi Etefaghi Tarikhi Bood va Omidvaram Edame Peyda Bokonad" [Sports minister: Women's presence at the Azadi Stadium was historic and I hope it continues], April 8, 2020, shorturl.at/bvx01.

51. *Aftab* newspaper compiled the front pages of the papers than ran after the game. All of the covers referenced here are available at the following link: *Aftab News*, October 12, 2019, shorturl.at/ptzHT.

52. *Hamshahri*, "Namey-e Jadid-e Fifa: Tamashaye-e League Baray-e Zanan as Khordad-e 1399" [FIFA's new letter: Women to watch league games from June 2020], February 17, 2020, shorturl.at/ezFG6.

53. *Aftab News*, "Parvaneh Salahsouri: Hame Kar Kardeem ta Dokhtaran Baray-e Vorood be Varzeshgah Niyaz be Tagheer-e Chehre Nadashte Bashand" [Parvaneh Salahashouri: We did all we could so that girls wouldn't need to disguise themselves to get into stadiums], February 18, 2020, shorturl.at/puxyS.

12. QATAR'S BEIN SPORTS AND FOOTBALL BROADCASTING IN THE MIDDLE EAST: INTERNATIONAL INFLUENCE AND REGIONAL RANCOR

1. BeIN's origins are in Al Jazeera Sport, which launched in MENA in 2003. Subsidiary BeIN Sports first launched in France in 2012 and became a separate entity the next year when it launched operations in Asia.

2. According to its corporate site, BeIN broadcasts sixty channels on five continents and in forty-three countries, including the world's two most valuable sport markets, the United States and the United Kingdom.

3. The countries served by BeIN MENA are Algeria, Bahrain, Chad, Djibouti, Egypt, Iran, Iraq, Jordan, Kuwait, Lebanon, Libya, Mauritania, Morocco, Oman, Palestine, Qatar, Saudi Arabia, Somalia, South Sudan, Sudan, Tunisia, the United Arab Emirates, and Yemen.

4. An important question, though not the focus of this paper, is why Qatar created BeIN Sports in the first place and why it funds a company that has never been profitable and which industry analysts believe annually loses tens of millions of dollars. The commonly heard explanation for Qatar's investments in international sport and sport broadcasting is that they are an exercise in soft power, an attempt, in Joseph Nye's original formulation, "to attract and co-opt" other states "to want what you want" as an alternative or complement to the exercise of military and economic hard power. See Joseph Nye, "Soft Power and American Foreign Policy," *Political Science Quarterly* 119, no. 2 (2004): 256.

5. According to a BeIN executive interviewed by the author in 2019, BeIN was the largest sports broadcaster in the world at that time, holding $15 billion in rights agreements and spending between $1–3 billion annually to maintain them. The company's Doha facility has nine studios, two of them large enough, at 800 square meters, to allow rights partners the ability to produce their own branded programming. In the MENA region BeIN broadcasts primarily in Arabic, but also in English, French, and Spanish. Yasser Hamdi, interview with the author, October 8, 2019.

6. The $600 million BeIN paid for Super Lig rights instantly made it the twentieth most valuable sports property in the world. See Tim Lloyd, "Digiturk Lands Major Turkish Super Lig Rights Deal," *SportsProMedia*, November 21, 2016, www.sportspromedia. com/news/digiturk_lands_major_turkish_superlig_rights_deal; and Emre Sarigul, "What the $700m BeIN Takeover of Super League Broadcasting Rights Means for Turkish Football," *Turkish Football*, December 22, 2016, https://turkish-football. com/700m-bein-takeover-super-league-broadcasting-rights-means-turkish-football.

7. Qatar sought $1 billion in damages from KSA in a separate investment arbitration case, but the status of that case is unclear with the end of the blockade in January 2021. See Kevin McCullagh, "End of Saudi-Qatar Dispute Raises Hopes for BeIN Rapprochement," *SportBusiness*, January 6, 2021, www.sportbusiness.com/news/ end-of-saudi-qatar-dispute-raises-hopes-for-bein-rapprochement; and Vivian Nereim, "Qatar's BeIN Seeks $1billion from Saudi Arabia Over Piracy," *Bloomberg*, October 1, 2018, www.bloomberg.com/news/articles/2018-10-01/qatar-s-bein-sports-seeks-1-billion-damages-from-saudi-arabia.

8. See Joost Pauwelyn, "Enforcement and Countermeasures in the WTO: Rules are Rules, Toward a More Collective Approach," *American Journal of International Law* 94, no. 2 (2000): 335–47.

9. "Saudi Arabia Permanently Cancels License of Qatar's BeIN Sports," *Reuters*, July 14, 2020. www.reuters.com/article/us-gulf-qatar-saudi-bein/saudi-arabia-permanently-cancels-licence-of-qatars-bein-sports-idUSKCN24F1PB.

10. For a discussion of this topic, see Mahfoud Amara, *Sport, Politics and Society in the Arab World* (New York: Palgrave Macmillan, 2012), 55–71.

11. According to former BeIN employees interviewed for this research, the network was told by the Qatari government in 2015 to become profitable, but there is no way to know what progress BeIN has made toward that goal, if any, and no independent market analysis describes it as anywhere close. In 2016, the company's losses were estimated at €200 million annually. See "Comment Bein Sports Peut Devenir Rentable" [How BeIn sports can become profitable], *BMF Business*, February 7, 2016, www.bfmtv.com/economie/entreprises/culture-loisirs/comment-be-in-sports-peut-devenir-rentable_AN-201607020080.html.

12. See "Qatar National Vision 2030," General Secretariat for Development Planning, July 2008, www.gco.gov.qa/wp-content/uploads/2016/09/GCO-QNV-English.pdf; "Qatar's Position as International Sports Centre Supported by Investment, Partnerships," Oxford Business Group, https://oxfordbusinessgroup.com/overview/full-pelt-infrastructure-investment-and-business-partnerships-are-supporting-country%E2%80%99s-rise-become; and, for greater historical perspective, Mahfoud Amara, "2006 Qatar Asian Games: A 'Modernization' Project from Above?" *Sport in Society* 8, no. 3 (2005): 493–514. In 2016, Saudi Arabia announced its own 2030 national vision plan, which includes transforming its sports sector. While the plan focuses primarily on the domestic sports market, the kingdom has since 2017 attempted to bring many more international sports competitions to the country through its newly created General Sports Authority. See Jonathan Reardon, "Developments in Saudi Sports Following Saudi Vision 2030," Al Tamimi & Co., December 2016-January 2017, hwww.tamimi.com/law-update-articles/developments-in-saudi-sports-following-saudi-vision-2030/; Deema Al-Khudair, "Saudi Arabia's General Sports Authority Reveals Strategy to Support Sports," *Arab News*, July 22, 2019, www.arabnews.com/node/1528916/saudi-arabia.

13. Lorenzo Arrigoni, "Middle East and Africa Market Report, 2020," *SportBusiness*, January 27, 2020, https://media.sportbusiness.com/2020/01/middle-east-and-africa-market-report-2020.

14. No other sport rivals football for viewership in the region, though other popular sports to watch are basketball, motorsports, professional wrestling (of the dramatic variety), tennis, e-sports, and golf. See Dennis, Everette E., Justin D. Martin, and Fouad Hassan, "Media Use in the Middle East, 2018: A Seven-Nation Survey," Northwestern University in Qatar, 2018, www.mideastmedia.org/survey/2018.

15. Arrigoni, "Middle East and Africa Market Report, 2020"; see also "Global Media Report 2019," *SportBusiness*, 2019, www.sportbusiness.com/consulting/sportbusiness-consulting-global-media-report-2019.

16. Martin Ross, "BeIN Sports Retains Champions League Rights in MENA Region in Crucial Renewal," *SportCal*, July 20, 2017, www.sportcal.com/News/Featured News/111962.

17. Arrigoni, "Middle East and North Africa Report, 2020."

18. Internationally, BeIN is the leading broadcaster of South American football, with rights not only in MENA but also in Australia, New Zealand, Turkey, United States, and Canada.

19. Frank Dunne and Alex Taylor, "Rights-Holders Face Large Fee Cuts in MENA as Saudi-Qatar Rancour Grows," *SportBusiness*, July 24, 2020, https://media.sportbusiness.com/2020/07/rights-holders-face-large-fee-cuts-in-mena-as-qatar-saudi-rancour-grows.

20. Robin Jellis, "BeIN Renews Premier League and Snatches Rights from Main Middle-Eastern Rival ADM," *SportBusiness*, November 6, 2015, https://media.sportbusiness.com/2015/11/bein-renews-premier-league-and-snatches-rights-from-main-middle-eastern-rival-adm.

21. Stuart Thompson, "Premier League Stays with BeIN Sports for Entire MENA Region," *DigitalTVEurope*, December 18, 2020, www.digitaltveurope.com/2020/12/18/premier-league-stays-with-bein-sports-for-entire-mena-region.

22. AD Sports first bought EPL rights in 2009, for the 2010–13 seasons, paying a reported $360 million, three times more than the previous fee for the league in the region paid by Showtime Arabia. See Keach Hagey, "ADMC Wins Premier League TV rights," *The National*, July 4, 2009, www.thenationalnews.com/sport/admc-wins-premier-league-tv-rights-1.533128.

23. "J.League Unveils New Media-Rights Deals in Indonesia and MENA," *SportBusiness*, February 25, 2021, www.sportbusiness.com/news/j-league-unveils-new-media-rights-deals-in-indonesia-and-mena.

24. "OSN to Close Last Sports Channels in July Due to Piracy," *SportBusiness*, June 18, 2019, https://media.sportbusiness.com/news/osn-to-close-last-sports-channels-in-july-due-to-piracy.

25. See Gillian Appleton, "The Politics of Sport and Pay TV," *Australian Quarterly* 67, no. 1 (1995): 31–7; Tom Evens and Katrien Lefever, "Watching the Football Game: Broadcasting Rights for the European Digital Television Market," *Journal of Sport and Social Issues* 35, no. 1 (2011): 33–49.

26. See Paul Smith, Tom Evens, and Petros Iosifidis, "The Regulation of Television Sports Broadcasting: A Comparative Analysis," *Media, Culture and Society* 37, no. 5 (2015): 720–36; and Amara, *Sport, Politics and Society in the Arab World*, 55–71.

27. Amara, *Sport, Politics and Society in the Arab World*, 61–2.

28. Amara, *Sport, Politics and Society in the Arab World*, 61–2.

29. Two years later, in 2011, Al Jazeera Sport bought the rights to the 2018 and 2022 World Cups for an undisclosed amount that was thought to be as much as $500 million, nearly twice the previous deal for 2007–14. See "Al-Jazeera's Pre-Emptive Bid 'Too Big to Refuse,'" *SportBusiness*, January 28, 2011, https://media.sportbusiness.com/2011/01/al-jazeeras-pre-emptive-bid-too-big-to-refuse.

30. Amara, *Sport, Politics and Society in the Arab World*, 67.

31. Ian Black, "Jordan Denies Illegal Jamming of Al-Jazeera World Cup TV," *The Guardian*, September 30, 2010, www.theguardian.com/media/2010/sep/30/al-jazeera-world-cup-jordan.

32. See Walaa Hussein, "Egypt-Qatar Relations Sour Over World Cup Broadcast Rights," *Al-Monitor*, October 24, 2013, www.al-monitor.com/iw/originals/2013/10/egypt-qatar-soccer-relations.html?amp.

33. "CAF Hits Egyptian FA with Fine Over Broadcast Dispute," *SportBusiness*, January 5, 2015, https://media.sportbusiness.com/news/caf-hits-egyptian-fa-with-fine-over-broadcast-dispute.

34. "CAF Hits Egyptian FA with Fine Over Broadcast Dispute."

35. Jean-Paul Savart, "No Africa Cup of Nations for Maghreb-based TV Stations," *AIPS Media*, January 13, 2017, www.aipsmedia.com/index.html?page=artdetail&art=20141&2017-Africa-CupNationfootballGabonTV.

36. "BeIN Bows to Pressure by Opening Up World Cup Coverage," *SportBusiness*, June 15, 2018, https://media.sportbusiness.com/news/bein-bows-to-pressure-by-opening-up-world-cup-coverage.

37. Brett Hutchins and David Rowe, *Sport Beyond Television: The Internet, Digital Media and the Rise of Networked Media Sport* (New York: Routledge, 2012).

38. A March 2021 report by market research firm Synamedia/Ampere Analysis estimates that sports piracy costs broadcasters $28.3 billion annually—more than half the value of the 2020 global sports rights market. See "Charting Global Sports Piracy: Understanding Sports Fans and What Drives Their Behaviors," Synamedia, March 2021, www.synamedia.com/whitepapers-reports/charting-global-sports-piracy. Generally, see Michael Mellis, "Internet Piracy of Live Sports Telecasts," *Marquette Sports Law Review* 18, no. 2 (2008): 258–84; Kanchana Kariyawasam and Matthew Tsai, "Copyright and Live Streaming of Sport Broadcasting," *International Review of Law, Computers and Technology* 31, no. 3 (2017): 265–88; and Hutchins and Rowe, *Sport Beyond Television*.

39. Before BeoutQ, piracy was widespread in the Middle East but no more prevalent than anywhere else. In 2017, before the blockade began, digital security firm Irdeto reported that about 20 percent of respondents in a MENA survey admitted to watching pirated live sports, mostly on P2P networks, and a third of respondents claimed not to know that piracy was illegal. In the Gulf states, with their large expat worker populations, there has long been a strong market for illegal decoding boxes and satellite dishes with which to watch international sports. See "Millennials Shaping Video Piracy in the Middle East and North Africa," Irdeto, March 20, 2017, https://irdeto.com/news/irdeto-survey-millennials-shaping-video-piracy-in-the-middle-east-and-north-africa; and Steve Bainbridge, "A Guide to Piracy Protection for Sports Broadcasting Rights in the UAE," *LawinSport*, December 8, 2015, www.lawinsport.com/topics/item/a-guide-to-piracy-protection-for-sports-broadcasting-rights-holders-in-the-uae.

40. Tariq Panja, "For Qatar Network BeIN Sports, Political Feud Spills into Stadiums," *New York Times*, September 11, 2017, www.nytimes.com/2017/09/11/sports/soccer/saudi-arabia-qatar-bein-sports.html.

41. Robin Jellis, "Dan Markham, Executive Director of Sports Content, and Cameron Andrews, Anti-Piracy Counsel," *SportBusiness*, November 2, 2018, https://media. sportbusiness.com/2018/11/dan-markham-executive-director-of-sports-content-and-cameron-andrews-anti-piracy-counsel-bein-media-group.

42. These details are in the report of the World Trade Organization's investigation of Qatar's claim against Saudi Arabia. See "Saudi Arabia—Measures Concerning the Protection of Intellectual Property Rights—Communication from Qatar," World Trade Organization Doc WTD5567/8, October 5, 2020.

43. See Lulwa Shalhoub, "Saudi-Egyptian Sports Alliance to Replace Blocked Qatar BeIN Sports," *Arab News*, June 20, 2017, www.arabnews.com/node/1117646/med; Ibrahim Ouf, "Arab Countries Move to Tackle Qatar Monopoly of Sports' Broadcast," *Arab Weekly*, August 13, 2018, https://thearabweekly.com/arab-countries-move-tackle-qatari-monopoly-sports-broadcast; and "Saudi Arabia to Launch Largest Sports Network," *Morocco World News*, June 18, 2017, www.moroccoworldnews.com/2017/06/220229/saudi-arabia-launch-largest-sports-network.

44. "Qatar's BeIN Sports Network Back on Air in UAE," *Arab News*, July 22, 2017, www.arabnews.com/node/1133316/sports.

45. "Expert Tests Prove Arabsat Not Involved in Illegal Broadcasts of World Cup," *Arab News*, July 16, 2018, www.arabnews.com/node/1339796/media.

46. See Jellis, "Dan Markham"; and "Expert Tests Prove Arabsat Not Involved in Illegal Broadcasts of World Cup," *Arab News*, July 16, 2018, www.arabnews.com/node/1339796/media.

47. One of BeIN's early efforts to combat BeoutQ included placing random audio and video messages in its broadcasts decrying the piracy. These were the "political bulletins" Saudi officials and media complained about, and they forced BeoutQ to monitor and screen the stolen stream of signals.

48. Hamdi, personal interview, 2019.

49. Jellis, "Dan Markham."

50. Hamdi, personal interview, 2019.

51. "FIFA Statement on BeoutQ," FIFA, July 11, 2018, www.fifa.com/worldcup/news/fifa-statement-on-beoutq.

52. "Saudi Welcomes FIFA Move on BeoutQ, Calls for Alternative to BeIN in MENA," *Al Arabiya*, July 12, 2018, https://english.alarabiya.net/en/sports/2018/07/12/Saudi-hails-FIFA-move-on-beoutQ-calls-for-alternative-to-beIN-in-MENA.

53. Tariq Panja, "FIFA and Premier League Document Saudi Link in BeIN Piracy Fight," *New York Times*, September 16, 2019, www.nytimes.com/2019/09/16/sports/fifa-beoutq-premier-league-uefa.html.

54. "BeoutQ Investigation," MarkMonitor, April 2019, https://premierleague-static-files.s3.amazonaws.com/premierleague/document/2019/09/16/2816a9d6–5ea2–4065–822c-7507d436e825/MarkMonitor-beoutQ-Report-April–2019.pdf

55. Alex Taylor, "Arabsat Hits Back at Rights-Holders in BeoutQ Dispute," *SportBusiness*, September 20, 2019, www.sportbusiness.com/news/arabsat-hits-back-at-rights-holders-in-beoutq-dispute.

56. See "What Lies Beneath?" [in Arabic], Al Jazeera Channel, September 22, 2019,

www.youtube.com/watch?v=ljgIcGIXey4; and "Qatar Charges 3 BeIN Sports Staff with Spying for Saudi, Egypt," *Middle East Monitor*, September 24, 2019, www.middleeastmonitor.com/20190924-qatar-charges-3-bein-sports-staff-with-spying-for-saudi-egypt.

57. Jellis, "Dan Markham."

58. Hamdi, personal interview, 2019.

59. The boxes are typically exported or imported to markets without any software on them, so when they go through customs they raise no IP issues even though the boxes have virtually no alternative use and are later sold as devices for accessing content illegally. IP issues arise when distributors and users load software on them. In 2018, Oman and Kuwait banned the import of BeoutQ boxes at Qatar's request. See "BeIN Sports Returns to Du Screens, Oman Takes Action Against BeoutQ," *SportBusiness*, June 5, 2018, https://media.sportbusiness.com/news/bein-sports-returns-to-du-screens-oman-takes-action-against-beoutq.

60. See Andrew McDonald, "MENA Pay TV Impacted by BeIN Dispute," *DigitalTVEurope*, January 21, 2019, www.digitaltveurope.com/2019/01/21/digital-tv-research-mena-pay-tv-impacted-by-bein-dispute.

61. David Hellier, "Qatar Sportscaster Fires Hundreds After Losing Markets to Piracy," *Bloomberg*, June 17, 2019, www.bloomberg.com/news/articles/2019–06–17/sports-broadcaster-bein-cuts-staff-as-piracy-hits-pay-tv-income.

62. Eventually, sports broadcasters around the world joined BeIN in condemning BeoutQ. See, for example, Rebecca Hawkes, "NBC Universal blasts BeoutQ for stealing World Cup feed," *RapidTVNews*, June 19, 2017, www.rapidtvnews.com/2018061952554/nbcuniversal-blasts-beoutq-for-stealing-world-cup-feed.html#axzz6tQ1mN000. Paul Nicholson, "'Your Worst Nightmare.' BeIN's Al-Obaidly Tells 'Sleep-Walking' Rights Owners the TV Bubble Has Burst," *Inside World Football*, December 31, 2020, www.insideworldfootball.com/2019/10/08/worst-nightmare-beins-al-obaidly-tells-sleep-walking-rights-owners-tv-bubble-burst.

63. Formula One, for example, received about $40 million per season from BeIN, but also earned $125 million in annual race hosting fees from Bahrain and the UAE, and another $35 million from sponsor Emirate Airlines. Though Formula One publicly accused BeoutQ of piracy in June 2018, BeIN terminated its contract in February 2019, angry about its failure to make a legal challenge against BeoutQ. Formula One is now held by Saudi majority-owned Middle East Broadcast Center (MBC), the region's largest FTA broadcaster.

64. Tariq Panja, "Mystery Consortium is Said to Offer FIFA $25 Billion for Control of 2 Tournaments," *New York Times*, April 9, 2018, www.nytimes.com/2018/04/09/sports/soccer/fifa-club-world-cup.html.

65. BeIN's decision to punish Serie A harshly, while three years earlier tripling its fee to retain UEFA rights in the region, reflects BeIN's changed approach to BeoutQ over time, but almost certainly also BeIN's fury at Serie A for keeping its contract to play Supercoppa matches in Saudi Arabia. See Anthony Harwood, "Serie A Issued US$500m Threat as BeIN Flexes Muscle Over Saudi Supercoppa Deal," *SportsProMedia*, November 28, 2019, www.sportspromedia.com/news/serie-a-bein-

sports-tv-rights-saudi-arabia-supercoppa-italiana-beoutq; "Adam Nelson, "Serie A Chief Executive Breaks Silence Over BeoutQ, Says League Will Take Legal Action Against Pirate Broadcaster," *SportBusiness*, June 13, 2019, www.sportbusiness.com/ news/italian-super-cups-saudi-future-called-into-question-as-serie-a-takes-stand-against-beoutq.

66. See "BeIN Sports blocks Serie A broadcasts over Saudi dispute," *Besoccer.com*, June 22, 2020, www.besoccer.com/new/bein-sports-block-serie-a-broadcasts-over-saudi-dispute-850316; and Reginald Ajuonuma, "BeIn Strikes Serie A Piracy Compensation Deal to Lift Blackout," *SportBusiness*, June 29, 2020, www.sportbusiness.com/news/bein-strikes-serie-a-piracy-compensation-deal-to-lift-blackout.

67. Martin Ross, "No Bid from BeIN in Serie A's MENA Rights Tender," *SportBusiness*, March 2, 2021, www.sportbusiness.com/news/no-bid-from-bein-in-serie-as-mena-rights-tender.

68. "Lega Serie A Braced for Sizeable Drop in International Rights Value," *SportBusiness*, March 23, 2021, www.sportbusiness.com/news/lega-serie-a-braced-for-sizeable-drop-in-international-rights-value. As of this writing, December 2021, Serie A has no regional rights partner for its games, but rather broadcasts on a YouTube channel.

69. Paul Nicholson, "AFC Re-tenders Saudi Media Rights Sparking BeIN Fury and a Broadcast Power Play," *Inside World Football*, May 9, 2019, www.insideworldfootball.com/2019/05/09/afc-re-tenders-saudi-media-rights-sparking-bein-fury-broadcast-power-play.

70. Martin Ross, "AFC Launches Territory-by-Territory TV Rights Sales in 10 MENA Countries," *SportBusiness*, June 11, 2020, www.sportbusiness.com/news/afc-launches-territory-by-territory-tv-rights-sales-in-10-mena-countries.

71. Jonathan Easton, "Saudi Arabia Reportedly Looking to Snatch Bundesliga Rights from BeIN Sports," *DigitalTVEurope*, June 25, 2020, www.digitaltveurope.com/ 2020/06/25/saudi-arabia-reportedly-looking-to-snatch-bundesliga-rights-from-bein-sports.

72. "AFC Enters into Landmark Agreement with Saudi Sports Company," *AFC Spotlight*, April 5, 2021, www.the-afc.com/news/afcsection/afc-enters-into-landmark-agreement-with-saudi-sports-company.

73. Kevin McCullagh, "AFC Resets Revenue Expectations with FMA as Sales Drag On," *SportBusiness*, April 22, 2021, www.sportbusiness.com/news/afc-resets-revenue-expectations-with-fma-as-sales-drag-on.

74. See World Trade Organization, "TRIPS: Agreement on Trade-Related Aspects of Intellectual Property Rights," Marrakesh Agreement Establishing WTO, Annex 1C, 1869 UNTS 299, 33 ILM 1197, April 15, 1994, www.wto.org/english/docs_e/ legal_e/31bis_trips_01_e.htm. For a succinct scholarly explanation of the TRIPs Agreement, see Daniel J. Gervais, "The TRIPS Agreement: Interpretation and Implementation," *European Intellectual Property Review* 21, no. 3 (1999): 156–62.

75. World Trade Organization, "Request for the Establishment of a Panel by Qatar, Saudi Arabia—Measures Concerning the Protection of Intellectual Property Rights," WTO Doc WT/DS567/3, November 19, 2018.

76. US Trade Representative for the Middle East, background interview with the author, March 1, 2020. The US government's view of the BeoutQ controversy was that it was not a trade dispute at all but rather a political dispute that involved trade-related issues, and therefore that the WTO was not the proper venue for resolving the problem.

77. US Trade Representative, "2020 Special 301 Report," USTR, April 2020, https://ustr.gov/sites/default/files/2020_Special_301_Report.pdf.

78. See "Report on the Protection and Enforcement of Intellectual Property Rights in Third Countries," European Commission, January 8, 2020, https://trade.ec.europa.eu/doclib/docs/2020/january/tradoc_158561.pdf.

79. World Trade Organization, "Request for Consultations by Qatar, Saudi Arabia—Measures Concerning the Protection of Intellectual Property Rights," WTO Doc. WT/DS567/1, October 4, 2018.

80. World Trade Organization, "Request for Establishment of a Panel by Qatar, Saudi Arabia," 2018

81. World Trade Organization, "Article XXI: Security Exceptions. GATT 1994: General Agreement on Tariffs and Trade, April 15, 1994, Marrakesh Agreement Establishing the World Trade Organization," www.wto.org/english/docs_e/legal_e/gatt47_01_e.htm; see also World Trade Organization, "Report of the Panel, Saudi Arabia—Measures Concerning the Protection of Intellectual Property Rights," WTO Doc WT/DS567/R, June 16, 2020; and Tania Voon, "Can International Trade Law Recover? The Security Exception in WTO Law: Entering a New Era," *AJIL Unbound* 113 (February 2019): 45–50. See also Tom Miles, "Saudi Cites National Security to Block WTO Case Brought by Qatar," *Reuters*, December 4, 2018, https://fr.reuters.com/article/uk-saudi-qatar-wto-idUKKBN1O31QQ.

82. Voon, "Can International Trade Law Recover?"

83. World Trade Organization, "Russia—Measures Concerning Traffic in Transit," WTO Doc WT/DS512/R, April 5, 2019.

84. World Trade Organization, "Report of the Panel, Saudi Arabia," 2020

85. The Berne Convention for the Protection of Literary and Artistic Works is the foundation of international copyright law and was first adopted in 1886 by ten countries in Bern, Switzerland. Today 179 states are parties to the convention.

86. World Trade Organization, "Saudi Arabia—Measures Concerning the Protection of Intellectual Property Rights—Communication from Qatar," WTO Doc WTD5567/8, October 5, 2020.

87. See, for example, "WTO Report on Qatar-Saudi Arabia's Case is a 'Full Victory' for the Kingdom: Legal Expert," *Al Arribiya*, July 17, 2020, https://english.alarabiya.net/features/2020/06/17/WTO-report-on-Qatar-Saudi-Arabia-s-case-is-a-full-victory-for-Kingdom-Legal-expert; and "WTO Rules that Saudi Arabia's Actions Against Qatar Justified," *Al Arribiya*, June 16, 2020, https://english.alarabiya.net/News/gulf/2020/06/16/WTO-rules-that-Saudi-Arabia-s-actions-against-Qatar-justified-SPA.

88. "Saudi Arabia Permanently Cancels License of Qatar's BeIN Sports," 2020.

89. Jonathan Easton, "Saudi Arabia's BeIN Ban Indicates that Newcastle Takeover Has

Wider Ramifications on Global Piracy," *DigitalTVEurope*, July 17, 2020, www.dig-italtveurope.com/comment/saudi-arabias-bein-ban-indicates-that-newcastle-take-over-has-wider-ramifications-on-global-piracy.

90. "Saudi Crown Prince 'Called On' UK PM to Intervene in PIF's Newcastle Takeover Bid," *SportBusiness*, April 15, 2021, www.sportbusiness.com/news/saudi-crown-prince-called-on-johnson-to-intervene-in-pifs-newcastle-takeover-bid.

91. Ben Cronin, "Ashley Still Committed to Newcastle's Saudi Takeover Despite High Court Setback," *SportBusiness*, March 5, 2021, www.sportbusiness.com/news/ashley-still-committed-to-newcastles-saudi-takeover-despite-high-court-setback.

92. See, for example, Mohammed Osman Ali, "Qatar-Saudi ties enjoy strong, histor-ical bonds of affection," *The Peninsula*, October 25, 2021.

93. See "BeIN lands Arab Cup Rights in MENA region ahead of kick-off," *SportBusiness*, November 29, 2021. The tournament has been held sporadically since 1963, but 2021 was the first time under the auspices of FIFA. Previously, the tournament had been held by the Union of Arab Football Associations, and last played in Saudi Arabia in 2012.

94. See Aziz Yaakoubi, "Saudi Arabia Allows Broadcast by Qatar-Based BeIN Sports Channel," *Reuters*, January 18, 2021, www.reuters.com/article/saudi-qatar-tv-int-idUSKBN29N1WY; and Ben Cronin, "Saudi Arabia to Lift BeIN Blockade and set-tle BeoutQ Dispute," *SportBusiness*, October 6, 2021, www.sportbusiness.com/news/saudi-arabia-to-lift-bein-blockade-and-settle-beoutq-dispute.

95. See Owen Lloyd, "Increased Saudi-Qatari Relations Pivotal to the PIF Takeover of Newcastle United," *Inside the Games*, October 8, 2021, www.insidethegames.biz/articles/1113968/saudi-qatari-newcastle-pif-takeover; and "Saudi-led Consortium Completes Newcastle United Takover," *SportBusiness*, October 8, 2021, www.sportbusiness.com/news/saudi-led-consortium-completes-newcastle-united-takeover.

96. In April 2020, in response to the loss of live sports caused by COVID-19, BeIN launched two additional subscriber video-on-demand services, one of them an on-demand archive of sports programming that includes old World Cup, EPL, and UEFA Champions Leagues matches, and its own documentaries. Like sports broad-casters everywhere during the pandemic, BeIN had to fill time—and attract view-ers—with non-live sports content, a trend that is expected to continue. Having laid off so many staff, however, the company may not be well positioned to do that: its news department has been decimated by cuts, and it does few if any sports fea-tures or documentaries.

97. Rebecca Hawkes, "Fluctuating Fortunes," *DigitalTVEurope*, November 27, 2018, www.digitaltveurope.com/longread/fluctuating-fortunes. A mystery of BeIN foot-ball broadcasts noticeable to any viewer is the scarcity of advertising, ordinarily a major revenue source.

98. "How BeIN Sports Can Become Profitable," 2016.

99. "Global Media Report 2020."

100. "Welcome to the 3rd Age of Sport: A Manifesto," Mailman/Seven League, October 14, 2020, www.3rdageofsport.com; and Ben Cronin, "83 Percent of Sports

Executives Believe Media Rights Have Peaked," *SportBusiness*, October 14, 2020, www.sportbusiness.com/news/83-per-cent-of-sports-executives-believe-media-rights-have-peaked.

101. See, for example, Adam Nelson, "Simon Green, BT Sport: Closed-Door Matches "Not the Product We Paid For," *SportBusiness*, August 12, 2020, www.sportbusiness.com/2020/08/simon-green-bt-sport-closed-door-matches-not-the-product-we-paid-for; Reginald Ajuonuma, "Rebates, renegotiations and non-live content: The year in sports media," *SportBusiness*, December 17, 2020, www.sportbusiness.com/2020/12/rebates-renegotiations-and-non-live-content-the-year-in-sports-media; and Alex Taylor, "LaLiga Agrees Broadcaster Rebates of Around €100m After Covid-19 Hit Season," *SportBusiness*, November 10, 2020, www.sportbusiness.com/news/laliga-agrees-broadcaster-rebates-of-around-e100m-after-covid-19-hit-season.

102. Steven Impey, "Covid-19 Now Set to Cost European's Soccer Elite €5bn, says ECA," *SportsProMedia*, November 5, 2020, www.sportspromedia.com/news/european-club-soccer-eca-coronavirus-2020-21-revenues-losses-study. The ECA is now led by Qatari Nasser al-Khelaifi, the chairman of both BeIN Media Group and Qatar Sport Investments, and owner of Paris Saint-Germain in France's Ligue 1.

103. Martin Ross, "UEFA Revenues Drop to €3bn as Fewer Matches, Rebates Take Effect," *SportBusiness*, April 20, 2021, www.sportbusiness.com/news/uefa-revenues-drop-to-e3bn-as-fewer-matches-rebates-take-effect.

104. "Global Media Report 2020."

105. Among the shortcomings of the short-lived European Super League was that it was neither very European nor very super, as it included no French or German clubs. Even more amazingly, the league was announced without a single broadcast partner. Instead, several companies, among them BT Sport, Sky Sports, and Amazon spoke out against the deal. See, for example, Jonathan Easton, "One of Super League's Biggest Sins was Alienating Broadcasters," *DigitalTVEurope*, April 23, 2021, www.digitaltveurope.com/comment/one-of-the-super-leagues-biggest-sins-was-alienating-broadcasters.

106. Mohammad Elzoheiry, "Egyptian Channel to Exclusively Broadcast Handball World Championship 2021," *SeeNews*, December 24, 2020, https://see.news/egyptian-channel-to-exclusively-broadcast-handball-world-championship-2021.

107. Sam Carp, "Saudi Arabia Set to Launch Sports Rights Media Company," *SportsProMedia*, November 6, 2020, www.sportspromedia.com/news/saudi-arabia-sports-media-rights-company.

108. See, for example, Andrew England, "Saudi Arabia Media Group to Make Play for Elite Global Sports Events," *Financial Times*, November 5, 2020, www.ft.com/content/179c9125-f2fc-4fcf-9eeb-61b1da03ce25.

109. The controversy began with a profane chant directed against Fenerbahce and almost (but not quite) imperceptibly buried in the audio of BeIN game broadcasts. When BeIN fired the two employees determined to be responsible, they turned out to be Fenerbahce fans, making matters worse.

110. Though Turkey is typically included in the literature on Middle East sports, the

Super Lig is part of European competition. Turkey has competed in four UEFA championships since 1996. See Emin Ozkurt, "How the Collective Sale of Broadcasting Rights Works in Turkey," *LawinSport*, October 6, 2017, www.lawin-sport.com/topics/item/how-the-collective-sale-of-broadcasting-rights-works-in-turkish-football; "Global Media Report 2019."

111. "Fenerbahçe ile beIN Sports arasındaki gerginlik ve dava süreci dünya basınında" [The fight between Fenerbahce and BeIN sports is getting bigger! They are in court], *SonDakika*, February 22, 2021, https://t24.com.tr/haber/fenerbahce-ile-be-in-sports-arasindaki-gerginlik-ve-dava-sureci-dunya-basininda,935109; Frank Dalleres, "BeIN Sports Takes Legal Action against Fenerbahce over Turkish Club's 'beFAIR' Campaign," CITYA.M, February 22, 2021, www.cityam.com/exclusive-bein-sports-takes-legal-action-against-fenerbahce-president-ali-koc-over-turkish-clubs-befair-campaign.

112. Martin Ross, "Turkish Football Federation and BeIN's Digiturk at Odds Over Super Lig Payments," *SportBusiness*, December 21, 2020, www.sportbusiness.com/news/turkish-football-federation-and-beins-digiturk-at-odds-over-super-lig-payments.

113. For an excellent and entertaining tour of Turkey's football history and culture, see John McManus, *Welcome to Hell? In Search of the Real Turkish Football* (London: Weidenfeld and Nicolson, 2018).

114. See Alex Taylor, "TFF and BeIN Settle Latest Fee Dispute with New Payment Plan," *SportBusiness*, January 4, 2021, www.sportbusiness.com/news/tff-and-bein-settle-latest-fee-dispute-with-new-payment-plan; David Hellier, "BeIn Set to Shun Auction to Renew Turkish Soccer TV Rights," *Bloomberg*, April 2, 2021, www.bloomberg.com/news/articles/2021–04–02/bein-is-said-to-shun-auction-to-renew-turkish-soccer-tv-rights.

115. Tariq Panja, "The Conspiracy Talk Threatening a $360 Million Deal," *New York Times*, March 10, 2021, www.nytimes.com/2021/03/10/sports/soccer/fener-bahce-bein-sports-turkey.html.

INDEX

Note: Page numbers followed by "*n*" refer to notes, "*f*" refer to figures and "*t*" refer to tables

395

INDEX

Ali La Pointe, 95
Ali, Almoez, 116–17, 133, 135*f*
  support for Sudan, 137*f*, 144
Al-Ittihad, 258
Alizadeh, Kimia, 292
Almond, Gabriel, 152
Al-Ram stadium (Palestine), 172
Al-Rayyan, 267
Al-Sadd (Qatari club), 254, 267, 275
Al-Wahda, 275
al-Wehdat SC football club, 155, 159
Amara, Mahfoud, 79, 81
Amed Sportif Faaliyetler, 101
'Āmer, Abdel-Ḥkīm, 44
Amer, Abdelhakim, 50
American University of Beirut (AUB), 159
Amīn, Moḥmmad, 18
Amman, 163, 193
Amnesty International, 75, 228, 235
anasheed (traditional Islamic songs), 80
Anderson, Benedict, 121
Anis, Rami, 177, 183
El Anka, El Hadj M'hamed, 83, 84
Ankara, 100
anti-apartheid movement, 199–200, 203, 204–8
anti-colonialism, 5, 26
antiracism, 187
Antranik (Armenian club), 163
"Anwa wigui? Imazighen" ("Who are we? Amazigh people"), 81
Aouf, Abderrahmane, 80
apartheid, 366n55
  apartheid South Africa, 12, 50–1, 199–200, 201–8, 210, 218, 220, 221

  See also anti-apartheid movement
Arab Radio and Television (ART), 308–9
Arab Rugby Sevens, 163
Arab Spring/Arab uprisings, 96, 70, 88, 90
Arab Weekly, The (newspaper), 166
Arabian Gulf Cup, 307
Arabian Gulf League, 306
Arabic newspapers, 28–9
Arab-Israeli war (1973), 209
Arabsat, 304, 310, 311, 312, 313–14, 319
Archetti, Eduardo, 283
Argentina, 217, 222, 275, 278
  World Cup (1978), 72
Arman-e Melli (newspaper), 299
Armenia, 162
Arsenal, 257
art, football-related. *See* football-related art
Ashley, Mike, 317
Asian Champions League, 154, 254, 258
Asian Football Confederation (AFC), 52, 116, 208, 209, 287, 305, 307, 314
Asian Cup (1996), 281–2
Asian Cup (2007), 1–2
Asian Cup (2015), 156
Asian Cup (2019), 116, 127, 164, 258
Champions League, 314, 301
  Women's Futsal Championship, 292
Asian Games Federation, 209
Asian Nations Cup, 254
Aspire Academy, 141
al-Assad, Hafez, 53
"As-Salam al-Amiri", 145–6, 148

397

INDEX

Dakhliyya, 43
Dart, Jon, 155, 171, 203, 210, 214
Davidson, Alastair, 138
decolonization, 49, 203
Deloitte, 262–3
Denmark, 108
Depetris-Chauvin, Emilio, 282
Dey Boys, 90
Dey, N.A. Hussein, 81
Dibba Al-Fujairah, 259
DigitalTVResearch, 318
Digiturk, 304, 320
Dinarsu, 99
Dodd, Moya, 288
Doha, 228, 254, 261, 268, 272, 278
Doidge, Mark, 86
Doroodgar, Sadeq, 286
Dorsey, James M., 46–7, 88–9, 220
Drogba, Didier, 187–90
Druze community, 166
Du (telecom provider), 311
Dubai Sports, 307
Dubai, 257, 266, 304
Duerr, Glen M. E., 155, 170–1
Dugout (UK), 308
Dukalskis, 53
Dukic, Darko, 181–3

Eagle Capital, 66
"East Bank first policy", 155
East Jerusalem, 152, 212
Eastern Africa, 187
East-West highway (Algeria), 93
EEFA. *See* English Egyptian Football Association (EEFA)
EFA. *See* Egyptian Football Association (EFA)
effendis, 22–3, 25

club for compete in physical games, 25
and Egyptian revolution (1919), 25–6, 35
hierarchies in football stadiums, 35–6
interest in football, 22–5
negotiating nationalism, 34–9
riyāḍa, interest in, 24, 26
youth practiced football at schools, 23
effendi clubs
Coptic Christian minority inclusion, 36–7
inviting non-effendis as spectators, 35
non-effendis inclusion, 35–6
riyāḍa venue for Muslim and Christian, 37
See also effendis
Egypt, 7, 49, 67, 90, 309, 310, 311, 313
anti-coup sit-in (2013), 64
British military's introduction of football, 20–1
bureaucratization of football, 23–5
cabinet crisis (1948), 17
club and city hierarchy, emergence of, 40–1
club directors promoting *riyāḍa*, 25
clubs integration into national football space, 40
dictators support for the sport, 76
eighth anniversary of coup (July 1952), 50
fan violence, 60–1
football, introduction of, 20–1
friendly games, cost of travelling, 39

401

hierarchies in football stadiums, 35–6
hosting African Cup of Nations, second (1959), 51
National Party, zero tolerance policy towards, 37
national team, assembling, 28
nationalism, 19–20, 26
Olympic Games (1920 and 1924) participation, 5
people on football matches, 28
professional football, conceptualization of, 45
provincial competition, 41
provincial football zones, 38–43
provincial leagues, 43
sport's governing bodies, Egyptianizing, 27–8
sports club establishment, 8, 19–20, 23–5, 26
sports club membership, 24
streets named after sport icons, 44
Tahrir Square protest (Cairo), 3–4, 88
banned Ultra groups, 4, 89
Ultras, role of, 3–4, 88
war with Israel (Jun 1967), 6
women's participation in club activities, 37–8
World Cup (2017), Congo vs., 63–4
See also Ahly Sporting Club; Mixed Football Association (MFA); Port Said Stadium massacre (Feb 2012)
Egypt's football league, genealogy of, 17–47
clubs' role in organizing the nation, 20, 34–8

early days of football, 20–5
Egypt's football league establishment, 17–19, 20
Egyptianization of football clubs, 26–9, 38–43
Egyptianization of football, 20, 25–9
See also Egypt; Egyptian Football Association (EFA)
EgyptAir, 65
Egyptian Football Association (EFA), 6, 27–8, 39, 50
clustering of clubs (1929), 40, 41
consolidation of EFA power, 33–4
inaugural game (Fārūq vs. Dakhliyya), 17–19, 43
membership, 34
national football domain, creation of, 28
national league organizing plans approval, 42–3
player identification cards, issuing, 34
support for el-Sisi, 64–5
World Cup preparations, 66
Egyptian Media Group, 66
Egyptian Radio, 41–2
Egyptian revolution (1919), 20, 24
clubs as launching pads for effendi protests, 25
nationalism after, 34–5
nationalization of football after, 25–9
outbreak of, 25–6
El Watan, 85
Elias, Norbert, 117, 120
Emirates Airlines, 52, 257
Emirati Pro League, 258–9
employees, 238–9, 310, 312

free-to-air (FTA), 304, 308, 309, 319
French Football Federation, 80
Friedman, Uri, 177
"friendly" games, 33, 39
"From the Moorish Café to the Sports Café" (Fates), 83–4
Front de Liberation (FLN), 5–6, 78, 80–2, 95
Algerian youth riot (Oct 1988), 82
Funk, Daniel C., 265
FutbolNet, 190, 192, 193, 195

Galatasaray (GS), 86, 101
Galilee (Israel), 185
Galily, Yair, 209, 210, 211, 214
GATT. *See* General Agreement on Tariffs and Trade (GATT)
Gaza Strip, 154, 187, 212
GCC. *See* Gulf Cooperation Council (GCC)
GDP. *See* Gross Domestic Product (GDP)
gender discrimination, 8, 73, 288
gender equality, 192, 193, 284
gender inequality, 10, 97, 104–5, 112–14
General Agreement on Tariffs and Trade (GATT), 315, 316
General Federation of Trade Unions (Nepal), 247
Generation Amazing, 187
Generations For Peace (GFP), 191, 196
Gengler, Justin, 238
Germany, 177, 181, 307
Gerschewski, 53
Gezira, 36
Ghali, Butrus, 37
Ghandour, Hind, 166
"Gheniet U.S.M.O" ("The songs

of U.S.M. Oran") (L'Oranais), 84
Ghyasvand, Ahmad, 293
Giro d'Italia (2018), 202
Girona (Spain), 268
Giulianotti, Richard, 195
Gladden, James M., 265
Glasgow Celtic, 217
global brands, localization of, 13
global human rights campaign, 225
"Global North", 12, 176, 194–5, 197
"Global South", 12, 194–5
globalization, of football, 6–7
goalkeepers, 11, 105
"God, the homeland, the Emir" caption, 128
Goodwill Ambassador (UNHCR), 177
Government Communication Office (Qatar), 248
Graeber, David, 22–3
graffiti, 79, 80, 95, 96
Greece, 177
Green Boys, 86
Griezmann, Antoine, 150
Gross Domestic Product (GDP), 173
Gruffydd-Jones, Jamie J., 245
Gruppo Aquile, 87
Guangzhou Evergrande, 266
Guardian, The (newspaper), 70, 71, 101, 167, 169, 224, 229, 242, 247–8
Guermah, Massinissa, 77
Guerouabi, El Hachemi, 85
Gulf Cooperation Council (GCC), 13, 55, 67, 238, 253, 254, 255, 256, 258t, 272–3, 280
fan attendance, 258–9

405

fan engagement, 13, 260–4
fan engagement, motives of,
274–9
fan portfolios, 268
fans characteristics, 265–7
fans, typologies of, 269–71
rentier states, 257
See also Qatar blockade
Gulf Cup (2019), 146
Gulf states
hosting regional and international football tournaments,
52
national football teams,
purchase of, 7

Haaretz (newspaper), 155
Haddad, Ali, 93
Al Haftaa, Muflih, 311
Haftar, Khalifa, 70
Haifa, 217
Haiti, 278
Hakkari, 100
Hamad, Adnan, 60
Hamas, 164, 218
Hamdeli (newspaper), 299
Hamshahri (newspaper), 301
Hanafi, Sari, 167
ha-Po'el Taibeh, 153
Hapoel Be'er Sheva, 217
Hapoel Hadera (Israeli team), 157
Hariri, Rafik, 166
El Harrachi, Dahmane, 84
Hashemite monarchy, 5
Hassan, Abbas, 164
Hassan, Abdulkarim, 128–30,
129f, 143
Al-Haydos, Hassan, 124–7,
125f, 126f, 127f
Hayhurst, Lyndsay, 194
Ḥegāzī, Hussein, 30–4, 326n60,
326n61

joined Ahly, 30
Mukhtalat. offer, acceptance
of, 30–1
rejoined Ahly, 31
warned against violating the
club's bylaws, 32–4
Henna Ahl Al-Samla, 130
Higher Schools Students Club
(HSSC), 24
hijab, 290–1, 292
Hirak mass protest movement
(Algeria, 2019–20)
anthems, 96
defining characteristic of, 91
football-related art in, 90–5
football-related chanting, 9,
77–8, 81–2
"La Casa Del Mouradia" ("The
Mouradia House") anthem,
92
locations, 91–2
outbreak of, 77–8
reason for, 90
Ḥishmat Cup, 25
Ḥishmat, Aḥd, 24–5
Homenetmen (Armenian club),
163
Homenmen (Armenian club), 163
Hugo, Victor, 93
human rights activists, 241–2,
245, 247
Human Rights Watch, 71–2,
213, 224, 228, 235, 298
humanitarianism, 185, 198
Hunā al-Qāhira, 41
Hussein, Saddam, 56
Hussein, Uday, 57
Hutchins, Brett, 122
Hyde, Marina, 242

IAAF Athletics World
Championship (2019), 254

Newcastle United, purchase
of, 54, 73
"sportswashing", 54–5
support for the military coup
(Egypt), 73
war in Yemen, 54
women's football league, first,
75
vs. WTO, 304–5, 315–17
See also Mohammed bin
Salman (Crown Prince of
Saudi Arabia); Qatar
blockade
Saudi Arabian Football
Association, 263
Saudi Football Federation, 314
Saudi Professional League, 258*t*,
306
Saudi Sports Company, 314, 319
Scandinavia, 240
Schaillée, Hebe, 183
Schmitt, Carl, 18
scholarship (subject of football),
8–15
school teams, 23
Schwabe, Siri, 155–6
Scott, David, 183
Scottish Professional Football
League, 307
SDP. *See* "sports for development
and peace" (SDP) movement
"sectarianization", 57, 332*n*22
Serie A (Italy), 257, 307, 314,
318
Seven League, 319
sexism, 104, 109
Shabhay-e Footballi ("Football
Nights") (television program),
290
Shankly, Bill, 14
Shargh (newspaper), 286
Sharjah, 261

Sharpeville massacre, 206
Shawqī, Aḥmad, 23
Al Sheeb, Saad, 143
'Sherwood Foresters', 28
Shiroudi Stadium, 285
"Shoomilah Shoomilah", 146–7,
148–9
Shor, Eran, 153, 211, 212
Siblin Training Centre, 169
Sichuan Juniu (China), 268
Sidon, 164, 165
Sikka Ḥadīd (Railways), 31, 33,
40
Silver, Chris, 84
Simon, Martin, 282
el-Sisi, Abdel Fattah/el-Sisi
regime, 54, 56
banned Ultra groups, 4, 89
EFA's support for, 64–5
Egyptian national team co-opt
attempt, 64
reelection (2018), 64
rise to power, 64, 70, 89
Salah's status, exploiting,
65–7
SKDWF. *See* Sandigan Kuwait
Domestic Workers Federation
(SKDWF)
Sky Sports, 312
Skype, 159
Smith, Aaron C. T., 269
social inclusion, 178–9, 181,
183, 187, 192
soft power
concept, 51
limits of, 52–3
Soltanifar, Masoud, 299
Somali community activist,
178–9
Sorek, Tamir, 152–3, 211
South Africa, 12, 49, 50–1, 60,
213–14, 218, 221

INDEX

INDEX

INDEX

- equal distribution of work
- whole taking what part
- no visuals
- how our papers consist
- roundtable about spots in middle East
- 3 mins per paper · 3 collecte
-

Jewish identity

- Jewish community → formation of Jewish
  late ottoman empire, eary mandate   community through
                                        sport
                                        jewish spotiz
                                        bodies

Ofer idels

@